Recent Developments in the Design, Construction, and Evaluation of Digital Libraries:

Case Studies

Colleen Cool
Graduate School of Library and Information Studies, Queens College, USA

Kwong Bor Ng
Queens College, CUNY, USA

A volume in the Advances in Library and Information Science (ALIS) Book Series

Information Science REFERENCE

Managing Director:	Lindsay Johnston
Editorial Director:	Joel Gamon
Book Production Manager:	Jennifer Yoder
Publishing Systems Analyst:	Adrienne Freeland
Assistant Acquisitions Editor:	Kayla Wolfe
Typesetter:	Christina Henning
Cover Design:	Jason Mull

Published in the United States of America by
Information Science Reference (an imprint of IGI Global)
701 E. Chocolate Avenue
Hershey PA 17033
Tel: 717-533-8845
Fax: 717-533-8661
E-mail: cust@igi-global.com
Web site: http://www.igi-global.com

Library of Congress Cataloging-in-Publication Data

Recent Developments in the Design, Construction, and Evaluation of Digital Libraries : Case Studies / Colleen Cool and Kwong bor Ng, Editors.
pages cm.
Includes bibliographical references and index.
Summary: "This book addresses the challenges with digital libraries, as well as describes the recent developments in the design, construction, and evaluation of these libraries in various environments"-- Provided by publisher.
ISBN 978-1-4666-2991-2 (hardcover) -- ISBN (invalid) 978-1-4666-2992-9 (ebook) -- ISBN (invalid) 978-1-4666-2993-6 (print & perpetual access) 1. Digital libraries. 2. Digital libraries--Case studies. 3. Electronic information resources--Case studies. 4. Computer network architectures--Case studies. 5. Libraries--Special collections--Electronic information resources--Evaluation. 6. Libraries--Information technology. I. Cool, Colleen, 1952- editor of compilation. II. Ng, Kwong Bor, editor of compilation.
ZA4080.R43 2013
025.042--dc23

2012040364

This book is published in the IGI Global book series Advances in Library and Information Science (ALIS) Book Series (ISSN: 2326-4136; eISSN: 2326-4144)

British Cataloguing in Publication Data
A Cataloguing in Publication record for this book is available from the British Library.

Advances in Library and Information Science (ALIS) Book Series

ISSN: 2326-4136
EISSN: 2326-4144

Mission

The **Advances in Library and Information Science (ALIS)** book series is comprised of high quality, research-oriented publications on the continuing developments and trends affecting the public, school, and academic fields, as well as specialized libraries and librarians globally. These discussions on professional and organizational considerations in library and information resource development and management assist in showcasing the latest methodologies and tools in the field.

The ALIS book series aims to expand the body of library science literature by covering a wide range of topics affecting the profession and field at large. The series also seeks to provide readers with an essential resource for uncovering the latest research in library and information science management, development, and technologies.

Coverage

- Academic libraries in the digital age
- Blogging in libraries
- Cataloging and classification
- Collection development
- Community outreach
- Digital literacy
- Ethical practices in libraries
- Green libraries
- Librarian education
- Mobile library services
- Remote access technologies
- University libraries in developing countries

IGI Global is currently accepting manuscripts for publication within this series. To submit a proposal for a volume in this series, please contact our Acquisition Editors at Acquisitions@igi-global.com or visit: http://www.igi-global.com/publish/.

The Advances in Library and Information Science (ALIS) Book Series (ISSN 2326-4136) is published by IGI Global, 701 E. Chocolate Avenue, Hershey, PA 17033-1240, USA, www.igi-global.com. This series is composed of titles available for purchase individually; each title is edited to be contextually exclusive from any other title within the series. For pricing and ordering information please visit http://www.igi-global.com/book-series/advances-library-information-science-alis/73002. Postmaster: Send all address changes to above address.

Titles in this Series

For a list of additional titles in this series, please visit: www.igi-global.com

Robots in Academic Libraries Advancements in Library Automation
Edward Iglesias (Central Connecticut State University, USA)
Information Science Reference • copyright 2013 • 341pp • H/C (ISBN: 9781466639386) • US $175.00 (our price)

Advancing Library Education Technological Innovation and Instructional Design
Ari Sigal (Catawba Valley Community College, USA)
Information Science Reference • copyright 2013 • 339pp • H/C (ISBN: 9781466636880) • US $175.00 (our price)

Recent Developments in the Design, Construction, and Evaluation of Digital Libraries Case Studies
Colleen Cool (Graduate School of Library and Information Studies, Queens College, USA) and Kwong Bor Ng (Queens College, CUNY, USA)
Information Science Reference • copyright 2013 • 275pp • H/C (ISBN: 9781466629912) • US $175.00 (our price)

Design, Development, and Management of Resources for Digital Library Services
Tariq Ashraf (University of Delhi, India) and Puja Anand Gulati (University of Delhi, India)
Information Science Reference • copyright 2013 • 438pp • H/C (ISBN: 9781466625006) • US $175.00 (our price)

Public Law Librarianship Objectives, Challenges, and Solutions
Laurie Selwyn (Law Librarian [Ret.], USA) and Virginia Eldridge (Grayson County, Texas Law Library, USA)
Information Science Reference • copyright 2013 • 341pp • H/C (ISBN: 9781466621848) • US $175.00 (our price)

Library Collection Development for Professional Programs Trends and Best Practices
Sara Holder (McGill University, Canada)
Information Science Reference • copyright 2013 • 504pp • H/C (ISBN: 9781466618978) • US $175.00 (our price)

Library Automation and OPAC 2.0 Information Access and Services in the 2.0 Landscape
Jesus Tramullas (University of Zaragoza, Spain) and Piedad Garrido (University of Zaragoza, Spain)
Information Science Reference • copyright 2013 • 409pp • H/C (ISBN: 9781466619128) • US $175.00 (our price)

Planning and Implementing Resource Discovery Tools in Academic Libraries
Mary Pagliero Popp (Indiana University, USA) and Diane Dallis (Indiana University, USA)
Information Science Reference • copyright 2012 • 342pp • H/C (ISBN: 9781466618213) • US $175.00 (our price)

Remote Access Technologies for Library Collections Tools for Library Users and Managers
Diane M. Fulkerson (University of South Florida Polytechnic Library, USA)
Information Science Reference • copyright 2012 • 232pp • H/C (ISBN: 9781466602342) • US $175.00 (our price)

IGI GLOBAL
DISSEMINATOR OF KNOWLEDGE
www.igi-global.com

701 E. Chocolate Ave., Hershey, PA 17033
Order online at www.igi-global.com or call 717-533-8845 x100
To place a standing order for titles released in this series, contact: cust@igi-global.com
Mon-Fri 8:00 am - 5:00 pm (est) or fax 24 hours a day 717-533-8661

Editorial Advisory Board

Table of Contents

Detailed Table of Contents

Digital Libraries have evolved from a digital counterpart of traditional libraries to highly dynamic environments conceived to provide a community with the data and services needed to accomplish its tasks. This trend is particularly frequent in the context of scientific research communities, whose members are scattered among multiple organizations across the world, with requirements that are very large, multidisciplinary, and evolving with innovation. The realization of such Research Digital Libraries calls for innovative approaches, capable of handling the inherent complexity of such systems while keeping their realization and maintenance costs under sustainable thresholds. Digital Library Infrastructures have been recently proposed as suitable candidates for the realization of Research Digital Libraries. They build on service-oriented infrastructure technologies to offer an environment where organizations can share and exchange their data and service resources to grow in synergy, exploiting an economy of scale approach. This chapter describes the peculiar challenges that designers, developers, and administrators have to face when realizing Research Digital Libraries, and presents the concepts and technologies of Digital Library Infrastructure as possible solutions to these issues.

This case study reports the activities, findings, and lessons learned during a project that replaced the legacy Digital Asset Management (DAM) system of The Portal to Texas History[SM] at the University of North Texas Libraries with an open source system. This unique system decouples the application development framework from the backend infrastructure, effectively relieving the development and growth constraints inherent in the legacy system. In a novel approach for an academic library, genealogists participated in the user-centered, iterative approach used to prototype, develop, and test the user interface. The resulting system promoted productivity gains by enabling programming staff to work in parallel from specialized areas of expertise. A post-project review process identified a number of lessons learned, including the importance of representing the requirements and priorities of internal and external stakeholders. The review process also informed an application development model that may be useful to other digital libraries.

This study examines the content in CONTENTdm item level records and their aggregated metadata in WorldCat. The research ascertains some amount of loss of contextualization in semantic meaning of digitized primary resources. Data was collected from non-probability sampling of CONTENTdm item records selected randomly from CONTENTdm's Collection of Collections Web page. The same aggregated digitized resources were retrieved in WorldCat, and the data was recorded and analyzed against the CONTENTdm records. Evidence shows that the value of the metadata is altered or ambiguous when the local field name is divorced from the descriptive metadata. Contextual meaning is lost when metadata is shared. In fact, the study reveals that the de-contextualization problem is two-fold: some inconsistent mapping from aggregated metadata and lack of clarity in the metadata itself.

Research into digital libraries has been carried out from two perspectives being libraries as contents and as services/organizations. The authors approach this topic from the service perspective. They argue that existing academic libraries in most parts of the world have augmented their services to include digital library services. This chapter discusses the development and components of a digital library and types of digital library services. It also discusses partial research findings on the integration of digital library services in blended learning environments at Open University Malaysia (OUM), focusing on issues and challenges encountered by librarians, which are: the need to provide both digital and physical resources, synchronous and asynchronous interaction with users, and engagement in continuous improvement. Information professionals at tertiary institutions are recommended to: keep abreast with the changing learning environments, maintain cooperation with users, and equip themselves with the new user-centric roles, knowledge, and skills that are required in this era of technological advancement.

This chapter addresses the question of how the analysis of results retrieved from online bibliographic information systems changed over the last 32 years as digital libraries have evolved. It demonstrates that Digital Libraries of the future will enable knowledge discovery by providing direct access to the semantic content of documents through the implementation of text mining tools. To achieve this research with IR systems and text-mining tools, pipeline pilot (Bandy, et al., 2009), I2E (Vellay, 2009), and BioText will need to be conducted by experts in information retrieval not just subject scientific specialists.

This chapter explores a pilot project investigating the development of audio descriptions to accompany an academic library's digital image collection. The project was introduced in selected classes and directly involved faculty and students in the creation and delivery of audio descriptions. The collaborative project initiated by the art librarian was in answer to a legislative act requiring accessibility for vision-impaired users. The discussion will specifically examine developing descriptions for images from Illinois State University's International Collection of Child Art a resource that presents a fascinating challenge to use language to broaden access to the content and construct a compelling representation with the spoken word for individuals with print disabilities such as vision impairment.

The purpose of the Sternberg Museum-Forsyth Library Fossil Digitization Pilot Project was to determine the feasibility of conducting a large-scale fossil digitization program at Fort Hays State University, Hays, Kansas. Conducted in early 2011, the pilot examined such aspects as fossil digitization techniques, metadata development and best practices, scope and timelines, and overall digitization goals. This chapter focuses on the digitization landscape of the natural sciences, including an overview of major fossil digitization projects and analyses of issues related to these projects. Conclusions from the Sternberg-Forsyth pilot are also recounted and discussed. Also included is an appendix outlining costs and time needed for the recommended small-scale digitization project that will begin in late 2011 or early 2012.

The intent of this chapter is to identify constructs and criteria for Digital Library (DL) evaluation based on document analysis. Eighty-five relevant articles and five websites were reviewed to generate the evaluation constructs and criteria. The findings consist of ten constructs, including collection, informa-

Preface

Over the past several decades, there has been an evolutionary change in the world of libraries from mostly print-based collections to today's current environment in which the phrase digital library is no longer new, but rather is synonymous with the library itself. Scholars no longer debate the various meanings of the concept "digital library" as practitioners routinely work in environments that have seen radical transformations in the nature of traditional library functions resulting from developments in digital technology. Within the academic universe, the subject of "digital libraries" has been the topic of much disciplinary-based discussion within the boundaries of library science, computer science, and engineering, each contributing a valuable piece to what is now recognized as a hybrid area of academic study, perhaps better characterized as "digital library systems." Digital library systems as such transcend the technologies that have so radically transformed the creation, organization, preservation, management, and use of information to encompass the larger sphere of digital library users, content, and evaluation—all within a social, political, and economic environment. In such a context, we believe that a better understanding of the evolving problems of digital libraries and their users will take place under the spotlight of practical and real world experience rather than solely that of theoretical scholarly debate. The chapters in this volume bring together academics and practicing professionals to address recent developments in the design, construction, and evaluation of digital libraries in a variety of library environments. Throughout, the emphasis is on practical strategies and lessons learned from real world case studies, with strong representation from the international community.

PURPOSE

In this volume, we have put together diverse writings of designers, content builders, and evaluation specialists in the digital libraries arena in order for scholars and practitioners to have a unified and better understanding of this multifaceted topic area. This work will inform both theory and practice, with the following objectives:

- To present a critical analysis of the subject in such a way as to assist faculty and practicing librarians.
- To present case studies displaying innovation and creative use of technology in libraries in and outside of the United States.
- To bring to the attention of scholars and practitioners some of the global perspectives on digital libraries represented in these practical case studies.
- To synthesize current approaches to the evaluation of digital libraries, from both user- and system-oriented approaches.

ORGANIZATION OF THIS BOOK

Section 1 contains chapters addressing issues related to content management infrastructure design. We start with an excellent chapter written by Candela, Castelli, Manghi, and Pagano. It discusses the design of digital library infrastructure built on service-oriented technologies, to offer an environment where organizations can share and exchange their data and service resources to grow in synergy, exploiting an economy of scale approach. Chapter 2 is a case study reporting the activities, findings, and lessons learned during a project that replaced a digital asset management system at the University of North Texas Libraries with an open source system. The new design decouples the application development framework from the backend infrastructure, effectively relieving the development and growth constraints inherent in the old system. Expert users participated in an iterative approach used to prototype, develop, and test the interface. The resulting system promoted productivity gains by enabling programming staff to work in parallel from specialized areas of expertise. In Chapter 3, aiming for a robust metadata infrastructure for digital library, Lee and Tyson investigate the problem of de-contextualization and reveal how metadata schemes may cause loss of contextualization in semantic meaning of digitized primary resources.

Chapters in Section 2 move away from content management and infrastructure issues to explore methods for designing effective access, novel preservation methods, and expanded library services in newer digital library environments. In Chapter 5, Amin, Ramly, and Gerbic bring the reader's attention to the changing nature of academic library services in the current digital library environment. Specifically, they describe how traditional academic library services in the Open University Malaysia have been expanded to include digital library services within the context of blended learning environments. Also, writing from the perspective of academic libraries, Lonbom addresses problems and opportunities associated with connecting sight-impaired users with the world of increasingly available image databases, in this case, art images. This chapter reports on a project in the use of audio descriptions to accompany images from Illinois State University's International Collection of Child Art. Also dealing directly with the design of more effective access to materials in digital databases is the chapter by Harrison, who describes experiences with the creation of novel search access methods to information retrieval systems in the pharmaceutical realm. Rounding out this section, the chapter by Weiss presents an overall discussion of the planning, design, and implementation of a large-scale fossil digitization program at Fort Hays State University, Hays, Kansas. This chapter provides the reader with important insights into the collaborative activities that were necessary between members of the Forsyth Library and the Sternberg Museum of Natural History in order to make this project successful.

Section 3 takes a look at the importance of developing appropriate methods for the evaluation of digital libraries. While evaluation methodology has always been an important subject in the assessment of traditional libraries and information retrieval systems, the digital library arena creates its own set of unique challenges for the design of appropriate evaluation metrics. The chapters in this section approach this from several perspectives. Joo and Xie begin with a description of key differences between traditional and digital libraries, arguing that the methods traditionally used to evaluate libraries must not be simply transferred to digital libraries. In order to develop appropriate relevant constructs and concepts for digital library evaluation, they use the technique of document analysis. Eighty-five relevant articles and five websites were reviewed to generate the evaluation constructs and criteria. The findings consist of ten constructs, including: collection, information organization, interface design, system performance, effects on users, user engagement, services, preservation, sustainability/administration, and context of use with associated criteria for each dimension. Taking a different perspective to the specification of evaluation principles for digital libraries, Petras, Stiller, and Gade focus on the cultural heritage domain, noting that cultural heritage information systems can be evaluated from a system-centric or a user-centric perspective. Their chapter discusses evaluation methods in cultural heritage collections and their distinctive features, interaction patterns, and challenges. The authors then illustrate these state-of-the-art methods with examples from Europeana, the European portal for access to digital library, museum, and archive collections, and other projects from within the cultural heritage domain. The final chapter in this section, by Li, takes yet another angle on the subject of evaluation in digital libraries. This chapter focuses explicitly on the cognitive dimension of users' experiences with digital libraries as the focus of investigation. The author proposes the technique of cognitive task analysis as relevant to the evaluation of digital libraries, based on its applicability for understanding iterative and formative processes. After presenting the theoretical framework and features of cognitive task analysis, the procedure of carrying out this type of evaluation is detailed. This chapter concludes with a discussion of future directions for digital library usability evaluation, especially for the purpose of iterative design processes.

The final section of this book looks at the larger social environment in which digital libraries are created and some aspects of the relationship between this context and the processes of digital library construction and use. Tobar, writing in the first chapter of this section, takes a decidedly political stance on what digital libraries are, directing our attention away from the purely academic or scholarly notion of these new library forms and arguing instead that digital libraries can be "of the people" and "for the people." The author documents her activities in the creation of a digital oral history archive documenting the Welfare Rights Initiative (WRI), a grassroots student activist and community leadership training organization located at Hunter College. The WRI was founded to aid student welfare recipients in becoming agents of social change and to actively involve them with policymaking. From this perspective, the digital library is conceptualized as a political tool that can be instrumental in social change. Perry and Valero give a detailed account of their lessons learned as educators teaching digital imaging techniques to Master's students in Library Studies, from the perspective of using digital imaging to foster experiential learning. Here, the digital library is understand to provide an opportunity for change in educational practices. Finally, in this section, Sofronijevic discusses the digital library within a larger context of communication and collaboration enhanced by Web 2.0 technology. He discusses the process of "intrapreneurship," which is the practice of applying entrepreneurial skills and approaches within an organization such as the library. This concept is currently utilized in many industries, but so far, rarely in librarianship, and the author argues for its usefulness there as well.

TARGET AUDIENCE

We have targeted this book to faculty, students, professionals, and researchers working in the field of digital libraries and electronic archives. It is our hope that the chapters contained in this volume will provide a valuable reference for all of those seeking a better understanding of the changing landscape of digital library environments.

Colleen Cool
City University of New York, USA

Kwong-Bor Ng
City University of New York, USA

Section 1
Behind the Scenes:
Creating Infrastructure and Metadata for Digital Libraries

Chapter 1
Infrastructure-Based Research Digital Libraries

Leonardo Candela
Istituto di Scienza e Tecnologie dell'Informazione "Alessandro Faedo" Consiglio Nazionale delle Ricerche, Italy

Donatella Castelli
Istituto di Scienza e Tecnologie dell'Informazione "Alessandro Faedo" Consiglio Nazionale delle Ricerche, Italy

Paolo Manghi
Istituto di Scienza e Tecnologie dell'Informazione "Alessandro Faedo" Consiglio Nazionale delle Ricerche, Italy

Pasquale Pagano
Istituto di Scienza e Tecnologie dell'Informazione "Alessandro Faedo" Consiglio Nazionale delle Ricerche, Italy

ABSTRACT

Digital Libraries have evolved from a digital counterpart of traditional libraries to highly dynamic environments conceived to provide a community with the data and services needed to accomplish its tasks. This trend is particularly frequent in the context of scientific research communities, whose members are scattered among multiple organizations across the world, with requirements that are very large, multi-disciplinary, and evolving with innovation. The realization of such Research Digital Libraries calls for innovative approaches, capable of handling the inherent complexity of such systems while keeping their realization and maintenance costs under sustainable thresholds. Digital Library Infrastructures have been recently proposed as suitable candidates for the realization of Research Digital Libraries. They build on service-oriented infrastructure technologies to offer an environment where organizations can share and exchange their data and service resources to grow in synergy, exploiting an economy of scale approach. This chapter describes the peculiar challenges that designers, developers, and administrators have to face when realizing Research Digital Libraries, and presents the concepts and technologies of Digital Library Infrastructure as possible solutions to these issues.

DOI: 10.4018/978-1-4666-2991-2.ch001

INTRODUCTION

The Digital Library (DL) concept can be traced back to the famous papers of visionary scientists like Vannevar Bush (1945) and J. C. R. Licklider (1965) identifying and pursuing the goal of innovative technologies and approaches toward knowledge sharing as fundamental instruments for progress. However, research and development activity on digital libraries actually started in the early 1990s; with the Internet proliferation since such technology created unprecedented possibilities to discover and deliver human knowledge.

During these years, a variety of different types of information systems—called "digital libraries"—have been developed in diverse contexts. These systems are very heterogeneous in scope and functionality and their evolution does not follow a single path. In fact, when DL evolve changes happened this has not only meant that a better quality system was been conceived by superseding the "preceding" ones but also meant that a new conception of digital libraries was born corresponding to new raised needs (Candela, Castelli, & Pagano, 2011).

In the last decade, Digital Libraries have achieved a fundamental role in our knowledge-based society, especially in the context of "scientific research." In this context, the novel multidisciplinary forms of research and the need for immediate and contemporary access to heterogeneous and independently grown content, brought up new and challenging requirements for DLs. DLs evolved from stand-alone systems supporting data storage and provision for the users of one organization, to possibly very-large, cross-domain, cross-organization DL systems tailored to serve continuously evolving needs. In general terms, these new generation of *Research DLs* (RDLs) are requested to provide user communities with (*a*) a wealth of content aggregated from existing knowledge providers such as libraries, museum, data archives, and any knowledge repository; and (*b*) the dynamically evolving applications they need to accomplish their tasks (study, work, leisure) by processing, exploring, accessing and interacting with such content.

Traditional DL development approaches based on from-scratch realization of the entire system proved to be unsuitable. In such scenarios, the costs of design, development, administration and maintenance (e.g., refinement, adaptation to evolution) tend to be not sustainable for organizations responsible of the resulting RDLs (Manghi, Mikulicic, Candela, Castelli, & Pagano, Realizing and Maintaining Aggregative Digital Library Systems: D-NET Software Toolkit and OAIster System, 2010), which are often faced with the trade-off between user satisfaction and lack of funding required to satisfy them.

In order to support this vision, new *infrastructure-based* approaches, fostering sharing of data and services started to be regarded as valuable solutions. In a broader sense, an "infrastructure" offers to a community a "service" that consists of a set of tools for managing, exchanging and accessing a set of *resources*—to be intended here as any asset worth to share across the boundaries of a specific institution or community—according to a set of participation and interaction *policies*. Infrastructures vary depending on the context of usage, which determines the kind of resources, services and policies they support. In particular, Digital Library Infrastructures (hereafter, for simplicity, DLIs) are software systems that provide tools for (*1*) sharing of resources such as datasets (e.g., digital objects, metadata, scientific datasets) and functionality services (e.g., storage, processing, export, access), and (*2*) facilitating the construction of RDL applications out of such resources. In this novel context, DLs are conceived as dynamic and flexible sets of such applications, whose nature can adapt in time to integrate new data or functionality resources from the underlying DLI with minimal costs. This vision changes completely the traditional design of digital library systems as monolithic blocks of code addressing initial user requirements and introduces a dynamic paradigm where often the DLI and its resources precede and can inspire the community at devising new RDL applications out of them. To ease this process, DLIs offer tools for the run-time and driven construction of applications (e.g., wizards) and for their run-time administration – in the literature, such applications are also referred as *Virtual Digital Libraries* (Candela, et al., 2007) or *Virtual Research Environments* (Allan, 2009; Candela, Castelli, & Pagano, 2009; Carusi & Reimer, 2010) (See Figure 1).

This chapter presents concepts and technologies underlying Digital Library Infrastructures. In particular, it motivates their conception as solutions to the sustainable realization and maintenance of Research Digital Libraries. To this aim, the chapter gives a background of DLs and infrastructure research initiatives, describes RDLs in terms of their requirements, elaborates on the inability of "traditional" DL technologies to meet them, and finally introduces the DLI approach as a valuable solution. DLIs are introduced from a functional perspective, in terms of the notions of "resources" and "enabling functionality," and from a technological perspective, illustrating the underlying programming paradigms and two existing implementations: the D-NET Software Toolkit and the gCube System. Concluding remarks and a discussion on future research directions complete the chapter.

BACKGROUND

There is an intense discussion at international level on e-Infrastructures and data infrastructure serving scientific work—digital library infrastructures falls in these categories. The European Strategy Forum on Research Infrastructures (ESFRI) presented the first European roadmap for new, large-scale Research Infrastructures (European Strategy Forum on Research Infrastructures, 2010). These are modeled as layered hardware and software systems which support sharing of a wide spectrum of resources, spanning from networks, storage, computing resources, and system-level middleware software, to structured information within collections, archives, and databases. The e-Infrastructure Reflection Group (e-IRG) has proposed a similar vision. In particular, it envisions e-Infrastructures where the principles of global collaboration and shared resources are intended to encompass the sharing needs of all research activities(e-Infrastructure Reflection Group,

Figure 1. Digital library infrastructure overview

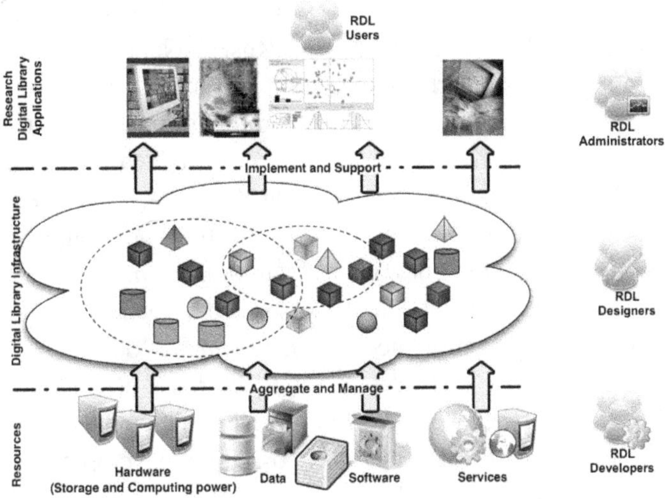

2010). In the framework of the Joint Information Systems Committee (JISC) e-infrastructure programme, e-Infrastructures are defined in terms of integration of networks, grids, data centers and collaborative environments, and are intended to include supporting operation centers, service registries, credential delegation services, certificate authorities, training and help-desk services (Joint Information Systems Committee, 2006). The Cyberinfrastructure programme launched by the US National Science Foundation (NSF) plans to develop new research environments in which advanced computational, collaborative, data acquisition and management services are made available to researchers connected through high-performance networks (Cyberinfrastructure Council, 2007). More recently, the vision for "global research data infrastructures" has been drawn by identifying a number of recommendations for developers of future research infrastructures (Thanos, 2011). This vision document highlighted the open issues affecting data infrastructures development—both technical and organizational—and identified future research directions. Besides these initiatives targeting "generic" infrastructures there are others oriented to specific domains, e.g. the European commission promotes the INSPIRE initiative for an e-Infrastructure oriented to the sharing of content and service resources of European countries in the ambit of geospatial datasets (European Parliament Council, 2007).

Although different in scope and requirements, all the initiatives listed above agree on characterizing infrastructures as means for effective consumption of shared resources. In some cases, motivations and design (sharing, on-demand resource provision, economies of scale) align with the principles of *grid computing* and its ecology of *virtual organizations* (Foster & Kesselman, The Grid: Blueprint for a New Computing Infrastructure, 1998) as well as with *cloud computing* (Foster I., Zhao, Raicu, & Lu, 2008). All of them endorse a holistic approach to resource sharing through the infrastructure, where the spectrum of shareable resources includes hardware-bound or physical resources (i.e. networks, storage, instruments, and computational resources) and digital resources, including content and application functionality resources (i.e. datasets, software, services). In particular, these initiative ground on the common assumption that sharing and reuse of resources is possible by means of infrastructure functionality, also called "core services," capable of dealing with management (e.g., registration, security, combination) of a dynamic set of resources.

Among the resources worth to share, the Digital Library domain focused primarily and for long time on content—in many cases by relying on metadata. At the end of the 1990s, the experiences of using distributed architectures to implement proper digital libraries and the proliferation of independent repositories of valuable content stimulated the idea of reusing content already collected (and curated) in existing independent repositories so as to reduce the effort to build (large-scale) digital libraries. To address these scenarios it was developed a protocol promoting the cooperation between content providers and service providers, the *Open Archive Initiative Protocol for Metadata Harvesting (OAI-PMH)*(Lagoze & Van de Sompel, 2001). This is a simple protocol made by six protocol requests and responses and because of its simplicity and relatively low cost of adoption it is so diffuse as to become a sort of *de-facto* standard solution that is still broadly diffused. Notable examples of Digital Library Infrastructures conceived to serve multiple user communities by aggregating the harvested records into centralized metadata repositories and serving the community needs through vertical DLs applications built on such shared content include *National Science Digital Library* (Lagoze, Krafft, Cornwell, Dushay, Eckstrom, & Saylor, 2006) and *Europeana* (2008).

The reuse of content is not the only strategy that has been put in place in order to reduce the cost of DL development. Another important step toward this aim has been the conception of Digital Library Management Systems (DLMSs), i.e. systems that provide the appropriate framework to both (1) produce and administer a Digital Library System incorporating the suite of functionality considered fundamental for Digital Libraries and (2) integrate additional software offering more refined, specialised or advanced functionality (Candela, et al., 2011). Thus, a DL can be built by configuring and deploying a DLMS and then operating the functionality to ingest or harvest content in it. In principle, depending on the flexibility and openness of the DLMS, this approach is in some sense aligned with the infrastructural one since it largely simplifies and reduces the effort required to set up a DL and, generally, guarantees a better quality-of-service. Unfortunately, as of nowadays there is a relatively low number of systems that can be reasonably considered as "true" DLMSs. Most of them fall in the category of stand-alone software systems equipped with management functionality supporting the operation of customised DLs. Examples are repository platforms, such as Fedora (Payette & Lagoze, 1998), DSpace (Smith, et al., 2003), Eprints (Millington & Nixon, 2007), and Greenstone (Witten, Bainbridge, & Boddie, 2001) or OAI-PMH aggregation systems, such as DLXS (University of Michigan – Digital Library Production Service). As we shall see in the next sections, Digital Library Infrastructure systems represent the first evolutionary attempt to deliver highly dynamic, flexible and open DLMSs, where designers and developers can find fully-fledge mechanisms and tools to realize their community-specific DLs.

RESEARCH DIGITAL LIBRARIES

To better understand the peculiarities of RDLs let us consider the community of marine biologists. Let us assume that researchers from several cooperating organizations need to set up an RDL for supporting research on environmental pollution in the Mediterranean's sea. The DL should offer a report management application, which includes multi-hand drafting, storage, and search of reports, where reports are obtained by dynamically integrating data resulting from processing input satellite images and sensor data of various forms and from several sources. To meet the continuous evolution of data and experiments, the DL should be able to integrate anytime new or better processing functionality and new applications, beyond that of report management, obtained as combination of data and functionality available to the RDL.

As suggested in this example, the purpose of RDL applications is typically to mediate/exchange data with existing data sources, store it, process it, and provide access to the resulting data to third-party consumers, such as end-user portals or external applications. This involves realization and maintenance costs, for deployment of servers, design, development, refinement, and installation of software on such hardware and production system administration activities. However, when compared to traditional DLs, the realization of RDLs has strong evolutionary requirements, driven by their worldwide, multidisciplinary, and transient nature. In particular, independently from the application domain, RDLs are characterized by one or more of the following requirements:

- **Evolving Content and Functional Requirements:** Application requirements can vary along time as new types of content, functionality, implementation or technology is demanded.
- **Large-Scale Requirements:** Communities may include an arbitrary, unforeseeable number of users, datasets, objects in datasets, and functionalities.
- **Quality of Service Requirements:** The physical resources to be consumed, e.g., storage and computing resources, may vary along-time, depending on the community demand.

- **Time-Frame Requirements:** The lifetime of an application may be short as well as the time expected to satisfy new sudden requirements.

Clearly, realization and maintenance costs of RDLs are much higher than in traditional DLs, where evolution is generally limited to minimal numbers of changes. As we shall see in the next section, the choice of the proper DLMS technology plays a crucial role in this context, since its ability to flexibly and dynamically integrate applications with new functionality or mediate with and process arbitrary numbers and typologies of data sources determines the sustainability of the resulting RDL. The adoption of inadequate DLMSs or, more in general, the realization of systems not adhering to standard and flexible design patterns may lead to likely unaffordable maintenance costs and therefore compromise the success of the RDL.

DIGITAL LIBRARY INFRASTRUCTURES

Digital Library Infrastructures (DLIs) are advanced DLMSs, conceived to offer to designers, developers and administrators of RDLs the tools for *(1)* managing a dynamic pool of dataset resources (e.g., satellite images, reports), functionality resources (e.g., services for processing images, editing reports, searching reports), and physical resources (e.g., servers), *(2)* constructing and supporting a number of RDL applications (e.g., report management). In line with the accepted intuition of "infrastructures," the underlying idea is that of an "enabling system" to which several "resources" can be dynamically added or removed and where these can be combined ("LEGO-like approach") to obtain the applications needed by the user community at a given time. Unlike most DLMS approaches, the components (i.e., resources) of the resulting DLs (i.e., RDLs) are not necessarily known in advance, can be offered by different actors (i.e., organizations, end-users), and can change dynamically, to the extent permitted by the technology. Accordingly, the organization responsible of the DLI is not necessarily the one that provides or administrates the individual resources part of the RDL. As such, DLIs should be intended as "active" DLMS, where:

- RDL developers are involved when new instances or kinds of functionality resources need to be made available;
- RDL designers are involved when existing applications need to modify the subset of resources they are built out of, or when new applications need to be constructed;
- RDL administrators are involved in monitoring the quality of service of applications.

In such scenario, the intervention of developers is limited to realization or refinement of individual and combinable functionalities, while the activity of RDL application designers and administrators is supported and facilitated by DLI's *enabling functionality*. Enabling functionality is provided through a set of tools operated by the Organization Responsible (RO) of the DLI. Such tools pre-exist the resources and the applications that will form the RDL and give life to a dynamic and distributed environment, where multiple Participating Organizations (POs) and the relative users can share, sell, exchange their content or functional resources according to given access and usage policies (depending on the RDL, resource usage can be free as well as toll-gated, thereby leveraging a "market" or an "ecological system," where "better" resources naturally supersede to "obsolete" resources). More specifically, enabling functionality covers resource and application management. On the side of resources it provides capabilities for: resource "registration" to the DLI (for resources to be used by RDL applications), resource "discovery" (for resources to be found and used by applications), resource handling (resource processing functionality, e.g., services for processing images, which operate on image resources), and resource policies enforcement (for resources to be safely handled by POs). On the side of applications they provide high-level functionality, e.g., user interfaces, for definition of applications out of resource handling functionality, the automatic execution of application workflows ("orchestration"), and the automatic and assisted monitoring (QoS) of applications.

In the following sections, we shall illustrate the resource typologies typically supported by DLIs and give a classification of the enabling functionalities that are typically supported by DLIs.

Resource Models

Observing existing DLIs out there, it is generally possible to classify their resources in the following main categories:

- **Hardware Resources:** Servers connected to the network and providing computing and storage capabilities for functionality service resources and dataset resources. Their number and "power" plays a critical part in the RDL quality of service.
- **Service Resources:** Resource-handling services, which run on hardware resources, used to create, delete, update, and process dataset resources. Services are accessible through the network and implement a set of publicly declared functions. Examples of such resources are DL services such as full-text index services, storage services, recommender Services, Transformation Services, etc. Service resources typically join the pool of resource handling capabilities available to the enabling functionality.
- **Software Resources:** Software packages relative to service resources; once deployed on a given hardware resource, software resources give life to a new service resource available to the RDL.
- **External Dataset Resources:** Data sources under the control of third-party data providers, whose content is accessible from the network. Examples are institutional repositories, archives, databases.
- **Internal Dataset Resources:** Data collections whose content is managed by RDL services and is stored within RDL hardware resources. Different kinds of such resources may exist and be specialized, depending on the specific domain of the RDL. Examples are: metadata record collections, compound objects, documents, images, videos, etc.

In general, all entities described above are part of RDL systems, needed to form their applications (except from instrumentations, which may not be required by the community at hand). However, the underlying DLI DLMS may or may not be capable of supporting their management as resources. For example, as we shall see in the next section, D-NET DLIs do not support software resources, while gCube DLIs do so. In D-NET, service software entities exist, but it is up to designers to download them from the D-NET software repository and manually install them on hardware resources to create a new service resource. In gCube, the same operation can be performed by designers through DLI enabling functionalities, which are capable of discovering the required software resources and automatically deploying them on hardware resources.

The resource categories supported by a DLI are specified in the DLI's *resource model*, which further describes a specialization of resource categories into a number of *resource types*. For example, the D-NET resource model features several service resource types, including index, store, transformation, feature extraction, etc. Moreover, in order to participate to a DLI, i.e., to be used as part of applications, resources must be registered to the system. As it happens in a SOA or in P2P systems, resource registration occurs by submitting a *profile* to the enabling functionalities. A profile is a machine-consumable description of the resource in terms of properties considered relevant for discoverability and reuse of the resource. Examples of profile properties are the resource unique identifier, its geographical location, the functionalities it offers, aspects of its internal status, its access point (e.g., URL for services, DOI for documents), its quality-of-service parameters, etc. Finally, to complete the scenario, resources are typically associated with a "security context," which defines the conditions of their usage, i.e., the organizations, applications, or resources authorized and not authorized to share/use the resource.

Enabling Functionalities

In the context of a DLI, RDL applications are defined as dynamic sets of resources (as described by the DLI resource model) interacting with each other in respect of given security policies. In particular, the construction, operation, and administration of applications are possible thanks to the DLI enabling functionalities. Such functionalities take inspiration from SOA's enabling middleware, which implement standard facilities for (Web) service registration, discovery, security, orchestration, and monitoring. DLIs extend this set of functionality to (*1*) apply to all resource categories described above (generally not supported by SOAs, e.g., datasets, hardware, software) and to (*2*) include the extra capabilities of service dynamic deployment, application construction and application monitoring. In particular, DLIs are characterized by the following enabling functionality:

- **Registry Functionality:** The purpose of registry functionality is keeping an up-to-date map of the resources registered to the DLI and of the applications living within the RDL. The map consists of all resource profiles, provided and kept up-do-date by the organizations responsible of the resources. Since resources can be dynamically added, removed, or change their status, service resources in the need of consuming resources of given type rely on the registry's resource discovery functionality (profile search) to search among the available resources the ones they are willing to consume.
- **Policy Enforcement Functionality:** Functionality addressing resource access security, that is ensuring resources are assigned a security context defining the terms of their usage and access by others and their ability (roles) to use or access other resources.
- **Application Design Functionality:** Functionality providing UIs for the creation of an application based on existing resources and available resource types. Design functionality UIs may offer different level of abstraction, depending on the skills of the targeted end users. For example, UIs may offer high-level functional views of applications, where end users can select from several pre-crafted application templates (e.g., report drafting application). In other cases, they can offer low-level views of the system and provide end users with resource browsing and handling tools. Examples are UIs for the dynamic deployment and configuration of software resources onto given hardware resources to create the relative service resources. Design functionality users, i.e., RDL designers, can personalize their applications by customizing functionality to be provided, internal processing workflows, quality of service and delegating the service to perform application deployment based on the availability of resources on the infrastructure. Once applications are deployed

and running, monitoring functionality may allow for their run-time administration to verify that quality of service is respected.

- **Application Monitoring Functionality:** In the construction of an application, RDL designers must specify the quality of service parameters, measured in terms of degree of robustness (availability), performance, and aliveness. An application defines its robustness level by specifying the minimal number of instances for each resource type it includes, its performance by specifying the kind of hardware resources (e.g., computational resources, RAM, disk space) required for executing given software resources, and its liveness through a number of resource-related conditions whose satisfaction determines the application liveness degree. An example of combination of robustness, performance, and liveness conditions may be that of an application requiring that at least 3 instances of Index Status Resources are available across different Hardware Resources supporting expected X CPU power, Y of RAM and Z of disk, and that these are full replicas of each other. The monitoring functionality supports RDL administrators at continuously verifying that application robustness, performance and aliveness conditions are respected. When this is not the case (e.g., only 2 of the 3 Index Status Resources expected are available), the functionality may attempt corrective actions (e.g., a new Index Status Resource is created on an existing Index Service resource) or, when this is not possible (e.g., only 2 Hardware Resourccs with such features are available), sends warning messages to RDL administrators (e.g., installation of a new Hardware Resource with such properties, so that the fix can be applied by the Monitoring Service).

DIGITAL LIBRARY INFRASTRUCTURE TECHNOLOGIES

Given the functional requirements of RDLs and the sustainability issues they entail, computer and information science research have recently opened a new research avenue, that of digital library infrastructures. The mission is to devise DLMS technology capable of facilitating RDL designers, developers, and administrators at accomplishing their tasks, while reducing the costs of the funding organizations.

As stated above, traditional DLMS technologies—such as repository platforms, e.g., Fedora (Payette & Lagoze, 1998), DSpace (Smith, et al., 2003), Eprints (Millington & Nixon, 2007), Greenstone (Witten, Bainbridge, & Boddie, 2001)—are not devised to cope with the realization of sustainable RDLs. Indeed, these are either conceived to deliver specific DL repository functionality, hence cannot be customized to match different needs, or instead are conceived to offer pure DL object storage functionality and leave the matter of functionality realization to further DLMS technologies. Accordingly, RDLs have been often realized from scratch, by integrating several open source or licensed technologies. Known examples are Europeana (Purday, 2009), OAIster-DLXS(Hagedorn, 2003), BASE (Pieper & Summann, 2006), and others, RDLs built to aggregate metadata records of publications collected from heterogeneous repositories and deliver homogeneous information spaces. As discussed in a previous work (Manghi, Mikulicic, Candela, Castelli, & Pagano, Realizing and Maintaining Aggregative Digital Library Systems: D-NET Software Toolkit and OAIster System, 2010) such systems are designed to successfully realize the expected aggregation functionality, but are not designed to facilitate functionality refinement and extension. In fact, they can cope with arbitrary large sets of aggregated records, unpredictable numbers of repositories, and in some cases deal with any input metadata formats, but their internal data processing workflows and end-user functionalities tend to be rather immutable. In other words, changes or updates to processing workflows and end-user functionalities imply expensive design and development human intervention on the code.

In the last few years, Service-Oriented Architecture (SOA) solutions have been also explored and adopted for the realization of RDLs. In fact, service-oriented applications can be run-time defined, modified, and automatically monitored thanks to the loosely coupled nature of services, encapsulation of service implementation, service sharing, service distribution, and service orchestration. Enabling functionality is implemented by so-called "enabling services" or "middleware," which implement the resource management functionalities of registry, security and orchestration. For such reasons, SOAs represent a good candidate for RDL construction, since they facilitate the evolution of applications and improve their ability to scale in size. On the other hand, when RDLs face quality-of-service and time frame requirements, SOAs still entail considerable development and administration costs and generally fail to meet them in a sustainable way. Moreover, the resulting DLMSs are tailored to support the given RDL scenario and generally fail at being reused in contexts where RDL requirements are distinct.

DLIs were conceived in attempt to overcome such limits and move to a new frontier of DLMSs. DLI technology is designed marrying general-purpose patterns, where sharing and reuse are the core characteristics (Manghi, Mikulicic, Candela, Artini, & Bardi, 2010). The objective is that of providing the tools and programming paradigms that can support designers and developers operating in different areas at realizing and maintaining their RDLs. To this aim, DLIs exploit ICT infrastructure principles, based on the notion of *Service-Oriented Infrastructures* (SOI) (Dimitrakos, Martrat, & Wesner, 2010). In SOIs, the RDL requirements depicted above are addressed by supporting enabling services that offer SOA's flexibility and autonomicity over richer resource models, which include, beyond services, all ICT resources involved in the chain of hardware deployment, software installation, service configuration, data management, and application deployment and monitoring. SOI resource models can include physical resources, such as servers, instruments, storage, computing resources, and digital resources, such as software, datasets, configuration packages, and real-world entity representations. In a running SOI, resources belonging to one organization (resource provider) are not limited in number and typology and, other than being available to the applications serving that organization, can be discovered, shared and reused by other organizations (resource consumers) as part of their applications, thereby supporting an *economy of scale* principle. Participation, interaction, and authorized sharing of resources are ruled by strict enabling services policies. In such an environment, several service-oriented applications can co-exist and their construction and part of their maintenance can be delegated to the SOI enabling services, which autonomically assemble resources to deploy applications and monitor resources to ensure quality of service thresholds. Moreover, by exploiting resources models and policies, SOI platforms can provide infrastructure administrators with advanced tools capable of abstracting over actions normally delegated to developers and system administrators in the process of application construction and maintenance:

- **Application Construction Tools:** On-demand and on-the-fly deployment of customized applications, out of the available resources or by automatically creating the missing ones. At a lower level, such tools may open to administrators or rely on "dynamic deployment functionality," capable of installing software resources over hardware resources in order to create new service resources.

- **Application Maintenance Tools:** Application quality of service can be autonomically and continuously monitored by the enabling middleware by exploiting resource management capabilities.

DLIs are domain-specific SOIs supporting the construction of RDLs. In this context, software and services resource categories are instantiated to offer functionality such as storage, indexing and processing of DL dataset resources, which in turn can be metadata records, payloads, compound objects, etc. Therefore, DLIs combine the benefits of SOIs (i.e., holistic approach, economy of scale, and flexibility and autonomicity applied to application construction, deployment and maintenance), with a rich set of ready-to-use DL functionality services, capturing the general requirements of RDL functional components. By construction, DLIs aim at matching evolving, time frame, quality of service, and large-scale requirements of RDLs, thereby drastically decreasing realization and maintenance costs.

In the following sections, we shall present the main features of two DLI enabling technologies, namely the D-NET Software Toolkit and the gCube system. Such systems have been used to operate a number of very-large RDLs in the context of European Projects or national initiatives. Among the most important ones, are to be mentioned DRIVER and OpenAIRE infrastructures for D-NET, and DILIGENT and D4Science infrastructures for gCube.

The D-NET Software Toolkit

The *D-NET* software toolkit[1] (Iatropoulou, Lebesis, Manghi, Manola, & Mikulicic, 2010) is a software system specifically conceived to support the realization of RDLs focussing on data aggregation aspects in the context of publications and relative metadata. Such RDLs, also known as data aggregators or repository federation systems, generally consist of two connected tiers: an aggregation system for populating an information space of metadata records by collecting and transforming (e.g., cleaning, enriching, curating) records from a set of data sources (e.g., OAI-PMH repositories); and a number of vertical applications (e.g., Web portals), providing groups of end-users with custom functionality over such information space (search, browsing, annotations, recommendations, collections, user profiling, etc). Typically, information spaces also offer access to third-party consuming systems through standard APIs and protocols, such as OAI-PMH, SRW, OAI-ORE.

The D-NET software toolkit, realized in the context of the DRIVER and DRIVER-II projects,[2] is a general-purpose and cost-efficient DLMS solution for the construction of RDLs supporting repository infrastructures. To this aim, it supports a service-oriented framework, whose services can be combined by developers to easily construct customized aggregation systems and personalized Web portals. The resource model of D-NET includes service and dataset resource categories: the former consists of several service types, covering data curation—including compound object management, authority file management, metadata transformation, full-text indexing, OAI-PMH/OAI-ORE export facilities—and end-user functionality aspects—including user profiling, recommendations, faceted search; the latter currently includes OAI-PMH repository resource types and FTP resource types. D-NET services can be run-time customized (e.g., to deal with metadata formats and transformations of interest), combined into workflows to match domain specific scenarios and new services can be added to the suite to compensate missing functionality. Besides, distribution, sharing, and orchestration of services enable the construction of scalable, robust and autonomic RDLs. As to autonomicity, D-NET enabling services (Candela, Castelli, Manghi, & Pagano, 2007) are capable of interpreting service workflows, which are manually defined out of existing services by RDL designers to construct applications (Sarasvati[3] workflow engine). Similar workflows can be defined to specify the application monitoring actions to be performed. Tools to help designers at designing their workflows from user interfaces are part of future work.

D-NET is open source and based on java Web Service technology. Currently it is the enabling software of a number of RDLs resulting from European projects and national initiatives. These include the DRIVER infrastructure (the European infrastructure of open access publications), the EFG system (the European portal of movie material), the HOPE system (the European portal of social history material), the OpenAIRE infrastructure (the European portal connecting scientific articles with EC project funding), and the Spanish-Recolecta aggregator (national repository aggregator of Spain). The ability to customize services and data processing workflows, as well as that of introducing new services, to match the directives of the specific application domain, has proved to be extremely effective. Development efforts have been limited to the realization of the missing services, while design and administration were limited to the definition of workflows and the customization of existing services.

The gCube Framework

gCube[4] (Candela, Castelli, & Pagano, 2010) is a software system specifically conceived to develop and operate large scale e-Infrastructures, enabling the declarative definition and automatic deployment and operation of Virtual Research Environments. It is the result of the collaborative efforts of researchers and developers from academic and industrial research centres including the Institute of Information Science and Technologies ISTI-CNR (IT), University of Athens (GR), University of Basel (CH), Engineering Ingegneria Informatica SpA (IT), University of Strathclyde (UK), CERN European Organization for Nuclear Research (CH), 4D SOFT Software Development Ltd (HU).

gCube facilities for e-Infrastructure development include a rich array of mediator services for interfacing with existing infrastructure enabling technologies including grid (e.g. gLite/EGEE), cloud (e.g. Hadoop) and data source (e.g. OAI-PMH) oriented approaches. Via these mediator services, the storage facilities, processing facilities and data resources of the external infrastructures are conceptually unified to become gCube resources. Facilities for deploying *gCube Nodes*, i.e. servers offering storage and computing facilities—similar to the *Infrastructure as a Service Cloud* (Foster, Zhao, Raicu, & Lu, 2008)—are also offered together with the dynamic deployment of gCube services—similar to the *Platform as a Service Cloud* (Foster, Zhao, Raicu, & Lu, 2008). These resources are complemented by the *Software as a Service Cloud* (Foster, Zhao, Raicu, & Lu, 2008) approach, i.e. offering software frameworks for data management, data integration, workflow definition and execution, information retrieval, and user interface building.

By relying on this impressive amount of resources and services, gCube based e-Infrastructures enable scientists to declaratively and dynamically build the *VREs* they need while abstracting on the implementation details (Assante, et al., 2008; Assante, Pagano, Candela, De Faveri, & Lelii, 2011). gCube technology implements a user friendly Platform as a Service Cloud "function" where the content, application services, and computing resources needed by a scientist are automatically aggregated and deployed, and made available through a Web based interface. The aggregated resources are also monitored to guarantee the VRE service.

FUTURE RESEARCH DIRECTIONS

The implementation of Digital Library Infrastructures is a challenging activity for a series of reasons including technical and organisational aspects. These aspects include all those underlying the implementation of (large-scale) information systems expected to serve scenario and users crossing the boundaries of multiple organisations. This includes a wide array of problems ranging from resources descriptions, distributed resources management, policy enforcements. Digital Library Infrastructure challenges include and extend those of Global Research Data Infrastructures (Thanos, 2011).

Digital Library Infrastructures should be designed, since the beginning, to *promote uptake, ensure usability, and guarantee sustainability*. These three aspects form a virtuous circle that if properly managed ensures the success of a specific Infrastructure. As regards *uptake*, it is fundamental that the community served by the specific Infrastructure, although virtual and aggregated by the Infrastructure itself, is provided with tools and facilities for managing and maintaining the Infrastructure services that have limited requirements with respect to community expertises. Moreover, the conceivers of the Infrastructure should plan how to engage the broader community of practice that can be served by the Infrastructure, e.g. it might be possible to build a core team that sustains the Infrastructure itself in the medium and long term by awareness raising, targeted training and other engagement events tailored to attract and convince key representatives of the community of practice. As regards *usability*, infrastructures building should be mainly a community building process rather than a technology development process. This implies that the focus should be primarily on using technology in identifying and rationalising workflows, procedures, and processes characterising a certain research scenario rather than having technology invading the research scenario and distracting effort from its real needs. As regards *sustainability*, it is fundamental that the resulting Infrastructure service is conceived as a vital tool in the community of practice it is dedicated to. Moreover, sustainability is further enhanced whenever the Infrastructure is perceived as a useful tool in the context of larger research initiatives and communities so to benefit from *economies of scales*, i.e. savings gained by an incremental level of production, and *economies of scopes*, i.e. savings gained by producing two or more distinct goods when the costs of doings so is less than that of producing each of them separately. Approaches and models oriented to promote uptake, ensure usability and guarantee sustainability of Digital Library Infrastructures should be identified.

CONCLUSION

Digital Libraries have achieved a fundamental role in our knowledge-based society, especially in the context of "scientific research." In this context, the novel multidisciplinary forms of research and the need for immediate and contemporary access to heterogeneous and independently grown content, brought up new and challenging requirements for Digital Library developers. This chapter discussed Digital Library Infrastructure as an approach for implementing such Digital Library effectively and efficiently. In particular, it discussed how an approach promoting sharing and reuse of a wide and evolving array of "assets" ranging from data sets to services and software components implementing various facilities, hardware supporting the operation of digital library constituents.

ACKNOWLEDGMENT

This work has been partially supported by the following EU projects: DILIGENT (FP6 of the European Commission, call FP6-2003-IST-2, Contract No. 004260, Sep. 2004 – Nov. 2007), D4Science (FP7 of the European Commission, call INFRA-2007-1.2.2, Contract No. 212488, Jan. 2008 – Dec. 2009), D4Science-II (FP7 of the European Commission, call INFRA-2008-1.2.2, Contract No. 239019, Oct. 2009 – Sep. 2011); DRIVER (FP6 of the European Commission, call FP6-2005-IST-5, Contract No. IST-034047, Jun. 2006 – Nov. 2007), DRIVER-II (FP7 of the European Commission, call INFRA-2007-1.2.1, Contract No. 212147, Dec. 2007 – Nov. 2009),

OpenAIRE (FP7 of the European Commission, call FP7-INFRASTRUCTURES-2009-1, Contract No. 246686, Dec. 2009 – Nov. 2012).

REFERENCES

Allan, R. (2009). *Virtual research environments: From portals to science gateways*. Oxford, UK: Chandos Publishing.

Assante, M., Candela, L., Castelli, D., Frosini, L., Lelii, L., & Manghi, P. (2008). An extensible virtual digital libraries generator. *Lecture Notes in Computer Science, 5173*, 122–134. doi:10.1007/978-3-540-87599-4_14

Assante, M., Pagano, P., Candela, L., De Faveri, F., & Lelii, L. (2011). An approach to virtual research environment user interfaces dynamic construction. In *Proceedings of Research and Advanced Technology for Digital Libraries - International Conference on Theory and Practice of Digital Libraries, TPDL 2011,* (pp. 101-109). Berlin, Germany: Springer.

Blanke, T., Candela, L., Hedges, M., Priddy, M., & Simeoni, F. (2010). Deploying general-purpose virtual research environments for humanities research. *Philosophical Transactions of the Royal Society A, 368*, 3813–3828. doi:10.1098/rsta.2010.0167

Bush, V. (1945). As we may think. *Atlantic Monthly, 176*, 101–108.

Candela, L., Akal, F., Avancini, H., Castelli, D., Fusco, L., & Guidetti, V. (2007). Diligent: Integrating digital library and grid technologies for a new earth observation research infrastructure. *International Journal on Digital Libraries, 7*(1-2), 59–80. doi:10.1007/s00799-007-0023-8

Candela, L., Athanasopoulos, G., Castelli, D., El Raheb, K., Innocenti, P., Ioannidis, Y., et al. (2011). *The digital library reference model.* D3.2b DL.org Project Deliverable.

Candela, L., Castelli, D., Manghi, P., & Pagano, P. (2007). Enabling services in knowledge infrastructures: The driver experience. In *Proceedings of the Third Italian Research Conference on Digital Library Systems, IRCDL 2007,* (pp. 71-77). Padova, Italy: DELOS.

Candela, L., Castelli, D., & Pagano, P. (2009). On-demand virtual research environments and the changing roles of librarians. *Library Hi Tech, 27*(2), 239–251. doi:10.1108/07378830910968191

Candela, L., Castelli, D., & Pagano, P. (2010). Making virtual research environments in the cloud a reality: The gCube approach. *ERCIM News, 83*, 32–33.

Candela, L., Castelli, D., & Pagano, P. (2011). History, evolution and impact of digital libraries. In Iglezakis, I., Synodinou, T.-E., & Kapidakis, S. (Eds.), *E-Publishing and Digital Libraries: Legal and Organizational Issues* (pp. 1–30). Hershey, PA: IGI Global.

Candela, L., Castelli, D., Pagano, P., & Simi, M. (2005). From heterogeneous information spaces to virtual documents. In *Proceedings of Digital Libraries: Implementing Strategies and Sharing Experiences, 8th International Conference on Asian Digital Libraries, ICADL 2005*. Bangkok, Thailand: Springer.

Carusi, A., & Reimer, T. (2010). Virtual research environment collaborative landscape study. *JISC*. Retrieved from http://www.jisc.ac.uk/media/documents/publications/vrelandscapereport.pdf

Cyberinfrastructure Council. (2007). *Cyberinfrastructure vision for the 21st century discovery*. Washington, DC: National Science Foundation.

Dimitrakos, T., Martrat, J., & Wesner, S. (Eds.). (2010). *Service oriented infrastructures and cloud service platforms for the enterprise*. Berlin, Germany: Springer. doi:10.1007/978-3-642-04086-3 e-Infrastructure Reflection Group. (2010). *Blue paper.* E-IRG.

European Parliament Council. (2007). *Directive 2007/2/EC of the European parliament and of the council of 14 March 2007 establishing an Infrastructure for spatial information in the European community (INSPIRE).* Brussels, Belgium: European Parliament.

European Strategy Forum on Research Infrastructures. (2010). *Strategy report on research infrastructures.* Brussels, Belgium: Publications Office of the European Union.

Europeana. (2008). *Website.* Retrieved from http://www.europeana.eu

Foster, I., & Kesselman, C. (1998). *The grid: Blueprint for a new computing infrastructure.* San Francisco, CA: Morgan Kaufmann.

Foster, I., Zhao, Y., Raicu, I., & Lu, S. (2008). Cloud computing and grid computing 360-degree compared. In *Proceedings of Grid Computing Environments Workshop, 2008, GCE 2008.* GCE.

Hagedorn, K. (2003). OAIster: A "no dead ends" OAI service provider. *Library Hi Tech, 21*(2), 170–181. doi:10.1108/07378830310479811

Hey, T., Tansley, S., & Tolle, K. (2009). *The fourth paradigm - Data-intensive scientific discovery.* New York, NY: Microsoft Research.

Iatropoulou, K., Lebesis, A., Manghi, P., Manola, N., & Mikulicic, M. (2010). On constructing repository infrastructures - The D-NET software toolkit. In *Proceedings of the International Conference on Open Repositories.* Open Repositories.

Joint Information Systems Committee. (2006). *e-Infrastructure briefing paper.* New York, NY: JISC.

Lagoze, C., Krafft, D., Cornwell, T., Dushay, N., Eckstrom, D., & Saylor, J. (2006). Metadata aggregation and "automated digital libraries": A retrospective on the NSDL experience. In *Proceedings of the 6th ACM/IEEE-CS Joint Conference on Digital Libraries,* (pp. 230-239). ACM/IEEE.

Lagoze, C., & Van de Sompel, H. (2001). The open archives initiative: Building a low-barrier interoperability framework. In *Proceedings of the 1st ACM/IEEE-CS Joint Conference on Digital Libraries,* (pp. 54-62). Roanoke, VA: ACM/IEEE.

Lave, J., & Wenger, E. (1991). *Situated learning: Legitimate peripheral participation.* Cambridge, UK: Cambridge University Press. doi:10.1017/CBO9780511815355

Licklider, J. (1965). *Libraries of the future.* Cambridge, MA: The MIT Press.

Manghi, P., Mikulicic, M., Candela, L., Artini, M., & Bardi, A. (2010). General-purpose digital library content laboratory systems. In *Proceedings of Research and Advanced Technology for Digital Libraries, 14th European Conference, ECDL 2010,* (pp. 14-21). Springer.

Manghi, P., Mikulicic, M., Candela, L., Castelli, D., & Pagano, P. (2010). Realizing and maintaining aggregative digital library systems: D-NET software toolkit and OAIster system. *D-Lib Magazine, 16*(3/4). doi:10.1045/march2010-manghi

Millington, P., & Nixon, W. J. (2007). EPrints 3 pre-launch briefing. *Ariadne,* 50.

Payette, S., & Lagoze, C. (1998). Flexible and extensible digital object and repository architecture (FEDORA). In *Proceedings of Research and Advanced Technology for Digital Libraries, Second European Conference, ECDL 1998,* (pp. 41-59). Heraklion, Greece: Springer.

Pieper, D., & Summann, F. (2006). Bielefeld academic search engine (BASE): An end-user oriented institutional repository search service. *Library Hi Tech*, *24*(4), 614–619. doi:10.1108/07378830610715473

Purday, J. (2009). Think culture: Europeana.eu from concept to construction. *The Electronic Library*, *27*(6), 919–937. doi:10.1108/02640470911004039

Smith, M., Barton, M., Bass, M., Branschofsky, M., McClellan, G., & Stuve, D. (2003). DSpace - An open source dynamic digital repository. *D-Lib Magazine*, *9*(1). doi:10.1045/january2003-smith

Thanos, C. (2011). *Global research data infrastructures: The GRDI2020 vision.* GRDI2020.

University of Michigan – Digital Library Production Service. (2012). *Website.* Retrieved from http://www.dlxs.org

Wenger, E. (1998). *Communities of practice: Learning, meaning and identity*. Cambridge, UK: Cambridge University Press.

Witten, I. H., Bainbridge, D., & Boddie, S. J. (2001). Greenstone - Open-source digital library software. *D-Lib Magazine*, *7*(10). doi:10.1045/october2001-witten

ADDITIONAL READING

Beivold, H. P., & Larsson, M. (2007). Component-based and service-oriented software engineering: Key concepts and principles. In *Proceedings of the 33rd EUROMICRO Conference on Software Engineering and Advanced Applications*, (pp. 13-20). EUROMICRO.

Belkin, N. (1999). Understanding and supporting multiple information seeking behaviors in a single interface framework. In *Proceedings of the Eighth DELOS Workshop: User Interfaces in Digital Libraries*, (pp. 11-18). European Research Consortium for Informatics and Mathematics.

Borgman, C. (1999). What are digital libraries? Competing visions. *Information Processing & Management*, *35*(3), 227–243.

Borgman, C. L. (2010). *Scholarship in the digital age: Information, infrastructure, and the internet*. Cambridge, MA: The MIT Press.

Fox, E., & Marchionini, G. (1998). Toward a worldwide digital library. *Communications of the ACM*, *41*(4), 29–32. doi:10.1145/273035.273043

Fox, E. A., Akscyn, R. M., Furuta, R. K., & Leggett, J. J. (1995). Digital libraries. *Communications of the ACM*, *38*(4), 23–28. doi:10.1145/205323.205325

Ioannidis, Y. (2005). Digital libraries at a crossroads. *International Journal on Digital Libraries*, *5*(4), 255–265. doi:10.1007/s00799-004-0098-4

Karande, A., Karande, M., & Meshram, B. B. (2011). Choreography and orchestration using business process execution language for SOA with web services. *International Journal of Computer Science Issues*, *8*(2).

Kuny, T., & Cleveland, G. (1996). The digital library: Myths and challenges. In *Proceedings 62nd IFLA General Conference*. IFLA.

Lesk, M. (2004). *Understanding digital libraries* (2nd ed.). San Francisco, CA: Morgan Kaufmann.

Papazoglou, M. P., Traverso, P., Dustdar, S., & Leymann, F. (2007). Service-oriented computing: State of the art and research challenges. *IEEE Computer, 11*.

Papazoglou, M. P., & van den Heuvel, W. J. (2007). Service-oriented architectures: Approaches, technologies and research issues. *The VLDB Journal*, *16*(3), 389–415. doi:10.1007/s00778-007-0044-3

Sengupta, S., Nellitheertha, H., & Sundarrajan, S. (2007). Service oriented infrastructure. *SETLabs Briefings, 5*(1).

Thomas, E. (2005). *Service-oriented architecture: Concepts, technology, and design*. Upper Saddle River, NJ: Prentice Hall PTR.

Witten, I. H., Bainbridge, D., & Nichols, D. M. (2009). *How to build a digital library* (2nd ed.). San Francisco, CA: Morgan Kaufmann.

KEY TERMS AND DEFINITIONS

Community of Practice: A group of people who share an interest, a craft, and/or a profession. The group can evolve naturally because of the members' common interest in a particular domain or area, or it can be created specifically with the goal of gaining knowledge related to their field. It is through the process of sharing information and experiences with the group that the members learn from each other, and have an opportunity to develop themselves personally and professionally (Lave & Wenger, 1991).

Digital Library: A potentially virtual organisation, that comprehensively collects, manages and preserves for the long depth of time rich digital content, and offers to its targeted user communities specialised functionality on that content, of defined quality and according to comprehensive codified policies (Candela, et al., 2011).

Digital Library Management System: A generic software system that provides the appropriate software infrastructure both (1) to produce and administer a Digital Library System incorporating the suite of facilities considered fundamental for Digital Libraries and (2) to integrate additional software offering more refined, specialized, or advanced facilities (Candela, et al., 2011).

Digital Library System: A deployed software system that is based on a possibly distributed architecture and provides all facilities required by a particular Digital Library. Users interact with a Digital Library through the corresponding Digital Library System (Candela, et al., 2011).

Infrastructure: An "operative" environment offering to a set of actors the services supporting management (i.e. creation, removal, and discovery) and handling (i.e. consumption or usage) of infrastructure resources in respect of given policies.

Research Digital Libraries: A Digital Library tailored to serve the needs of a scientific research community. Its functionality has typically to do with supporting the research life cycle, from storing and processing experimental data, to support drafting, sharing, and discovery of research publications.

Virtual Research Environment: A Web-based working environment conceived to provide scientists with a collaborative framework enabling them to produce and exchange results with peers around the globe in cost-efficient manner. A VRE not only offers capabilities for accessing cross-disciplinary data and knowledge, it also provides services for exploiting a multiplicity of other disparate tools and computing resources enabling innovative analysis, simulation and domain specific knowledge generation processes (Candela, Castelli, & Pagano, 2009).

ENDNOTES

1. http://www.d-net.research-infrastructures.eu/
2. http://www.driver-community.eu
3. http://code.google.com/p/sarasvati/
4. http://www.gcube-system.org

Chapter 2
Reengineering The Portal to Texas History℠: A Case Study

Kathleen Murray
University of North Texas, USA

William Hicks
University of North Texas, USA

Mark Phillips
University of North Texas, USA

Neena Weng
University of North Texas, USA

Dreanna Belden
University of North Texas, USA

ABSTRACT

This case study reports the activities, findings, and lessons learned during a project that replaced the legacy Digital Asset Management (DAM) system of The Portal to Texas History℠ at the University of North Texas Libraries with an open source system. This unique system decouples the application development framework from the backend infrastructure, effectively relieving the development and growth constraints inherent in the legacy system. In a novel approach for an academic library, genealogists participated in the user-centered, iterative approach used to prototype, develop, and test the user interface. The resulting system promoted productivity gains by enabling programming staff to work in parallel from specialized areas of expertise. A post-project review process identified a number of lessons learned, including the importance of representing the requirements and priorities of internal and external stakeholders. The review process also informed an application development model that may be useful to other digital libraries.

INTRODUCTION

The Portal to Texas History℠ is a gateway to a significant set of humanities collections within the digital library of the University of North Texas (UNT) Libraries (http://texashistory.unt.edu/). In collaboration with over 200 content partners, the Portal provides access to collections from Texas libraries, museums, archives, historical societies, and private collectors. The Portal archives and provides access to more than 165,000 digital objects, comprising over 2.3 million image files.

DOI: 10.4018/978-1-4666-2991-2.ch002

The range of primary source materials includes maps, books, manuscripts, newspapers, diaries, photographs, and letters. While materials primarily concern the 254 Texas counties, there are items related to most of the states in the USA and to over 40 other countries.

Materials include a fascinating array of rare and invaluable items that document Texas's history, such as handwritten correspondence between Santa Anna and Lorenzo de Zavala from the early 19th century and photograph collections covering seminal events, including the Dallas Police Department's investigation of the 1963 John F. Kennedy assassination and the Texas City Disaster of 1947. Historic newspapers represent a large segment of the materials, with over half a million searchable pages dating from 1829 to the present. This significant collection is not only used in traditional research by scholars and lifelong learners, but also forms the basis for a collaboration between UNT and Stanford University in text mapping research that is exploring new methods for programmatically finding and analyzing meaningful patterns.

Development of the Portal began in 2003 when the UNT Libraries selected a system vendor for its digital library, and, as is typical of many digital libraries, based design decisions largely on the requirements of librarians and what they imagined end users would need. When the reengineering project began in 2008, the number of unique visitors per month had grown from 1,000 in 2004 to over 20,000. This success was accompanied by operational and management challenges, which affected the Portal's content partners, users, and other stakeholders.

Scale issues created by the continuous addition of content and the increased usage required constant attention and distracted the systems team from other areas of development. The underlying data model for both the digital objects and descriptive metadata were limiting the kind of items that could be ingested into the system. Development constraints associated with the underlying technical infrastructure also emerged. In particular, the design and implementation of new features and functions was limited by outdated software and changing vendor priorities. It was often not feasible to make interface design changes without programmatic changes in the supporting infrastructure.

In 2007, a decision was made to replace the legacy asset management system with a digital library infrastructure and framework based largely on modern open source components widely used throughout the world. This approach distinguishes the UNT Libraries within the broader library community, in which libraries generally employ single-vendor, integrated systems for their digital libraries. Replacing the legacy system also presented an opportunity to include users directly in the design process.

The UNT Libraries received a National Leadership Grant from the Institute of Museum and Library Services (LG-06-07-0040-07) for a two-year study (2007-2009) to redesign the Portal's interface. At the outset of the project, an application development model was drafted to guide the project's work. The model employed user-centered design methods within a rapid development framework. The framework required reengineering the underlying technical infrastructure, which was undertaken in conjunction with this project. The model involved three teams within the Digital Libraries Division: (1) system designers and programmers, (2) user interface designers, and (3) user study researchers. The user group involved in the project was genealogical researchers, a significant and growing user group of both libraries and archives. Genealogists participated in needs assessment activities at the start of the project and in usability testing at three points over the course of the project. The goals of the project were:

- Implementation of a rapid development framework within the UNT Libraries, Digital Libraries Division.

- Implementation of an iterative user-centered design process to create a user interface to The Portal to Texas History℠ optimized for genealogists.
- Identification of the information context and information needs of genealogists interacting with The Portal to Texas History℠.
- Creation of an application development model for digital libraries that incorporates user-centered design principles.

The redesigned Portal was launched in two public releases: Release 1 in June of 2009 and Release 2 in October of 2009. Following the second release, project team members participated in a post-project review. From this review, a revised application development model was created. Both the model and the infrastructure resulting from this project have supported the rapid growth of digital collections within the UNT Digital Library and the further enhancement of the user interface.

Objectives

This chapter is a case study of how one large, public university library dealt with growth and technology challenges within its digital library. The first objective is to describe the application development-working model and the specific activities and findings involved in each of the three phases of work within the project: (1) requirements definition, (2) application development, and (3) usability testing. The second objective is to illustrate the value of a post-project review process by including the key lessons learned as well as the final application development model that resulted from the review process. The third objective is to report the project outcomes and impact. In closing, reflections on the experience gained during the project are stated, as well as implications for other digital library application development projects.

BACKGROUND

Digital Asset Management Systems

Most libraries use asset management systems to manage the end-to-end processes that support their digital collections, which may be comprised of multiple object types and formats including photographs, maps, documents, audio recordings, newspapers, video, and books. Digital Asset Management (DAM) systems provide storage for a library's digital objects and their associated metadata, as well as tools to manage and provide access to these assets (Kim, et al., 2007).

Some DAM systems are add-on products that leverage the investment libraries have made in Integrated Library Systems (ILS). These systems interface with an ILS product from the same vendor and generally include tools to import, catalog, edit, store, search, retrieve content and metadata, and generate statistics (Boss, 2009). Examples include Media Management from Innovative Interfaces, Portfolio™ from SirsiDynix®, and DigiTool® from Ex Libris. CONTENTdm® from OCLC® is an example of a DAM system that is not an ILS add-on product but does offer libraries a similar set of tools for the storage, curation, and distribution of their digital collections.

Summarizing from a previous study (Marchionini & Fox, 1999), Marchionini, Plaisant, and Komlodi state that, "most research and development projects to date have been devoted to technology and content" (2003, p. 123). Matuskiak (2006) asserts that most digital library research concentrates on infrastructure and metadata. Early development of DAM systems is consistent with these observations. Historically, development of DAM systems concentrated on providing workflows for content providers, such as libraries, and for persons creating the digital assets, while particularly emphasizing metadata tools. DAM systems have offered little design flexibility to local developers in terms of customization and enhancement of the user interface to meet local requirements (Salo, 2008).

More recent open source DAM-related projects offer increased flexibility for local developers interested in customizing the user interface to meet local requirements (Jansson, 2010; Uzwyshyn, 2008). Open source DAM systems have been created by in-house programming efforts such as the New Zealand Digital Library Project at the University of Waikato, which developed Greenstone, a suite of open source software for building a digital library. Other open source DAM systems have been built through collaborations between libraries and private companies. The Portal to Texas History^{SM} at UNT Libraries was originally built with Index Data, a software development company.

In the digital repository arena, DuraSpace supports two open source platforms: DSpace, a turnkey institutional repository application, and Fedora, a framework for building digital repositories. Two open source projects, FEZ, developed by the University of Queensland Library as a front end to Fedora, and Manakin, developed by Texas A&M University for DSpace, enable customization of the user interface. Of course, not all libraries have the staff with Web application development expertise to support advanced customization, even with tools such as Manakin (Janssen, 2010). Many libraries continue to require turnkey DAM solutions with a limited set of options for interface customization.

Rapid Application Development

Rapid application development strives to complete development in as few steps as possible and in a relatively short timeframe (e.g., 30-90 days) (Fernandez, Martinez-Prieto, de la Fuente, Vegas, & Adiego, 2008). Software solutions are usually based on standards and strive for simplicity and portability. Because solutions can be designed and developed in an accelerated timeframe, a website, such as The Portal to Texas History^{SM}, can be more responsive to changing needs.

Rapid application development occurs within a Web framework, such as the open source frameworks of Ruby on Rails® and Django®. Web frameworks are configured using modules, components, and tools, which are easily interchangeable, robust, highly cohesive, and loosely coupled. This is sometimes referred to as shared nothing architecture. Components in a Web framework are supported by flourishing active user communities and audited by a large base of users, whereas components developed for niche communities are generally avoided. Within the framework, components at each level are highly scalable to allow costs to be distributed across the framework as increased capacity is needed in particular areas.

Application development within a Web framework tends to follow an established flow in which functional requirements are first identified and generally remain unchanged during the application development process. Developers use prototyping tools to create functional designs based on the requirements. Using an iterative process, the prototypes can be revised in response to user feedback. Marchionini et al. (2003) state that digital library development is well-served by an iterative, process-oriented approach; however, only a few studies (Norberg, Vassiliadis, Ferguson, & Smith, 2005; Van House, Butler, Ogle, & Schiff, 1996) have included an iterative user-centered design approach for creation or redesign of user interfaces to digital library collections. Within a Web development framework, this iterative process between developers and users continues until a final prototype is agreed upon. Subsequently, development and testing of the Web application occurs.

The project reported in this chapter replaced the legacy software development platform for The Portal to Texas History^{SM}, which had a development community with dozens of fellow developers, with an open source Web application framework, whose components have Web communities with thousands or tens of thousands of developers. This novel approach enabled developers within the UNT Libraries to solve problems by leveraging the solutions and innovations of developers from different disciplines and knowledge domains. The Web development framework made it possible to integrate these solutions and application code into the Portal's user interface, allowing more flexibility in implementing changes in response to user requirements.

Genealogists: A Significant User Community

Many stereotypes have a basis in fact and the view of genealogy as an avocation for those in middle to later life is generally supported in demographic research. A study of New Zealand genealogists revealed that 73% of respondents were female and 87% were aged 51 or over (Kuglin, 2004). The Fullerton Genealogy Study found that (1) 72.2% of respondents were female, (2) the average number of years spent pursuing genealogy was 14, and (3) the average age at the inception of their research was 40 (Drake, 2001).

This user community is poised to grow significantly in the coming years. In 1995 four out of ten Americans were somewhat interested in genealogy (Fulkerson, 1995) and by 2000, 60% of Americans were interested (Gallop-Gerdman, 2000). A 2005 study by Market Strategies, Inc. (MSI) indicated that the percentage of Americans interested in genealogy had grown to 73% (Generations Network, 2005). This trend indicates a growing interest in genealogical research.

Genealogists are also a significant percentage of the users of digital libraries, archives, and record repositories (Boyns, 1999; Cherry & Duff, 2002; Duff & Johnson, 2003). Despite this, only a few studies have investigated genealogists' information seeking behavior (Duff & Johnson, 2003; Fulton, 2009; Kuglin, 2004; Skinner, 2010; Yakel, 2004). The significance of this user group and the fact that it is growing, compel the digital library community to seriously examine this user group to better inform their services and user interfaces.

Butterworth (2006) declares that traditional information seeking models such as those put forward by Kuhlthau and Belkin break down when applied to information seekers pursuing personal history. When information seekers do research as a leisure activity, their motivations are significantly different—these users pursue "research undertaken primarily for pleasure" (Butterworth, 2006, p. 2). In a study of amateur genealogists around the world, Fulton (2009) identified leisure as an important information-seeking context.

Taylor (1991) asserts that effective design of information retrieval systems should be informed by an understanding of the unique information use environments of discrete user groups. This project investigated the information needs of genealogists and conducted initial usability tests with genealogists of the existing user interface to The Portal to Texas History[SM]. The results of these assessments informed the design of a prototype user interface optimized for use by genealogists and developed within a Web application development framework within the UNT Libraries.

THE REENGINEERING PROCESS

The reengineering project was guided by a draft application development model (Figure 1). Three teams were identified at the start of the project: System Development, Interface Design, and User Studies. Consistent with user-centered design, the three iterative phases of work over the course of the project included: (1) Requirements Definition, (2) Application Development, and (3) Usability Testing. The arrows identified the collaborative interfaces and the handoff points among the teams.

Project Teams

System Development Team

The system development team consisted of two programmers and a system architect. The system architect was experienced in architectural design

Figure 1. Draft application development model

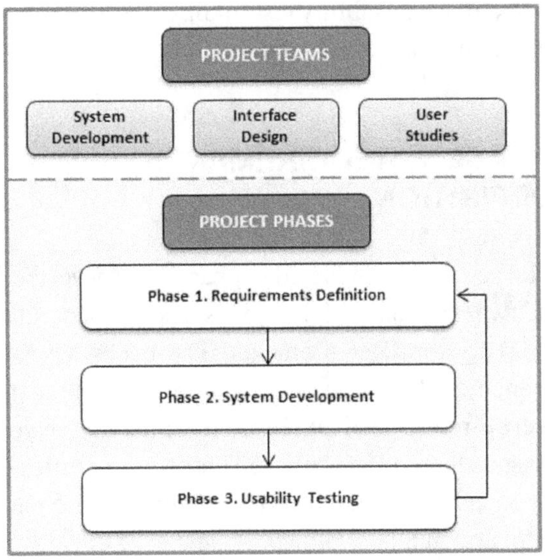

and proficient in data model specification. The programmers had the requisite skill sets to support the backend system components, in particular the search platforms, servers, and the Web development framework. System developers were responsible for configuring, coding, and testing infrastructure components. System developers took great care to identify and specify each component of the Portal system so that the key constraints of the legacy system were removed. The objective was to build a system and a development framework that would enable independent utilization of the expertise of the Libraries' Web interface designers, while at the same time accommodating future growth in both usage and content.

Interface Design Team

The user interface team consisted of two librarians whose singular focus was Web development. Both had experience with best-practices in information architecture, accessibility compliance, and were familiar with the processes of user-centered design. Interface designers created and coded the user interface components. As part of the overall design process, the user interfaces group helped guide the larger development team in their assessment of real world design issues and their application in the current project. After some initial work in needs assessment, the team was tasked with creating visual mock-ups for paper prototyping, and with generating and revising html wireframes. As other teams continued their development efforts, the user interface team transformed the incoming ideas, pseudo-code, wireframes, and requirements documents into the actual source code and presentation logic that would be used for the final deliverable, a working site.

User Studies Team

The user studies team consisted of one researcher, with experience in conducting interviews, focus groups, survey research, and usability testing, as well as a graduate research assistant. The researcher was responsible for all communication and interaction with the genealogists who participated in the project. The team developed all data gathering instruments (i.e., the focus group protocols, questionnaires, quality assurance tests, and usability tests), conducted the focus group discussions, and administered all tests. Subsequent to data gathering the team analyzed the data and reported the findings to the other project teams. These findings directly impacted the design and development activities, as well as measuring overall user satisfaction with the resulting system.

Project Phases

Phase 1: Requirements Definition

Infrastructure and interface requirements were created by the system development and user interface teams. Both teams also generated questions, ideas, and prototypes regarding possible features and functional enhancements to the existing Portal. The user studies team used these to develop a protocol for focus group discussions with members of genealogical societies. In addition to conducting focus groups, the user studies team (1) analyzed a log of comments submitted by the Portal's users over the previous three years and (2) conducted initial usability tests of the existing Portal with genealogists. After analyzing all of the data collected, the user studies team drafted a set of functional requirements for the user interface. These requirements were refined by members of the three teams and classified into implementation phases or releases.

Phase 2: System Development

The system development team designed and implemented the necessary hardware and software infrastructure to create the rapid development framework. This team created specifications for the framework's overall architecture, components, tools, and workflows. Likewise, system developers created required application specifications and code. The interface design team first translated user, non-functional, and functional requirements into paper prototypes, which were subsequently transformed into HTML mock-ups. These, in turn, informed the final design and its implementation in client-side code.

The system development and interface design teams created and refined workflows to support their separate but inter-dependent design and development work. These two teams also performed internal quality assurance tests. The user studies team conducted Quality Assurance (QA) tests of completed software releases with individuals external to the design and development teams (i.e., library staff, student workers, and users). The system development and interface design teams used the QA test findings to refine each software release prior to its public launch.

Phase 3: Usability Testing

Subsequent to the public launch of each release, the user studies team conducted usability tests with members of genealogical societies. The arrow from Usability Testing to Functional Requirements in Figure 1 indicates a key feedback loop in the work, that is, usability test findings became input for future functional requirements.

PHASE 1: REQUIREMENTS DEFINITION

The activities conducted in phase 1 are described in two sections: (1.1) Needs Assessment and (1.2) System Requirements. The needs assessment includes the activities in which genealogists were directly involved. Section 1.3 lists the major lessons learned in phase 1. These were identified by members of the three project teams who participated in a post-project review.

1.1. Needs Assessment

1.1.1. Identification of Innovative Features

After ample exploration and discussion, more than 15 innovative features, which might have great potential to enhance the user experience, were identified and considered by the team. These included navigation options and displays of metadata, objects, and search results. At the onset of the project, social networking sites were becoming popular on the Web and in keeping with this wider trend, it was anticipated that the new interface would include social features, such as commenting and tagging.

Additionally, a number of open source and freely available widgets and other easily implementable code libraries that could enable users to interact with websites had become available and could be readily adapted to local interface designs. MIT's SIMILE Timeline and the image magnifier code for Zoomify™ were two such examples. From within the world of libraries and booksellers, a number of sites had begun offering faceted displays of search results in order to provide users more choices for filtering and evaluating their results.

In order to assess the interest and usefulness of these new social and interactive functions, mock-ups were created for the focus group discussions conducted by the user studies team. Figure 2 is a mock-up of a possible comment function. Additionally, mock-ups of five object navigation designs were created for the focus group discussions. The options incorporated several of the proposed interactive functions including tabs, widgets, and collapsible menus.

1.1.2. Focus Group Discussions

During February and March of 2008, three focus group discussions were held. Nineteen genealogists from two northeast Texas genealogical societies participated in one of three focus group discussions. Participants were primarily females (84%; n=16) and all were over 50 years of age. On average, participants had been doing genealogical research for 21 years. Of the 19 participants, only three reported having professional genealogical credentials and these three were all members of the Association of Professional Genealogists (APG). However, about 70% reported having memberships and affiliations with local, state, and national genealogical organizations, including the National Genealogical Society, the USGenWeb Project, the TXGenWeb Project, the Hispanic Organization of Genealogy and Research (HOGAR de Dallas), and several local genealogical societies.

The focus group protocol included a semi-structured questionnaire and a slideshow illustrating features of the legacy system interface as well as ideas for new features. Marchionini et al. (2003) noted: "An inherent limitation in directly assessing the human needs for an innovation is the fact that potential users must imagine what the innovation can and will do for them" (p. 123). In order to address this limitation and to stimulate thinking, mock-ups were created by the user interface team to illustrate possible new features for the Portal. The discussions addressed each of the key functional areas within the Portal: (1) Search, both basic and advanced; (2) Browse; (3) Search results; and (4) Object navigation for photographs, maps, and multi-page documents. The discussions were recorded and the audio recordings were subsequently transcribed and analyzed.

In addition to providing input for the functional requirements discussed at the end of this section, the findings identified key information seeking characteristics of genealogical researchers. These include:

1. Genealogists, both hobbyists and professionals, research family histories as well as the historical and cultural context in which the individuals lived. In the former instance, genealogists primarily seek three types of data about major events in individuals' lives: names, locations, and dates. In the latter instance, genealogists seek information that situates individuals within a larger historical context in order to discover insights about the society and culture in which they lived.
2. Most often, genealogists will begin their information search using a surname, although many will start by using advanced search features to add a location (often a county name), as well as a date range.
3. Genealogists include people with a wide range of both research experience and computer skills. Less experienced researchers need visible features to successfully navigate the materials.
4. Some terms commonly used in digital library interfaces are generally misunderstood or not understood by most genealogical researchers. These include metadata, relevance, permalink, fulltext, and creator. Likewise, most genealogists do not understand distinctions among file formats, such as jpeg and tiff.
5. Genealogists often publish their family histories and are attentive to copyright restrictions and the need for permission from copyright holders prior to publishing the materials they discover. Likewise, genealogists are aware of

Figure 2. Example mock-up of a comment function

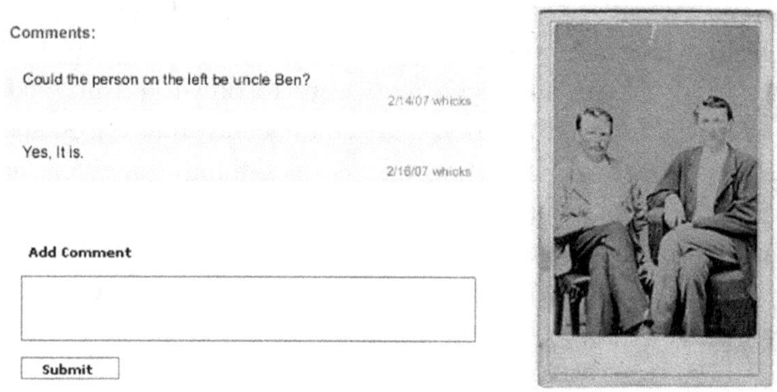

the importance of citing references for their information sources. However, in practice, many genealogists find this a difficult task and fail to obtain the data elements needed for adequate source citations.

6. Genealogists often wish to see the source objects whose digital surrogates they discover in libraries and archives. Having found items of interest to their research, they will often explore a digital collection more fully and may well visit the library or archive in person at a future date.

1.1.3. Feature Ranking Questionnaire

Participants in the three focus groups and the usability tests completed a questionnaire that measured their interest in specific features that the reengineered Portal might include. The results were tabulated and the features were ranked by the percentage of users indicating they were interested in each feature.

The top two features of interest to all participants were saving items and saving search results. These were followed by adding items to personal favorites and accessing the personal search history for an active session. Compared to the focus group participants, the participants in the usability tests were somewhat more interested in building lists of objects and somewhat less interested in commenting on items and annotating images. The features of less interest to all participants were receiving RSS feeds of search results, rating the historical significance of objects, and commenting on other users' comments.

1.1.4. Overall Design Characteristics

Members of the Digital Libraries Division staff, including system developers, programmers, metadata librarians, interface designers, program coordinators for the Portal, and staff involved in the digitization and preservation of materials, completed a brief questionnaire that included the questions listed below regarding: (1) general information about the Portal, (2) the audience the Portal serves, and (3) the desired perception the Portal should strive to elicit in visitors.

- **General Information**
    - What are the goals and objectives of the site?
    - What aspects of your current site do you like and/or not like?
- **Audience**
    - Describe the audience and typical user(s) of the Portal?
    - How often is the user online?
    - What does he/she generally use the Portal for?

- **Perception**
  - Use a few adjectives to describe how users should perceive the Portal (examples include prestigious, friendly, corporate, fun, forward thinking, innovative, and cutting edge).
  - Is this different than the current image perception?
  - List the URLs of any sites you find compelling and would like us to use in conceptualizing or for reference.
  - What specifically do you like about these sites?

The objective of the questionnaire was to stimulate thinking among internal stakeholders that would identify the Portal's major user groups and inform decisions regarding the overall design characteristics of the interface, as well as desirable features and functions.

1.1.5. Internal Stakeholders Group Discussion

Particularly important to the design effort was achieving a consensus among internal stakeholders regarding priorities for the Portal's overall information architecture, functionality, and design. An additional design goal was to achieve an optimal balance between the needs and priorities of users, content partners, and the library. To these ends a discussion among a group of internal stakeholders was conducted by the interface design team.

The group included current members of the Digital Libraries Division as well as members of the initial team within the UNT Libraries who had identified the need for the Portal, recruited the founding partners, obtained seed funding from external sources, selected the original asset management system, designed the original data model, and launched the first public system in 2004. This enabled a range of experiences and perspectives to be considered in the design of the user interface. Participants shared and discussed websites they particularly liked. Features, navigation, and aesthetic preferences were demonstrated.

Consensual decisions concerning the overall design, functions, and information architecture were identified. For example, the following user groups were identified as the audiences the Portal serves: researchers, historians, genealogists, educators/teachers, K-12 students, lifelong learners, family history enthusiasts, and the general public. However, consensus was reached that the needs and opinions of three expert user groups (researchers, historians, and genealogists) would outweigh the preferences of other groups when conflicting aspects of the design arose. Based on the experience of the design team, decisions based on consensus that are established early in the design process help clarify what is expected of the development team. Additionally, they prevent downstream scope creep that is always costly in terms of time and human resources.

1.1.6. Analysis of User-submitted Comments

Portal visitors submitted 425 comments to library staff via a link on object display pages between October 13, 2005 and January 8, 2008. Content analysis classified these into two groups: comments related to a specific object itself and other types of feedback (e.g., typos and requests for copies). About 60 percent of the comments in the log were classified as comments about objects and about 40 percent as other feedback. Analysis of the comments about objects proved more fruitful in terms of understanding the Portal's users.

The comment group was further classified into three categories: (1) pertaining to people depicted in an object; (2) pertaining to locations depicted in an object; and (3) pertaining to other object content, including descriptive metadata.

Within each of these three categories, comments were further classified as identifications, questions, notes, or errors (e.g., in the content of the descriptive metadata).

The analysis indicated that users were particularly interested in identifying people and locations, although their comments often included dates as well. About half (51%) of the object-specific comments related to people depicted in objects and 28% related to locations depicted. This interest echoed the importance of names, locations, and dates that emerged in the focus group discussions. Further analysis of this group found that user comments identifying people constituted the largest sub-category within the entire log (16%; *n*=71). Identifying locations ranked third within the entire log (10%; *n* = 44).

1.1.7. Initial Usability Testing

Consistent with usability testing practices (i.e., Nielsen, 2000), five volunteers from a genealogical society were recruited by a member of the project's advisory board to participate in usability testing of the legacy system. The participants were females between 40 and 70 years of age. On average, they had been doing genealogical research for 14 years. One person was a member of the Association of Professional Genealogists (APG) and two were members of the National Genealogical Society (NGS). Test sessions lasted one hour and a talk-aloud protocol was used.

A test script with four scenarios reflecting the types of research goals that genealogists commonly address was created. These goals were: (1) find an answer to a specific question about a person, (2) test a hypothesis concerning where an ancestor lived around a certain date, (3) find evidence to prove a statement from one ancestor about another ancestor, and (4) investigate a topic related to the history of a certain area. Participants read aloud a scenario and its associated tasks prior to searching or browsing the Portal to find an answer.

Audio, video, and screen recordings of each session were captured using Morae® Recorder software from TechSmith. Each recording was analyzed using Morae® Manager software to identify the duration of each task, key observations and problems, tester prompts, and illustrative video clips. Task completion was rated either 0 (*completed with ease*), 1 (*completed with difficulty*), or 2 (*not completed*).

Morae® Manager was also used to measure the Portal's effectiveness and efficiency in regard to the test scenarios. For the four scenarios tested, the Portal's efficiency, as measured by the average time participants engaged in each scenario, was clearly related to its effectiveness scores. The more difficulty participants encountered in effectively resolving a scenario, the more time they spent attempting to do so. Overall, participants were fairly motivated to resolve the scenarios, even though the records they might commonly use to do so (e.g., census records or burial registers) are not available on the Portal.

Among the findings was important feedback regarding the Portal's home page, which for new users of the system provided no clues regarding the types of information and records contained in the Portal. Other findings supported priorities that emerged in the focus group discussions: (a) name searches are a first priority for genealogists; (b) access to information needed for citations is important; and (c) saving and printing objects is important.

1.2. System Requirements

1.2.1. Functional Requirements

Analysis of the data collected from the various activities of the needs assessment resulted in a draft set of functional requirements for the Portal's user interface. The requirements were categorized into existing or new functions. Existing functions were grouped into the following categories: (1)

search (basic and advanced), (2) browse, (3) search results (list and grid views), (4) metadata, (5) object navigation, and (6) help. Six new functional categories were identified:

1. **Obtain:** Allow users to save and print objects, along with their citations and metadata. Users may order high-resolution prints of images.
2. **Comment:** Allow any user to submit error reports and allow registered users to add comments, view others' comments, and communicate with other registered users.
3. **Register:** Offer users a simple registration process.
4. **Create Lists:** Allow registered users to merge search result lists and create object lists.
5. **View Map:** Allow users to view search results on a map of Texas counties that visually indicates the variance in the number of hits for each county.
6. **View Timeline:** Allow users to view search results on a timeline.

The functional requirements provided a foundation for the redesign of the interface to The Portal to Texas History^{SM}. The requirements were classified by members of the three project teams into one of four development priorities: (1) Implement in Release 1; (2) Implement in Release 2; (3) Consider for Future Releases (i.e., not possible in the project's timeframe); and (4) No Development Planned (i.e., not feasible within the system).

At the time of this classification, existing workflows within the Digital Libraries Division did not include a formal review process for draft functional requirements. One oversight in the review process was the failure to include the Portal's program coordinators. As a result, some requirements that should have been clarified or omitted were not. Additionally, documentation activities (i.e., writing help content, modifying metadata practices, and updating partner and collection profiles) could have been better understood at an earlier date and assigned to appropriate staff members who were not directly involved on one of the three project teams.

A second issue with the draft requirements was with the initial wording of some them. For example, some requirements were redundant and could have been eliminated; other requirements were quite similar and could have been merged. Sometimes requirements included too much design specificity (e.g., "include a print icon on search results pages"). It would have been helpful to have spent more time and resources early in the project to resolve these issues prior to classifying the requirements.

Functional requirements identified for implementation in Release 2 of the Portal were revised in June 2009. The major modification resulted from a decision to defer development of a shared commenting feature, which required development of a registration capability that was beyond the development resources available for the project.

1.2.2. Structural Requirements

As a prerequisite for implementing the rapid development framework, system requirements included specifications and practices to enable implementation and testing of prototype technologies and standards prior to final implementation. The four key specifications are listed below.

1. **Digital Object Manifestations Model:** This is an extensible model that defines what a digital object entity is as well as a consistent naming convention for the possible manifestations of any digital object (e.g., various file formats such as TIFF, JPEG, and PDF for a specific digital object). Based on existing and future content, the object model allowed the development team to create standardized tools for reading and writing digital objects. METS (Metadata Encoding

and Transmission Standard) was used as a serialization format for this object model throughout the system.

2. **Persistent Identifiers:** Archival Resource Keys (ARKs) were implemented as part of the persistent identifier strategy. ARKs provide a globally unique naming system for objects in the digital library. Digital objects within the Portal were mapped to URLs, with ARKs playing a key role in providing logical, hackable, and bookmarkable identifiers for the system. For example, the thumbnail for each object in the system is available by appending/thumbnail/ to the end of the ARK URL, which always returns a thumbnail as in: http://texashistory.unt.edu/ark:/67531/metapth163241/thumbnail/.
3. **Metadata Scheme:** The UNT Libraries uses a locally qualified Dublin Core® metadata format (UNTL[1]) for all collections within its digital library. The UNTL input guidelines and formatting rules were updated to reflect the new data model. Additionally, all controlled vocabularies used within the UNTL metadata scheme, as well as in other parts of the system, were added to a controlled vocabulary management tool. The new metadata model allows for organic change within the scheme by adding qualifiers as needed to the vocabularies management tool. An example would be the addition of new types of dates associated with the lifecycle of an object (e.g., date harvested or date embargoed until).
4. **Edit Application:** Requirements for a new application (edit) to facilitate modification of records in the new system were specified for later development. The edit application provides a dashboard for collection maintainers (e.g., content partners) to interact with their objects in the system. They can search, browse, and limit records to a subset of all their records and edit each of those records through a user-friendly Web-based interface. When saved by the record maintainer, the edit application versions the record. This makes it available for future edits and re-indexes the new record, making any metadata changes available to the public instantly. Many of the record maintainers for the Portal are external partners not affiliated with UNT.

1.2.3. Architectural Requirements

As the number and complexity of digital objects in the Portal grew, it was apparent that key areas within the legacy system needed to be re-engineered to increase flexibility and to accommodate future growth. A major challenge within the legacy system architecture was that one application was responsible for both the access copies of objects as well as the preservation metadata associated with the master objects, which were managed by another system. Additionally, the legacy system made assumptions about the location of files within a traditional file system, which made adding storage resources challenging. The bottom-line result was a bottleneck within the system that limited the amount of new content that could be ingested. In order to address these inherent issues with the legacy system, architectural changes were needed in the core infrastructure. The fundamental change was to move from a monolithic system design to a decoupled, Web services approach to system architecture.

The reengineered system architecture specified two core infrastructure systems: external and internal systems (Figure 3). This architectural design effectively decoupled access services associated with digital library programs, such as The Portal to Texas History[SM], from preservation services associated with Libraries' digital repository. Doing so has allowed the UNT Libraries to manage the growth of its storage and processing components in a staggered, systematic manner that was not possible within the legacy system architecture.

The external system includes an administrative component, the *Metadata Editor*, for editing and adjusting records via the *edit* application. It also includes the *Complex Object Digital Archive* or

Figure 3. Core infrastructure systems and components

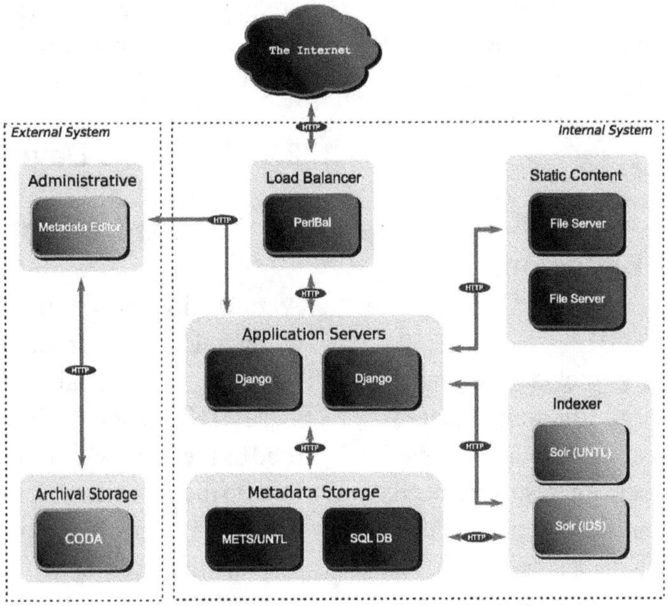

CODA, which is the archival storage component of the system that supports long-term preservation and curation of the Portal's digital objects. In addition to preservation management of the Portal's digital objects, *CODA* manages the master files for other digital library initiatives within the UNT Libraries.

When possible, open source software and tools were selected, for example, the Ubuntu® Linux operating system, the Apache HTTP Server™, the Python programming language, and mod_python, an Apache™ module that embeds the Python interpreter within the server.

The internal system, named Aubrey, is comprised of the following five core components:

1. **Static Content Storage Servers:** These include the file servers for the Portal's digital objects (e.g., image files and OCR-text files).
2. **Servers for the Open Source Solr Search Platform:** These include indexes at both the digital object level (e.g., a photograph or book) as well as page-level indexes (e.g., pages within a book).
3. **Metadata Storage Servers:** These contain: (1) the METS files for the Portal's digital objects; (2) the UNT Libraries' (UNTL) standard metadata records for digital objects; and (3) the MySQL relational database management system, which includes collection and partner information for the user interfaces.
4. **The Perlbal HTTP Load Balancer:** This is a Perl-based open source application that distributes HTTP requests from the Internet across the Portal's application servers to optimize system performance.
5. **The Application Servers:** These are implemented within the open source Django® Web framework that supports the design and development of the Portal's website. The Django® framework includes the Portals three core applications, search, browse, and contribute, as well as the edit application that supports the Metadata Editor. The framework also includes the ARK component, which is responsible for mapping a digital object's features to the ARK URL presented to the end user. All interactions with the digital

objects are handled through the ARK component, which creates an application where the URL is the API for objects. The Django® framework and the application interfaces to system components are illustrated in Figure 4.

1.3. Requirements Definition: Lessons Learned

1. External stakeholders include the Portal's content partners and funding agencies. Program coordinators are in the best position to represent their interests and needs, which constitute significant input for design and implementation decisions.
2. Internal stakeholders include the Portal's program coordinators and the various departments within the UNT Libraries. Departments need to be informed of changes that might impact their operations. Communicating with them early on would lessen any impacts from changes.
3. User needs should be stated as general cases in requirements documents and broad classes of users, for example, novices and experts, should be identified.
4. It would be advantageous to add a formal review process for draft functional requirements into the workflows.
5. Stakeholders, both inside and outside the library, need to be represented and/or included in the requirements review process and in the process of establishing development priorities.

PHASE 2. SYSTEM DEVELOPMENT

System development activities are described in two sections: (2.1) Prototype Development and (2.2) Application Development. Descriptions of the system architecture and the open source tools are included. Section 2.3 lists the major lessons learned by members of the three project teams during phase 2.

2.1. Prototype Development

2.1.1. Content Migration

A conversion script was written for the migration of digital objects from the proprietary format specified in the content model of the Portal's legacy TKL system to the new METS data model used by the Aubrey system. This conversion transformed the previous descriptive metadata into the new UNTL specification and legacy structural information into the METS specification for the Aubrey system. A number of inconsistencies were encountered in the legacy format, which required a substantial amount of code to be written to test the conversion.

The bulk of the work required in the conversion was in the change from the proprietary XML format for storing metadata and structural information about files (i.e., sequence, page numbers, and OCR-text) to the new METS format. In the legacy system, some content, such as OCR-text, was stored inline whereas in the new system this

Figure 4. Django applications and interfaces

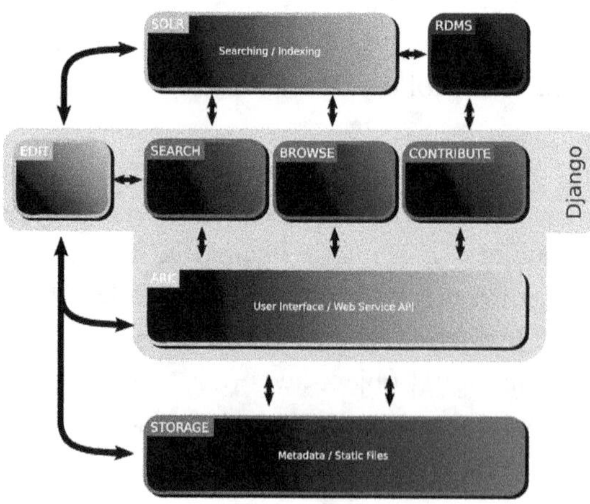

content was stored as static content outside of the METS files. The conversion script was refined during successive migration trials and successful migration of a subset of the Portal's digital objects was completed for use by developers in the prototype system. Prior to public launch of the reengineered Portal, smaller sets of objects than those used in trial migrations were converted in order to further ensure a successful, error-free migration of the Portal's entire content to the new system.

Creating and implementing new backend workflows for moving digital objects in and out of the system took a great deal more time than anticipated. As a consequence, the amount of time and resources required were not adequately estimated. However, these workflows had to be in place prior to beginning development of the user interface, which consequently was delayed.

2.1.2. Prototype System

Since the legacy Portal was a production system, a separate development system was installed for application development. The development environment was defined for multiple developers, each working in different areas of the project. It was decided that separate development, staging, and production environments would be used for the project and they were created using a combination of virtual machines and physical servers. This separation of environments allowed changes to be made in different areas in the architecture that would not interfere with other areas. Additionally, deployment of code to the different environments uncovered bugs based on assumptions of one system versus another.

Servers were installed and configured for the Portal's static content (i.e., digital objects, including image files and OCR-text files). The digital objects were stored using the hierarchical file system specification, Pairtrees for Object Storage. A Pairtree file system enables an application, for example the *search* application within the Portal, to locate digital objects by mapping an identifier string to the file location. As part of Phase 1, Archival Resource Keys (ARKs) were implemented as persistent digital object identifiers within the system. The ARK application within Aubrey maps the identifier strings to specific file locations in the static content storage servers. An example of this mapping occurs in a request for the item *ark:/67531/metapth125323*. The Aubrey system includes the logic to convert this to a file path, *me/ta/pt/h1/25/32/3/metapth125323/*, which is appended to the location of a static content server where all files associated with that object are located.

Servers were also installed and configured for digital object metadata, including both METS and UNTL metadata. These files were again written to disk using the ARK identifiers mapped to the Pairtree file system. The Aubrey application converts the incoming requests for an identifier into a file location where it can access the metadata files. The *edit* application, developed after Release 1 was launched, interacts with the metadata files to both read and write metadata. All changes to the metadata are versioned and stored on the metadata servers in the Pairtree file system.

The metadata files and static content were located on different servers because of their rate of change and expected growth. Metadata files in the Aubrey system are considered *business data* and are part of the Libraries' daily backup procedures, whereas the static content is replicated using other technologies tailored for the high number of files and disk space required.

2.1.3. Search Platform and Indexer

The Solr search platform includes documents (or indexes) that represent the Portal's digital objects at both the object and page levels. A new document schema was specified and implemented to support future user interface features, such as search facets and collection pages. Many of the features of a digital object in the new data model were mapped to the document schema. This allows quick lookups of features in the index that can be used for system functionality or other types of functions. For example, inclusion of the number of files comprising an object allows statistics about the Portal's content to be generated. Likewise, inclusion of a field designating the access policy for an object allows user interface features to display different information based on an object's access policy. As the project progressed and new requirements were identified through the iterative process, new fields were added to the document schema.

The UNT Digital Library uses an in-house digital object indexer (Irex) which is responsible for the conversion of UNTL and METS records into the format needed by Solr for indexing. A new version of Irex was developed to support the METS and the UNTL metadata models. Additional logic was added to this indexer to improve the experience of end users, for example, removal of the end-of-line hyphenation present in OCR files that splits words across lines. This transformation occurs at index time and is not volatile to the original OCR files. Another example of additional logic used by Irex is the conversion of the various date formats used in an object into standardized machine-readable versions. This is an important process because the Solr platform requires certain formats for sorting and date range searching.

2.1.4. Prototype Designs

Paper prototyping is an essential component of an iterative user-centered design process in that it allows the interface design team to identify design flaws early, to iterate inexpensively, and to adjust aspects of the design rapidly. Additionally, due to their low-fidelity, the paper prototypes present users who test them with a malleable product that is free of aesthetic distractions and largely approachable. Because the product is clearly incomplete, people can be more honest about problems and are apt to think about the items under study rather than adapt to a finished-looking model. As noted by Spool, "real-life representations will likely contain critical flaws. Since the reason we're prototyping is to identify those flaws, we find it essential to draw everything out" (Spool, 2005).

To this end a paper prototype depicting the navigational structure for the redesigned Portal interface was created; although, instead of using paper and pen, the team decided to present cleaner lines drawn with Adobe® Fireworks® since they were intimately familiar with this graphics program. A tree diagram illustrated the top-level functions (i.e., browse, search, help, and about) for the site as well as the navigational flow through the site, for example, from a basic search page to a search results page(s), to the digital object and brief metadata page. The content layouts for specific screens were also drafted as prototypes. These screens included the Portal's home page (Figure 5), the six explore (i.e., browse) pages, basic and advanced searches, and grid, list, and brief views of search results. For individual objects, an *about the object* screen and a *view/read the object* screen were created. Documentation pages for *help*, *FAQ*, and user *guides*, as well as an *about* page for the Portal itself, were also created.

2.1.5. HTML-Based Mock-Ups

HTML-based mock-ups, as a testing medium that more closely resembles the final product than paper prototypes, were deployed as the next interface design step. A non-functional, HTML-based mock-up of the Portal was created using standard Web development tools like Adobe® Dreamweaver® and the Blueprint CSS code library. While not fully implementing all required functionality, the mock-up illustrated possible user interaction flow as well as options for the Portal's overall look and feel, for example, the color choices, image sizes, and fonts. Using a CSS framework ensured that important design aspects such as whitespace, typography, and grid-design were consistent and would be complimentary to the content on pages. The purpose of the mock-ups

Figure 5. Initial paper prototype for the home page

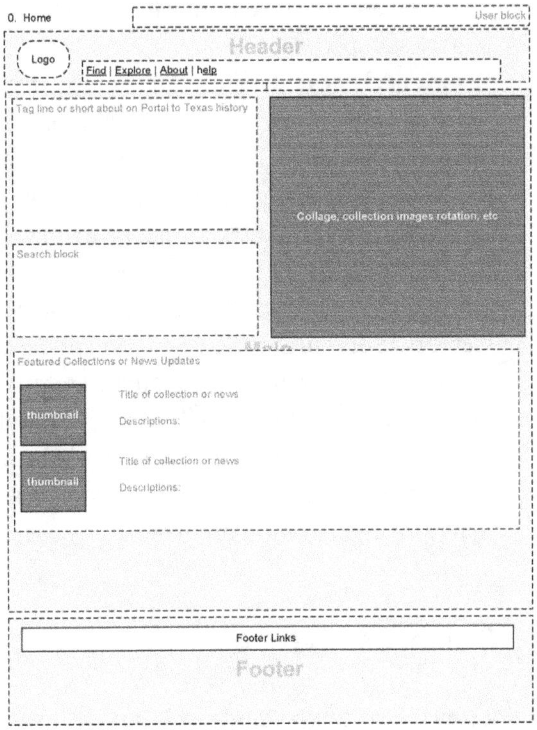

was to visualize all interface related requirements and to expose potential user-interface related issues. As a partially working model, screens within the HTML mock-ups were interlinked and search forms, though not functional, behaved by forwarding correctly through any given scenario.

The goal of the mock-ups was to ensure that the features that would be implemented would satisfy the requirements of both users and internal stakeholders. Unfortunately, genealogists were not included in the prototyping and mock-up activities. In the future, clarification of user requirements would be better achieved with continued involvement of the user community through this stage. However, designers did test several storyline walkthroughs. Likewise, digital library staff members reviewed the mock-ups and provided feedback to the design team, who revised the mock-ups. This pattern of design, review, and revision was repeated until consensus on the designs was achieved.

2.2. Application Development

2.2.1. Collaboration and Management

The system development and user interface teams used two open source systems to manage application development: Apache Subversion® and Trac. Subversion, a project of the Apache Software Foundation, is an open source version control system. And Trac, an open source project of Edgewall Software, is an issue tracking system for software development projects that provides an interface to Subversion. Together these tools facilitated typical software development activities such as check-in and checkout of source code and creating and merging code branches. Trac provided tools for submitting bugs and managing milestones within the project. The project team found both indispensable during the development cycles.

Actual development occurred on two independent testing servers, one primarily devoted to the development of business logic within the Django® application and the other to presentation, which would occur at the browser-level. As the need arose, systems and interface developers created tickets and, upon completion of requested features, checked-in code for updating the other's system. As an example, on individual object navigation screens, there was a requirement for text highlighting of instances of OCR-text that matched a user's search query. The interface designer requested a list of coordinates be returned as an array that could be parsed in JavaScript. While the systems developer built this list in python, the interface developer generated the necessary display logic and, once the code was available, hooked the elements together. Collaborating in this manner allowed each development team a measure of stability in their daily work since the codebase was typically stable.

2.2.2. Software Development

1. **Branding Application:** Requirements for this application were coded and the application was implemented in the prototype system. This application allows a subset of records held by Aubrey to be designated for presentation to an end user community. For example, The Portal to Texas History^{SM} is a uniquely branded system comprised of a subset of the digital objects held by the UNT Libraries in the Aubrey system. Likewise, the UNT Digital Library is a separately branded system comprised of other digital objects, also held by Aubrey. It is possible for content to be shared among more than one branded system. Each brand has custom variables, which define the layout, style, and text used in its user interface.
2. **ARK Application:** Modifications were made to the ARK application to support the newly implemented Pairtree directory structure. As a request is made to the ARK application, it is mapped to an underlying data structure built from the UNTL and METS metadata records. This application provides a consistent and stable URL structure for the end user and abstracts the filenames and storage platform providing more flexible content management.
3. **Edit Application:** The requirements specified in Phase 1 for the edit application were coded. This application enables an authorized user (or metadata maintainer) to create or edit descriptive metadata associated with a digital object and save the edits, which are automatically re-indexed in the Solr platform. The edit application includes features that allow an authorized user to manage their collections on the Portal. Unfortunately, there were insufficient resources to develop this application in parallel with other essential infrastructure work. It was necessary to suspend the Portal partners' ability to edit their metadata records while the application was developed.
4. **Content Ingest Tools:** Three tools were created and tested: SIPmaker, AIPmaker, and ACPmaker. These tools enable new content additions to the system. The tools are used by the Aubrey system to ingest content of all types into both the Aubrey and CODA systems. There are several ingest servers used during the ingest process and these three tools are used to create archival and access packages which are then stored in either the CODA system or the Aubrey system. Preservation metadata and access derivative generation are handled by these tools.

2.2.3. Interface Development

Guided by the prototypes and mock-ups, the interface design team implemented the Portal's Web interface. Building on the HTML wireframes as an actual skeleton for the site's markup, the team constructed the site using a number of established code libraries and best practices from the larger Web-design community. Using code libraries gave designers a degree of flexibility, in that they provided well tested, community supported foundations upon which to build. In essence, the model that applied to the larger site's framework, using tools such as Django® and Perlbal, could be applied to the design as well.

Having initially employed Blueprint for its CSS framework, the designers employed a more adaptable and robust framework for styling called Compass CSS. Built by Christopher Eppstein, this library expanded on Blueprint's strengths to (a) allow for better semantics within the site's markup and (b) aid in the abstraction of styles into a more programmatic environment using Sass and the Ruby programming language. Because this was code that could be processed, it was written using

DRY (Don't Repeat Yourself) principles and its output could be tested, compressed, and optimized for distribution.

For client-side behaviors, the interface team employed several existing JavaScript libraries, most notably jQuery and OpenLayers. To actually make use of these libraries, several contributed plugins were employed and the interface team wrote several thousand lines of JavaScript to create fully-functional features, such as the page zoomer, text highlighting, and a number of other visual and functional enhancements.

2.2.4. Documentation Creation

Documentation was needed in support of several areas within the reengineered system. Relying on both the functional requirements developed in Phase 1 of the project as well as content design requirements for the Portal interface, an ad hoc team of digital library staff members was established to develop documentation. This documentation related to information about collections and content partners, as well as information regarding internal practices within the digital library, for example, digitization standards, metadata practices, and partnership options.

The metadata for all content partners and collections was updated in a consistent manner that would support ease of future editing and consistent display within the interface. This important work contributed to the dramatic improvement in the visibility of content partners and their contributed materials. Additionally, information regarding options for becoming a content partner and the practices and standards employed for digitization and digital object metadata creation were reviewed and revised in conjunction with Release 1.

A second important documentation area was the user documentation for each of the major functional areas within the Portal. The *Help* feature of the reengineered Portal included specific guides for each major function (e.g., basic and advanced searches), FAQs, and a glossary of terms. Guides for discovering educational materials and genealogical materials were also created. This was a greatly expanded feature within the reengineered Portal and steps were taken to outline the documentation needed and to review any existing documentation prior to creating new content.

Two issues emerged in the process of creating user documentation. The review of existing documentation and the creation of an outline for specific content that needed to be written went smoothly. However, with a team of six individuals creating documentation, inconsistencies in scope, style, and format emerged. Additionally, it became apparent that functional guides could not be completed until the functions themselves were fully operational. Attempting to do so beforehand resulted in unmanageable version control and multiple re-writes.

2.2.5. Quality Assurance (QA) Testing

Subsequent to completion of Release 1 on the development system and prior to its public launch, a Quality Assurance (QA) test was created by the user studies team and completed by members of the UNT digital library staff and student employees. Testers reported an overall success rating of 84% for the 46 tasks. Unsuccessful test results for several tasks were influenced by the limited number of digital objects available in the development system. Test feedback and results informed a set of design and development tasks for implementation. With the objective of optimizing information display and improving the user experience, various solutions were considered, tested, and implemented prior to the public launch of Release 1.

The public version of Release 1 included the whole complement of the Portal's digital objects and a second round of QA testing was conducted in June 2009 after the system was launched. Testers included practicing genealogists in addition to

UNT digital library staff and student employees. Participants reported an overall success rating of 90% for the 37 tasks tested. As with the initial QA test findings, testers' feedback and results informed a set of system design and development tasks.

Prior to the public launch of Release 2, QA testing was conducted with 22 UNT digital library staff members and student employees. With the exception of one task, 73% or more of the testers indicated they successfully completed each task, although some noted issues and problems with some tasks they completed. As before, test feedback informed design changes, which were implemented prior to the public launch of Release 2.

2.2.6. Migration to Production System and Release 1

The production system's infrastructure was configured and the prototype system was replicated and tested prior to the public launch of Release 1 of the new Portal. This infrastructure meets current needs and provides capacity for growth both in terms of throughput and content. From a user perspective, the migration from the legacy system to the Aubrey system was seamless; user requests were automatically forwarded from the legacy system to the new system's ARK-based URLs. It was important to the project team that all existing URLs that users might access continue to lead them to the expected digital object. To complete the testing of the redirect feature, old access logs were used to provide previously requested URLs, which were then fed into the new application. Developers monitored the server logs to make sure that all URLs resolved to the appropriate ARK-based URLs used by the Aubrey system. The code for the redirects was adjusted until all requests were correctly forwarded.

After the initial launch of the system, log files were monitored and additional redirect rules were added as needed. Google Analytics was switched to the new system for continued data collection. Google, bing™, and Yahoo® began including links from the new system within 24 hours of the switch to the new URL structure. A second release of the Portal was launched four months after Release 1.

By staging the required features of the system across two releases, it was possible to deliver a new system to the end user in pieces instead of waiting until the final application had been developed and tested. In the implementation stage of any project, it is challenging to balance the desire to add new functionality with the need to deliver a product at a given time. The hardest part of the process is deciding which features will not be included in one release and will be rolled out in subsequent releases. The use of version control software and tools like Trac are helpful both for tracking bugs as they occur and for tracking feature requests to consider for development in future releases.

2.2.7. Release 2 Implementation

Usability testing of Release 1 of the Portal interface by the user studies team identified additional areas for revisions to the interface, primarily in regard to secondary navigation features. Different design changes were considered, mock-ups were developed, and feedback was solicited from the project team. Once consensus on the design direction was achieved, the changes were implemented, tested, and included in Release 2 of the Portal.

Additionally, two major features were developed for Release 2. The first was the addition to search results pages of a number of facets for limiting search results. Optional designs for the display of facets were investigated and tested. The second feature added a function that allowed users to return to their search results from object display pages.

2.3. System Development: Lessons Learned

1. It is very important to identify the resources required, in terms of people and time, for infrastructure work upon which an application development project is dependent. In

this project, the time and resources required to finalize the migration process from the legacy file format to the new data model were not adequately estimated. This delayed both establishment of the development framework and writing the edit application. In consequence, a decision was made to launch Release 1 prior to developing the edit application, which in turn necessitated a three-month suspension of metadata editing while the application was coded. Better estimation of time and resources would have helped set more realistic stakeholder and partner expectations.

2. Clarification and refinement of user requirements might be better achieved with more user involvement in the prototyping work that follows the assessment of user needs. Ideally, users' involvement would begin with a needs assessment to inform a set of general functional requirements. The requirements would then be translated into mock-ups of user workflows (either paper-based or online), which would be used in usability testing with a set of representative users. The findings of the usability tests would shape the final design requirements.
3. When constructing digital libraries on open source frameworks, development plans should take into account the evolutionary nature of the open source components. Because code libraries and tools come into and fall out of favor with communities of developers over time, the development team needs to consider the ramifications of choosing one library over another. The team might consider: How reliant is the system on any single component? Are there enough developers using it to ensure long-lived support? Regarding the open source project for any tool: Is it being actively developed? Is it stable? Has it fallen out of favor for a different tool? Is the tool well documented? How easily can a new team member learn and begin working with the tool?
4. Specialization allowed technical team members to develop expertise at each of two levels: (1) interface design or system design and (2) specific applications or technology areas within each design area.
5. De-coupling of interface design and development from the underlying system is a key to easily making changes, including upgrades. For example, the look and feel of the portal, along with client-side functionality, could be changed as needed, without impact to the underlying system. Likewise, system changes could be made independently of the user interface.
6. The Subversion system worked well in terms of providing a running log of all changes and informing work ticket assignments for developers. However, shared modules can be problematic. For example, with three developers working in the Django® framework, each one needed to understand who had access to what modules and who needed to be informed of module changes. With even more developers, workflows and additional rules would need to be enforced.
7. Given finite resources, it is prudent for a development organization to follow the design leadership of leading enterprises like Google and amazon.com, which invest heavily in usability testing; following their leadership, in terms of features and design, effectively leverages their investment in testing. The sophistication commercial enterprises bring to the presentation of large masses of information often becomes the intuitive approach that their consumers and digital library users become accustomed to using.

8. Technology changes over the lifetime of a project, as do user expectations. Users adopt new habits through their interactions with leading websites (e.g., Google). This reality particularly impacts user interface design. Several user interaction features, navigation layouts, and underlying technologies changed throughout the course of this project.
9. Quality assurance testing with users prior to publicly releasing a system is one activity that will be incorporated into the workflow for future application development as a result of this project. The testing was both valuable and affordable. Users brought issues to light that internal tests would not have uncovered. For example, developers tend to have a set of searches they use to test; a wider pool of testers will use different queries and therefore uncover different problems. In addition, software development tools often have testing limitations. For example in Django® and Python, internal tests of the search application will not uncover character problems, such as problems with diacritics or ampersands.
10. Including partners and library stakeholder groups in the QA tests would hopefully foster a sense of the Portal as their system. Additionally, they might uncover problems that others did not find.
11. Service interruptions may happen with any major technology implementation or change, such as occurred between June and September 2009 while the edit application was being written. Content partners effectively could not add new metadata records or edit existing ones, and they received inadequate notice of this service outage. Advance notice to stakeholders should make these types of disruptions more acceptable. Ongoing communications with partners and other stakeholders should routinely advise them of system upgrades, expected disruptions, and fairly accurate estimates of completion dates. Internal stakeholders, including program coordinators, need to be cognizant of system development plans and activities that may impact the external stakeholders with whom they interface.
12. The amount of staff time required to develop supporting documentation, such as help guides and FAQs, was also underestimated. The application development workflow needs to include a documentation activity prior to the public launch of a new system or new software release.
13. An ad-hoc group was needed to create the online documentation accessible from the Portal interface. It was noted that while Portal users infrequently access the help guides, they are very helpful reference tools for Portal support staff.

PHASE 3. USABILITY TESTING

Subsequent to both Releases 1 and 2 of the reengineered Portal, the user studies team conducted usability tests with volunteers recruited from three North Texas genealogical societies by members of the project's advisory board. The participants (*N*=7 for Release 1; *N*=6 for Release 2) included 10 females and 3 males, ranging from 31-80 years of age. Most participants (85%) were over age 50. Participants had been doing genealogical research an average of 17 years.

The test scripts utilized scenarios that corresponded to the four research goals or information problems that genealogists typically address: (1) questions to answer, (2) hypotheses to test, (3) statements to prove, and (4) topics to investigate. As with the initial usability tests, a talk-aloud protocol was used in each test session and recordings were captured using Morae® software from TechSmith. For each release, the tasks in the test script were targeted to evaluate specific features and functions of the user interface. Morae® software was used to analyze each test session and to produce video clips illustrating user behavior.

In the interest of communicating the findings of the Release 1 tests in a timely manner, they were reported in a project team meeting and a number of short videos were produced to illustrate users' behaviors. While the video clips highlighted problems, they did not assign a severity level to the illustrated problems (e.g., critical, moderate, or mild), which would have been useful to developers. Likewise, it would have been useful to have measured task completion.

Findings from the Release 2 usability tests did include a measure of task completion for each of the 42 tasks in the test script. Each task was rated on a 3-point scale: *1* (completed with ease), *2* (completed with difficulty), or *3* (failed to complete). All participants completed 17 (40%) of the 42 tasks with ease. An additional 22 tasks were completed by most users, although some had difficulty doing so. The average completion scores for only three tasks were in the *failed to complete* range (i.e., average score greater than 2). Similar tasks had been identified as problem areas in the Release 1 tests, in particular, tasks that tested users' ability to locate secondary navigation features.

OUTCOMES

In the legacy system, both the addition of storage resources and the development of application enhancements were protracted and time-consuming processes. The reengineered system overcame these constraints. Within the new system architecture, storage servers for both metadata and content can be added as needed, thereby accommodating content growth. Likewise, the Django® framework enables user interface design and development to proceed independently from the underlying system, thereby enabling more agile application development.

The redesigned Portal was launched in two public releases: Release 1 in June of 2009 and Release 2 in October of 2009. The reengineered system readily scaled to meet the Portal's digital object growth. In 2010, the number of digital objects doubled, from 68,344 to 137,111 (Figure 6).

The infrastructure also proved robust at handling an ever-increasing numbers of visitors. The number of Portal visits per month increased by 59% from June 2009 (21,775), when the new Aubrey system was first released, to January 2010 (34,680), when the project ended. The reengineered system handled this increase in visitors with ease. By January 2011, this number had grown to 45,000 visitors per month.

FUTURE RESEARCH DIRECTIONS

In addition to reengineering The Portal to Texas History^{SM} to eliminate the constraints of its legacy infrastructure by replacing it with an open source development framework, a major goal of this project was to create a model for digital library application development that included an iterative user-centered design approach. The project was initially guided by a draft application development model (Figure 1), which identified three teams: System Development, Interface Design, and User Studies. The internal post-project review identified areas for improvement in the model and these were incorporated into a revised application development model (Figure 7).

Figure 6. Digital object growth

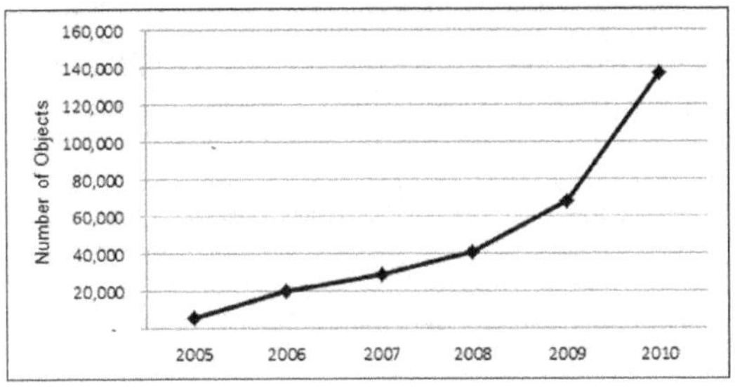

Perhaps most importantly, the revised model includes a fourth project team: Program Management. Specific digital library programs, such as The Portal to Texas History^{SM}, are often managed by program coordinators who are not system developers or designers. Program coordinators have responsibilities similar to business account executives. These include marketing products to clients and also providing customer service by conveying clients' needs and issues to the product team. Academic library liaisons have a similar role between the library and the departments and faculty within a university.

Program coordinators within a digital library are effectively library liaisons for a specific digital library program. At the University of North Texas, program coordinators' clients include significant user groups, both internal and external to the university, as well as content partners and funding agencies. As academic libraries increasingly provide digital access to their unique collections and collaborate with other content providers to develop new digital collections, program coordinators will continue to play critical roles within the library. Identification of the skill set needed for successful program coordination within an academic library is an area for further research.

The revised model also incorporates an understanding that, in the application development process, some requirements are addressed by metadata documentation (e.g., updating input guidelines and formatting rules) and program documentation (e.g., user guides). In order to complete a project on time and within budget, explicit identification of the resources for these activities must be included in project management plans. In the revised model, creation of user documentation occurs after quality assessment of an application is completed and prior to usability testing with external users. In this manner, documentation, in addition to application features and functions, can be included in usability testing. This should allow problems to be corrected prior to publicly launching an application. Creating documentation can be resource-intensive. Understanding to what extent user documentation is needed in a digital library application is an area that could be further investigated to evaluate both its effectiveness and utility for system users and library staff.

With its commitment to open source components throughout the reengineered Portal, the UNT Libraries reflects the acceptance of open systems in the wider academic community. Increasingly, faculties are requiring open access to research publications and funding agencies are requiring open access to research data. As academic libraries adapt their infrastructures and services to address these requirements, it is likely that open source-based systems will become more common in libraries that can provide the necessary technical infrastructure and support. In such libraries, the model resulting from this project supports a relatively low-cost approach to creating and redesigning user interfaces to digital libraries when compared to integrated, tightly-coupled, single-vendor, system solutions.

Applying the model will hopefully promote the design and development of user interfaces that are

Figure 7. Revised application development model

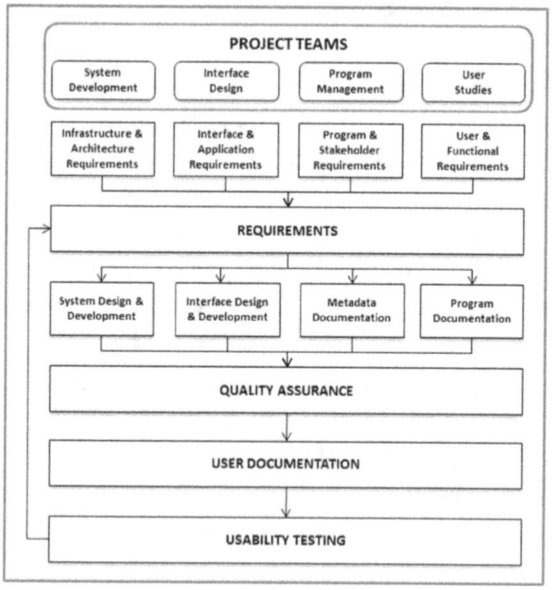

informed by the information needs and contexts of targeted user communities. As group needs and contexts change, responsive interface redesign will be enabled by the development framework. The advantages of open source frameworks for application development include design flexibility in the local library environment and access to a robust community of developers. These benefits are highly desirable for digital libraries seeking to optimize their user interfaces for key user communities. Because digital libraries built by academic libraries often serve user communities beyond their traditional users, models for how to meet user needs are needed. Testing the applicability of the model developed in this project with user communities of other academic libraries is an area for further research.

CONCLUSION

In order to overcome the application development constraints of the legacy asset management system on which The Portal to Texas History^{SM} was built, the UNT Libraries reengineered the system. To coordinate activities, the project team drafted a working model consisting of three teams: system developers, user interface designers, and user studies researchers. The model incorporated user-centered design methods, involving genealogists in the design process beginning with an assessment of their information needs and continuing through usability testing of the redesigned Portal interface.

Substantial amounts of time and effort were invested in the specification of a new data model and in the migration from the legacy data model to the new model. The model defined a digital object entity and a consistent naming scheme for each manifestation of a digital object within the system. Archival Resource Keys (ARKs) were established and incorporated into persistent identifiers for each object. These building blocks enabled applications within the system to read and write digital objects in a consistent manner and were prerequisites for de-coupling design and development of the user interface from core infrastructure components.

Subsequent to successful migration of a test set of digital objects to the new data model, a development framework comprised largely of open source components was established. This allowed the Libraries' interface design team to implement prototype designs based in part on the findings of the user needs assessment with genealogists and usability testing of the legacy system. Coordination of activities between programmers supporting core infrastructure components and those developing the user interface was facilitated by two open source tools: Subversion®, a project of the Apache Software Foundation, and Trac, a project of Edgewall Software.

The accomplishments of this project are unique in academic digital libraries. This project successfully implemented a digital asset management system comprised largely of open source components, which are supported by a very large and robust community of developers outside of those who typically support this type of system in libraries. Open source digital asset management systems for libraries are more often supported by relatively small library-centric communities.

This project was also atypical of many digital library application development projects in terms of including users who are external to the university in the process. In professional meetings and conferences, librarians often report their inability to involve users in their design and development work and many digital libraries base their interface designs on librarians' requirements. Likewise, few data collection efforts involve users outside of the academic community on the scale accomplished in this project. There are several reasons for this. Many libraries simply lack the resources to involve users. Others have neither the staff with requisite skills nor the necessary technical infrastructure to do so. Often, libraries have no programming staff at all, forcing them to choose more turnkey digital asset management systems that constrain local modifications to the user interface.

Importantly, the project also demonstrated the value of including internal program coordinators in the application development process, as well as the need for including external stakeholders in quality assurance testing prior to public releases of new and revised interfaces. As the UNT Digital Library's collections grow and become more integral to teaching and research at the university, new digital library programs will be identified. The need for management of these programs is clear so that the requirements of external stakeholders and end users inform application development, operational decisions, and strategic direction.

Reflecting on the success of this project in terms of its original objectives, the constraints of the legacy system were removed and the technical infrastructure has scaled to meet growth requirements. The UNT Libraries have leveraged the infrastructure and development framework engineered for this project to other projects within the university's Digital Library. The rate of collection growth in the UNT Digital Library would not have been possible without the investments made in this project.

REFERENCES

Boss, R. W. (2009). Digital asset management systems. *Tech Notes*. Retrieved August 10, 2011 from http://www.ala.org/ala/mgrps/divs/pla/tools/technotes/DigitalAssetManageme.pdf

Boyns, R. (1999). Archivists and family historians: Local authority record repositories and the family history user group. *Journal of the Society of Archivists*, *20*(1), 61–74. doi:10.1080/003798199103730

Butterworth, R. (2006). Information seeking and retrieval as a leisure activity. In A. Blandford & J. Gow (Eds.), *First International Workshop, DL-CUBA 2006, JCDL 2006, Digital Libraries in the Context of Users' Broader Activities*, (pp. 29-32). Chapel Hill, NC: JCDL. Retrieved August 11, 2011 from http://citeseerx.ist.psu.edu/viewdoc/download?doi=10.1.1.96.8745&rep=rep1&type=pdf#page=43

Cherry, J., & Duff, W. (2002). Studying digital library users over time: A follow-up survey of early Canadiana online. *Information Research, 7*(2). Retrieved August 16, 2011 from http://informationr.net/ir/7-2/paper123.html

Drake, P. J. (2001). *Findings from the Fullerton genealogy study*. Retrieved August 11, 2011 from http://psych.fullerton.edu/genealogy/

Duff, W. M., & Johnson, C. A. (2003). Where is the list with all the names? Information-seeking behavior of genealogists. *The American Archivist, 66*(1), 79–95.

Fernandez, J. D., Martinez-Prieto, M. A., de la Fuente, P., Vegas, J., & Adiego, J. (2008). Agile DL: Building a DELOS-conformed digital library using agile software development. In B. Christensen-Dalsgaard, D. Castelli, B. A. Jurik, & J. Lippincott (Eds.), *Research and Advanced Technology for Digital Libraries, 12th European Conference, ECDL 2008*, (pp. 398-399). Berlin, Germany: Springer-Verlag.

Fulton, C. (2009). The pleasure principle: The power of positive affect in information seeking. *Aslib Proceedings*, *61*(3), 245–261. doi:10.1108/00012530910959808

Gallop-Gerdman, G. (2000). We are family. *American Demographics*, *22*(9), 24.

Generations Network. (2005). *Americans' fascination with family history is rapidly growing*. Retrieved August 11, 2011 from http://corporate.ancestry.com/press/press-releases/view/?id=406

Jansson, E. (2010). *DSpace manakin UI: Case study of value and costs*. Retrieved August 11, 2011 from http://hdl.handle.net/10090/12618

Kim, Y., Ahronheim, J., Suzuka, K., King, L. E., Bruell, D., Miller, R., & Johnson, L. (2007). Enterprise digital asset management system pilot: Lessons learned. *Information Technology & Libraries*, *26*(4), 4–16.

Kuglin, H. (2004). *Granny hunting: The information seeking behaviour of genealogists in open access libraries: A quantitative study*. Paper presented at the Lianza Conference 2004. Auckland, Australia. Retrieved April 14, 2010 from http://www.lianza.org.nz/library/files/store_018/Granny_Hunting_Kuglin.pdf

Lancaster, F. W. (1986). Why vocabulary control? In *Vocabulary Control for Information Retrieval* (2nd ed., pp. 1–4). Arlington, VA: Information Resources Press.

Marchionini, G., & Fox, E. (1999). Progress toward digital libraries: Augmentation through integration. *Information Processing & Management*, *35*(3), 219–225.

Marchionini, G., Plaisant, C., & Komlodi, A. (2003). The people in digital libraries: Multifaceted approaches to assessing needs and impact. In Bishop, A., Buttenfield, B., & VanHouse, N. (Eds.), *Digital Library Use: Social Practice in Design and Evaluation* (pp. 119–160). Cambridge, MA: MIT Press.

Matuskiak, K. (2006). Information seeking behavior in digital image collections: A cognitive approach. *Journal of Academic Librarianship*, *32*(5), 479–488. doi:10.1016/j.acalib.2006.05.009

Mills, E. S. (2007). *Evidence explained: Citing history sources from artifacts to cyberspace*. Baltimore, MD: Genealogical Publishing Company.

Nielsen, J. (2000). *Why you only need to test with 5 users*. Retrieved August 12, 2011 from http://www.useit.com/alertbox/20000319.html

Norberg, L. R., Vassiliadis, K., Ferguson, J., & Smith, N. (2005). Sustainable design for multiple audiences: The usability study and iterative redesign of the documenting the American south digital library. *OCLC Systems & Services*, *21*(4), 285–299. doi:10.1108/10650750510629625

Salo, D. (2008). Innkeeper at the roach motel. *Library Trends*, *57*(2), 98–123. doi:10.1353/lib.0.0031

Skinner, J. (2010). Does greater specialization imply greater satisfaction? Amateur genealogists and resource use at the state historical society of Iowa libraries. *Libri: International Journal of Libraries & Information Services*, *60*(1), 27–37.

Spool, J. (2005). *Looking back on 16 years of paper prototyping*. Retrieved August 15, 2011 from http://www.uie.com/articles/looking_back_on_paper_prototyping/

Taylor, M. (2008). *Genealogy research process*. Retrieved August 15, 2011 from http://www.thinkgenealogy.com/wp-content/uploads/genealogy-research-map.pdf

Taylor, R. S. (1991). Information use environments. In Dervin, B., & Voight, M. J. (Eds.), *Progress in Communication Science* (*Vol. 10*). Norwood, NJ: Ablex Publishing.

University of Chicago. (2003). *The Chicago manual of style*. Chicago, IL: University of Chicago Press.

Uzwyshyn, R. (2008). Repurposing open source software for agile digital image library development: The University of West Florida libraries model. *D-Lib Magazine, 14*(9/10). Retrieved August 12, 2011 from http://www.dlib.org/dlib/september08/uzwyshyn/09uzwyshyn.html

Van House. N. A., Butler, M. H., Ogle, V., & Schiff, L. (1996). User-centered iterative design for digital libraries: The cypress experience. *D-Lib Magazine, 2*(2). Retrieved August 11, 2011 from http://www.dlib.org/dlib/february96/02vanhouse.html

Yakel, E. (2004). Seeking information, seeking connections, seeking meaning: Genealogists and family historians. *Information Research, 10*(1). Retrieved August 11, 2011 from http://informationr.net/ir/10-1/paper205.html

ENDNOTES

1 The UNT Libraries metadata guidelines are available at http://www.library.unt.edu/digitalprojects/metadata/.

Chapter 3
Content Analysis of CONTENTdm Item Level Records and Their Aggregated Metadata in WorldCat

Iris Lee
American Museum of Natural History, USA

Mary Tyson
Whitney Museum of American Art, USA

ABSTRACT

This study examines the content in CONTENTdm item level records and their aggregated metadata in WorldCat. The research ascertains some amount of loss of contextualization in semantic meaning of digitized primary resources. Data was collected from non-probability sampling of CONTENTdm item records selected randomly from CONTENTdm's Collection of Collections Web page. The same aggregated digitized resources were retrieved in WorldCat, and the data was recorded and analyzed against the CONTENTdm records. Evidence shows that the value of the metadata is altered or ambiguous when the local field name is divorced from the descriptive metadata. Contextual meaning is lost when metadata is shared. In fact, the study reveals that the de-contextualization problem is two-fold: some inconsistent mapping from aggregated metadata and lack of clarity in the metadata itself.

INTRODUCTION

The purpose of this study is to understand how interoperable metadata is shared and used through gathering evidence of problematic mapping. More illumination on issues that arise from using Dublin Core (DC) as the schema to describe archival collections has the potential to help managers and data providers. This study examines records made from OCLC's digital content management system, CONTENTdm. We made a content analysis of 241 unique CONTENTdm collections. Data was

DOI: 10.4018/978-1-4666-2991-2.ch003

gathered from one randomly sampled item-level record from each of the 241 collections to determine how metadata descriptions help or hinder their access on the World Wide Web via WorldCat.

The justification for this exploration is to evaluate how data providers customize and use DC elements to describe their digitized material. Because CONTENTdm items can also be easily published to WorldCat using Digital Collection Gateway, the resources become more visible to potential researchers. An important change is noted that the platform on which the metadata is presented is very different. It is important to understand how the descriptive information is read when mapped to another cataloging format, in this case, Machine-Readable Cataloging (MARC).

Tested metadata crosswalks are available for transforming DC records to MARC. However, the DC element set does not always meet data providers customized needs for special collection and archival descriptions. They then create semantically appropriate local field names. Even when crosswalks are applied, meaningful descriptors are dissociated, which render the metadata incomplete or ambiguous. Good metadata is shareable. Shareable means that a cultural object projects metadata that is aggregated in a meaningful and contextual way (Shreeves, Riley, & Milewicz, 2009). Descriptions for item-level records should be read and understood completely from one catalog to the next.

Libraries and archives seek to cast a wide net on the World Wide Web for increased accessibility of their primary source material. As Riley and Shepherd (2009) say, "The concept that records exist to be used is a core archival value" (p. 94). This study aims at observing the accessible view of CONTENTdm records aggregated in WorldCat. As Greenberg (2011) says now there is a concept of the *macroscope*: large views of things from potentially aggregating vast amounts of available data. This study points out where there are pitfalls in aggregating today and the importance of mending them.

BACKGROUND AND LITERATURE REVIEW

A full color giga-pixel photograph is a much richer visual experience than a high-contrast black and white copy. As Coyle (2005) says, "... metadata is not the world, it is how we see the world at some moment in time for some purpose" (p. 160). The full information in a record is a surrogate for the real thing, and as such, metadata is a surrogate for the real thing found online (Coyle, 2005). However, when at one time, a user would sit in the library and look up resources in the ILS, now many kinds of users, from many locations, with many different purposes, from people to crawlers, all access metadata through the World Wide Web.

Research on metadata spans interoperability to the implementation of standards with quality and shareability at the center. Howe (2011) said about quality that to have good metadata you must *make* good metadata meaning automatically generated metadata will not suffice. Metadata that is shareable means it can be mapped to schemas such as DC and others. Riley and Shepherd (2009), as well as Suleman (2001), describe shareable as a known concept distinct from *local*. It is with this shareable structure that metadata can be mashed up outside of relational mapping (included in commercial sources such as Google, Wikipedia, the Atlas Initiative).

The Challenge of Metadata Creation

What seems challenging for many metadata creators is to comprehend the value of using standards. Librarians have long been trained to adhere to cataloging rules and standard practice. The concept of metadata standards is to help search functionality work better. According to Reese (2009), the lack of national standard or shared best practices has contributed to a high level of inconsistency in the metadata currently being produced. This makes capturing subtle relationships expressed within the metadata difficult.

Dublin Core (DC) is a standard for metadata creation. It organizes both the descriptive metadata and the technical metadata into an open common framework. Tillet (2003) says DC has no inherent rules and that it is open. DC's design is known for prioritizing simplicity. Coyle (2005) states, the simplicity was designed as an inclusive standard: everyone could use it. DC has fifteen "core" elements—five can be given further detail using some qualifiers. There are mapping issues when using DC elements. Han et al. (2009) said that using Simple DC as a minimum requirement in the OAI-PMH environment is problematic because it is "semantically limited and has a flat structure" (p. 215). Tillet (2003) states, in contrast to AACR2, "DC is emerging as its own standard and as a National Information Standards Organization (NISO) standard for metadata" (p. 108).

Riley et al. (2008) recommend guidelines for metadata creation best practices. One of the signature subtleties and difficulties in metadata work is keeping a descriptive record focused on a single object. Consistency is challenging. Some metadata applies specifically to a physical item, some only to a digital surrogate, and some to the intellectual content of a resource spanning all versions. For one example, metadata on physical location of a primary resource material would naturally apply only to an analog original. Technical metadata is for the digital surrogate. The place or person depicted in an image would apply to both versions. The DC Metadata Initiative (DCMI) has long maintained a dictum of a one-to-one relationship between record and object (Hillmann, 2005, section 1.2). Shreeves, et al. (2006) say the missteps metadata creators make are not enough information about the context is included in the record while too much information can cloud coherence. Too much means details about the scanning equipment, the digital file, etc. They cite Lagoze and Van de Sompel's (2001) advice to avoid making a monolithic record, but to make a multifaceted one. They say this kind of structured metadata has the ability to project multiple perspectives on the World Wide Web rather than just one.

Kurth, Ruddy, and Rupp (2004) use an organizing model for the process: mapping, transformation, and metadata management. Mapping is defining the relationship between schemes. Transformation is the movement of data between schemes. Metadata management is the coordination of both the intellectual activity and the resources.

Kurth et al. (2004) found that mapping work should have plenty of documentation, planning, and communication with the aggregators in order to be discoverable. Reese (2009) said, "The one-size-fits-all approach to metadata is problematic because of issues related to granularity and consistency" (p. 122).

There are standards for choosing and using formats to give a primary resource material a rich record to represent it, i.e., *information representation*. DC is so widely adopted of a standard because it is an ISO Standard 15836: 2009 of February 2009 [ISO15836] and is harvestable by OAI's structure called the Protocol for Metadata Harvesting (PMH) (OAI-PMH). The flexibility is found in two measures: one, no field is required and, two, every field is repeatable. Reese (2009) says this flexibility causes a relaxed adherence to best practices.

The Dublin Core Metadata Initiative (DCMI) (1997) mandated that all open archives be able to generate metadata in unqualified DC. This will ensure that service providers (aggregators) who do not understand any other metadata format will at least be able to glean basic information about resources from their DC renditions. DC is almost never the best choice for metadata for any given repository, but its generality makes it suitable for interoperability in the context of the OAI and its application to various different types of repositories.

CONTENTdm is popular software that is librarian- and archivist-friendly (Online Computer Library Center (OCLC), 2006). CONTENTdm provides users with a means to customize metadata descriptions to local needs (Han, 2009). In doing so, metadata creators do not have to use the DC field names to describe their collections. However, in order to make these records interoperable, locally defined field names should be mapped to DC elements. By using CONTENTdm in this way, the metadata records become available to external metadata aggregators. Han reinforces the argument that semantic meaning has to be applied where DC does not do the job. Our research results provided in this chapter supports this. While the flexibility and customization of field names is an attractive aspect of CONTENTdm, it does not augment the use of standards. Han's research confirms CONTENTdm allows collection curators to extend the CONTENTdm base metadata scheme with locally defined fields to fully describe the resources.

Creating Context in the Digital Realm

Content contextualization is considered the central tenet of metadata creation (Roel, 2005). Items at a sub collection level almost always have metadata that is part and in relation to the collection-level metadata. Archival practice is a constant contextualization of content to background (p. 23).

Latham (2010) reiterates what John Swan and others over twenty years said of de-contextualization: the translation from printed material to an electronic form is a "de-contextualization and disembodiment" of the printed work—"an inevitable part of the electronic metamorphosis of information" (Fraistat, p. 108; as cited by Latham, 2010). Even so, Bruce and Hillmann (2004) and Shreeves et al. (2006) found with Simple Dublin Core, metadata quality could be improved to support interoperability. Park (2005), Chan and Zeng (2006), Zeng and Chan (2006), Jackson et al. (2008), and Han et al. (2009) support improvement through the consistent and correct mapping of custom local metadata to Dublin Core and/or to other widely adopted standards. Jackson et al. (2008) found native metadata records are meaningful locally, but lose richness in the aggregated environment due to the mapping errors and misuse of DC elements (p. 18). Since no single metadata standard works for every digital collection, this study shows it is unavoidable for collection curators to develop and use locally defined unique fields. Fear (2010) found the most frequently misunderstood elements are *source*, *publisher*, and *relation*. Figuring out how to help fellow archives with the development of more meaningful metadata formats (such as Encoded Archival Description (EAD), VRA Core, and Natural Collections Description (NCD), to name a few), and to coordinate with OAI usability requirements is the future. OAI is designed with room to grow to support increased interoperability (Suleman, 2001).

MAPPING METADATA: CONTENTDM DC TO WORLDCAT

Statement of the Problem

CONTENTdm as a management system is very flexible and uses DC as the base schema. The DC mapped fields are then aggregated through OAI-PMH and transformed to WorldCat as MARC records (See Figure 1).

The flexibility of customizing field elements in CONTENTdm has its advantages: cultural institutions can create semantically meaningful metadata tailored to the needs of local audiences. The disadvantages are: the same semantically meaningful metadata descriptor is lost when aggregated and seen in other union catalogs, in this case, WorldCat.

This loss of contextual meaning is due to three possibilities: (1) incorrect mapping to DC in CONTENTdm; (2) field name variations (with

Figure 1. Data flow of metadata from CONTENTdm to user

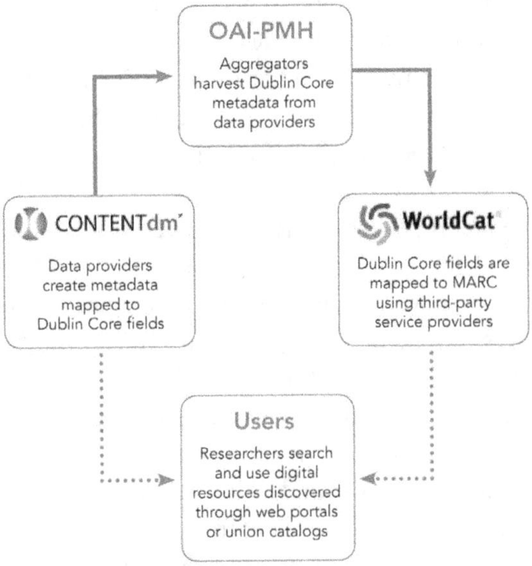

local semantic meaning) that are meaningless to the harvester; or (3) incorrect mapping by the service provider for record creation in WorldCat. In this case, the service provider is the same entity as the data provider.

A Measure for Analysis

Using spreadsheets, native metadata was systematically transcribed from the CONTENTdm publicly displayed record item. We randomly sampled browseable items from a systematic selection of CONTENTdm collections. Metadata was transcribed with repeated field entries logged as separate lines. In the same spreadsheet, we created corresponding columns for the WorldCat record, logging the results of the mapping. Many items, 49%, did not have WorldCat records. An early harvester, "OAIster was one of the early 'one-stop-shopping' user interfaces that aimed to . . . connect end-users with OAI-PMH harvested metadata for relevant digital resources anywhere on the World Wide Web" (Beisler & Willis, 2009, pp. 67-68). In 2009, OCLC moved to a single harvesting process facilitated by Digital Collection Gateway, which uses OCLC's WorldCat Metadata Harvesting Program (MHP). Subscribers could use self-service harvesting tools using this Gateway interface (Beisler & Willis, 2009; OCLC, 2011). Of the 124 records that were found on WorldCat, OAIster harvested 51 while MHP harvested 73.

Once the information was recorded, the data was sorted and filtered according to field names and mapping patterns. We quantified frequency in use for field elements and mapping hits. Items with no WorldCat equivalent were indicated "no WC record." For these, we quantified local field names appearing in CONTENTdm only.

Preparing the information in a spreadsheet allowed us to calculate usage of Dublin Core fields against modified local field names. It also facilitated a strategy for measuring how the aggregated record mapped to WorldCat. If trends emerged in the frequency of particular field names, a connection could be made with the semantic values assigned for that customization. Variations of DC field names appeared, as did several unique local names that describe the resource more precisely or address the audience for the content.

A closer examination of digital resources and their attendant metadata was reviewed both in their local environments and in the WorldCat records where context from meaningful labels have been lost through harvesting. Comparing the records identified a disparity of meaning for the metadata descriptions in the separate platforms. Analysis of how structured data loses shape in an aggregated environment may help identify issues with metadata creation.

Which DC Fields Were Used

Illustrated in Table 1, the most used DC field name used in the native environment was *Title*. Appearing 216 times in 241 records, not surprisingly <dc:title> is the least ambiguous element in the DC set and resulted in the least amount of variation on the element name. The remaining 25

Table 1. DC field names used in metadata (n = 241)

Dublin Core Used (15 simple elements)	Frequency
Title	216
Description	146
Subject	134
Type	115
Rights	112
Publisher	99
Creator	97
Language	95
Format	93
Date	87
Source	63
Identifier	61
Contributor	46
Relation	26
Coverage	10

Title field names employed some modification of the word, such as "Article Title" (AcadLib-116) or "Image Title" (UnivArc-083).

Description appeared in approximately 60% of the items slightly ahead of *Subject* with 56%. *Coverage* and *Relation* were least employed in a local environment resulting in only 11% and 4% (respectively) of the total number of units sampled. We observed limited use of Qualified DC, with *Subject (LCSH)* being the most frequently used (See Figure 2).

The Crosswalk Not Taken

As evidenced in the frequency of the field *Title* in CONTENTdm, *Title* was just as frequently mapped to WorldCat *Title*. *Creator* and *Contributor* both mapped consistently to *Author* and *Author; All Contributors*.

A sizeable amount of fields do not map anywhere in the WorldCat record for public display. Three of the fifteen DC elements were consistently not mapped to WorldCat: *Subject*, *Rights*, and *Source*. Table 2 lists the DC fields and the frequency of mapping to the most widely used crosswalk element in WorldCat. When computing these results, we only looked at CONTENTdm units using simple DC field names for labels.

The frequency by which a clear crosswalk exists and not taken by data providers raises some questions. One would expect to see DC *Subject* fields mapped to WorldCat *Subject* fields with much more frequency than observed in this study. Out of 75 records, no mapping was chosen for this field more than half the time. The high frequency reflects the repeated use of the field. In one record, *Subject* was repeated 50 times (ConsLib-108).

This may indicate a problem mapping DC to a more granular descriptive metadata set, in this case MARC. With Library of Congress hierarchical subject headings complying with AACR2 Cataloging rules, it may be difficult to map a subject string to a single subfield in MARC. For example, this data taken from AcadLib-010's *Subject* field "Poetry—Ozark Mountains Region; Folk art—Ozark Mountains Region; Mothers—Death" identifies two problems. First three distinct subjects separated by semicolons ran as a line in a single *Subject* field. Secondly, the subject string does not map well to a MARC 650 topical term field because the service provider cannot break the string into more granular MARC subfields. AcadLib-010 chose not to map DC *Subject* to WorldCat. Perhaps for similar reasons, other institutions made the same decision as AcadLib-010 resulting in the high frequency of DC *Subject* not being mapped to WorldCat at all.

Figure 2. Usage of qualified DC fields

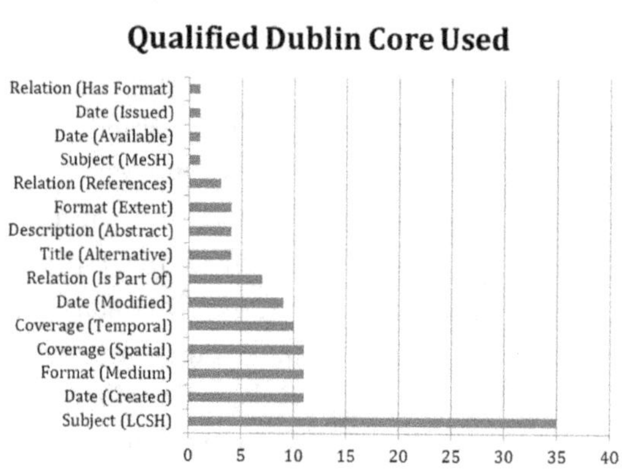

Table 2. The frequency of DC field elements mapped to the most used WorldCat field

Dublin Core Field Elements	WorldCat Mapping most used	Frequency
Subject*	None	169
Title	**Title**	**125**
Date	Publisher	82
Publisher	**Publisher**	**65**
Creator	Author; All Authors/Contributors	61
Description	**Summary**	**53**
Type	Genre/Form	51
Rights	**None**	**44**
Source	None	41
Language	**Language Note**	**38**
Format	Notes	36
Identifier	**Notes**	**26**
Contributor	Author; All Authors/Contributors	12
Coverage	**Subject**	**3**
Relation	Notes	1

**Subject* here represents 75 units, logged 169 times in WorldCat None because it is a heavily repeated field.

Mapping of Local Fields

In the local environment, many DC fields were modified to enrich the semantic meaning of metadata. Figure 3 and 4 illustrate the metadata records for AcadLib-233. In the CONTENTdm record view a user can see a rich set of metadata that speaks to a scientific community: *Kingdom*, *Phylum*, *Genus*, *Habitat*, *Reproduction*, *Social Structure*, and *Diet* are all local field names assigned to this resource. Not one DC element would satisfy the specificity given to this digital item. The field names here are just as informative as the data assigned to the field names. To have a full understanding of the resource, a user needs to read both together.

WorldCat displays this metadata very differently: 19 out of 25 of the local fields mapped to WorldCat *Notes*. *Height*, *Weight*, *Diet*, and *Reproduction* each had the value "unavailable." While unavailable is not very useful information on its own, being attached to meaningful designators give "unavailable" more context: what exactly is "unavailable"? The answer in this case is *Height, weight, reproduction,* and *diet*. Additionally "unavailable" makes perfect sense when combined with other descriptors such as *Behavior*: "Very little is known about this squirrel species. It is very shy and difficult to find in the wild." Unfortunately much of this richness and context is lost in the WorldCat record where the data is read in *Notes*. A user sees a list of information with the word "unavailable" repeated four times. Observe the measurement listed with no reference to what is exactly measured (35-40cm = *Head-Body Length*).

The full record in CONTENTdm is rich in information, the metadata in both assigned meaning and data create a concise record for a specific audience. However when describing digital resources designed to be harvested and shared, the data provider should consider the readability of the created metadata. How much meaningful context is lost when the original field name is swapped for another field name? Without the label does the description still make sense? These are important questions to ask.

Mapping of Fields Borrowed from Standards Other Than DC

Consistently, we observed a fair frequency of DC field element usage with some modification to the field name in the local environment. Field names from other metadata standards were used in some of the items we sampled. *Collection*, a

Figure 3. Example of metadata with many local field names displayed in CONTENTdm

Title:	Malabar squirrel feeding on ground
Identifier:	G13593
Kingdom:	Animalia
Phylum:	Chordata
Class:	Mammalia
Order:	Rodentia
Family:	Sciuridae
Genus:	Ratufa
Genus Species:	Ratufa indica
Common Name:	Malabar squirrel; Indian giant squirrel
Subject:	Squirrels; Sciuridae; Rodents; Mammals; Vertebrates; Chordata
Physical Characteristics:	
Head-Body Length:	35-40 cm
Height:	unavailable
Weight:	unavailable
Identification:	The Malabar squirrel has a deep brown coat with buff-colored underparts.
Geographic Range:	Southern Central Asia; Northern Africa
Habitat:	Deciduous, mixed deciduous, and moist evergreen forests
Diet:	unavailable
Reproduction:	unavailable
Social Structure:	Malabar squirrels live alone or in pairs
Behavior:	Very little is known about this squirrel species. It is very shy and difficult to find in the wild.
Status:	Threatened
Interesting Facts:	unavailable
Keyword:	rodent

Add to My Favorites View My Favorites

Figure 4. Example of metadata mapped to WorldCat notes

Notes: Animalia
Chordata
Mammalia
Rodentia
Sciuridae
Ratufa
Ratufa indica
35-40 cm
unavailable
unavailable
The Malabar squirrel has a deep brown coat with buff-colored underparts.
Deciduous, mixed deciduous, and moist evergreen forests
unavailable
unavailable
Malabar squirrels live alone or in pairs
Very little is known about this squirrel species. It is very shy and difficult to find in the wild.
Threatened
unavailable
G13593

Visual Resources Association (VRA Core) XML element (Visual Resources Association, 2007), was used 180 times in 241 records (75%). Some of the modifications made to *Collection* include: *Repository Collection*, *Source Collection*, *Collection Name*, *Archival Collection*, and *Digital Collection*. *Material* was used 15 times (6%).

Use of other standards with DC suggests that data providers are aware of the best practices for creating shareable metadata. Though CONTENTdm defaults to DC, subscribers may want to express their items using other schemas. With *Collection* appearing 75% of the time, it is evident that metadata creators feel they need to supplement DC with elements from other standards.

Other fields that appeared with much frequency described digitization methods and general notes. *Digitization Specifications* and *Digitization Process* appeared 38 times (16%) and *Note/Notes* was used 52 times (22%). While *Digitization Specifications/Process* do not comply with other standards, *Note/Notes* is a Metadata Object Description Schema (MODS) and Encoded Archival Description (EAD) element (Library of Congress, 2010; Library of Congress, 2006). *Contact* and *Contact Information*, also EAD, was used 25 times (10%).

Figure 5 shows how *Collection* is mapped in WorldCat records. Overwhelmingly, *Collection* does not get mapped at all (74%). The information maps to WorldCat *Notes* 17% of the time with the other fields at 1-2%. For as frequently as the field name *Collection* is used in the native environment (75%), it is equally not crosswalked into other catalogs. This shows a discrepancy in the value of this data. It is important enough to provide context in the local environment, but is either too confusing when mapped to WorldCat, or does not have an appropriate corresponding field. *Collection* appears largely in WorldCat *Notes* when it is mapped, but is there a more appropriate corresponding field for this information?

Possible Mismapping and Inaccuracies Observed

While we cannot accurately state that errors occurred in mapping DC harvested elements to WorldCat, we did observe many fields mapped to *Notes* in WorldCat. Over 100 unique field names map to *Notes*. The most frequent mapping occurs with the field *Format* and its variation in name (14%). *Description* and *Identifier* also map heavily with 11% and 10% respectively. Other fields with a wide variation of local names mapped to WorldCat *Notes*. See Table 3 for a full list. This indicates a misunderstanding of the MARC *Notes* field, or a tendency to use the *Notes* field for information that does not appear to have a direct crosswalk, such as *Title* and *Creator*. Here we see that several DC elements are mapped to WorldCat *Notes*: *Format*, *Description*, *Relation*, *Identifier*, *Date*, *Language*, *Source*, *Publisher*, *Rights*, *Coverage*, and even one instance of *Title*. That counts for an astounding 12 out of 15 of the Simple Dublin Core element set.

Unless the WorldCat display compounds several MARC fields into one umbrella category called *Notes*, this is an area that should be addressed in best practices for shareable metadata.

Figure 5. Collection mapped to WorldCat (n = 104)

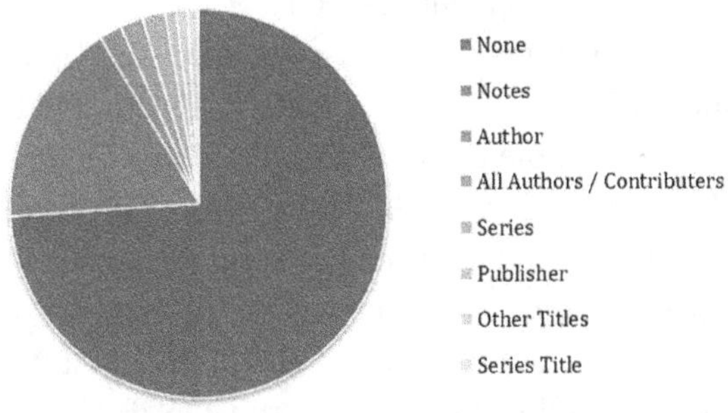

Table 3. The frequency of local field names in CONTENTdm mapped to WorldCat notes (n = 258)

CONTENTdm local field name	Frequency	CONTENTdm local field name	Frequency
Format; Format - Digital; Format-Extent; Format.Creation; Format.Use; Original Format; Video Format; Additional Physical Formats Held by UO	37	Competition Year:	1
Description; Description/Notes; Summary/Description	28	Contributing Institution	1
Identifier; Identification; Object ID; Digital ID; Resource Identifier; Collection Identifierl Original Item ID; PHOTO ID; Photo Number	26	Detail	1
Note; General Notes; TCI Notes	18	Diet	1
Citations/Bibliography	8	Family:	1
Digital Collection; Digital Collection Title	8	Genre	1
Relation	7	Genus Species:	1
Repository	7	Genus:	1
Accession Number	4	Habitat:	1
Caption	4	Head-Body Length:	1
Collection; Collection Name; Collection Title	4	Height:	1
Date Created; Date-Original; Date.Digital; Event Date	4	Image Dimensions	1
Image Number; Item Number; Slide Number; Negative Number	4	Interesting Facts:	1
Learning Standards	4	Interpretation	1
Location Depicted	4	Kingdom:	1
Original Collection; Original Collection Name	4	Language	1
Display Dimensions; Overall Dimensions; Original Dimensions	3	Lesson Plans / Themes	1
Location	3	Order:	1
Related item(s); Related Objects	3	Part of Collection	1
Rights	3	Photographer's Note/Description	1
Coverage	2	Phylum:	1
File name	2	Provenance	1
Finding Aid	2	Reference	1
Folder Name; Folder Title	2	Region / Country	1
Media & Support	2	Regional Arts Council	1
Number of pages	2	Relates to Artwork	1
Original Item Location	2	Reproduction:	1
Publisher	2	Series	1
Source	2	Size of Original	1
TIF Filename	2	Social Structure:	1
Type; Object Type	2	Source Collection	1
Abstract	1	Source Container	1
Album	1	Source physical description	1
Artwork Description	1	Source Relation	1
Artwork Site	1	State / Province	1
Award Date(s)	1	Status:	1
Behavior:	1	Technique	1
Bit Depth	1	Title	1
Building Style	1	Transcription	1
Call Number	1	Transmission Data	1
Class:	1	View	1
Comment	1	Weight	1

In "Best Practices for CONTENTdm and other OAI-PMH compliant repositories," OCLC recommends <dc:format> map to <wc:notes> or MARC 500 (p. 14). The most frequently mapped field to *Notes* as visible to the user on the WorldCat display page is *Format*. But many other DC fields are represented with high frequency. In some cases, the information for several different fields may be collapsed into *Notes*. Out of the 124 items total mapped to WorldCat from CONTENTdm, mapping occurred for 258 unique instances. This reveals that several local field names associated with one item mapped to *Notes*. It is an area that needs more research as it proves to be a misunderstood crosswalk.

Many of the records violated the DC 1:1 principle by including technical information about the digital resource. This principle states "related but conceptually different entities, for example a painting and a digital image of the painting, are described by separate metadata records" (Dublin Core Metadata Initiative, 1995-2011). 57% of the total sample units describe some process of digitization or include information about digital characteristics. (Note: Instances of *Identifier* was not included when it was not qualified with the term "digital.")

One of the typical problems in creating shareable metadata is the inclusion of technical information, for instance, date of digitization and scanner used (Shreeves, et al., 2006). It is recommended that the institution save the technical details of a digital resource for internal use only (and not map to DC elements). Manifestations of the field name *Date Digital* appeared 61 times out of 241 records. Out of those 61 records, 8 map to WorldCat *Publisher*, 1 maps to WorldCat *Notes*, and 51 do not map or have WorldCat records. When the item does map to the WorldCat *Publisher* field, both the digital date and the resource's original date appear side-by-side. This combination of dates is confusing to a user because the semantic labels assigned in the local environment have been removed in the harvested record. Both years, 1938 and 2003, appear together in a single line with no qualifying text. Shareable metadata should be created to describe a single manifestation of the resource (OCLC, 2010, p. 15).

Additional Findings

An encouraging observation: many CONTENTdm item records mapped well to WorldCat. We provided our best guess DC mapping for CONTENTdm field names and descriptors in a separate column. When the mapping was obvious, the corresponding WorldCat record generally displayed a record with little ambiguity in the descriptive metadata.

Thumbnails of the digital resource, in 55 out of 124 instances, did not display in WorldCat. Most of these records were harvested by the OAIster database (51 out of 55 records), which may indicate a problem with the harvester. Fortunately, items harvested by MHP consistently displayed thumbnail images.

Links to the original CONTENTdm item displayed in the WorldCat record. Some links were broken, others loaded the correct CONTENTdm page but did not display the image, and the majority linked back to the original item correctly. Over time, if the CONTENTdm hosted site moves, links could become dead if not updated in the WorldCat record.

In some cases, only collection-level records for the sampled items were available in WorldCat. In CONTENTdm collection-level metadata records describe associated digital items as a group. Created by the data provider, collection metadata were distinct from the discreet units we sampled and gave more contextual meaning for the digital items as a whole while also listing the constituent items within.

Limitations of the Study

While the study illuminates problems in mapping, without harvesting the samples directly, we cannot see an accurate view of how aggregated data is mapped. We do not infer the decisions that may have been made in terms of mapping local fields to DC elements. Instead, this study focused on the result of a record that has been harvested and reused.

Normally service providers do not have the full context of the digital resource. However, using Gateway, the data providers are fully aware of the content and context of their records. For the purpose of this study, it was assumed that the data provider is also acting as the service provider for the mapped WorldCat entries. In this light, the problems that surfaced addressed the lack of understanding DC elements and the best practices for creating shareable metadata.

Lastly, the pool of sampling units only makes up a portion of the total CONTENTdm collections. Because a collection record is not required to submit to the Collection of Collections site, there is an unknown quantity of CONTENTdm collections that we were unable to include. While this limited our range of sample units, a non-biased analysis was still conducted for a significant group of collections.

STUDIES BEYOND THE RECORD DISPLAY

The digital future is to increasingly aggregate and share information. The main reason for rethinking, observing, and noting the occurrence of inaccurate metadata display, is to enhance the visibility of primary source material to researchers. Creating metadata for materials is very labor-intensive (Howe, 2011). In order for this effort to count, and to be cost-effective, research on the mis-mapping needs to be explored further. The study samples we observed in the aggregated WorldCat record varied in accuracy. A technical analysis of the same samples pulled from an OAI repository at the harvesting stage could be done to observe the mapping. In addition, case studies with CONTENTdm subscribers would show mapping decisions.

The model of relational mapping has been highly valued. Roel (2005) states content contextualization in metadata creation practice is of supreme importance and is the central tenet of archival practice. This includes metadata of a resource's background, topographic place, and relationship to the archive as a whole. Counter to this, she argues that libraries use the model of incrementally building metadata so that minimum metadata is assigned to the largest volume of materials. Libraries trail archives because often items within collections lack strong relational mapping (p. 22). A better understanding of metadata creation will lead to more comprehensive relational metadata coverage.

Earlier this year, Society of American Archivists (SAA) adopted the Encoded Archival Context-Corporate Bodies, Persons, and Families (EAC-CPF) to accentuate the EAD standard (2011). EAC-CPF will provide a multi-layered approach to archival description that enables "the sharing, discovery and display" of information about the creator entities in an electronic environment (EAC-CPF, 2012, para. 2). The creation of shareable metadata is increasingly in the foreground for facilitating access to archival materials as these new ways of delivering information take shape and become standardized. Shreeves et al. (2006) recommend creating metadata in six "Cs": content, consistent, communication, context, coherence, and conformance to standards.

CONCLUSION

Metadata was collected from non-probability sampling of CONTENTdm item records (n = 241) selected randomly from CONTENTdm's Collection of Collections Web page. The same aggregated digitized resources were retrieved in WorldCat (51%, n = 124) and the data was recorded with the CONTENTdm sampling units.

Evidence in the aggregated WorldCat records showed that certain DC fields mapped consistently to WorldCat fields, but WorldCat *Notes* proved to be largely problematic with 12 out of the 15 Simple DC elements mapped to it, one instance including DC *Title*. *Subject*, with a direct crosswalk to WorldCat *Subject*, did not map over half of the units represented in WorldCat. Guidelines and best practices specifically for mapping these fields may help data providers create better metadata for seemingly straightforward, yet problem-prone crosswalks.

In qualitative analysis, the use of local field names showed intent to create semantically contextual information. Both field names and their qualifiers were appended to DC field names. In the CONTENTdm environment, the displayed metadata was rich in meaning and sometimes had a specific audience in mind. In the aggregated WorldCat records, these rich metadata sets often lost important contextual meaning when the display omitted their assigned labels. When creating shareable metadata, data providers should understand how the metadata might become devalued in meaning once it is transformed from native catalog.

This content analysis of digital items in CONTENTdm illuminated many issues that arise when creating metadata for interoperability. Initially we hypothesized that DC did not meet the needs for describing primary resources that may require a richer set of semantic field names or labels. However, the research showed that a lack of awareness for creating shareable metadata on the part of the creator might override the limitations of using this general yet flexible schema. Using other metadata standards with DC to describe these resources may result in more accurate metadata transformations. Unless OAI-PMH adopts other standards for metadata harvest, data providers should be aware of the importance for creating shareable metadata using DC as a way to extend their resources to a wider audience through the World Wide Web.

REFERENCES

Beisler, A., & Willis, G. (2009). Beyond theory: Preparing Dublin core metadata for OAI-PMH harvesting. *Journal of Library Metadata*, *9*(1/2), 65–97. doi:10.1080/19386380903095099

Bruce, T., & Hillmann, D. (2004). The continuum of metadata quality: Defining, expressing, exploiting. In Hillmann, D., & Westbrooks, E. (Eds.), *Metadata in Practice* (pp. 238–256). Chicago, IL: American Library Association.

Coyle, K. (2005). Understanding metadata and its purpose. *Journal of Academic Librarianship*, *31*(2), 160–163. doi:10.1016/j.acalib.2004.12.010

DiConsiglio, J. (2010). *Connecting to collections: A report to the nation*. Retrieved from http://www.imls.gov/resources/year.shtm.

Dublin Core Metadata Initiative. (2004). *DCMI glossary*. Retrieved from http://dublincore.org/documents/usageguide/glossary.shtml

EAC-CPF. (2012) *Welcome to the EAC-CPF homepage*. Retrieved from http://eac.staatsbibliothek-berlin.de

Fear, K. (2010). User understanding of metadata in digital image collections: Or, what exactly do you mean by "coverage"? *The American Archivist*, *73*, 26–60.

Greenberg, J. (2011). *Keynote*. Paper presented at the Webwise 2011. Baltimore, MD. Retrieved from http://www.tvworldwide.com/events/webwise/110309/globe_show/default_go_archive.cfm?gsid=1585&type=flv&test=0&live=0

Han, M. J., Cho, C., Cole, T. W., & Jackson, A. S. (2009). Metadata for special collections in CONTENTdm: How to improve interoperability of unique fields through OAI-PMH. *Journal of Library Metadata*, *9*(3), 213–238. Retrieved from http://hdl.handle.net/2142/15415. doi:10.1080/19386380903405124

Hillmann, D. (2005). Using Dublin core. *Dublin Core Metatdata Inititative*. Retrieved from http://dublincore.org/documents/usageguide/elements.shtml

Howe, K. (2011). *Session #3: Tapping into science: Promoting collections for use in teaching, learning and research*. Paper presented at the Webwise 2011. Baltimore, MD. Retrieved from http://www.tvworldwide.com/events/webwise/110309/globe_show/default_go_archive.cfm?gsid=1576&type=flv&test=0&live=0

Jackson, A. S., Han, M. J., Groetsch, K., Mustafoff, M., & Cole, T. W. (2008). Dublin core metadata harvested through OAI-PMH. *Journal of Library Metadata*, *8*(1), 5–21. Retrieved from http://hdl.handle.net/2142/9091. doi:10.1300/J517v08n01_02

Kurth, M., Ruddy, D., & Rupp, N. (2004). Repurposing MARC metadata: Using digital project experience to develop a metadata management design. *Library Hi Tech*, *22*(2), 153–165. Retrieved from http://proquest.umi.com.queens.ezproxy.cuny.edu:2048/pqdlink?did=679670391&Fmt=7&clientId=13031&RQT=309&VName=PQD doi:10.1108/07378830410524585

Lagoze, C., & Van de Sompel, H. (2001). The open archives initiative: Building a low-barrier interoperability framework. In *Proceedings of the ACM/IEEE Joint Conference on Digtial Libraries*, (pp. 54-62). ACM/IEEE. Retrieved from http://www.openarchives.org/documents/papers.html

Latham, K. F. (2010). Medium rare: Exploring archives and their conversion from original to digital part one: Lessons from the history of print media. *LIBRES: Library & Information Science Research Electronic Journal*, *20*(2), 1–14.

Library of Congress. (2006). *Encoded archival description tag library, version 2002: Appendix d: Index by element name*. Retrieved from http://www.loc.gov/ead/tglib/appendix_d.html

Library of Congress. (2010). *Outline of elements and attributes in MODS version 3.4*. Retrieved from http://www.loc.gov/standards/mods/mods-outline.html

OCLC. (2010). *Best practices for CONTENTdm and other OAI-PMH compliant repositories: Creating shareable metadata*. Retrieved from http://www.oclc.org

OCLC. (2011). *WorldCat digital collection gateway: Overview*. Retrieved from http://www.oclc.org/gateway/overview/default.htm

Park, J. (2009). Metadata quality in digital repositories: A survey of the current state of the art. *Cataloging & Classification Quarterly*, *47*, 213–238. doi:10.1080/01639370902737240

Reese, T. (2009). Automated metadata harvesting: Low-barrier MARC record generation from OAI-PMH repository stores using MarcEdit. *Library Resources & Technical Services*, *53*(2), 121–134.

Riley, J., Chapman, J., Shreeves, S., Akerman, L., & Landis, W. (2008). Promoting shareability: Metadata activities of the DLF aquifer initiative. *Journal of Library Metadata*, *8*(3), 221–247. doi:10.1080/19386380802397083

Riley, J., & Shepherd, K. (2009). A brave new world: Archivists and shareable descriptive metadata. *The American Archivist*, *72*, 91–112.

Roel, E. (2005). The MOSC project: Using the OAI-PMH to bridge metadata cultural differences across museums, archives, and libraries. *Information Technology and Libraries*. Retrieved from http://www.ala.org/lita/ital/sites/ala.org.lita.ital/files/content/24/1/roel.pdf

Shreeves, S. L., Riley, J., & Milewicz, L. (2006). Moving toward shareable metadata. *First Monday*, *11*(8), 1–9. Retrieved from http://firstmonday.org/issues/issue11_8/shreeves/index.html

Society of American Archivists. (2011). *SAA council adopts EAC-CPF standard, calls for member comments on draft code of ethics and proposed constitutional amendments*. Retrieved from http://www2.archivists.org/news/2011/saa-council-adopts-eac-cpf-standard-calls-for-member-comments-on-draft-code-of-ethics-and-

Suleman, H., & Fox, E. (2001). The open archives initiative: Realizing simple and effective digital library interoperability. *Journal of Library Administration*, *35*(1/2), 125–145.

Tillett, B. B. (2003). AACR2 and metadata: Library opportunities in the global semantic web. *Electronic Cataloging: AACR2 and Metadata for Serials and Monographs, 36*(3/4), 101-119.

Visual Resources Association. (2007). *VRA core 4.0 outline*. Retrieved from http://www.loc.gov/standards/vracore/VRA_Core4_Outline.pdf

ADDITIONAL READING

Arlitsch, K., & Jonsson, J. (2005). Aggregating distributed digital collections in the mountain west digital library with the CONTENTdm™ multi-site server. *Library Hi Tech*, *23*(2), 220–232. doi:10.1108/07378830510605179

Bearman, D., Rust, G., Weibel, S., Miller, E., & Trant, J. (1999). A common model to support interoperable metadata: Progress report on reconciling metadata requirements from the Dublin core and INDECS/DOI communities. *D-Lib Magazine*, *5*(1). Retrieved from http://www.dlib.org/dlib/january99/bearman/01bearman.html. doi:10.1045/january99-bearman

Chapman, J. W., Reynolds, D., & Shreeves, S. A. (2009). Repository metadata: Approaches and challenges. *Cataloging & Classification Quarterly*, *47*, 309–325. doi:10.1080/01639370902735020

Colati, J., Dean, R., & Maull, K. (2009). Describing digital objects: A tale of compromise. *Cataloging & Classification Quarterly*, *47*, 326–369. doi:10.1080/01639370902737331

Daniels, C. (2009). Providing online access to oral histories: A case study. *OCLC Systems & Services: International Digital Library Perspectives*, *25*(3), 175–185.

Han, M., Bair, S., & Lee, J. (2010). Creating metadata best practices for CONTENTdm users. *International Conference on Dublin Core And Metadata Applications*. Retrieved from http://dc-papers.dublincore.org/ojs/pubs/article/view/996

Han, M. J., Cho, C., Cole, T. W., & Jackson, A. S. (2009). Metadata for special collections in CONTENTdm: How to improve interoperability of unique fields through OAI-PMH. *Journal of Library Metadata*, *9*(3), 213–238. Retrieved from http://hdl.handle.net/2142/15415. doi:10.1080/19386380903405124

Harpring, P. (2010). Development of the getty vocabularies: AAT, TGN, ULAN, and CONA. *Art Documentaries*, *29*(1), 67–72.

Huthwaite, A. (2003). AACR2 and other metadata standards: The way forward. *Electronic Catalogingd: AACR2 and Metadata for Serials and Monographs*. Retrieved from http://www.haworthpress.com

John, N. (2005). Digital repositories: Not quite at your fingertips. *Libri*, *55*(4), 181–197. doi:10.1515/LIBR.2005.181

Lampert, C., Dolski, A., & Egan, B. (2010). dmBridge: Building a collaborative solution for streamlined digital library design and development. *OCLC Systems & Services*, *26*(2), 103–113. doi:10.1108/10650751011048470

Latham, K. F. (2010). Medium rare: Exploring archives and their conversion from original to digital part one: Lessons from the history of print media. *LIBRES: Library & Information Science Research Electronic Journal*, *20*(2), 1–14.

Lopatin, L. (2010). Metadata practices in academic and non-academic libraries for digital projects: A survey. *Cataloging & Classification Quarterly*, *48*(8), 716–742. doi:10.1080/01639374.2010.509029

McBride, R. (2011). Look what we got! How inherited data drives decision-making: UNC-Chapel Hill's 19th-century American sheet music collection. *Code4Lib, 13*. Retrieved from http://journal.code4lib.org/articles/4916

Miller, S. (2010). The one-to-one principle: Challenges in current practice. *International Conference on Dublin Core And Metadata Applications*. Retrieved from http://dcpapers.dublincore.org/ojs/pubs/article/view/1043/992

Park, J., & Childress, E. (2009). Dublin core metadata semantics: An analysis of the perspectives of information professionals. *Journal of Information Science*, *35*(6), 727–739. doi:10.1177/0165551509337871

Park, J., & Tosaka, Y. (2010). Metadata creation practices in digital repositories and collections: Schemata, selection criteria, and interoperability. *Information Technology and Libraries*, *29*(3), 104–116.

Shreeves, S. L., Kaczmarek, J. S., & Cole, T. W. (2003). Harvesting cultural heritage metadata using the OAI protocol. *Library Hi Tech*, *21*(2), 159–169. doi:10.1108/07378830310479802

Simeoni, F., Yakici, M., Neely, S., & Crestani, F. (2008). Metadata harvesting for content-based distributed information retrieval. *Journal of the American Society for Information Science and Technology*, *59*(1), 12–24. doi:10.1002/asi.20694

Suleman, H., & Fox, E. (2001). The open archives initiative: Realizing simple and effective digital library interoperability. *Journal of Library Administration*, *35*(1/2), 125–145.

Toy-Smith, V. (2010). UALC best practices metadata guidelines: A consortial approach. *Journal of Library Metadata*, *10*(1), 1–12. doi:10.1080/19386380903543734

Van de Sompel, H., Young, J. A., & Hickey, T. B. (2003). Using the OAI-PMH ... Differently. *D-Lib Magazine*, *9*(7/8). doi:10.1045/july2003-young

Warner, S. (2001). Exposing and harvesting metadata using the OAI metadata harvesting protocol: A tutorial. *High Energy Physics Libraries Webzine, 4*. Retrieved from http://library.web.cern.ch/library/Webzine/4/papers/3/

Zick, G. (2009). Digital collections: History and perspectives. *Journal of Library Administration*, *49*(7), 687–693. doi:10.1080/01930820903260465

KEY TERMS AND DEFINITIONS

Aggregated Metadata: Metadata seen in the service provider's environment dissociated from its local field name and attached only to its Dublin Core mapped element.

Best Practice: A set of guidelines to help create commonality in the activity across a disparate group of practitioners.

Data Provider: The publisher of the digital resource creating structured metadata and making them visible to harvesters. Body who maintains repository and allows access.

Element: A category of information defined by a metadata schema. In this study, we refer mostly to Dublin Core elements, but elements can make up other metadata schemas. Elements and field are used interchangeably, or sometimes expressed together as "field elements."

Harvest(ing): A service provider accesses metadata from digital resources through the process of pulling structured metadata from a data provider. The process makes the metadata available in the World Wide Web and makes it accessible by queries.

Interoperability: The ability to exchange metadata between data providers and service providers in a shareable environment—the exchange of metadata between (libraries).

Item: One unit of many digital resources making up a digital collection. Metadata is used to describe the content and context of the item. Also item is the unit of study in this research. "Unit" and "item" may be used interchangeably.

Local Field Names: The field element name assigned in the local environment by the metadata creator. These are labels created for display in a user environment and may or may not be mapped to a Dublin Core element for OAI harvesting.

Metadata Standard: Agreed upon replicable measures and actions. The set is authorized and publicized by an acknowledged working group.

Service Provider: Requests the harvests and collects metadata from data providers.

Section 2
Preservation, Access, and Services

Chapter 4
Issues and Challenges of Integrating Digital Library Services in Blended Learning Environments:
A Case Study of Open University Malaysia (OUM)

Norasieh Md Amin
Auckland University of Technology (AUT), New Zealand

Ruzita Ramly
Open University Malaysia (OUM), Malaysia[1]

Philippa Gerbic
Auckland University of Technology (AUT), New Zealand[2]

ABSTRACT

Research into digital libraries has been carried out from two perspectives being libraries as contents and as services/organizations. The authors approach this topic from the service perspective. They argue that existing academic libraries in most parts of the world have augmented their services to include digital library services. This chapter discusses the development and components of a digital library and types of digital library services. It also discusses partial research findings on the integration of digital library services in blended learning environments at Open University Malaysia (OUM), focusing on issues and challenges encountered by librarians, which are: the need to provide both digital and physical resources, synchronous and asynchronous interaction with users, and engagement in continuous improvement. Information professionals at tertiary institutions are recommended to: keep abreast with the changing learning environments, maintain cooperation with users, and equip themselves with the new user-centric roles, knowledge, and skills that are required in this era of technological advancement.

DOI: 10.4018/978-1-4666-2991-2.ch004

INTRODUCTION

The concept of digital libraries has gained much attention over the last two decades from researchers and information professionals. There are many debates about what constitutes a digital library, with people perceiving it differently based on their expertise and practice. We view the digital library from a services perspective. We contend that existing academic libraries in most parts of the world have augmented digital library services to varying extents and this has changed the landscape of the library environment.

In this chapter, we discuss different perspectives and definitions of the digital library, its development and components as well as varying types of the digital library services. Based on qualitative case study research in a university in Malaysia, we draw attention to issues and challenges of integrating digital library services in blended learning environments as experienced by the librarians of this institution.

POSITIONING THE DIGITAL LIBRARY

An Introductory Historical Glimpse

The concept of libraries as systems for storing knowledge arose hundreds of years ago (Lerner, 1998). However, the concept of having a technology driven system (using machines) whereby humanity's knowledge could be stored, searched, and displayed was first coined by Bush (1945) who introduced a mechanized system based on microfilm technology which he called the "Memex." This concept was further crafted by Licklider (1965) whereby he envisaged a computer-based library called the "Procognitive System." This system, according to him, transmitted information "without transporting materials" and "not only present[ed] information to people but also process[ed] it for them." It is "a meld of library and computer" (p. 6).

Computer technology began to emerge in the 1970s and librarians were early adopters of computers. The development of computer technology during this time has impacted on almost all aspects of the library profession, including the ways in which librarians acquire, organize and manage library resources and the ways in which library services are delivered to customers. Librarians have been 'digital' for some time, but it was not until 1990s that the concept of digital libraries began to receive significant attention. The term 'digital library' was first used in print in 1988 in the report of the Corporation for National Research Initiatives (Kahn & Cerf, 1988).

Digital Library Definitions

There are various synonymous terms including 'virtual library,' 'library without walls,' 'electronic library,' 'ubiquitous library,' 'hybrid library,' 'cyberlibrary,' 'cybrary,' and 'ebrary' as well as other related terms such as library 'gateway' and 'portal.' Various authors and researchers have attempted to define 'digital library' within their perspectives which has lead to a plethora of definitions because each perspective is shaped by the background, discipline and professional expertise and practice of the author. There are basically two main perspectives of the digital library found in the literature. In many instances, authors refer particularly to Borgman (1999, 2000) to explain these two perspectives (such as Johnson & Magusin, 2005; Rowlands & Bawden, 1999; Saracevic, 2000). Although Borgman (2007) also mentions a third perspective—digital libraries as websites and databases—this perspective somehow resembles the first one.

The first perspective is a technical focus, put forward primarily by digital library researchers from computer science, information system and computer engineering backgrounds. The emphasis is on digital libraries as contents collected on behalf of user communities. As sets of electronic resources and associated technical capabilities for creating, searching, and using information, digital libraries are extensions and enhancements of information storage and retrieval systems that manipulate digital data in any medium (text, images, sounds; static or dynamic images) and exist in distributed networks. The content of digital libraries includes data, metadata that describe various aspects of the data (e.g. representation, creator, owner, reproduction rights) and metadata that consist of links or relationship to other data or metadata, whether internal or external to the digital library (Borgman, 2007).

A second perspective focuses on digital libraries as institutions/services and addresses the practical challenge of transforming information institutions. As institutions/services collected and organized by and for a community of users to support their information needs, digital libraries are an extension, enhancement, and integration of a variety of information institutions such as physical places where resources are selected, organized, preserved, and accessed in support of a user community's information need. These information institutions include not only libraries but also other institutions such as museums, archives, schools, laboratories, etc. (Borgman, 2007).

Varying definitions of the digital library from seventeen authors are listed in Table 1, arranged by year of publication. We highlight definitions that support our view of the digital library. We construct the following definition, which is based on the experience of some of us who are university librarians, and is drawn from the definitions in Table 1, especially that of Gapen (1993) and the Digital Library Federation (1998). In our view, on the basis of this definition, many academic libraries nowadays would be considered as a digital library:

A form/concept of library organizations/services that provide remote and ubiquitous access to their contents, resources and services, that are selected, organized, stored, preserved and managed by specialized staff, who optimize technology usage, and combine an on-site collection of current and heavily used materials available in a variety of formats (print, electronic, etc.), with an electronic network which provide access to, and delivery from, external worldwide library and commercial information and knowledge sources.

Development and Augmentation from a Traditional to a Digital Library

The library concept has gone through various transformations throughout the centuries. Conventional libraries accumulate and maintain printed and non-printed materials, which are not easily accessible and have limited physical boundaries. In the past, users would travel to the library and refer to catalogue cards in order to retrieve materials. With the development of computers, it has become easy to search through Online Public Access Catalogue (OPAC) and CD-ROM databases later provided an alternative for information storage and wider accessibility through Local Area Network (LAN) within limited geographical boundaries. Online databases then developed, providing a wider spectrum of resources to users. Eventually information became accessible globally through the Internet. The digital library concept is now seen and accepted as the fastest and easiest way to deliver and access information in many societies. The following factors have contributed to the development of the digital library:

- **Information Explosion:** Information technology advancement has created changes in socio-economic and cultural needs. Information centers including libraries must store, maintain, provide, and disseminate information as fast and accurately as possible. In this era of information explosion (Sharifabadi, 2006), it is impossible for any library to keep all information and publications under one roof. Today, more libraries are shifting into developing digital information cooperation by mutual

Table 1. Definitions of the digital library by various researchers/authors

Source	Definitions of the Digital Library
Garrett (1991)	A comprehensive electronic 'highway' which would link information to the widespread community of users.
Gapen (1993)	The concept of remote access to the contents and services of libraries and other information resources, combining an on-site collection of current and heavily used materials in both print and electronic form, with an electronic network which provide access to, and delivery from, external worldwide library and commercial information and knowledge sources.
Lynch and Molina (1995)	A system that provides a community of users with coherent access to a large organized repository of information and knowledge.
Lesk (1997)	Organized collections of digital information. They combine the structuring and gathering of information, which libraries and archives have always done, with the digital representation that computers have made possible
Kuny and Cleveland (1998)	Include a collection of both digital and non-digital objects and include all the process and services – collection development and management, subject analysis, index creation, reference work and preservation – that are the backbone and nervous system of contemporary libraries.
Leiner (1998)	Collections of information objects and services that support users in dealing with information objects, and the organization and presentation of those objects, available directly or indirectly, via electronic/digital means.
Lang (1998)	The use of digital technologies to acquire, store, preserve and provide access to information and materials originally published in digital form or digitized from existing print, audio-visual and other forms.
Digital Library Federation (1998)	Organizations that provide the resources, including the specialized staff, to select, structure, offer intellectual access to, interpret, distribute, preserve the integrity or, and ensure the persistence over time of collections of digital works so that they are readily and economically available for use by a defined community/set of communities
Chowdhury and Chowdhury (1999)	An assemblage of digital computing, storage and communications machinery together with the content and software needed to reproduce, emulate and extend the services provided by conventional libraries based on paper and other material means of collecting, cataloguing, finding and disseminating information. A full service digital library must accomplish all the essential services of traditional libraries and also exploit the well-known advantages of digital storage, searching and communication.
Arms (2000)	A managed collection of information, with associated services, where the information is stored in digital formats and assessable over a network
Marchionini (2000)	Extension and augmentation of physical libraries
Bargellini and Bordoni (2001)	The creation and management of electronic information sources, the movement of information across global networks and the effective use of this information by a wide range of users
Yusof & Mohd (2003)	A vast and organized collection on digital information in various form (combination of text, graphic, audio and video) which allows timeless and borderless access through network with optimum use of information technology
Witten and Bainbridge (2003)	A focused collection of digital objects, including text, video, and audio, along with methods for access and retrieval, and for selection, organization and maintenance of the collection
Secker (2004)	Collections of information and materials originally published in digital form or digitized from existing print, audio-visual and other forms by using digital technologies, that enable any citizen to access all human knowledge anytime and anywhere, in a friendly, multi-model, efficient, and effective way, by overcoming barriers of distance, language, and culture and by using multiple Internet-connected devices
Jeng (2005)	An organized and managed collection of digital information; are accessible over a network; and may include service
DELOS (2006)	Systems that are very heterogeneous in scope and provide very different functionality. These systems span from digital object and metadata repositories, reference-linking systems, archives, and content administration systems (mainly developed by industry), to complex systems that integrate advanced digital library services (mainly developed in research environments).

agreements of shared usage. Services are becoming more user-centric oriented.

- **New Generation Need:** As socio-economic conditions and culture have changed over time, the acceptance of a different delivery mode has occurred. Digital information in itself is an attraction to the public apparently for the reason that it is associated with advantages of the Internet. The availability of hyperlinks helps users to read multiple screens simultaneously and to navigate from one screen to another. The Internet offers texts, sounds, graphics, and interactivity and most importantly scholarly information that is available sometimes for free (Johnson & Magusin, 2005).
- **Searching, Browsing, and Retrieval:** Even though OPAC allows easy searching through author, title or subject to locate material, online accessibility used to be limited, for example within the campus or the library. Users were required to go to the library to use OPAC. With the Internet, searching using Web-base OPAC allows users to search for library materials and ensure availability of materials prior to coming to the library. The availability of full text materials over the Internet further allows users to retrieve them anytime anywhere at the comfort of users' home or office (Arms, 2000; Kaske, 2004).
- **Access to Library Resources:** Libraries do not purchase printed resources including books and journals in large numbers. Normally, acquisitions of library materials follow certain ratios that have been

specified in libraries' policy. The availability of online databases, especially with full text, allows users to retrieve the same document simultaneously and avoids waiting time over the same reading material (Sharifabadi, 2006).

- **Low Technical Cost:** Printed and non-printed materials (including audio visual, and digital) involve large storage spaces and a work force for loan processing and daily maintenance. Subscribing to online databases, therefore, reduces daily staff responsibilities in borrowing, returning, and shelving activities. It also reduces maintenance cost for preservation and conservation processes in the long term (Arms, 2000).
- **Current of Information:** Information on the availability of library resources is automatically updated using library systems. News, alert services, and changes related to library services and collections can be updated on a regular basis. The Internet allows a currency of information that was previously impossible (Arms, 2000).

Components of a Digital Library

The components discussed below are a synthesis of ideas from the authors delineated in Table 1 and others including Anderson and Maxwell (2004), Borgman (1999), Herold (2004), Ochs and Saylo (2004), Sharifabadi (2006), Secker (2004), and Tedd and Large (2005), and also draw on the experience of the librarian authors. These components are not of physical but rather constructed from a pragmatic management point of view. Hence, a digital library should have all these components.

1. **Purpose(s) of the Digital Library:** There are purposes (including objectives/aims) behind the creation of a digital library. They include: to provide remote access of on-site collection of current and heavily used materials in both printed and digital form; to offer intellectual access, preserve the integrity of digital contents and ensure their persistence over time; and to provide better delivery of information than was possible in the past. The digital library does not replace existing physical collections, but enhances usability and accessibility of information to meet users' information needs.
2. **Role of Information Professionals and Librarians:** A digital library is created by information professionals, librarians, specialized staff, and experts of many disciplines using the technology (hardware and software) to enable collections of information stored in digital formats and retrieved over networks. These people can be from outside the organization/library when digital library projects are outsourced or they are electronic publishing companies. They follow certain steps, standards, and procedures in order to: select, structure, organize and distribute digital works; make it available to users and archive digital contents so that purposes of creation are achieved. They also work on associated areas such as library resources, budget, storage capacity, etc. and carry out planning.
3. **Digitization Process:** Technically, this involves attaching or uploading contents that are readily available in a digital format to the library homepage/website, and digitizing contents from text/printed materials using certain software/hardware and later uploading them. The digitizing of contents is possible through the availability of scanners and optical character recognition software. It is preceded by a selection process of identifying appropriate contents based on users' demand for the information, importance, and appropriateness of contents to be preserved

and the need to abide by the copyright law. Contents are categorized and managed in a manner that will provide easy retrieval and this normally involves the creation of contents typology, which is usually supported by features of the software used in the digitization process.

4. **Contents of the Digital Library:** The digital library contents or objects vary according to the institutions it serves. They include data, metadata that describe various aspects of the data and metadata that consist of links or relationship to other data or metadata, whether internal or external to the digital library. They come in various formats including text, audio, video, and image and include various types of collections (such as e-books, e-journals, databases and journal indexes, scholarly commons, course reserved materials and online databases) and various services (such as loan services, library catalogue, inter library loan and document delivery, information literacy, and reference services). Appropriate hardware, software, and applications are used to store and preserve the contents.
5. **Access to the Digital Library:** Access is vital so backup servers are normally created to enable 24/7 accessibility to contents. The digital library is accessed via the library homepage or website. Access is made possible via system/s equipped with searching interfaces and retrieval features following certain standards, specifications, and access management.
6. **Users Accessing the Digital Library:** Most digital libraries exercise usage control and authentication such as ID control using proxy for a defined community of users. Few libraries allow general users to access digital contents. A common practice is a combination of both: allowing general users to access some part of the services and resources; and exercising usage control over specific digital objects. This is mainly due to copyright issues and library policies.
7. **Usage of the Digital Library:** Usage of the digital library contents is evaluated from time to time. Evaluation becomes significant because it allows continuous improvement and ensure budget for the library remain or increase. A special purpose committee may be formed for this purpose and they would use the previous six components as points of reference in the process of usage evaluation.

Digital Library Services: Two Classifications

Most academic libraries have augmented their services to include digital library services and these can be categorized into two main services (Figure 1). The first is the provision of various customer and information services, which include: Online Public Access Catalogue (OPAC), loan services, interlibrary loan and document delivery services, information literacy and user education, and reference services. The second is the provision of access to various kinds of library resources, available in physical/digital formats. These include but are not confined to e-books, online journals and databases, local repository, electronic and Internet resources, course reserve materials, audio-visual materials, etc. Figure 1 illustrates this augmentation process, whereby all arrows indicate this process from traditional to current status of services.

INTEGRATING DIGITAL LIBRARY SERVICES IN BLENDED LEARNING ENVIRONMENTS

The term 'integration' in this research is generally viewed as expanding the use of electronic databases and journals, raising library users' awareness of existing digital library services and resources (Joint, 2006) and positioning library

Figure 1. Two types of digital library services as augmentation of existing services, arrows indicate augmentation process

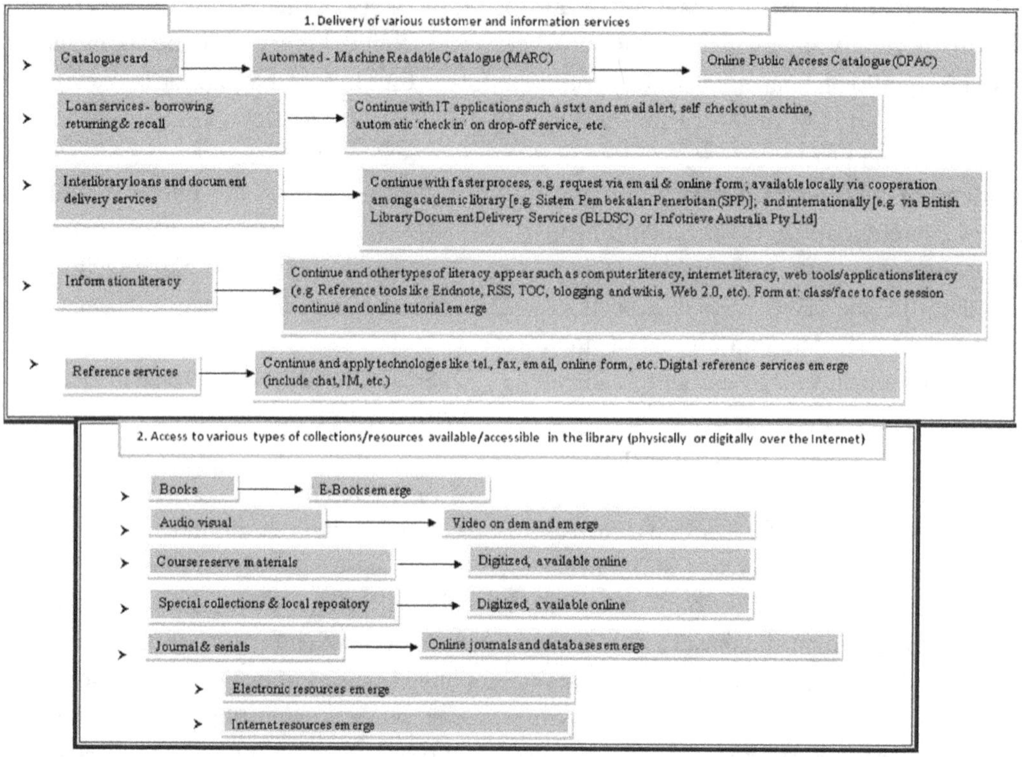

information services within emerging online learning environments (McLean & Lunch, 2004). Blended learning is now constantly positioned as one of the emerging trends in higher education (Stacey & Gerbic, 2009). A plethora of perspectives exist on what people actually blend to create a blended learning environment and there is not yet a consensus about its definition. Various perspectives and definitions reflect its complexity. One of the simplest and most widely used is that of a combination of face-to-face learning with online or technology mediated learning (Graham & Dzuiban, 2008; Stacey & Gerbic, 2009a). This was later extended to include "the thoughtful integration" (Garrison & Kanuka, 2004) of face-to-face and online learning, thus indicating the significance of pedagogical design in learning.

Complexity arises with blended learning at different levels. We must not only understand the strengths and weaknesses of the two different environments and how to make meaningful connections between them (Gerbic, 2009) but also be able to respond to different settings, such as the discipline and its learning outcomes, the institutional and community context, and the students and their needs and expectations. This conceptual flexibility has led to wide variation in practice with blended learning occurring across a continuum, which ranges from conventional fully face-to-face learning at one end to fully online (distance) at the other end. This has resulted in a wide range of learning designs (Stacey & Gerbic, 2009) which include enhancing face-to-face teaching, replacing selected face-to-face elements and increasing online activities and including some face-to-face elements in traditional off-campus courses. A practice of including residential courses within distance programs was identified (Moore, 2006), but the advent of blended learning has now meant that the role of face-to-face sessions can be more purposefully added to establish social presence and build a sense of community for off-campus students (Stacey & Gerbic, 2007).

The role of the library, and especially their digital library services, is becoming more important in blended learning environments. University libraries nowadays have augmented their digital services and have incorporated the use of ICT into various library operation and services provision. While university libraries have becoming increasingly digital, their future role and challenges is well articulated in concepts such as blended librarianship and the Library 2.0. The vision of blended librarianship (Bell & Shank, 2007) was one of an increasing integration of services and practice into the teaching and learning process. This included the challenges of improved support for academic staff but also, reaching out to students by integrating the library into their learning spaces. The concept of Library 2.0 (Casey, 2005) reinforces the blended nature of future libraries by describing the ubiquitous library which supports learners by overcoming current physical limitations through blending flexible 'best of breed' systems to communicate, collaborate and learn online.

There has been very little reported research on integration of digital library services into blended learning environments and this has mostly occurred in the United Kingdom. Identified key issues and challenges include the importance of seamless universal access and responding to the needs of different learners, enabling teachers to embed their own pedagogy rather than a systemic approach, moving away from 'spoon-feeding' and encouraging online resource discovery by students, the need for strong collaboration between library and academic staff and a commitment to teaching and learning as well as technical development (Currier, 2002; Robert & Davey, 2002).

THE RESEARCH PROJECT

A research project was conducted in 2010 by the first author exploring the integration of digital library services into blended learning environments from the perspectives of various library stakeholders. The research utilized a qualitative case study methodology to understand stakeholders' perspectives. A case study is "an in-depth exploration and empirical inquiry of a contemporary phenomenon within its real-life context or bounded system" (Creswell, 2005). The Open University Malaysia was chosen as the project case because: first, it offers blended learning opportunities, and second, the library is a digital one since its commencement in year 2000.

After ethics approval, data collection began in January 2010 utilizing interviews and documents as data collection methods. A total of 26 (individual, pair, and focus group) interviews with 43 participants (comprising of librarians, lecturers, tutors, a programmer, an instructional designer and students) were carried out, of between 15 to 75 minutes in duration. Participants were recruited based on purposive random sampling and using snowballing approach. Interviews were audio-recorded and conducted in Malay/English. Documents gathered include a module sample, university and library reports, and first author's personal journal. Data analysis was assisted by the use of a Computer-assisted-qualitative-data-analysis-software (CAQDAS), NVivo. Data analysis steps (Creswell, 2005) and an interactive model of qualitative data analysis (Miles & Huberman, 1994) were employed during the analysis and themes emerged. The partial findings reported in this chapter focus on issues and challenges for librarians.

The Research Context: The Open University Malaysia and its TSDAS Digital Library

Established in 2000, the University is an institution owned by a consortium of 11 public universities in Malaysia. The Open University's creation was a response to the Malaysian government call for the democratization of education. It is a challenge to help Malaysia advance into a developed nation by the year 2020 and open and distance learning is one of the emerging delivery systems, which are becoming a way of providing education for all levels of the Malaysian society. The University capitalizes on Information and Communication Technology (ICT) capabilities in teaching and learning through this system to achieve the Vision 2020.

With the University motto "University for all," OUM offers opportunities to diverse groups of society to obtain higher academic qualifications by providing a quality-learning environment through an internationally recognized blended learning pedagogy using multimodal learning approaches. In essence, the University uses a blended mode of learning—a combination of online, face-to-face, and self-paced learning. Online learning is conducted via a Virtual Learning Environment (myVLE) for discussion with tutors and peers. Face-to-face tutorials are conducted on-campus at the main campus and various learning centers across the country. For self-paced learning, students are supplied with modules for each course they enroll. Modules are available in printed and electronic format (pdf, cd, or html). OUM began with 753 students during its first intake in 2001 and now has over 40,000 active students attending various programs at diploma, undergraduate and graduate levels. In addition to its main campus in Kuala Lumpur, OUM has more than 40 learning centers for students beyond the capital city. These learning centers are selected for their strategic locations and telecommunication facilities. OUM owns 16 regional centers and most others are located at teacher institutes.

The TSDAS Digital Library began in January 2002. Obtaining its name from the OUM founding president and vice-chancellor Tan Sri Dato Abdullah Sanusi, the Library envisions becoming the pioneer digital library in Malaysia. The digital library functions as the foundation for learning, teaching, and researching activities: where students look for references, textbooks, and other learning materials; and academics seek information for their research activities. The Library is operated from the main campus. Most collections are in digital format in the form of e-books and online resources/journals. There are limited physical collections located in the library and some of them are distributed through selected learning centers across Malaysia.

The shift from a traditional library to the digital is not merely a technological evolution, but requires a change in the ways in which people access and interact with information. As an open and distance learning university, with local and international students, the Library aims to apply the concept of "anytime, anywhere" where interactions with the library and access to collections is available at all time and from anywhere. The library uses a combination of computers and Wi-Fi to provide access. OUM has also increased the Internet bandwidth, considering the increasing number of students, to cater for myVLE and digital collection accessibilities.

Unlike conventional universities where the main campus is the hub for students' activities, OUM has to deal with a 'floating' campus in the digital environment where students, both local and international such as in the Middle East and Maldives, communicate using myVLE and access library resources via the Internet. In order to facilitate this learning environment, the digital collection provides: (1) a borderless environment – the digital collection is accessible globally through the Internet; (2) seamless availability – the digital collection is accessible 24 hours a day, 7 days a week (although the physical library has its closing hours); (3) simultaneous access – databases are simultaneously accessible by several users; and

(4) single sign-on portal – registered students and staff of OUM must login at the OUM portal to access all facilities and services and they are able to navigate to the library portal through myVLE without a second time login.

THE FINDINGS ON ISSUES AND CHALLENGES FOR LIBRARIANS

With regards to issues and challenges for librarians in providing digital library services in blended learning environments, three themes emerged from the analysis of data conducted by the first author. The second author adds commentary based on her professional reflection and experiences and these additions are clearly indicated. Most figures in this section are supplied by the second author. Parts of sentences in *italic* are quotes taken from interviews and all names reported in this chapter are pseudonyms.

1. The Provision of Digital and Physical Resources

The librarians reported some issues with regards to providing both digital and physical collections. The TSDAS Digital Library aimed to apply the concept of "anytime, anywhere" where access to collections is available at anytime. Most collections were in digital formats such as local electronic repository, e-books, and e-journals. However, the Library still purchased physical collections due to existing demand from users and the requirement from the Malaysian Qualification Agency (MQA). This highlights the continuing needs to provide both types of resources. Consequently, librarians faced the following issues:-

- **Limitations of Digital Resources:** Some databases providers were reported to allow users to *print/view a page at a time* which caused *inconveniences among users* (Seri, Lecturer). Frustration regarding retrieval of digital resources discouraged users from using them again. Moreover, some students suggested a *scarcity of digital collections for specific subjects, especially those relating to the Malaysian context* (Zul, Student), mainly because these collections were mostly internationally published. *Almost all* collections were *written in English* and some students had *language difficulties in grasping the meaning* of texts or they might *spend more time* in their learning (Sam, Student).
- **Internet Access:** Internet access was reported to be *an issue for some rural students* (Sam, Student). Those who do not have the Internet at home had to access their learning materials and *work in online learning environments from computers at the learning centers* (Chong, Lecturer). Some students were reported to have Internet at home but *access may take longer time at certain areas* even if they were using *Internet broadband* (Sam, Students). Although ICT infrastructures in remote areas are beyond librarians or OUM's ability to control or change, this significantly influences users' information seeking behavior.
- **Access During Peak Hours:** It was reported that access to the Library digital resources might be affected or took a longer time than usual due to *overloaded logins into myVLE*, especially during *peak hours* such as registration or assignment submission (Irene, Programmer). Although the IT Department has prepared a *mechanism to control access traffic* (Irene, Programmer), users might be discouraged from coming back if they *experienced long waiting to access the Library digital resources* (Liza, Student).
- **Staying Compatible with Physical Resources:** *Demands for physical collections* were reported to *remain* despite the

fact that the Library aimed to provide digital resources accessible anytime anywhere (Zety, Librarian). Some users were reported to *prefer to hold and feel their reading materials more than reading from a computer screen* (Dina, Students). Moreover, the *approval from MQA,* prior to offering any new course, indicated that the Library should provide *sufficient reading materials* for each courses and subjects they offered (Faiz, Librarian). Unfortunately, a librarian suggested that *some textbooks are not available in digital format* (Daud, Librarian). The Library had no choice but to acquire printed materials. Hence, many issues emerged including: (1) *limited spaces* – the Library faced an acute *shortage of storage space* due to increasing number of physical collections and additional shelves to place them (Daud, Librarian); (2) *limited availability for readers* – the drawback of printed materials was viewed as providing *limited users at a time* (Zaini, Librarian); (3) *additional cost – acquiring printed on top of digital materials* was viewed as additional *cost* to the Library (Zety, Library); and (4) *processing time – acquiring printed books take between 1 to 3 months depending on availability while e-books takes a week or less to be processed* (Zety, Librarian).

Other issues were also identified from professional experience and reflection:

- **Storage Capacity and Cost for Digitization of Local Materials:** The Library has built an in-house database consisting of: books, articles and conference papers written by academic and non-academic staff; theses written by students; and newspaper clippings related to OUM. To digitize these materials, the library has had to take into account storage capacity and the cost. HTML format requires lesser storage space as compared to PDF files whereas scanning and converting to PDF is technically much easier but costly.
- **Cost of Digital Resources:** The Library has over 115,000 e-books and over 28,000 e-journals. Subscribed digital resources are accessible while they are still in subscription whereas 'perpetual' e-books belong to the Library, just like printed books. Although the cost for perpetual e-books is relatively higher than subscribed e-books, this is cost effective in the long run. There are times when the Library acquires perpetual e-books in 'bundles,' offered by publishers at a lower price, only to discover later that very few of those bundles are fully utilized by users.
- **Databases Subscription Cost:** Subscription to online databases is expensive. Subscription cancellation due to limited budget is not viable because of its repercussions to teaching and learning activities. Hence, the Library makes precautionary decisions by considering subscription cost, suitability of databases to courses offered by OUM and the percentage of courses covered by a particular database. A database that covers a greater number of subjects or is multidisciplinary is preferred over a database specializing in a few specific subjects.
- **Copyright and Legal Issues:** Copyright permission from publishers to digitize printed textbooks available in the Library is hardly available. Commercial databases allow downloading and printing activities, making documents vulnerable to be distributed by library users to non-subscribers.

2. Providing Synchronous and Asynchronous Interaction

Data suggested that OUM librarians realized that with the advance in ICT, the Library needed to utilize both synchronous and asynchronous interaction techniques to communicate with users during reference enquiries, loan services and other purposes. In the early years of the library operation, *emails, telephones, or in-person consultation* (at the information counter or during workshops) were used. *In 2006, the Library started using an online forum (in myVLE)* called *ODLibrary* (Figure 2). *All questions posted in the forum receive an immediate response* and students were reported to *appreciate* the Library support they received in the forum (Faiz, Librarian).

Email, telephone, and personal consultation were reported as important communication techniques by librarians. In many instances, even when users send emails, librarians would make *follow-up telephone calls directly to users*. This practice was taken particularly for issues that require *immediate attention*. If users made phone calls and the dialogue (via telephone line or mobile) was prolonged, librarians would ask them to stop and instead *return their call* to continue the dialogue (Daud, Librarian).

After a few years of using the ODLibrary, the Library decided to use *Facebook* as it has becoming a *widely used* social online networking application among Malaysians (Zaini, Librarian). According to the second author, all OUM librarians have their own Facebook account but interactions with users are conducted through the Library Facebook page. The page, created on April 2009, quickly went from a few hundred to over 2000 followers in less than a year and now has more than 4500 fans (See Figure 3). While OUM has a total 40,000 active students every semester, the student response to the Facebook initiative was viewed as promising enough to continue its usage.

Figure 2. ODLibrary, the online forum in myVLE

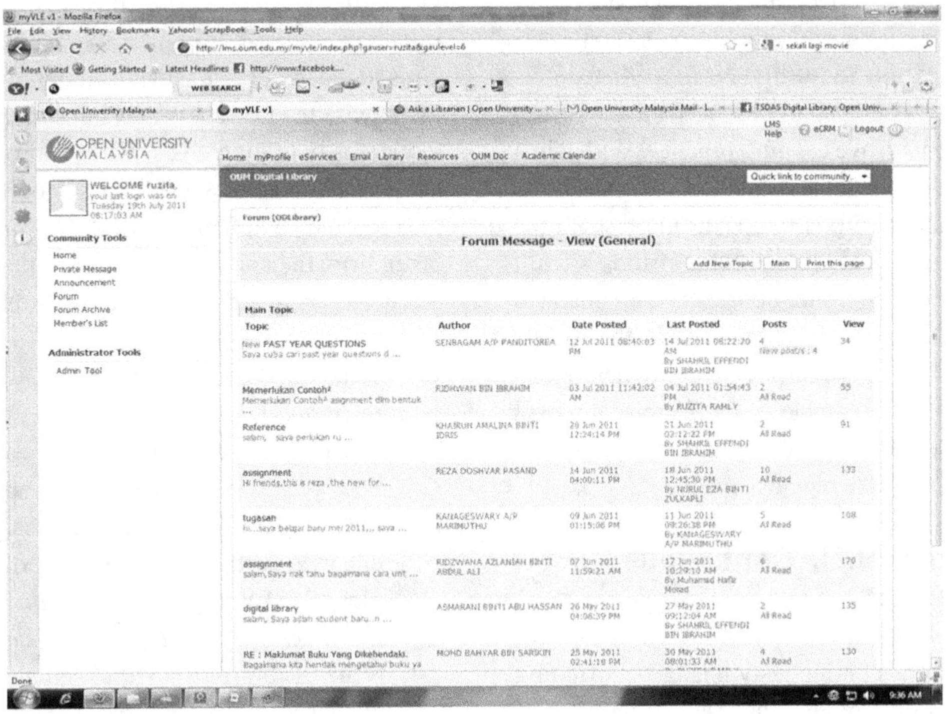

Figure 3. TSDAS digital library on Facebook

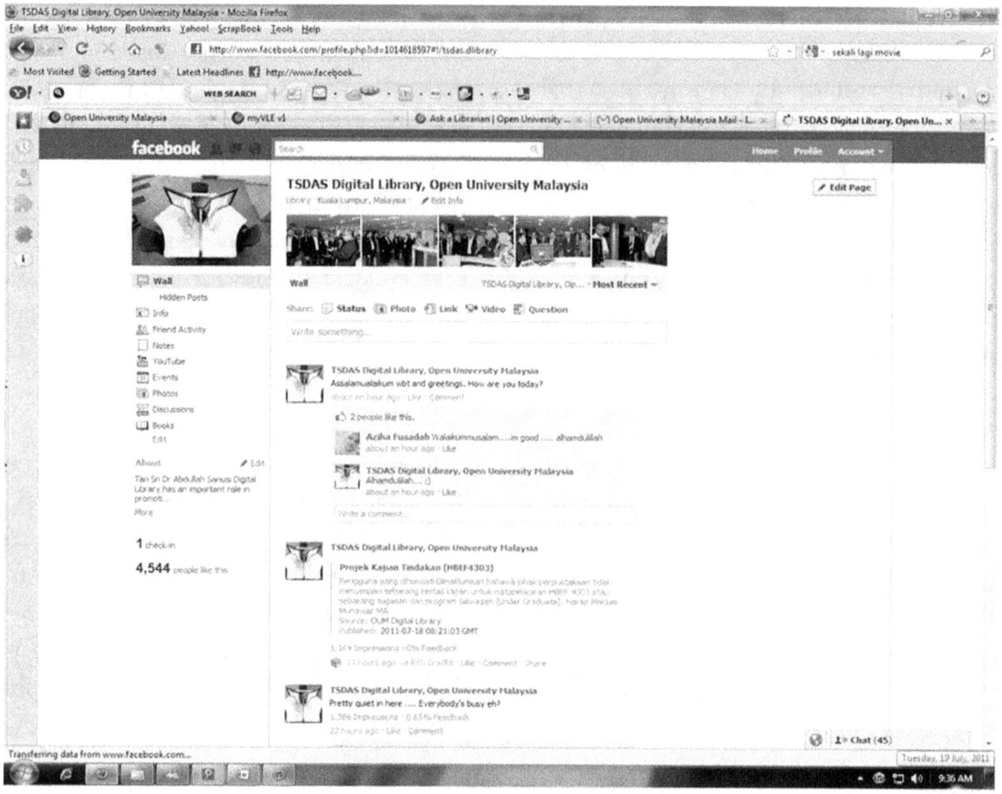

Professional reflection by the second author suggests that librarians' interaction with users is meant to not only to fulfill their immediate information needs but also to seek feedback and suggestions to improve existing practices and gain a better understanding of users' changing demands for information. OUM librarians understand the constraints of OUM students who are mostly adult working learners. Continuous efforts are made to allow students to reach librarians in the easiest ways possible, particularly using synchronous interaction. An example is the Library's recent initiatives of online chatting and mobile library which are discussed in next theme.

3. Engagement in Continuous Improvement

The Library is continuously engaged in finding better ways of providing access, delivering services, and communicating with users. Continuous improvement, according to the second author, aims to reach out to a wider user community and to increase the Library usage, but simultaneously reduce its operating costs. Various projects have been undertaken to achieve these goals and they are reported next. Only the first three projects are taken from the research data while other projects are additions given by the second author.

- **Reading Lists:** OUM has *developed its own modules* for students' self-paced learning. These modules are *available* in both *electronic* (via myVLE) and *printed format* (Farid, Instructional Designer). To enhance further reading beyond the modules, the Library provides a *direct hyperlink from the reading list in each module* (Faiz, Librarian) to the actual materials available in the Library collection (Figure

Figure 4. Direct links from the reading list project

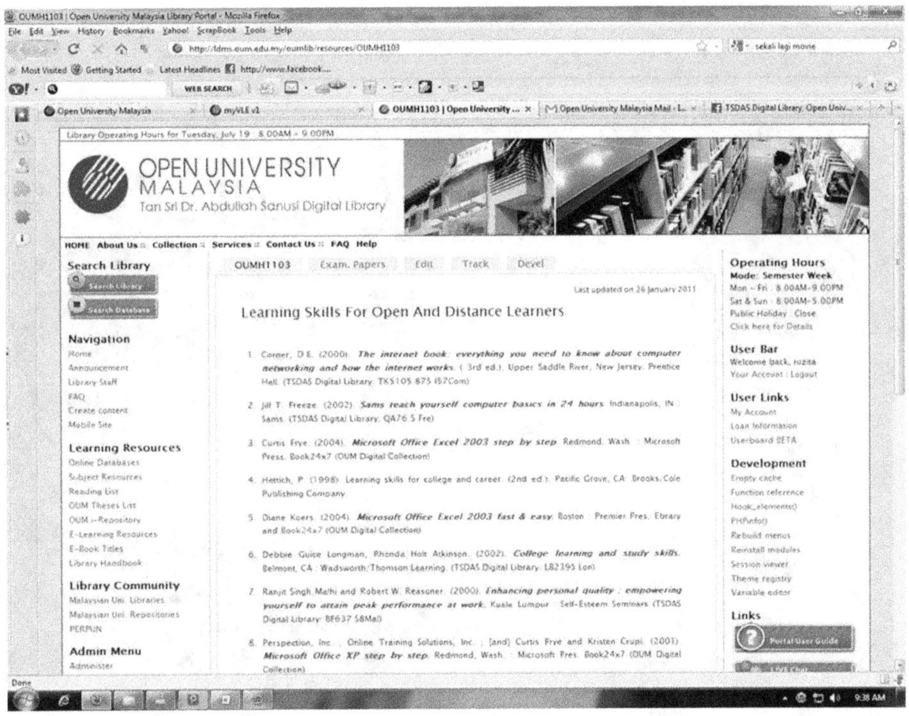

4). These links are available in myVLE for most courses offered in OUM. Students can use these links to either read e-books or borrow printed books.

- **Online Library Guides:** The Library used to organize periodical user education workshops at the main campus and learning centers. Since 2004, the number of workshops *reduced* and *organized based on request* by respective learning centers. The Library created *online guides*, which include *general guidelines* about the Library and *guidelines on how to use specific databases*. They are *accessible* through the *Library portal,* and *YouTube* (Md Zaini, Librarian). Figure 5 is an example of the online guide.
- **iRadio Library Slot:** iRadio OUM, launched in March 2007, broadcast a variety of shows and programs that bridge education and information with entertainment (Figure 6). The *Library segment every Tuesday afternoon* provided *updated Library news* as well as Library discussion and guidelines such as on *how to use specific database*. Previous segments were reported to be *archived* and students could listen to them anytime and anywhere they want (Siham, Librarian).
- **Focus on Synchronous Interaction with Users**: The Library has recently introduced two new platforms to enhance its interaction with users. Firstly, the mobile library is created whereby this platform allows users to access the Library portal using their mobile devices with simple menu and shortcuts. The application is still limited to the Library portal. It is not available in the actual online database interfaces since most online databases do not support mobile access, apart from EbscoHost. Users can download the Ebsco applications (from Ebsco website) onto their smart phones and search the Library's Ebsco collection

Figure 5. Online guides on YouTube

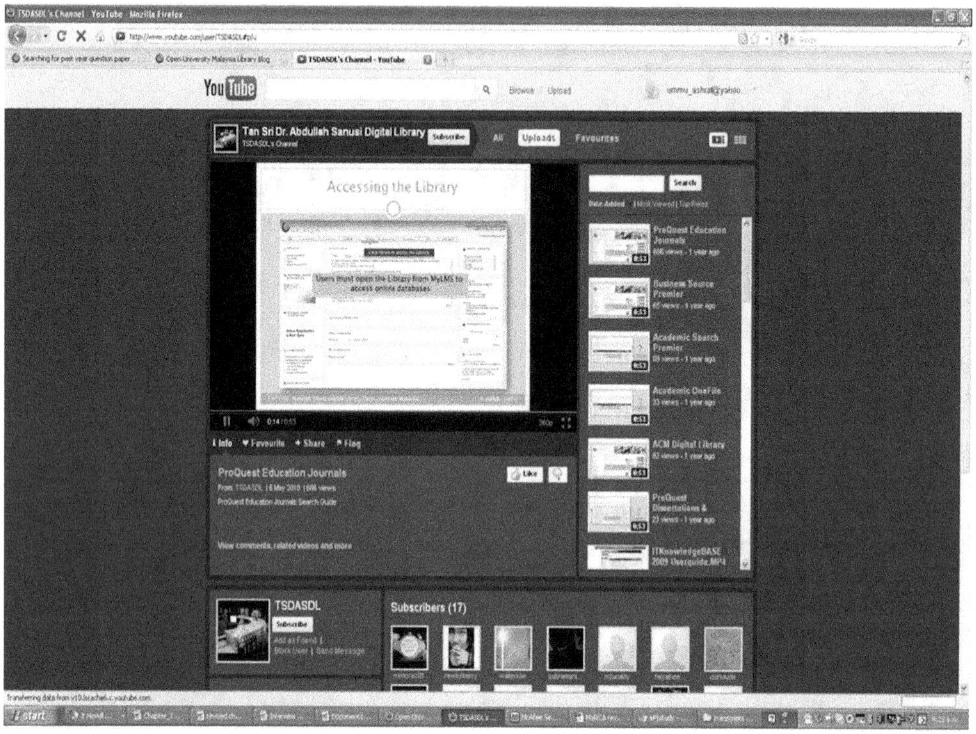

Figure 6. OUM iRadio

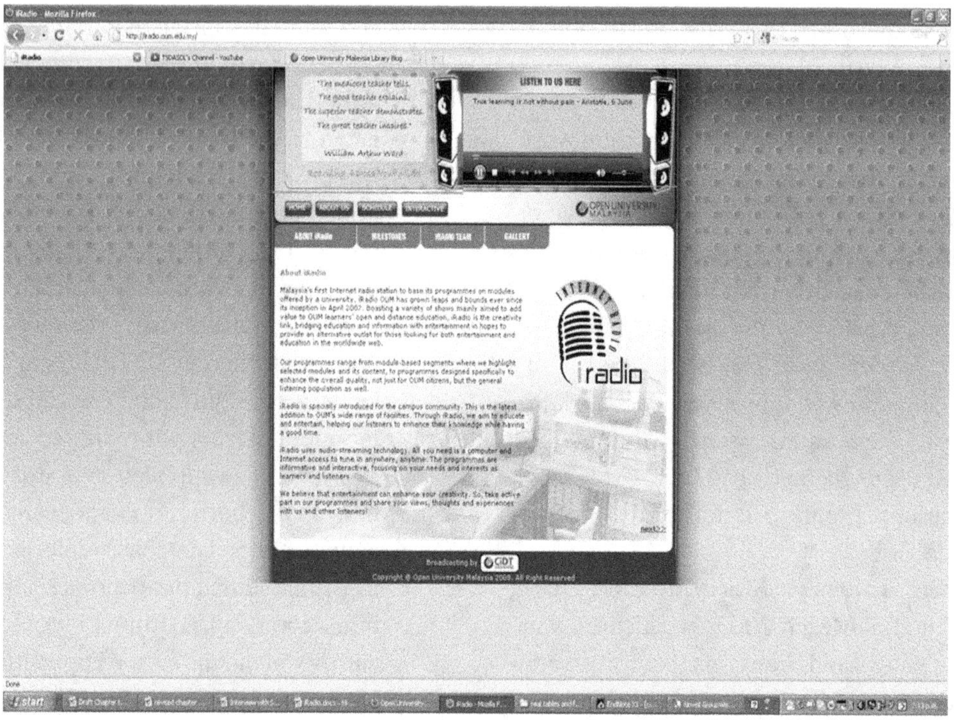

from their mobile devices. Secondly, an online chatting platform has been introduced. This platform, developed using Meebo.com (Figure 5), allows users with Yahoo and MSN Messenger accounts to communicate synchronously by adding the Library's user ID. With the Library Facebook and Meebo chat system, the Library has been able to extend and provide information and reference services almost around-the-clock (See Figure 7).

- **Distribution of 'Space':** When the Library was established, the concept was to develop a digital library - with a digital collection and students mostly accessing the collection online. The physical space of the Library is fairly small and now, it has become constrained with the growing number of printed materials and the sharp increase in student numbers. However, the recent construction of three Learning Centers within the vicinity of Klang Valley allows the Library to minimize this issue by distributing some printed books to these centers. With the printed collection being dispersed, the students are no longer only using the Main Campus Library but are also visiting their respective centers.

REFLECTION ON ISSUES AND CHALLENGES

Despite the fact that digital resources are ubiquitous and widely accessible to users, issues for the library concerning storage, cost, copyright,

Figure 7. Online chatting using Meebo

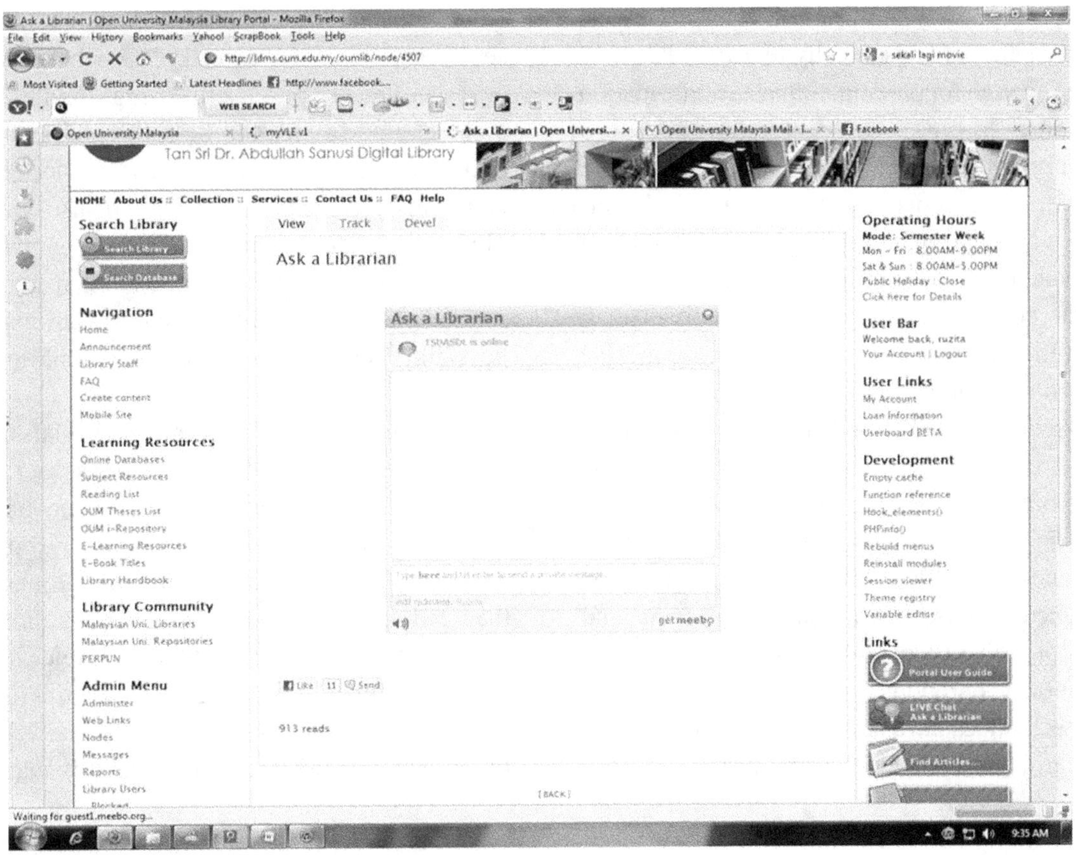

access, etc. are unavoidable. Physical resources have some limitations particularly for students from diverse localities. The digital and physical presence of academic libraries continues to be relevant for today's tertiary teaching and learning. Beyond providing contents, the libraries' social role in providing physical space for people to meet remains unchanged, as there will always be a need for social setting and physical objects in learning (Marchionini & Maurer, 1995).

Regardless of the Library's efforts to provide digital resources and their advantages for open and distance learning, for some students there is a digital divide. They may have technical difficulties in accessing digital resources or language barriers in understanding them and these influence their learning. This issue of the 'digital divide' (Hawkins, 2005) requires not only policy makers' involvement to further enhance ICT diffusion all over the country but also the involvement of librarians. The main challenge is to enhance information literacy skills because "without these skills, merely being able physically to access ICT will not be enough for participating in the information economy" (p 178).

Information literacy, according to Warschauer (2003), is a 'practice'—more than a skill—of effective acquisition and appropriate utilization of information and this practice varies depending on the culture and context of the individual. It is an important component of access alongside with other components: devices and conduits (Warschauer, 2003). While librarians emphasize resources/contents, access and usage, their role in information literacy means inculcating that 'practice' among user communities. User education and information skills workshops should be designed to assist users to effectively acquire and appropriately utilize information.

Both synchronous and asynchronous interaction techniques have advantages and limitations. Synchronous techniques particularly in-person consultation, online chatting and phone calls allow high level of interaction, immediacy of responses and timely feedback. On the other hand, asynchronous techniques such as email allow librarians to have ample time to reply appropriately to queries (Norasieh & Fadzilah, 2011).

Librarians have the advantage of utilizing Web 2.0 social networking applications to interact and reach users in dispersed localities. Many academic libraries have adopted a similar concept—Library 2.0—and the data here demonstrates its four principles (Black, 2007, p. 10): the library is everywhere; the library has no barriers; the library invites participation; and the library uses flexible best-of-breed systems. Beyond synchronous and asynchronous interaction is an engagement in continuous improvement.

The Library's focus on synchronous interaction such as mobile library and online chatting align with Library 2.0. Indeed, the essence of Library 2.0 is closely related to engagement for continuous improvement. It is a model for library services (Casey & Savastinuk, 2006) that encourages constant and purposeful change, invites user collaboration in creating both the physical and digital services they want, and is supported by consistently evaluating services. It also guides libraries in their effort to win new users while, at the same time, acknowledging that current service offerings are insufficient and inflexible, possibility due to physical technological limitations (Crawford, 2006).

Convenient access to learning materials from the digital library is one of the reasons many working adults in Malaysia appreciate online learning (Wong, 2006). Embedding resources within myVLE such as providing hyperlinks for the Reading List allows OUM students to directly retrieve materials from electronic modules, thus, saving their time for learning. However, this raises concerns which are expressed as a 'spoon-feed attitude' and 'narrowly focused' research by students

(Roberts & Davey, 2002). It is advised that only essential set of recommended readings should be spoon-fed to students (Joint, 2006).

Due to the expensive cost of the digital library, librarians need to convince University management that resource allocations to the library are worthwhile. Management would be more persuaded if usage of resources was high or at least meeting their expectations. A high usage of library collections and services among users could be achieved if librarians rigorously market their resources and services, keep abreast with users changing learning needs, and continuously interact and attract users to utilize them. In other word, librarians need to keep abreast with the changing learning environments, maintain cooperation with users, and equip themselves with the new user-centric roles, knowledge, and skills that are required in this era of technological advancement.

In this chapter, we have identified three main issues and challenges of integrating digital library services in blended learning environments based on a case study of OUM. These issues and challenges may not necessarily exist in the traditional face-to-face and/or online learning. Physical space issue for example may not happen among institutions where face-to-face learning predominantly occurs because a physical library is normally established in each such institution and it has ample space to locate physical collections. Moreover, university libraries such as in Malaysia are better staffed and received sufficient funding as compared to other types of libraries (Wedgeworth, 1993). Some issues however such as cost, legal, and copyright are quite common among academic libraries.

With the increasing production of digital resources, librarians and information professionals of academic institutions nowadays must deal with both digital and physical resources. The degree of each type of resources within a library may vary but serving both types means they need to be proactive and innovative. Engagement in continuous evaluation and improvement is crucial in today's enormous technological progression (Casey & Savastinuk, 2006). The expansion of ICT and Library 2.0 allows them to continuously find new ways to reach users, improve usage of existing services and resources, and play new roles in today's changing landscape of library and learning environments. Librarians' roles are multiplying and expanding into areas such as becoming a user-centric 'access-assurer' of information. Librarians need to continuously engage in professional learning to develop the new user-centric roles, knowledge, and skills that are required in this era of technological advancement.

ADDRESSING FUTURE CHALLENGES

This chapter has focused on librarians' perspectives of digital library services and their attendant issues and challenges in Malaysia. However, in order to innovate and improve, librarians must work with academics and students, who are users of their digital services. To date, much of the research effort has focused on the technical and non-technical issues and challenges of linking digital libraries in virtual learning environments such as by Currier (2002) and Robert and Davey (2002). More insight is needed into academics views' of digital libraries and the ways in which its services might assist them to develop their students into information literate learners in their discipline. As we have discovered, not all users are comfortable using digital services and there is a larger issue of the digital divide and its impact on digital services. Earlier research by the first author has found that this is not only a matter of access, but also of language barriers particularly among students (Norasieh & Gerbic, 2010). More research is needed to identify approaches, which can increase digital inclusion (Warshauer, 2003).

While the concepts of blended librarianship (Bell & Shank, 2007) and the Library 2.0 (Casey, 2005) may appear to be somewhat visionary at the moment, they do provide an indication of the pathway for further research and development. A key facet of Library 2.0 is user collaboration in developing digital services and further research into student and academics perspectives of the recently introduced Web 2.0 initiatives would provide insights to support further innovation as well as identifying barriers to their further uptake. The focus in blended librarianship and Library 2.0 on innovation and organizational change means that adapting to change, design, and professional learning for librarians will become increasingly important. Further research into effective approaches in these areas would be valuable, especially those that preserve librarians' sense of agency and empower them to increasingly integrate their services and practice into the university's teaching and learning activities.

CONCLUSION

This chapter contributes to the view of the digital library from a services perspective. The concept of the digital library is no longer alien to many librarians and information professionals of academic institutions. As academic libraries are becoming more 'digital,' issues and challenges for digital librarians are intensifying. Constant review, re-thinking and re-designing of existing library practices will allow digital librarians to remain significant contributors to the teaching and learning agenda in higher education.

We have shared perspectives, definitions, and components of the digital library and the various types of digital library services. We conclude that while the following components of the digital library—purpose, creators, and creations—serve as the foundation of the digital library, other components—content, access, users, and usage—are of significance and require particular attention from information professionals in higher education to ensure ongoing relevance of the digital library. Integrating the digital library brings a huge potential to enhance learning particularly in today's changing learning environment. Our experience in Malaysia may offer insights for others involved with the integration of digital library services in blended learning environment.

REFERENCES

Anderson, C. G., & Maxwell, D. C. (2004). *Starting a digitization center*. Oxford, UK: Chandos Publishing. doi:10.1533/9781780630663

Arms, W. Y. (2000). *Digital libraries*. Cambridge, MA: MIT Press.

Bell, S. J., & Shank, J. D. (2007). *Academic librarianship by design: A blended librarian's guide to the tools and technique*. Chicago, IL: ALA.

Black, E. L. (2007). Web 2.0 and library 2.0: What librarians need to know. In Courney, N. (Ed.), *Library 2.0 and Beyond: Innovative Technologies and Tomorrow's Users* (pp. 1–14). Westport, CT: Libraries Unlimited.

Borgman, C. (1999). What are digital libraries? Competing visions. *Information Processing & Management*, *35*(3), 227–243.

Borgman, C. (2000). *From Gutenberg to the global information infrastructure: Access to information in the networked world*. Cambridge, MA: The MIT Press.

Borgman, C. (2007). *Scholarship in the digital age: Information, infrastructure, and the internet*. Cambridge, MA: MIT Press.

Bush, V. (1945). As we may think. *The Atlantic Monthly*. Retrieved from http://www.theatlantic.com/doc/194507/bush

Casey, M. (2005). *Working towards a definition of library 2.0*. Retrieved August 5, 2009 from http://www.librarycrunch.com/2005/10/working_towards_a_definition_o.html

Casey, M., & Savastinuk, L. C. (2006). Library 2.0. *Library Journal, 131*(14), 40–42.

Crawford, W. (2006). Library 2.0 and "library 2.0". *Cites and Insights, 6*(2), 1–32.

Creswell, J. W. (2005). *Educational research: Planning, conducting, and evaluating quantitative and qualitative research* (2nd ed.). Upper Saddle River, NJ: Merrill.

Currier, S. (2002). INSPIRAL: Digital library services and online learning environments: Issues for integration. In Brophy, P., Fisher, S., & Clarke, Z. (Eds.), *Libraries without Walls 4: The Delivery of Library Services to Distant Users* (pp. 50–61). London, UK: Facet Publishing.

Digital Library Federation. (1998). *A working definition of digital library*. Retrieved March 29, 2008 from www.diglib.org/about/dldefinition.htm

Gapen, D. K. (1993). The virtual library: Knowledge, society and the librarian. In Saunders, L. M. (Ed.), *The Virtual Library: Vision and Realities* (pp. 1–14). Westport, CT: Meckler.

Garrison, D. R., & Kanuka, H. (2004). Blended learning: Uncovering its transformative potential in higher education. *The Internet and Higher Education, 7*(2), 95–105. doi:10.1016/j.iheduc.2004.02.001

Hawkins, S. (2005). Beyond the digital divide: Issues of access and economics. *Canadian Journal of Information and Library Science, 29*(2), 171–189.

Herold, P. (2004). Teams and teamwork. In Barnes, S. J. (Ed.), *Becoming a Digital Library* (pp. 117–142). New York, NY: Marcel Dekker.

Johnson, K., & Magusin, E. (2005). *Exploring the digital library: A guide for online teaching and learning*. San Francisco, CA: Jossey-Bass.

Joint, N. (2006). Common principles in managing digital libraries and managing VLEs. *Library Review, 55*(4), 232–236. doi:10.1108/00242530610660771

Kahn, R. E., & Cerf, V. G. (1988). *The digital library project volume 1: The world of knowbots (draft): An open architecture for a digital library system and a plan for its development*. Retrieved February 9, 2009 from http://www.cnri.reston.va.us/kahn-cerf-88.pdf

Kaske, N. (2004). The ubiquitous library is here. *Libraries and the Academy, 4*(2), 291–297. doi:10.1353/pla.2004.0030

Lee, S. H. (Ed.). (1997). *Economics of digital information: Collection, storage and delivery*. New York, NY: Haworth Press.

Lerner, F. (1998). *The stories of libraries: From the invention of writing to the computer age*. New York, NY: Continuum.

Licklider, J. C. R. (1965). *Libraries of the future*. Cambridge, MA: MIT Press.

Marchionini, G., & Maurer, H. (1995). The roles of digital libraries in teaching and learning. *Communications of the ACM, 38*(4), 67–76. doi:10.1145/205323.205345

McLean, N., & Lynch, C. (2004). *Interoperability between library information services and learning environments - Bridging the caps*. Retrieved from http://www.estandard.no/tilgjengelig/CNI-andIMS_2004.pdf

Miles, M. B., & Huberman, A. M. (1994). *Qualitative data analysis: An expended sourcebook*. Thousand Oaks, CA: Sage.

Moore, M. (2006). Foreword. In Bonk, C., & Graham, C. (Eds.), *The Handbook of Blended Learning: Global Perspectives, Local Designs*. San Francisco, CA: John Wiley and Sons.

Norasieh, M. A., & Fadzilah, A. (2011). *Synchronous and asynchronous interaction between librarians and library customers: Where are we heading?* Paper presented at the meeting of the Seminar Kebangsaan Perpustakaan Akademik (National Academic Libraries Seminar). Kelantan, Malaysia.

Norasieh, M. A., & Gerbic, P. (2010). Exploring the use of digital library services in blended learning environments: A Malaysian higher education perspective. In L. G. Chova, D. M. Belenguer, & I. C. Torres (Eds.), *Proceedings of the International Conference of Education, Research and Innovation,* (pp. 1782-1792). Valencia, Spain: International Association of Technology, Education, and Development (IATED).

Ochs, M. A., & Saylor, J. M. (2004). Resources for the digital library. In Barnes, S. J. (Ed.), *Becoming a Digital Library* (pp. 49–80). New York, NY: Marcel Dekker.

Roberts, S., & Davey, J. (2002). VLEs and information services: Redefining distance learning and the role of information services within the virtual learning environment. In *Libraries without Walls 4: The Delivery of Library Services to Distant Users* (pp. 73–84). London, UK: Facet Publishing.

Rowlands, I., & Bawden, D. (1999). Digital libraries: A conceptual framework. *Libri, 49*(4), 192–202. doi:10.1515/libr.1999.49.4.192

Saracevic, T. (2000). Digital library evaluation: Towards an evolution of concepts. *Library Trends, 49*(3), 350–369.

Secker, J. (2004). *Electronic resources in the virtual learning environment: A guide for librarians.* Oxford, UK: Chandos. doi:10.1533/9781780630700

Sharifabadi, S. R. (2006). How digital libraries can support e-learning. *The Electronic Library, 24*(3), 389–401. doi:10.1108/02640470610671231

Stacey, E., & Gerbic, P. (2007). Teaching for blended learning - Research perspectives from on campus and distance students. *Education and Information Technologies, 12*(3), 165–174. doi:10.1007/s10639-007-9037-5

Stacey, E., & Gerbic, P. (2009). Introduction to blended learning practice. In Stacey, E., & Gerbic, P. (Eds.), *Effective Blended Learning Practices: Evidence-Based Perspectives in ICT-Facilitated Education.* Hershey, PA: IGI Global. doi:10.4018/978-1-60566-296-1.ch001

Stacey, E., & Gerbic, P. (Eds.). (2009a). *Effective blended learning practices: Evidence-based perspectives in ICT-facilitated education.* Hershey, PA: IGI Global. doi:10.4018/978-1-60566-296-1

Tedd, L. A., & Large, J. A. (2005). *Digital libraries: Principles and practice in a global environment.* Munchen, Germany: Saur, K.G.

Warschauer, M. (2003). *Technology and social inclusion: Rethinking the digital divide.* Cambridge, MA: MIT Press.

Wong, D. (2006). Fulltime students' and working adults' perceptions of e-learning in Malaysia. *Asian Journal of Distance Education, 4*(1), 67–84.

ADDITIONAL READING

Bargellini, M. L., & Bordoni, L. (2001). The role of the library in a new learning scenario. *The Electronic Library, 19*(3), 153–157. doi:10.1108/EUM0000000005480

Chan, G., & Ibrahim, M. Z. (2008). Conceptualising the network society in Malaysia. *Asian Journal of Social Science*, *36*, 773–791. doi:10.1163/156853108X364226

Chowdhury, G. G., & Chowdhury, S. (1999). Digital library research: Major issues and trends. *The Journal of Documentation*, *55*(4), 409–448. doi:10.1108/EUM0000000007154

DELOS. (2006). *The digital library manifesto: DELOS a network of excellence on digital libraries*. Retrieved from http://www.delos.info/index.php?option=com_content&task=view&id=496&Itemid=73

Garrett, J. R. (1991). Copyright compliance in the electronic age: Conceptual issues. *Publishing Research Quarterly*, *7*(4), 13–20. doi:10.1007/BF02678329

Jeng, J. (2005). What is usability in the context of the digital library and how can it be measured?. *Information Technology and Libraries*, *24*(2), 47(10).

Kuny, T., & Cleveland, G. (1998). The digital library: Myths and challenges. *IFLA Journal*, *24*(2), 107–113. doi:10.1177/034003529802400205

Lang, B. (1998). Developing the digital library. In Carpenter, L., Shaw, S., & Prescott, A. (Eds.), *Towards the Digital Library: The British Library's 'Initiatives for Access' Programme* (pp. 227–233). London, UK: British Library.

Leiner, B. (1998). *The scope of the digital library*. Draft prepared for the DLib Working Group on Digital Library Metrics. Retrieved from http://www.dlib.org/metrics/public/papers/dig-lib-scope.html

Lesk, M. (1997). *Practical digital libraries: Books, bytes, and bucks*. San Francisco, CA: Morgan Kaufmann.

Lynch, C., & Molina, H. G. (1995). *Interoperability, scaling and the digital libraries research agenda*. Reston, VA: US Information Infrastructure Technology and Application (IITA). Retrieved June 13, 2011 from http://www.sis.pitt.edu/~repwkshop/papers/DL1995.pdf

Marchionini, G. (2000). Evaluating digital libraries: A longitudinal and multifaceted view. *Library Trends*, *49*(2), 304–333.

Neal, J. G. (1996). Academic libraries: 2000 and beyond. *Library Journal*, *121*(12), 74–76.

Norasieh, M. A., & Yanti Idaya Aspura, M. K. (2009). *Understanding digital library services in the virtual learning environment in higher education*. Paper presented at the meeting of the International Conference on Teaching & Learning in Higher Education. Kuala Lumpur, Malaysia.

Rusbridge, C. (1998). Towards the hybrid library. *D-Lib Magazine*. Retrieved May 16, 2008 from http://www.dlib.org/dlib/july98/rusbridge/07rusbridge.html

Witten, I. H., & Bainbridge, D. (2003). *How to build a digital library*. London, UK: Morgan Kaufman.

Yusof, Z. M., & Mohd, M. (2003). Conceptual framework for digital library: A proposal and a study of understanding the concept among chief librarians in Malaysia. In C. Crawford, et al. (Eds.), *Proceedings of Society for Information Technology & Teacher Education International Conference 2003,* (pp. 2768-2775). Chesapeake, VA: AACE.

KEY TERMS AND DEFINITIONS

Digital Library: Is viewed from services/ organizations perspective from the context of higher learning institutions.

Blended Learning: A fusion of face-to-face, online, and self-paced learning.

Digital Divide: A situation whereby societal members are stratified by possession and usage of knowledge (including access to knowledge and access to means of acquiring the knowledge such as computer and the Internet), and, consequently, by possession of income and wealth acquired through the knowledge (Chan & Ibrahim, 2008).

ENDNOTES

1 Ruzita is ex-Chief Librarian, TSDAS Digital Library.

2 Philippa is a Researcher/Lecturer and Norasieh's main supervisor for her doctoral studies.

Chapter 5
Information Analysis in Digital Library Environments:
Lessons Learned in Pharma

Lauren Harrison
Roche Pharmaceutical Corp., USA

ABSTRACT

This chapter addresses the question of how the analysis of results retrieved from online bibliographic information systems changed over the last 32 years as digital libraries have evolved. It demonstrates that Digital Libraries of the future will enable knowledge discovery by providing direct access to the semantic content of documents through the implementation of text mining tools. To achieve this research with IR systems and text-mining tools, pipeline pilot (Bandy, et al., 2009), I2E (Vellay, 2009), and BioText will need to be conducted by experts in information retrieval not just subject scientific specialists.

INTRODUCTION

The process of searching and retrieving relevant data from bibliographic databases has relatively stayed the same. In the beginning Boolean logic and proximity searching (right and latter on left hand) are applied to online systems containing records that were created as surrogates for a publication/article. Indexing and thesauri were created to facilitate the identification of relevant articles. This has not changed. Experimentation with full text bibliographic databases resulted in statistical algorithms to rank search results. None of these relevance-ranking mechanisms were not adopted by the major vendors—Dialog, DataStar, STN.

Today, most online bibliographic database collections are now linked to the institutions licensed e-journal collection so that the database

DOI: 10.4018/978-1-4666-2991-2.ch005

record is directly linked to the pdf or html of the document it represents. This affords opportunities for experimentation in the post processing of information results not previously available. This is the greatest change in information analysis.

HISTORY OF POST PROCESSING OF RETRIEVAL RESULTS

In the beginning there was manual "cut and paste." The database records contained the text of a bibliographic citation—the title, author, journal, and keywords of the referenced article. A Boolean query matched specific words to the words in the fields of the database record. The hardware capacity of the mainframes of this period determined the functionality of the IR system. The corpus was a collection of database records rather than a collection of the full text articles. The output device was a paper teletypewriter. The network was a telephone line with a coupler. These systems were best suited to generating a bibliography—an exhaustive printout of all articles that contained the key words on a subject such as diabetes and insulin. These collections of records that online systems handled became known as bibliographic databases. These bibliographies databases (e.g. Medline in Biology and Medicine and STN in Chemistry) grew over time to include searchable abstracts of the articles as a result of the growth of the indexing and abstracting industry.

Harrison and Lacerna (1992) documented the process of producing annotated bibliographies in Pharma prior to 1989. A considerable amount of production time was spent in the content analysis and review of the abstracts or original articles to determine various topics relevant to the drug profile. Prior to 1989, the process by which bibliographies were created required manual manipulation of the exported in-house database records. A print out of all records on a substance was retrieved. Each record was then manually coded or indexed according to the categories.

If a record was indexed by two or more categories, two or more photocopies were made. References were then cut, pasted and sorted manually into alphabetical lists per category. The resulting report listed records alphabetically by author within each category. This process had to be repeated per category and each category was input in the logical order of appearance desired. An author index indicating the location of authors works within the subject section could be automatically generated. This process was tedious, laborious, and costly in terms of man-hours spent in compilation.

In 1987 research on a automated method of bibliography general using Sci-Mate Manager was initiated. This initiative went on to review all bibliographic manipulation software available at the time. Pro-Cite was ultimate chosen as the best tool to facilitate bibliography generation as on a daily basis it eliminated the need to edit downloaded data for search report generation. It provided an efficient means of electronically combining references from several sources, facilitating the review of data by providing duplicate detection assistance. It greatly reduced the amount of post processing required to produce the subject section of the bibliography. Most importantly, at the time, the application was programmer independent and the users (information scientists) had total control over the output appearance.

THE ADVENT OF PERSONAL VIRTUAL LIBRARIES

Since then many other tools of this genre have appeared—Endnotes, Ref works, References Manager to name a few. All have attributes comparable to Pro-Cite. However, the most recent tool in this arena, Quosa Platinum Manager, has a decided advantage. It was designed in the digital library age and it not only facilitates the import/download of bibliographic database records but it retrieves the pdf or html format of the full text of the article in as well (See Figure 1). This tool provides a level of text mining that may be applied to search result sets. The tool creates an algorithm based on the search phrase utilized on the online system. It then clusters the results by related terms.

The users can also develop their own algorithm for clustering of results. Figure 2 illustrates the use of this algorithm on a corpus of articles on diabetes to determine the most interesting ones for inclusion in an alert. The algorithm identified those articles in which the pharmacokinetic value for HbA1C was discussed which is the key pharmacokinetic to determine the control of blood glucose levels in diabetic.

Alternatively if your goal is to identify the most interesting articles published on diabetes for a certain period of time you can download a list of diabetes genes from ENTREZ and then use that list or any subset of this list as the basis of the custom concept clustering algorithm (See Figure 3).

This is a unique way to help find a needle in a haystack as it offers some aspect of text mining on search results. This is not to be compared with tools specifically developed for text mining such as I2E that are used on large data sets to determine if previously unidentified relationships can be found. In a search set of a maximum of 500 pdfs or less, where you expect to find the information required it is quite powerful.

Quosa Manager has a companion tool the Quosa Virtual Library where users can share their results with a wider community thus creating personalized virtual libraries for specific user communities. The Browser Plus tool provides these user communities a vehicle where they can annotate and search these custom virtual libraries created for their specific use. The application is also available on an IPAD for flexible use.

Quosa platinum manager allows the export of the xml format (database record and full text in html) compatible for import into text mining tools

Figure 1. The interface Quosa platinum manager

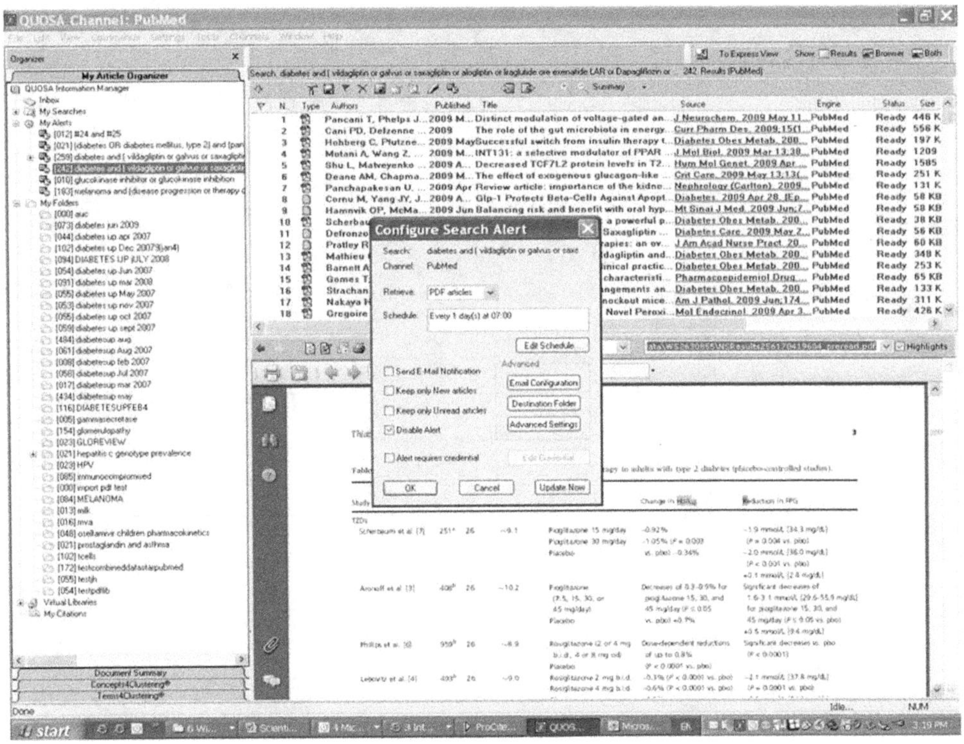

Figure 2. An example of application of the concept for clustering algorithm

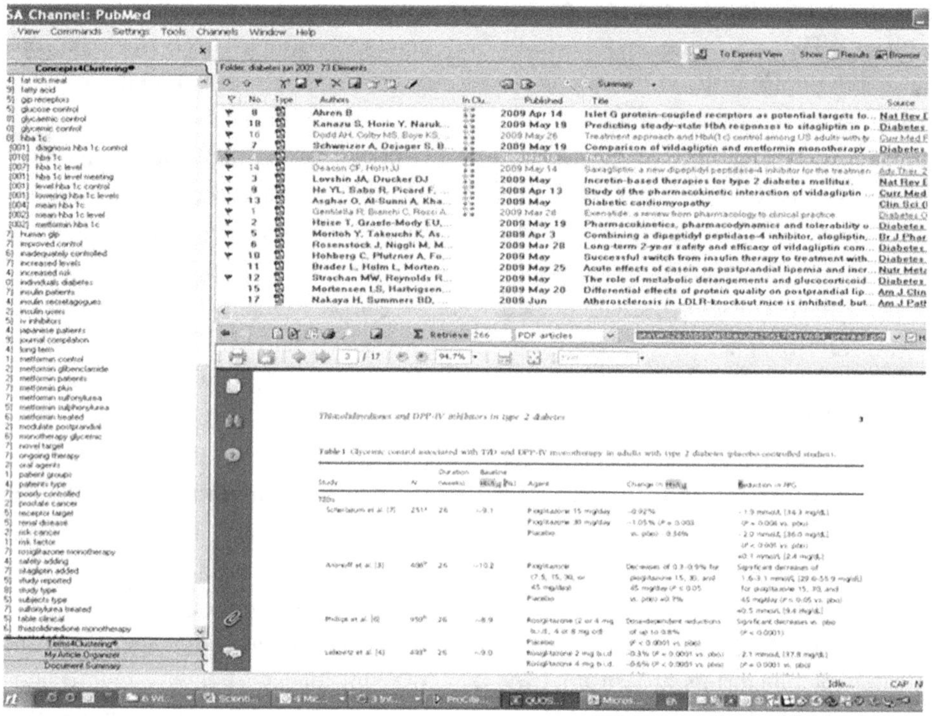

Figure 3. Custom concept clustering for relevance

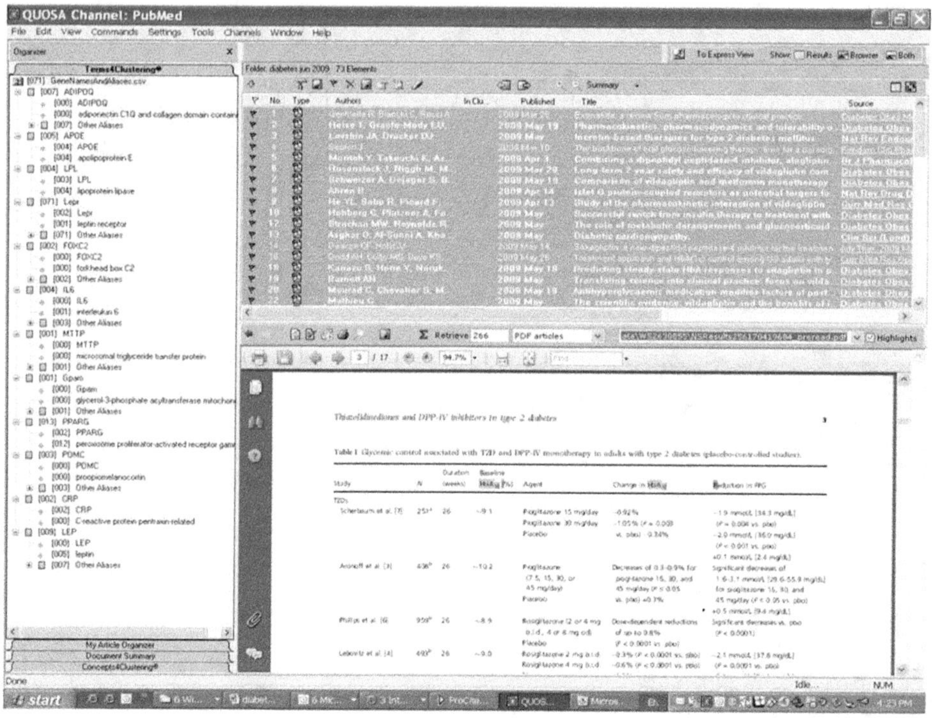

such as Pipeline pilot and I2E. Here large corpus of data can be easily downloaded and exported for text mining.

INFLUENCE OF TEXT MINING

What influence has text mining had on information analysis in digital library environments in Pharma? The overall goal of digital libraries is to facilitate the identification/analysis of relevant information. Vannevar Bush (1945) was the first to predict that growing mountain of research findings would eventually stagger the investigator with findings and conclusions that not only would he not have the time to grasp much less remember. His vision was that scientist should build systems for information manipulation. Many feel that this is the original vision for the field of information retrieval. Alternatively it has been suggested that a more accurate beginning to the field was presented by Licklider (1961), where he suggests that the research agenda for digital libraries was established (Schatze, 1997). Vellay et al. (2009) suggested that Bush's vision of a computerized method of knowledge associated was not clearly realized until Swanson's paper in 1989 where the relationship of fish oil to Raynauds' syndrome was extracted from published literature sources using text mining. This relationship was not previously known. The question is - will text mining and information retrieval continue to be considered different fields in the digital library age in Pharma?

Most of the initiatives in text mining have been across bibliographic database. The best example is the work at Berkeley by Marti Hearst with the BioText search engine. This tool searches full text of the open access journals of Pubmed and can search the tables and figures as well. To my knowledge, research with this tool across virtual

Figure 4. Visualization of related terminology from Leximine

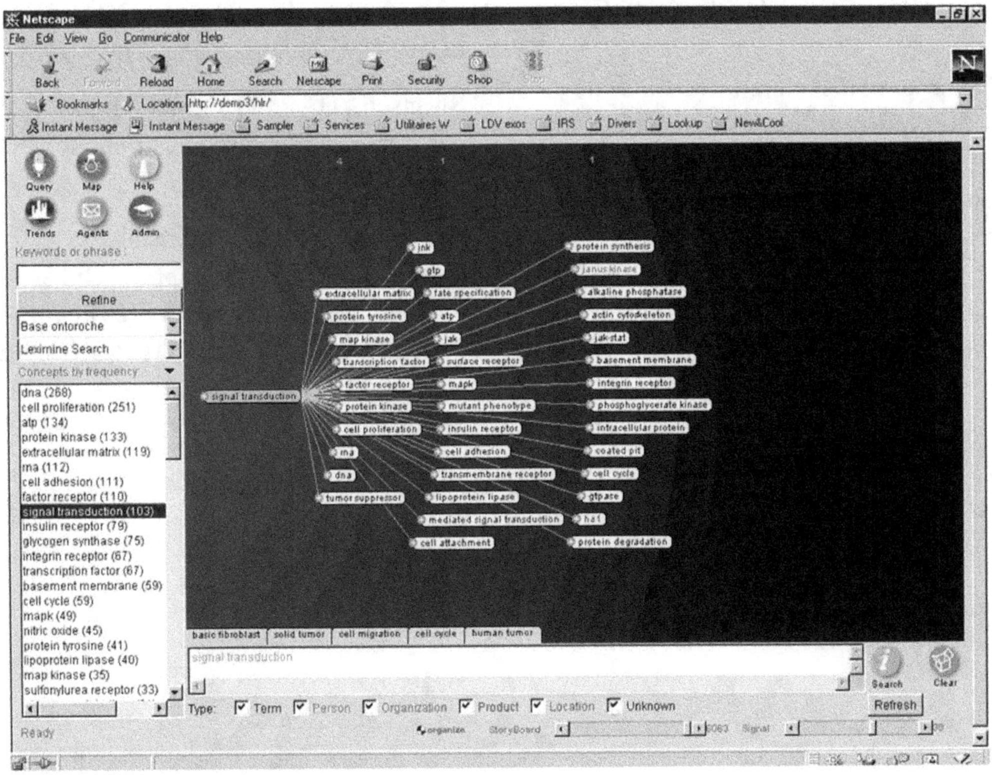

libraries designed for certain users may prove valuable. I believe that there is great opportunity for text mining to influence information analysis in digital libraries in Pharma.

Early efforts into text mining include a lexical approach to text mining for the integration of genomic information (Harrison, et al., 2001) with Lexiquest. This chapter described a case study of the utility of a lexical approach to text mining incorporating the GO ontologies into LexiMine—a tool produced by LexiQuest to facilitate information integration in Pharma. This research illustrated the value of text mining in the domain of genomics an area that was rapidly developing at that time and where the availability of indexing according to genomic criteria was limited. Text mining can be applied in a variety of ways. Where thesauri provide static vocabulary control, linguistic extraction can be used to visualize the evolution of terminology in new disciplines and thus support thesauri/ontology development (Figure 4).

PREDICTIONS FOR THE FUTURE

Digital Libraries of the future will enable knowledge discovery by providing direct access to the semantic content of documents through the implementation of text mining tools. To achieve this research with IR systems and Text mining tools, pipeline pilot (Bandy, et al., 2009), I2E (Vellay, 2009), and BioText will need to be conducted by experts in information retrieval not just subject scientific specialists.

REFERENCES

Bandy, J. (2009). Mining protein-protein interactions from published literature using linguamatics I2E. *Protein Networks and Pathway Analysis, 563*, 3–13. doi:10.1007/978-1-60761-175-2_1

Bush, V. (1945). As we may think. *Atlantic Monthly, 176*(101).

Harrison, L. D., et al. (2001). A lexical approach to text mining for the integration of genomic information. In C. Wu (Eds.), *Proceedings of the Atlantic Symposium on Computational Biology and Genome Information Systems & Technology*. Durham, NC: IEEE.

Harrison, L. D., & Lacerna, L. (1992). Reducing barriers to the utilization of literature at Hoffmann-La Roche. *Drug Information Journal, 26*(3), 433–443. doi:10.1177/009286159202600317

Hearst, M. A., Divoli, A., Guturu, H., Ksikes, A., Nakov, P., Wooldridge, A., & Ye, J. (2007). BioText search engine: Beyond abstract search. *Bioinformatics (Oxford, England), 23*(16), 2196–2197. doi:10.1093/bioinformatics/btm301

Swanson, D. R. (1986). Fish oil, Raynaud's syndrome, and undiscovered public knowledge. *Perspectives in Biology and Medicine, 30*(1), 7–18.

Vellay, S. G. P. (2009). Interactive text mining with pipeline pilot: A bibliographic web-based tool for PubMed. *Infectious Disorders Drug Targets, 9*(3), 366–374. doi:10.2174/1871526510909030366

Chapter 6
Listening to Images: Exploring Alternate Access to a Digital Collection

Kathleen C. Lonbom
Illinois State University, USA

ABSTRACT

This chapter explores a pilot project investigating the development of audio descriptions to accompany an academic library's digital image collection. The project was introduced in selected classes and directly involved faculty and students in the creation and delivery of audio descriptions. The collaborative project initiated by the art librarian was in answer to a legislative act requiring accessibility for vision-impaired users. The discussion will specifically examine developing descriptions for images from Illinois State University's International Collection of Child Art a resource that presents a fascinating challenge to use language to broaden access to the content and construct a compelling representation with the spoken word for individuals with print disabilities such as vision impairment.

INTRODUCTION

Imagine encountering a database filled with a collection of wonderfully rich, imaginative, and vivid artworks created by children and adolescents from around the world. The Web-based resource allows viewers unfettered access to the creativity and imaginings of young artists. The multicultural collection displays digital images encompassing worlds filled with family, friends, animals, home lives, activities, and observations from children's experiences. Colorful, bright, and frequently fantastical the collection is culled from the countries and cultures of six continents over a

DOI: 10.4018/978-1-4666-2991-2.ch006

period of more than forty years. Imagine the joy of viewing such a delightful collection. Now take a moment to imagine a world where your vision is limited or consider the possibility that you are legally blind. How do you experience a digital image resource such as the one described above? Do the creators of digital image archives, such as libraries and museums, build in mechanisms for meaningful access for all to these visual resources? A piece of state legislation sparked these thoughts and questions and set the course for a serendipitous journey of into the world of audio description. What is audio description and how does it fit into an image collection? How does audio describing an image collection enhance access for all users? What resources are required to describe a collection? Does the creation of audio description have a place in the collaborative and pedagogical environment of an academic library and university? The discussion that follows will describe an investigation into audio describing a digital image collection in an academic library and uncover preliminary observations that may begin to answer these questions.

In fiscal year 2009, Illinois State University's Milner Library was awarded a Library Service and Technology Act digitization grant through the Illinois State Library. This grant provided funding to digitize one of the library's collections, the International Collection of Child Art (ICCA). Just as the grant was awarded the state passed Public Act 095-0307, also known as the Illinois Information Technology Accessibility Act (IITAA). This act essentially requires that any state funded information technology, including development, purchase, or new provision, will be made accessible to users with disabilities. Due to this legislative act questions arose that had not been considered at the outset of the project. How do we, as art librarians and visual resource curators provide access to a digital image? At the outset of a project, do we consider our users with print disabilities such as vision impairment? How do we account for various modes of access to an image such as text, or the spoken word?

Following is a discussion of an audio description pilot project, in its early stages, including the implications of the IITAA. State funded grants in Illinois are required to prepare audio descriptions to accompany digital images to enhance access for individuals with print disabilities. The primary objective for this project was to develop strategies that will inform future digital image grant initiatives requiring audio description. Discussion will specifically examine developing descriptions for images from Illinois State University's International Collection of Child Art (ICCA). The ICCA presents a challenge to use language to broaden access to the content and to construct a compelling representation with the spoken word. Highlighted will be approaches to uncovering resources and options for writing and recording narratives for images. The collaborative efforts initiated between the librarian and selected teaching faculty to integrate the creation of audio description for digital images from the child art collection into their courses will be discussed.

BACKGROUND

Audio description, also referred to as verbal or narrative description, is the act of purposefully providing language to describe the visual elements of a theatre production, film, television program, museum exhibit or even an artwork to a primary audience of vision impaired individuals. The Audio Description Project (2011), an initiative of the American Council for the Blind, defines audio description as a spoken word service which provides "the accessibility of the visual images of theater, television, movies, and other art forms for people who are blind, have low vision, or who are otherwise visually impaired." Snyder (2003) further describes audio description as "a narrative technique that renders the visual images of theatre, media, museum exhibitions, and other endeavors more accessible to people who are blind or have low vision." Audio description is linked historically to the performing arts. The late Dr.

Margaret Phanstiehl, founded the Metropolitan Washington Ear in 1974 and served as a longtime activist for and educator of descriptive services to enhance quality of life by supporting access to venues such as television programming, theatre, and the daily newspaper for the visually impaired. Partnering with husband, Cody Phanstiehl, they are credited with providing the first continuing audio description service for the performing arts. Additionally, the non-profit Washington Ear played a long and active role providing volunteer led services reading and recording articles from popular publications. The Phanstiehls pushed accessibility through audio descriptive services into the mainstream (Ellis, 1991; Snyder, 2003).

Literature on accessibility and audio description of images and artworks indicate museums have been at the forefront making their visual collections accessible to vision impaired individuals offering audio or verbal description for artworks and exhibits. In addition to providing Braille and large print labels, touch and tactile tours, and three dimensional models, museum programming may include a tour, live or recorded, with narrative description. The Metropolitan Museum of Art in New York City has provided programming and service for the visually impaired since the 1970s (McGinnis, 2003). The Metropolitan Museum of Art (2011) website provides information for "verbal imaging tours" pairing a small group or an individual with a museum educator and also "Met audio guides" which are both available for vision impaired visitors as well as sighted visitors. Audio samples of selected descriptions for artworks, architecture, and featured exhibits, from more than one hundred hours of recorded narrative, and transcripts are available from the Metropolitan's website. Findings from a study conducted by the Royal National Institute of the Blind (2003) indicate when audio guides provided by institutions, such as Britain's Tate Museum, were created with quality recordings, well-crafted descriptions, and accessible technology, visually impaired users were satisfied and found the guides useful. Alternatively, simply because a museum provides audio description, does not guarantee the guides created are crafted with quality, good recording, or even good writing, which can contribute to a less than desirable experience for the user.

Although academic libraries have been at the forefront of digitizing image and cultural heritage collections and making them widely available there are few that have made their image resources accessible to vision impaired individuals through audio description. Peters and Bell (2006) suggest library audio collections that are available more frequently include sound collections, which are inherently oral or aural such as spoken word recordings, sounds, or music. For example, digital oral history collections such as Columbia University Center for Oral History's "Notable New Yorkers" provide audio and video interviews with influential New York politicians, activists, and innovators from the last half of the twentieth century (Clark, 2006). Cornell University's Macaulay Library and Lab of Ornithology, hosts an expansive online archive of animal sounds and video (2009). The University of California, Santa Barbara Davidson Library's Special Collections has digitized historic cylinder recordings from the early twentieth century (2002).

The Alliance Library System, (reorganized as RAILS, Reaching Across Illinois Library System) a regional library group, was funded in 2004 through the Illinois State Library to pilot a project exploring audio description for a collection of historic photographs documenting history in nineteenth century Illinois. The outcome of the grant, Illinois Alive! (2004) was a digital collection featuring historic photographs accompanied by audio descriptions and transcripts and film clips with narratives. Contributors to this project included public and academic librarians and individuals from related groups such as the Mid-Illinois Talking Book Center. The described photographs in this collection stand as a good example of providing access to images through audio. In 2007, the Alliance Library System was the recipient of a second related grant project, Audio Description Illinois, and was tasked with introducing audio description to libraries that were developing state funded digital initiatives. The Audio Description Illinois workshop served as the catalyst for the exploration of audio describing a digital image collection discussed in this chapter.

Genesis of the Audio Project

A brief description of the collection and recent grant initiatives which have helped successfully fund research and development of the resource will provide the background and context for the genesis of the audio project. The ICCA, initiated by former Illinois State University Museum Director Dr. F. Louis Hoover in the 1960s, became part of Milner Library's holdings in early 2000. The ICCA includes approximately 8,600 accessioned pieces of children's art from fifty-eight countries and cultures and has served as a teaching and learning resource for faculty, students, and researchers from across disciplines (Lonbom, 2010). Milner Library's art librarian administers and curates the ICCA and served as principal investigator and project manager for the grant funded digitization of the collection. As noted the passing of the IITAA reshaped state awarded digitization grants requiring the preparation of audio descriptions to accompany digital images. Due to the overlapping timelines of the fiscal year Milner Library was awarded the funding and the passing of the Technology Accessibility Act, grant recipients were only asked to submit audio files to accompany a sample of digital images. If the same grant were submitted today details for the provision of audio descriptions for each image digitized in order to comply with the legislation would have to be included in the proposal.

After attending an audio description workshop hosted by Illinois's Alliance Library System, I was overwhelmed but also intrigued by the concept of providing an alternate source of access—audio—to a visual resource. How can the spoken word be used to effectively describe an image when your audience has limited or no access to the image? How do you describe the color blue? Is there a need to describe the color blue? During a faculty workshop, I discovered the key to understanding the ultimate benefit of providing this level of access to an image was the introduction to the concept of universal design in learning. Originally conceived as a movement in architecture universal design principles espouse the concept of removing potential barriers at the design or beginning stage of the process. Innovative design, conceived at the outset of a project, considers a full range of potential users (Rose, Harbor, Johnston, Daley, & Abarbanell, 2008). A helpful analogy is to consider the sloping cut of a sidewalk curb, which benefits not only a person in a wheelchair but also a parent with a stroller, a person with a wheeled suitcase, or even a person walking down the sidewalk. Universal design in learning provides a framework that encourages multiple and flexible methods of presentation to support a range of different learning styles. Situating the development of audio descriptions within this lens of understanding opened up a much wider perspective on the ultimate outcomes of the work at hand. It became obvious that a recorded description could potentially benefit a much wider audience than the identified group—those with low vision or who are legally blind. In addition to descriptive text and the image represented audio descriptions might also enhance the learning experience for a range of users who respond to sound, or the quality and expressive nature of speech.

The audio description training, universal design workshop, further reading, and my innate curiosity, both as a librarian and an artist, led me to apply for additional, albeit small, grant funding from the university to provide support to continue researching the process of audio description. The project team consisted primarily of interested students including library interns, Honors students, and library faculty emerita serving as an external consulting editor. Fortunately, the library's digital imaging specialist has a professional background in voice-over and audio editing and has contributed her expertise to the project. Throughout the project, the group wrote, edited, and recorded transcripts for a small sample of images, and prepared digital recordings for inclusion in the image collection. Behind-the-scenes contributors included technical staff members who uploaded recordings to the library's streaming server and ultimately to the database matching the recorded description with the image.

The Alliance Library audio description workshop provided basic principles for preparing narratives for images and helped to develop a template appropriate for the child art image collection (Lyons & Peters, 2008). Elements for the description include an introduction to the image, identification of the primary elements, and a more detailed description of the image. The transcripts are brief, providing up to a one to two minute description averaging two hundred words (See Exhibit 1). Descriptive language attempts to provide a listener with a concise understanding of the image. Developing the descriptions is an exercise in writing concisely in a relatively structured environment (See Figure 1).

Earlier questions about the act of describing a color were answered in part by ongoing conversations with University's Director of Disability Concerns who referred to statistics provided by resources such as the Centers for Disease Control and Prevention (2004) which note, "most people who are vision impaired or legally blind have some usable vision that helps them navigate their everyday environment." Scott Nelson, an artist, curator, and advisor to Art Education for the Blind and the National Endowment for the Humanities was diagnosed with retinitis pigmentosa, an eye condition which leads to blindness. Nelson provides a framework of understanding from his perspective as vision impaired person.

It is commonly understood that of every ten Americans who are considered blind, one was born blind, another became totally blind later in life, eight have some remaining or "residual" vision, and, of these eight, five are in the process of losing their sight. This helps us to understand why a majority of people who are blind are able to respond in some way to a visual stimulus, and why their visual memory acts to enhance image making (Nelson, 2003).

There are a variety of research skills necessary for the students contributing to the project. Artwork in the international collection is primarily from the mid to late twentieth century, so there are historic, linguistic, religious, and cultural references a student may have to explore in order to accurately understand and explain what is depicted in the image. Research also involves learning about the nature of an audio description and its meaning to someone with impaired vision. Developing a transcript that is highly readable is part of the challenge. Guidelines suggested by the *Audio Description Illinois* workshop continued to be of assistance throughout the process of training the project team. Additional recommendations suggested writers imagine listening to the description and then read it aloud to someone else. Replace words you stumble over with words that are more easily spoken. Finally, be clear and concise and realize not everything needs to be described (C. Lyons, personal communication, July 26, 2009).

As I continued to explore resources and options for developing, writing, and recording narratives for images, working with the university community at hand was a natural step. The level of student engagement encountered with the original digitization project inspired me to consider building collaborative partnerships with teaching faculty to integrate the creation of audio description for images, into selected courses in related disciplines. Early in the process of deciding how to manage the creation of audio transcripts ISU's Director of Disability Concerns, Dr. Ann Caldwell, was consulted. She enthusiastically encouraged me to pursue working with faculty and to bring audio description into the classroom, acknowledging the challenge of developing an original transcript, but

Exhibit 1. Sample transcript

Introduction:
A Soldier is a painting on paper. The artist is a five-year-old boy from Wales. The brightly colored artwork features a smiling, round-bodied soldier boldly painted in large, thick brushstrokes.

Overview:
The soldier, who looks directly at the viewer, stands on the right side of the paper with both arms outstretched. His longer right arm reaches to the left edge of the paper where his oversized hand just barely touches an upright black rifle.

Details:
The soldier is painted a cheerful red on a white background. His eyes, nose, and mouth are smudged dots and lines of yellow paint. The soldier wears the red uniform of the British royal guard, with a line of brown buttons down the front, a white belt around his middle, and a thick blue stripe down each pant leg. His black boots are round like boulders. He wears a tall, black, furry hat with a wide, black chin strap—like the royal guards wear. In the bottom left edge, a piece of paper labeled "A Soldier" has been affixed. The young artist comments about his artwork quote "This is one of the soldiers we saw in our school pantomime" unquote.

Publication note:
This image is published by Milner Library at Illinois State University as part of the International Collection of Child Art.

Figure 1. A Soldier, boy, five years old, Wales. 1980. © Illinois State University, Milner Library, International Collection of Child Art. Used with permission.

also suggesting the project might diminish barriers and potentially cultivate an understanding of those who are differently abled.

In the Classroom

The process developed with the fledgling project team prepared me to work collaboratively with several classes in subsequent semesters. Selected classes included a 300 level Art for Diverse Populations, a 400 level Children's Literature and New Media, and an Art 290 Research Methods and Professional Skills. The faculty were colleagues I had worked with previously and each had some knowledge of or prior use and experience with the ICCA. In learning how to set the stage of understanding for the students when introducing the project several strategies and resources were employed. Responding to a request the Library of Congress/National Library Service for the Blind donated bookmarks with the Braille alphabet embossed on the surface and an explanation of how the Braille cells are arranged and numbered. At the beginning of class, each student receives a Braille bookmark, which serves as a graphic reminder of the primary audience of the created descriptions. Also circulated during the class are library copies of Cottin and Faria's *The Black Book of Colors* (2008). The Venezuelan artist and writer created a remarkable children's book that explores the experience of color from the perspective of one without sight. The book thoughtfully describes color through texture, sound, taste, and smell, using embossed images on black pages. The story is simultaneously told in Braille and white text. Similar to the bookmarks the publication serves not only as a reminder, but also as a bridge for students to gain a level of understanding of their audience.

Courses targeted for the project included those where the impact of learning to develop an audio description might extend beyond the classroom. The students in an upper level Art for Diverse Populations class were primarily seniors, art education majors, and future teachers. Prior to developing transcripts for the audio project the students were required by their professor to read from a related text about individuals who are visually impaired (Gerber, 2006). The faculty thought the project was a good fit for this class, as it would reinforce both the academic and clinical experience for the students. A similar session was planned for an Art Research Methods and Professional Skills class. The students in this course were upper level studio and art history majors who could appreciate being introduced to a skill that used their strengths as creators and researchers of art and was potentially meaningful in the professional environment of a museum or cultural institution.

The library sessions planned for the classes introduced the students to audio description, discussed the pilot project, and had them select an image and develop a transcript. A Webguide (http://ilstu.libguides.com/Art307) developed for the class included transcripts, images, and recordings for the students to sample. Dr Caldwell, ISU's Director of Disability Concerns, was invited to join the classes and shared her insights on the potential impact the students would have contributing to this project and how they would help provide access to a variety of users. Dr. Caldwell also thoughtfully participated in a critical critique of the students descriptions.

Students were given an option to record their transcripts at a separate session in the library with the art librarian and the library's digital imaging and voice over specialist. Recordings were made in the library's sound-booth where transcripts were recorded on a laptop computer using a USB Snowball microphone. At the outset of the pilot, the freeware Audacity was used to record WAV files. The project team has since upgraded to Soundbooth CS4 software which allows more control when editing the WAVs and creating MP3 files for uploading to the image database. The sound files average one megabyte each. About half of the students scheduled individual sessions lasting anywhere from thirty minutes to an hour depending on the student's ability to grasp the concept of using their voice to actively bring the image to life through their reading of the transcript. Anecdotally, students queried why they chose to come in and record. The students saw it as an opportunity to do something they had never done before, as an additional piece to add to their teaching portfolios or resumes, or they had someone in their lives with a disability and they saw the project as meaningful. No student seemed to know or care about the session counting for extra credit.

Solutions and Recommendations

A significant challenge noted for this project is the amount of time it takes to generate an audio description for each image. Because this pilot project was grounded in learning about the process of audio description, the overarching priority was quality not quantity. Introducing the project in a university classroom was rewarding for the librarian, faculty, and students who participated. Preparation, execution, and follow up with contributing classes was necessarily time consuming. The drafts created in class sparked informative discussions about what we see or do not see in an image. A consulting editor, project students, and the art librarian edited transcripts individually initially. The team soon realized that meeting together and having group editing sessions was a much more efficient and productive method of revising the transcripts. If asked to describe an entire collection at the outset of a project, time and resources would be a consideration that would require close review. If library staff are not familiar with concepts of accessibility for vision-impaired individuals and the creation of descriptions for images there are resources and professional groups such as the Audio Description Coalition or Art Education for the Blind who provide information, training, and services. Potentially a future project could include a hybrid model of introducing audio description into the classroom as described in this paper and also outsourcing part of the image collection to be described. Another challenge this pilot has not yet met is the assessment of the project by the very audience it is intended for—a vision-impaired user. At the outset of the project, attention was focused on learning a new set of information and skills over a short period of time and consideration was not given to assessment of the project in progress. Assessment is the next step for the current project, but prior to embarking on the next project a solution would be to invite a vision-impaired individual to be part of the project from the outset.

FUTURE DIRECTIONS

The initial thrust of this investigation focused on developing an understanding of developing access to a digital image collection through audio description. Bringing primary source material to the classroom and directly involving students in the creation and delivery of audio descriptions for an image collection has been received positively and collaborative work with faculty and students to develop transcripts in the classroom will continue. Additional grant funding to continue supporting the audio project into the future will be sought; however, ongoing fiscal constraints in the state of Illinois have curtailed the Library Services and Technology Act grant program, which funded the initial digitization project and sparked the audio pilot. Next steps for this pilot include implementing usability testing with vision-impaired users and incorporating feedback from these individuals to improve the descriptions being developed. Although primarily reporting on findings for audio description and closed captioning for live and media events Udo and Fels (2010) recommend building access for all into a project at the outset as universal design principles suggest. The library's provision of access to any digital image collection should be considered an integral part of the production process at the outset instead of a secondary action. Museums and cultural heritage institutions continue to explore models and new technologies that may inform paths for libraries to consider such as incorporating accessible mobile applications for personal devices that are increasingly ubiquitous (Ruiz, Pajares, Utray, & Moreno, 2010).

CONCLUSION

The outcome of the pilot project research may inform future digital imaging initiatives integrating audio descriptions with digital images. The requirement to provide enhanced access to image collections creates a new area for visual resource and art librarians to consider and has the potential to influence the way future image collections are constructed. Partnering with units across campus and beyond to develop methods to provide audio description for image collections will increase visibility at the institution and position the library as a leader in creating an environment of enhanced access. Audio description for digital image collections is not traditionally provided by libraries. Providing this enhanced level of access through the creation of audio files opens new doors for opportunity including implications for technology. Broadening access to the digital image collections being built will ultimately benefit all users.

REFERENCES

Audio Description Illinois. (2009). *Website.* Retrieved February 13, 2011 from http://www.alsaudioillinois.net/

Audio Description Project. (2011). *What is audio description?* Retreived August 11, 2011 from http://www.acb.org/adp/ad.html

CDC. (2004). *Vision impairment.* Retrieved February 1, 2011 from http://www.cdc.gov/ncbddd/dd/ddvi.htm

Clark, M. (2006). Notable New Yorkers. *Columbia University Libraries Oral History Research Office*. Retrieved August 1, 2011 from http://www.columbia.edu/cu/lweb/digital/collections/nny/index.html

Cottin, M., & Faria, R. (2008). *The black book of colors*. Toronto, Canada: Groundwood Books.

Donald, C. Davidson Library Special Collections. (2011). *Cylinder preservation and digitization project*. Retrieved July 29, 2011 from http://cylinders.library.ucsb.edu/

Ellis, F. (1991). *A picture is worth a thousand words for blind and visually impaired persons too!: An introduction to audiodescription*. New York, NY: American Foundation for the Blind.

Gerber, B., & Guay, D. (Eds.). (2006). *Reaching and teaching: Students with special needs through art*. Reston, VA: National Art Education Association.

Illinois General Assembly. (2007). *Illinois information technology accessibility act*. Retrieved February 14, 2011 from http://ilga.gov/legislation/publicacts/95/PDF/095-0307.pdf

Lonbom, K. C. (2010). Drawing on imagination: Children's art in the academic library. *Art Documentation*, *29*(1), 11–15.

Lyons, C., & Peters, T. (2008). Audio description Illinois: Workshop outline. *Audio Description Illinois*. Retrieved July 15, 2011 from http://www.alsaudioillinois.net/workshops.cfm

Macaulay Library and Cornell Lab of Ornithology. (2006). Online archive: The world's largest archive of animal sounds and videos. *Macaulay Library*. Retrieved July 29, 2011 from http://macaulaylibrary.org/index.do

McGinnis, R. (2003). Museum programs: Metropolitan Museum of Art. In Levent, N., & Axel, E. (Eds.), *Art beyond Sight* (pp. 454–457). New York, NY: AFB Press.

Metropolitan Museum of Art. (2011). *Programs for visitors with disabilities*. Retrieved August 1, 2011, from http://www.metmuseum.org/events/visitorsdisabilities/blind

Nelson, S. (2003). A professional artist and curator who is blind. In Levent, N., & Axel, E. (Eds.), *Art beyond Sight* (pp. 28–30). New York, NY: AFB Press.

Peters, T., & Bell, L. (2006). Audio description adds value to digital images. *Computers in Libraries*, *26*(4), 26–28.

Rose, D. H., Harbor, W. S., Johnston, C. S., Daley, S. G., & Abarbanell, L. (2008). Universal design for learning in postsecondary education: Reflections on principles and their application. In *Universal Design in Higher Education*. Cambridge, MA: Harvard Education Press.

Royal National Institute of the Blind. (2003). *The talking images research: Museums, galleries and heritage sites: Improving access for blind and partially sighted people*. Retrieved August 1, 2011 from http://www.rnib.org.uk/professionals/solutionsforbusiness/leisure/museumsgalleries/Pages/talking_images.aspx

Ruiz, B., Pajares, J. L., Utray, F., & Moreno, L. (2011). Design for all in multimedia guides for museums. *Computers in Human Behavior*, *27*, 1408–1415. doi:10.1016/j.chb.2010.07.044

Snyder, J. (2008). Audio description: The visual made verbal. J. Cintas (Ed.), *The Didactics of Audiovisual Translation,* (192-197). Philadelphia, PA: John Benjamins Publishing Company.

Udo, J., & Fels, D. (2010). The rogue poster-children of universal design: Closed captioning and audio description. *Journal of Engineering Design*, *21*(2-3), 207–221. doi:10.1080/09544820903310691

Chapter 7

Wrestling with Mosasaurs: Results of the Sternberg Museum of Natural History–Forsyth Library Fossil Digitization Pilot Project

Andrew Weiss
California State University, Northridge, USA

ABSTRACT

The purpose of the Sternberg Museum-Forsyth Library Fossil Digitization Pilot Project was to determine the feasibility of conducting a large-scale fossil digitization program at Fort Hays State University, Hays, Kansas. Conducted in early 2011, the pilot examined such aspects as fossil digitization techniques, metadata development and best practices, scope and timelines, and overall digitization goals. This chapter focuses on the digitization landscape of the natural sciences, including an overview of major fossil digitization projects and analyses of issues related to these projects. Conclusions from the Sternberg-Forsyth pilot are also recounted and discussed. Also included is an appendix outlining costs and time needed for the recommended small-scale digitization project that will begin in late 2011 or early 2012.

INTRODUCTION

Between January 27th, 2011, and March 5th, 2011, Forsyth Library and the Sternberg Museum of Natural History, both operating within Fort Hays State University, participated in a pilot project to determine the feasibility of digitizing a paleontology fossil collection. This chapter aims to discuss the results and conclusions of this collaboration between a nationally-recognized natural history museum and a medium-sized academic library serving a state comprehensive university in rural Kansas.

Sternberg Museum of Natural History

The Sternberg Museum of Natural History, first founded as an academic support facility in 1915, contains millions of specimens ranging from the Paleozoic to Cenozoic eras, including world-

DOI: 10.4018/978-1-4666-2991-2.ch007

class specimens of fossils from the Cretaceous period, and plants and animals from more modern periods. It is most well known for its specimen, *Gillicus* within a *Xyphactinus*, the "fish within a fish," found by Dr. George Sternberg, and its world-class collection of Vertebrate Paleontology specimens, including world-renowned specimens of *Pteranodons*. The museum's holdings are stored in various rooms dedicated to unique types of collections, including the wet collections (specimens held in liquid, jars), dry collections, and taxidermy collections. Additionally, the museum contains artifacts ranging from antique furniture, to old weapons, to images from other countries such as Borneo and Malaysia. Many of these miscellaneous collections are in the process of being moved to different locations or transferred to different organizations, including the Forsyth Library Archives and Special Collections (Sternberg, 2011).

Forsyth Library

The partnership to create digital images of the Vertebrate Paleontology exists as part of the ongoing collaborative efforts that have occurred between the library and the museum. Currently the Forsyth Library Archives contains a number of significant artifacts related to the founder of the Sternberg Museum. These holdings include a series of 8 personal photo albums created by Dr. Sternberg. They are significant because these images are from his original archaeological digs, which started in the 1910s and ran through to the 1950s, serving as both a primary source for Sternberg's paleontological discoveries and as a source for the history of Fort Hays State University. Additionally, the archives hold a series of glass-plate negatives and film negatives taken by Sternberg, some of which are found within the photo albums. These holdings represent some of the most sought-after materials in the archives and account for many of the research requests from patrons. The Sternberg Photo Albums, in particular, are a major priority item for digitization given their fragility and high patron demand. Both the albums and the negatives are in the process of being digitized and displayed online (FHSU, 2011).

Project Proposal and Time Frame

Given the overlap in collections housed at FHSU's Sternberg Museum and Forsyth Library, and the constant cooperation and collaboration between the two organizations, it was a natural progression to begin investigating the possibility of a digitization partnership. The project proposed by the Sternberg Museum was to begin a digitization partnership in order to digitize the vast collection of fossils from the Vertebrate Paleontology (VP) Room, a collection estimated to be at least 1 million specimens. From the discussions, it was determined that the Sternberg Museum was interested in digitizing the entirety of the fossils in the VP collection with the aim to give scholars a comprehensive picture of their holdings. It is envisioned as a service for scholars to more efficiently use the fossil holdings, who otherwise might not be able to visit Hays, Kansas.

From February – March 2010 preliminary discussions were initiated about the possibility of a partnership between Forsyth Library and Sternberg Museum, with both sides expressing interest in exploring a joint project. A preliminary 8-week pilot schedule was drawn up to begin June 2010. However, the start was delayed until January 2011 by several factors:

- Forsyth Library Digital Collections data storage backup was projected to reach full capacity by August 2010. Though sufficient space existed for current projects, adding significant amounts of data from new projects was not possible. A Network Area Storage (NAS) device was requested June, 2010, but not ordered until September, 2010. It was received by FHSU Center for Technology and Computing (CTC) in October and fully functional by mid-November 2010.

- Metadata records for fossils were not in digital format; they were in the process of being sent to the University of Kansas for ingestion into the new *Specify* content management system. As of January 2010, most records, with the exception of Vertebrate Paleontology, had been returned to Sternberg Museum.
- Equipment needed for digitization of fossils was not yet purchased (purchased between July and August 2010). This equipment included sufficient lighting, camera tripods, a laptop computer, and other miscellaneous items (50mm macro lenses, lens filters, close-up filters for small artifacts, image scales, etc.).
- Emergency exploration of alternative climate control options for the Forsyth library's archives needed to be addressed in June 2010, further delaying the start of the project.
- Other projects (digital and non-digital) were slated to begin at roughly the same time and given a higher priority due to minimal size and/or timeliness, including digitization of Sternberg Photo Albums and Sternberg Negatives, as well as preparations for the Kansas 150th Anniversary in January 2011.

Once these obstacles and priorities had been addressed, the potential for partnership could again be explored. Beginning in December 2010, with revitalized efforts from the Forsyth Library and Sternberg Museum staff, a new 8-week pilot proposal was drawn up to commence in January, 2011. The project began January 24th and ran for 6 weeks until March 4th. Originally planned as an 8-week project, it was truncated to 6 weeks after realizing the pilot project would not include training sessions.

The pilot's aim was to determine multiple objectives, including: (1) the proper photographing technique for fossils; (2) photographic workflows and setups; (3) fossil selection workflows; (4) quality-control workflows and procedures; (5) metadata schema policies and practices; and (6) time- and cost-analyses with benchmarks and timelines established for project implementation.

The results of the pilot suggested to project managers that a scaled-down, 6-month fossil digitization project would likely best serve both organizations. Rather than emphasizing a comprehensive scope, this preliminary digitization project would focus instead on digitally photographing 500-700 fossils from a well-preserved Mosasaur. This dinosaur represents one of the world-renowned specimens held by the Sternberg Museum of Natural History. The project will also look to refine digitization techniques in order to seamlessly render photographs taken from multiple angles into an inexpensively created, easily used, and downloadable 3D image. The project is slated to begin in mid-to-late 2011 and is expected to run through the first half of 2012.

While it is not the aim of this chapter to list all of the details of the pilot project and the resulting recommendations, we believe that many lessons related to digitization and digital collection development arise from it and can be applied in general to the librarianship in the digital age. In particular, after a general look at the role of digitization and information management in paleontology and archaeology, we will examine specific digitization predecessors. We will also examine a number of the issues with regard to improving digitization projects related to 3-dimensional objects/specimens and collaborations with libraries and museums of natural history. We will examine issues of low metadata granularity in the source collection and contrasts that with the need for higher granularity in the digital collection; finally, we will take a look at the organizational requirements (including costs, scope, labor and technical needs) for creating a successful multi-year, multi-project, multi-tiered, fully-implemented fossil digitization partnership.

BACKGROUND

Major Fossil Digitization Projects: Aspirational Peers and Leaders

Digitizing fossil collections is nothing new. A number of important fossil digitization projects have been developed over the years with outcomes varying from full-text searchable 3D-renderings to browsable database records without any accompanying images, and a full range of collections residing between both extremes.

The University of Texas at Austin's *Texas Natural Science Center*, funded by a National Science Foundation grant, has created a large searchable database for allowing scientists to search vertebrate and non-vertebrate fossils. (University of Texas at Austin, 2011) The NSF grant of $350,000 represents an aspiration of the Sternberg/Forsyth alliance; a similar proposal for long-term digitization funding is in the works for the Sternberg Museum and Forsyth Library.

Additionally, the *USGS* paleontology service contains a large number of digitized fossil records online. Working in tandem with the *National Geological Mapping Program*, they are attempting to "prepare the vast collections and data into searchable databases in a virtual repository" (USGS, 2006). Their fossil collection database, populated with fossils in various geo-locations, contains the records of thousands of localities within the United States, covering the Mesozoic, Cenozoic and Paleozoic eras (USGS). This collection is significant because it overlaps areas that the Sternberg Museum has traditionally focused on.

The University of Iowa has done extensive work digitizing a large amount of various fossils, including the *Neogene Marine Biota of Tropical America (NMITA)* project, and the *Iowa Repository Digitization Project*, starting from 2006. Specimens date back 25 million years. It includes a searchable database with accompanying 2-D representations of specimens (University of Iowa, 2006).

Other important institutions related to paleontology and fossil digitization projects include the Smithsonian Institute's Paleobiology collections (Smithsonian, 2011), and Ball State University's Digital Repository, which uses CONTENTdm, the same platform being used by Fort Hays State University Forsyth Library to manage digital content (Ball State University, 2007).

Essentially, there is no dearth of online fossil collections displaying some type of digitized content. However, there have been several major concerns raised by digitization: (1) preservation and access; (2) metadata and thoroughness of the digitized record; and (3) fossil rendering in 2D and 3D. The remainder of this section will examine these 3 issues.

Issue 1: Digital Preservation and Access

The concerns that have been raised by these projects dovetail completely into the issues that libraries have faced for years: access. The problem of inaccessible collections remains a looming issue as such collections have been considered useless by the end users/target community and therefore the impetus for improving access via digital media has been a main consideration. (MacLeod & Guralnik, 2000) The main issue with the Sternberg Museum's collection has been the digitization of records and metadata as well as the fossils themselves. Wolniewicz (2009) outlines the three main needs for improving the access of paleontology collections: (1) mass digitization of specimens, (2) acquisition of "reliable morphological" data (i.e. metadata), (3) contribution of data to open and searchable databases. Wolniewicz also outlines a thorough workflow for the digitization of paleontological collections. The Sternberg/Forsyth library collaboration attempts to meet all three of these major efforts by first photographing large quantities of fossils while at the same time transferring hand-written metadata (provided in the specimen boxes) into a database and content management system (SPECIFY and/or CONTENTdm) (Specify Software Project, 2011; OCLC, 2011).

Significant issues with multiple databases also arise with so-called "siloed" collections that do not link up and remain relatively isolated, causing some consternation and delay for researchers looking for more thorough search results. There has been a studied need for federated search ability across multiple platforms as explained by *Anthrodatadpa* (2009). The issue of siloing is one that is not new to the library world, with its emphasis on interoperable collections and the development of such standards as Z39.50, Dublin Core, and the OAI-PMH model for digital collection interoperability (NISO, 2011; DCMI, 2011; OAI-PMH, 2008). In the anthropological/archaeological world, emphasis has been on breaking down the siloes as well. However, it appears that much is needed to be done to ensure interoperability as well as preservation of digital metadata and digital objects of these anthropological/paleontological collections and archives.

There have been several attempts and studies at creating more interoperable digital fossil research databases. One of the most well known is *Digital Archive Network for Anthropology* (DANA), which was developed in the early 2000s (Clark, 2002). DANA links, via distributed, federated and interoperable databases, various types of data together, including 2D and 3D "visual representations of artifacts, fossils, and other objects, along with two-dimensional (2D) digitized documents (e.g. maps, plan views, excavation profiles, field notes, manuscripts, charts, graphs, and photographs) and associated content" (Clark, 2002). Espousing the model of "Virtual Archaeology," much of the direction taken for fossil access can be said to have started with the DANA model.

Another important contributor to the interoperability movement is *GBIF: Global Biodiversity Information Facility*, which is based on the open access model. It is essentially a Web-based index of "a globally distributed network of interoperable databases that contain primary biodiversity data—information on museum specimens, field observations of plants and animals in nature, and results from experiments—so that data holders across the world can access and share them" (GBIF, 2011); it also includes data tools, and training programs for allowing national/regional institutions to become active participants in the network. Other attempts at information integration and collaboration with fossil collections have been discussed by Meyer et al. and the U.S. Biological Collections report (Meyer, 2008; NIBA, 2010). Both discuss the need for more integrated databases for improved research service.

What each of these studies and initiatives point out is the generally fragmented body of scholarship that could be readily served by improving the workflows and best practices of fossil digitization projects. As Wolniewicz (2009) suggests, the answer to the problem lies in a three-pronged approach to improving the digital fossil record: mass digitization, metadata, and open-access, interoperable databases. The good news in all of this is that libraries, with expertise in metadata and access, are in prime position to help natural history museums and academic paleontology departments wrestle with the issues that arise with digitizing collections. In this regard, the collaboration between the Sternberg Museum and Forsyth library makes a lot of sense, and, while Forsyth Library does not have the content, it does have the ability to provide data management consultation and preservation that the Sternberg does not have. It also has the infrastructure and theoretical base to handle the mission of digital access and preservation of materials regardless of whether or not they are traditional library materials.

Issue 2: Metadata – Schema and Granularity, TMI (Too Much Information), and Too Little Information

Dublin core has been adopted by many digital libraries as a universal standard, despite the initial creation of DC for very different purposes as a method to archive and describe Web pages. The very ability to customize the standard and alter it to suit local needs while at the same time be able to suit needs of interoperability make it a flexible and useful metadata standard (DCMI, 2011). The natural history/biological sciences disciplines have adopted Dublin Core to suit their own data needs by altering it into Darwin Core. The main advantage to using Darwin Core for the scientific community is the ability to use certain types of data that library and Web communities are not entirely concerned with. Using the basic sample, one can see how the fossil information would be well represented by Darwin Core as opposed to the unqualified or even qualified DC schema (See Figure 1).

Adding certain information such as locality, improves the ability of researchers to piece together the fossil record. Barton et al., however, outline the problem of too much information regarding fossils being leaked to those who steal or vandalize fossil beds. He writes about the creation of a relational database for tracking such fossil specimens and damage to fossil beds (Barton, et al., 2006). The development of a more sophisticated database model helps to improve the ability of researchers to keep track of records, tables, and eventually, images for the fossils. This problem of theft raises the issue of how much digital information should be visible online. This issue will be explored in more depth in the next section.

On the other side of the issue, however, is the problem of too little information regarding the fossil collections. In the case of the Sternberg fossils, many of the fossils are considered to be fragments of the same item, or it is unclear whether the fragment should be considered the same or part of a different bone. This issue of granularity begins to affect the ability of the digitizer to make sure that there is an anchor to the real object and the metadata with the object. On occasion, it might be impossible for the collection to be entirely digitized due to very low granularity of the collection metadata. As a result, it might affect overall access if the metadata in question does not completely describe the items in the collection. Similar issues arise in digitizing archival collections that contain top-level descriptions but not item-level descriptions. Unlike papers, however, which are generally in sequential order and have a clearer provenance, fossils can often be lacking in clear provenance or might not truly be part of what they have been found lying with.

Issue 3: Fossil Rendering/ Representation – "2D or not 2D? That is the Question"

The simplest solution for digitizing fossil collections is creating basic 2-dimensional photograph images of a fossil and providing multiple angles of the specimen. The *Paleo Portal*, created in 2003, is a prime example of the simplicity of this method (Paleontological Portal, 2003). A large number of fossils can be photographed in order to give the researcher a good clear basic idea of the size, shape and proportion of the specimen itself. The visual record becomes a little more complete without an intensive reliance on technology and large digital files. Ball State University's repository of fossils, using CONTENTdm as its digital asset management platform, is another prime example of the usefulness of a 2D approach, and one that Forsyth Library adopted for the pilot project (Ball State, 2007). However, the drawback to this approach is a limited usefulness of the fossil specimen. Although flat fossil specimens are easily observed in a well-lit photograph, observing a 3-dimensional object such as a bone, with all of its nooks and crannies, is much more difficult in a 2D format.

Figure 1. Sample of Darwin core metadata in XML format


```
<?xml version="1.0"?>
<dwr:SimpleDarwinRecordSet
xmlns:xsi="http://www.w3.org/2001/XMLSchema-instance"
xsi:schemaLocation="http://rs.tdwg.org/dwc/xsd/simpledarwincore/
http://rs.tdwg.org/dwc/xsd/tdwg_dwc_simple.xsd"
xmlns:dcterms="http://purl.org/dc/terms/"
xmlns:dwc="http://rs.tdwg.org/dwc/terms/"
xmlns:dwr="http://rs.tdwg.org/dwc/xsd/simpledarwincore/">
<dwr:SimpleDarwinRecord>
<dcterms:type>PhysicalObject</dcterms:type>
<dcterms:modified>2009-02-12T12:43:31</dcterms:modified>
<dcterms:rightsHolder>Museum of Vertebrate Zoology</dcterms:rightsHolder>
<dcterms:rights>Creative Commons License</dcterms:rights>
<dwc:institutionCode>MVZ</dwc:institutionCode>
<dwc:collectionCode>Mammals</dwc:collectionCode>
<dwc:occurrenceID>urn:catalog:MVZ:Mammals:14523</dwc:occurrenceID>
<dwc:basisOfRecord>PreservedSpecimen</dwc:basisOfRecord>
<dwc:country>Argentina</dwc:country>
<dwc:countryCode>AR</dwc:countryCode>
<dwc:stateProvince>Neuquén</dwc:stateProvince>
<dwc:locality>25 km al NNE de Bariloche por Ruta 40 (=237)</dwc:locality>
</dwr:SimpleDarwinRecord>
</dwr:SimpleDarwinRecordSet>
```


One of the major developments in digitization of the fossil record has been in the 3D rendering of images. Rather than focus on the 2-dimensional image, which is generally the fastest and easiest way to digitize a fossil collection (though not without its drawbacks), some projects have seen value in creating 3-dimensional digital models of fossils in an attempt to improve upon the "virtual archaeology" philosophy.

University of Kansas has already taken the lead in digitization on multiple fronts, including institutional repository development in general and paleontology digitization in particular. KU's *Museum of Natural History and Biodiversity Research Center, Division of Invertebrate Paleontology*, has created several databases for searching three-dimensional images of macrofossils, trace fossils and two-dimensional images of invertebrate microfossil slides (University of Kansas Museum of Natural History and Biodiversity Research Center, 2006).

Others have worked on similar projects. Wilhite's (2003) study on 3D techniques points out the issues of low accuracy of digitized files and the inordinate amount of extra time it takes to build these digital models. Mallison et al. describe more recent innovative techniques for digitizing fossils using computer assisted tomography (CT) scanners; their results suggest that 3D rendering can be relatively inexpensive, but still show that 3D digitization techniques will require a large amount of specialization and technical expertise (Mallison, et al., 2009). Large quickly scanned automated digitization of collections may be out of the question with this method, further emphasizing the need for quality of specimens rather than quantity.

As impressive as the results are for 3D rendered fossils, major obstacles arise in the full digitization of these collections. First, costs, including equipment and training, are especially severe. The special equipment used, as outlined by Mallison, Wilhite, and others, is cost prohibitive; there is also a need for specialized labor, which will contribute to higher costs as well as slower digitization outputs. Given the immense size of many of these collections, some ranging into the millions of fossil specimens and fragments, the time needed to implement these projects can be staggering. Therefore, implementation of the project using 3D technologies can only represent a tiny fraction of the actual collection. Selection of proper specimens is therefore absolutely essential, calling for a dedicated professional who can select the right fossils for the projects. This expertise adds to the expense of the project, and as numerous specimens may to look the same to a layperson, experts must be relied upon to determine the most important representative samples.

DIGITIZATION OF A FOSSIL COLLECTION: FINDINGS FROM THE PILOT

The main goal for conducting the pilot project was to determine the feasibility of digitizing a large vertebrate paleontology fossil collection residing in the Sternberg Museum of Natural History. This section will attempt to describe a number of the issues and work-arounds that arose during the pilot. It will also describe many of the procedures that needed to be developed to ensure project sustainability. Though the project was particular to the needs of the two FHSU organizations, it is felt that these issues can be applied to other institutions interested in conducting similar fossil digitization projects.

1. Determining Representative Types of Fossils to Digitize

At the Sternberg Natural History Museum vertebrate paleontology fossils are housed in the cavernous Vertebrate Paleontology room; fossils are arranged by period and stored in labeled cabinets with drawers. The time period represented by the fossil record at Sternberg ranges from Cretaceous to Modern time periods. Metadata records are kept in each of the cabinet drawers in the form of hand-written cards, each comprised of data about the fossil's taxonomy, location, geospatial data, date of finding and/or processing, and other notes created by either the fossil's finder or the cataloger. Records have also been converted into a database and input into the SPECIFY content management system. Fossils are also marked with numbers [VP*n*] identifying their corresponding metadata records; some fossils have the same VP number and are therefore considered fragments of the same piece. For the purposes of the pilot, fossils with the same number were considered members of a unique set, but not necessarily unique items in the collection.

For a full-scale, comprehensive project that encompasses all of the fossils, a systematic approach would need to be initiated by starting at the first cabinets and following through to the end. Because of the immense scale of the project, there would be less flexibility in the project's methodology. Therefore, larger fossils, those over 45 cm and including those several meters long, would be worked on at a later date, after all the smaller fossils were photographed. Immediate concern would be centered on efficiently photographing as many fossils as possible, at the expense of the larger types in the collection. For a small-scale project, Sternberg staff would spend time creating a priority list of fossils that must be photographed above all others. A list would comprise between 2000 and 2500 of the most important fossils that would be of the most use for scholars to access. All sizes of fossil could be addressed with a small project because of the smaller sample size and inherent flexibility that this would provide.

Figure 2. Camera, lighting, and laptop setup

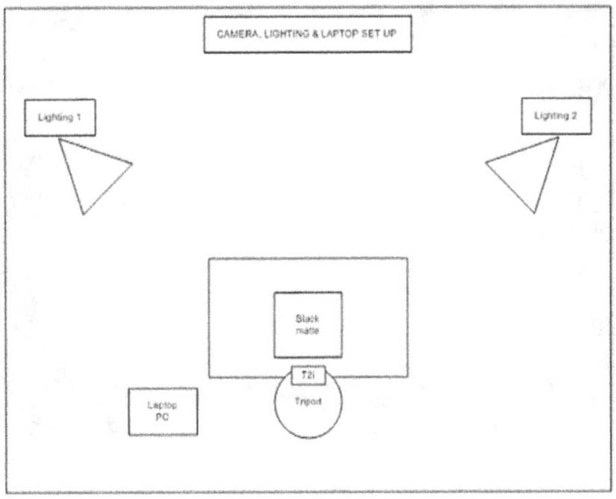

2. Photography Basics and Lighting

Basic Set Ups

During the pilot, a few days were taken to determine the best ways to photograph fossil specimens. Below is a list of the findings:

1. **Exposure and ISO Readings:** Camera was set at an ISO of 200 for good resolution. Shutter speed was set at 1/25 second with aperture readings set at f4. Flash was not used, but a lighting set-up was used instead (See Figure 2).
2. **Location:** Equipment was set up in the vertebrate paleontology room, in the student work area, allowing plenty of space for lights and all other equipment to be set up without any obstacles.
3. **Camera and Lighting Set Ups:** Lighting set up was placed with two lights at 45 deg angles to provide sufficient lighting and relief for the specimens; the camera's set up was generally an overhead shot using a tripod, whose arm bent down to shoot close up objects (if close-up filter is mounted). Objects were placed upon a black matte, which was further mounted upon a wooden platform. This set up was deemed to be appropriate for fossils less than 60 cm in length. For fossils of a larger size, a different set up would need to be developed, with the camera and lighting moved to the fossil's location in the VP room. However, the setup above was deemed sufficient to handle the majority of fossils stored in the cabinets and drawers.
4. **Scale:** All objects were photographed with a uniform scale to provide correct size-scale ratios (See Figure 3).
5. **Format:** All photographs were taken in Canon Raw (CR2) Format using a Canon T2i, 18 megapixel camera, and then converted to TIFF for use as master files; master files were then cropped, rotated and color-contrast optimized to create TIFF optimal files, from which all JPEG surrogates were then derived.
6. **Number of Photographs Per Shot:** 2 – 4 photographs were taken for each specimen depending on the complexity of item. Mostly flat items needed only front/back shots. Others specimens needed front and back shots as well as shots from the sides, bringing the total up to 4 or 5. Close up shots were also possible. Figure 4 shows four angles taken for a mastodon tooth.

Additionally, for sets of fossils contained in the same box and holding identical VP numbers,

Figure 3. Fossils with scale

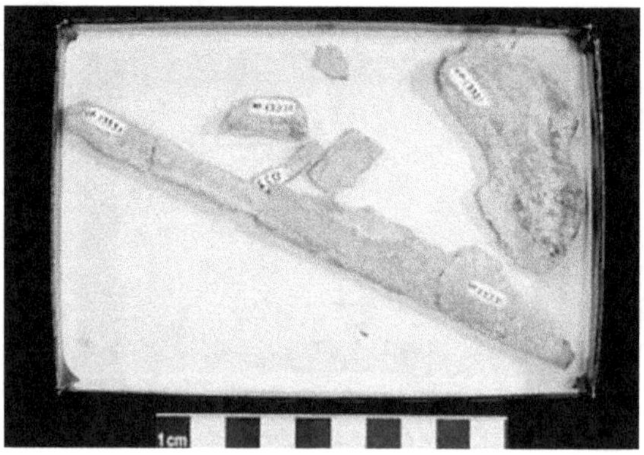

Figure 4. Sides of a mastodon tooth

it was necessary to take multiple photographs; 1 photograph contained the contents of an entire box, while the second photograph contained a close-up of one representative sample for that set. This is shown in Figure 5.

Since the collection items range greatly in sizes, from < 1 cm to > 60 cm (and up to 3+ meters) the set ups will need to change. In the case of items less than 1 centimeter, close up filters can be attached to a macro lens for greater magnifications, as shown in Figure 6.

7. **Digital Orphans and Granularity:** The biggest organizational problem with this digital collection will be the granularity of the original fossil cataloging. The decision to provide only one representative sample will not necessarily solve the problem, but it will allow users to see one part of a set in detail, which should prove satisfactory to most potential users of this collection. We do not recommend at this time to photograph more than one fossil as a detail, given the potential for the mislabeling of images with the originals. For example, sometimes up to 20 fragments would have the same VP number and many of those fragments looked similar, it was decided that photographing only one representative sample would best prevent loss of digital image due to insufficient source metadata.

2. Preservation and Access for Sternberg/Forsyth

It was determined during the pilot that using the CONTENTdm, which had already been set up and used by Forsyth Library, would be the best candidate for the housing and display of the digital fossil images. Though it is primarily meant to work for archival and 2D paper/photo collections, other institutions, notably Ball State University, have used CONTENTdm for their online fossil collections (Ball State, 2007). As a result, FHSU Forsyth Library decided to follow suit, as it represented the quickest and easiest solution to the problem of online access.

Currently, although the Sternberg museum has bought and installed a Specify content man-

Figure 5. Set of fossils with same VP number with representative sample

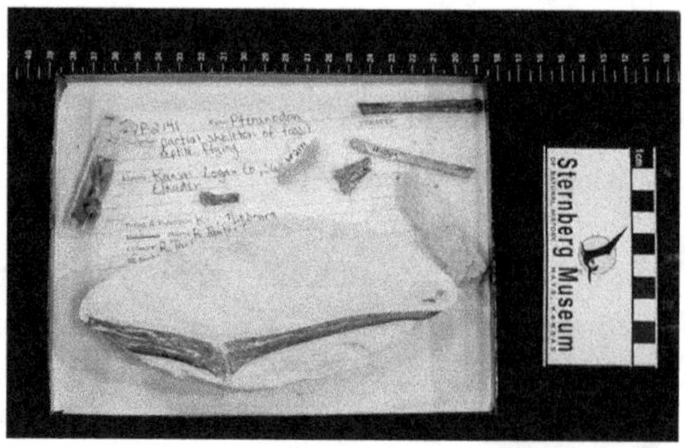

agement system, it was not being used and there was not anyone fully versed in using it (Specify, 2010). Specify is also a new and unproven system, without a large number of sample collections to vouch for its efficacy. As a result, since the library would be largely responsible for the development of the online collection, it was decided that using CONTENTdm would work best. The digital infrastructure to save and preserve data was in existence as well as the needed staff and workflows for saving, cataloging, and managing data.

Therefore, although an alternative system exists specifically for the management of digital fossil metadata records, the library made the decision to work as long as it could with the CONTENTdm system. The library, however, is keeping a flexible outlook and is willing to change over to Specify whenever the Sternberg Museum is ready to adopt it as their primary platform for digital asset management.

Figure 6. Fossil close-up (with VP number painted on side)

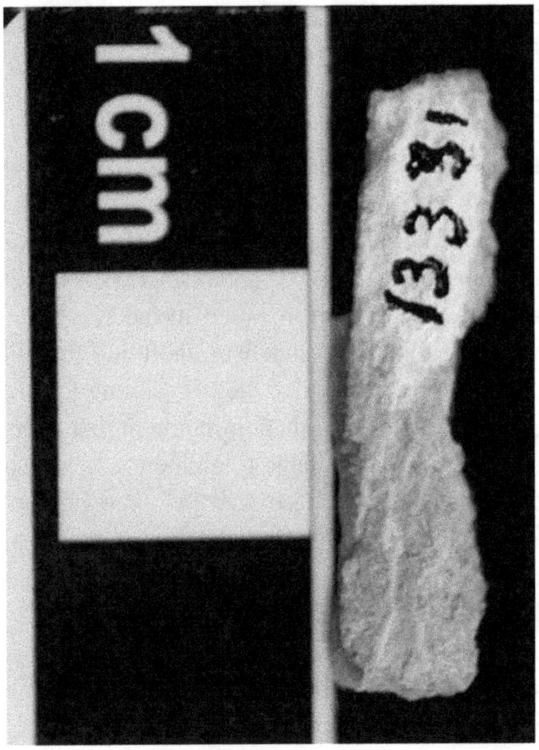

3. Developing the Metadata Schema and Its Policies

Brief mention was made above about the metadata scheme. This section will discuss some of the problems with the granularity of the fossil collection itself and how that impacts digitization.

Metadata Schema Development

Metadata development, quality control, and long-term integrity will be some of the most important aspects of this project. Most likely bottlenecks will occur at this point of the project due to the detailed and comprehensive aspects of the cataloging process. Crosswalking from one system to another (i.e. Sternberg analog metadata records to digital metadata schema) may be necessary, further complicating the metadata development process. It is recommended to use Darwin Core, which is a variant of the ANSI/NISO Z39.85 standard Dublin Core (Biodiversity Information Standards, 2009). The advantages to using this schema include: developed primarily to describe natural history objects, extends the standard DC, is interoperable, and is adopted as the basic standard for the natural history museum world. It is "based on the standards developed by… DCMI and should be viewed as an extension of the Dublin Core for biodiversity information" (Biodiversity Information Standards, 2009). The types of information found in the fossils' records mimics that of the typical Simple Darwin Core (SIMPLEDWC) element set: i.e. Taxonomic data, locality data, stratigraphic data, contextual information, provenance data, treatment history, and legacy data. However, more investigation of the metadata elements and how they relate to the simple Dublin Core metadata scheme is needed at this point. It remains to be seen how much customization will need to be applied to the metadata schema in order to tailor it to the needs of the Sternberg Museum and to synchronize it to the metadata schema used by Forsyth Library Digital Collections.

Metadata Policies: Control and Access Issues

As Barton et al. demonstrated in their study on tracking fossil beds and vandalism, access issues arise with providing detailed metadata online. With the threat of vandalism, theft and the all-too-common practice of illegally selling fossils, certain types of information should probably not be made freely available to online users, unless that information is restricted by some form of authentication to allow tracking of users. Information that would be potentially sensitive includes the following:

- Information about the storage environment;
- Storage room and specimen locations;
- Personnel information;
- Conservation and preparation techniques;
- Detailed locality information;
- Specimen status and value;
- Unpublished information on research being currently conducted by staff, students, scholars, and other visitors.

Copyright should also be included in the metadata to point out that Sternberg is the holder and owner of the original object as well as the digital object. Furthermore, in relation to copyright and its issues, the Sternberg ought to consider what its definition of "fair use" implies; if it has a predetermined definition, it would be useful to add such a definition to each record put online.

Metadata Integrity and Adherence to Uniquely Identifiable Physical Objects

Being unable to trace a digital image to its physical counterpart will be one of the biggest challenges this project faced. The danger of this issue is that if various people take photographs of fossils that have the same numbers, it could become impossible over time to trace that image back to its original physical specimen. The result could be that thousands of images become rendered essentially useless for archaeological research because of the loss of provenance. There are two solutions to this issue:

1. The digital collection can add new name variants to meet the problem of granularity in the fossil collection; i.e. new suffixes could be added to the file names of images for fossils that have the same VP numbers. This is not recommended. The problem with this method is that the responsibility of essentially recreating a new cataloging method will fall upon the untrained photography and metadata staff.
2. The digital collection can respect the fossil record's level of description and photograph fossils with the same number all together in the same image as a set; additionally, one image will be photographed to be the representative sample of that set of fossils.

It is essential, therefore, to understand that the digital collection must *complement* the physical collection; it is this writer's belief that a digital image for an archival collection cannot surpass the granularity of the cataloging of the physical collection without risking either the traceability or provenance of the digital image and creating a digitalized orphan work.

4. 2D/3D Rendering Results/Study

In the FHSU Sternberg/Forsyth Paleontology digitization pilot project, effort was made to create 2D images to demonstrate project feasibility, and then to begin 3D image development and experimentation using cheaper and newer means than had been tried in the past. The pilot project never attempted 3D imaging beyond the exploratory phase, however.

Some discussion has been raised about the possibility of using 3-dimensional imaging techniques to give users multiple sides of the original fossils. It is the opinion of this writer, given the scope of the project and the amount of time and data it will generate, that such a technology is not ready to be implemented for this project. A short pilot project might be tried at some later date, but it is not clear that doing such a project will have the intended result.

Beyond the use of CT scanning, which has been outlined by Willhite, MacLeod, and Guralnik, and others, and shown to wonderful results by one University of Michigan project, investigating ancient whale fossils, led by Professor Philip Gingerich at Wadi Al-Hitan in Egypt, there might be other possible cheap and simple alternatives (Mueller, 2010).

Forsyth Library Director John Ross, in looking for innovative ways to keep the Forsyth Library relevant to the needs of the 21st century campus, has investigated some 3D modeling solutions, including companies such as EON Reality, and GNS Science (EON Reality, 2011; GNS Science, 2011). The first of these solutions from EON Reality is being implemented as a learning center embedded within the library itself, with further development pending grant approval. The learning curve for this program and equipment is quite steep as well as cost-intensive. For immediate classroom consumption, this is a useful product, even though it requires 3D animation modelers. On the other hand, however, the second of these solutions, which involves merely photographing multiple angles of a fossil and rendering it into 3D in a PDF file, would be a more cost effective way to develop 3D content. The amount of equipment needed is limited to a medium-resolution digital camera, a sufficient lighting setup to keep ISOs low, and access to the Adobe PDF and GNS's software (GNS Science, 2011). It is the recommendation of this writer that the second solution be the subject of further collaborative research and development at Forsyth Library and the Sternberg Museum.

SOLUTIONS AND RECOMMENDATIONS

Final Results and Recommendations of Pilot

After conducting the 8-week pilot, essential needs for finishing the project became very apparent. Given the size of the collection, the nature of its specialized content, and the weak infrastructure that exists between the Sternberg Museum and FHSU's campus (the museum is located a few miles off-campus), it became obvious that a large-scale project cannot proceed without specific needs addressed in the following areas: staffing, funding, infrastructure. Below is a list of 8 recommendations that would need to be met in order to seriously tackle the proposed large-scale fossil digitization project.

Recommendation 1: Realistic Expectations – Limit Scope, Increase Staff, Increase Funding, Secure Infrastructure

The recommendation is that the Sternberg decides which important items it would like to digitize by creating a predetermined short list already prioritized for project staff to work on for the period of 6 months, or even a slightly longer period of 2 – 3 years. This should result in the creation of a collection of about 2500 new images and 4000-5000 previously photographed images (6000-8000 total) for a 6 month project, and roughly 20,000 – 40,000 for a 2- to 3-year project. Although not a complete record, it is sufficient to give researchers a good idea of Sternberg Museum's collection.

It is this writer's strong recommendation that the project be reshaped to meet smaller ambitions in addition to hiring the sufficient number of staff needed to complete the project in a reasonable amount of time. The selection of fossils needs to fall within the expertise of the Sternberg itself; the responsibility should not be placed on the shoulders of the library staff or other digitization project staff members.

A full scale project could be attempted, and for that reason full-scale project projections have been included, but it is *not recommended* that such a large amount of fossils be considered part of the project without sufficient staffing, infrastructure, metadata, time and funding and modeling upon the work of other institutions.

Recommendation 2: Sufficient Staffing

Below is an estimation of the staffing needs required for both the large, multi-year, full-scale fossil digitization project and the smaller-scale, 6-month project. The work is quite labor-intensive, yet requires highly specific skills.

For a full-scale project:

- Need 2 photographing workers, working a total of 40 hours/week.
- Need 1 full-time 40 hour/week project manager to oversee all aspects of project.
- Need 1 full-time 40 hour/week cataloger/metadata specialist to work with CONTENTdm or SPECIFY to create/add/revise/edit necessary metadata records.
- Need 1 part-time (10 hours per week) Web developer to design Web interface.
- Need 1 subject specialist (10 hours per week) to select fossils for weekly list and to provide expertise about which fossil in a set should be photographed over others.

For a small-scale project:

- Need 1 (at least) subject specialist to select fossils for short-list of 2000 – 2500 fossils (estimated at 2 weeks).
- Need 2 photographers (20 hours combined).
- Need 1 part-time project manager to oversee all aspects of the project (10 hours).
- Need 1 part-time metadata specialist to work with CONTENTdm or SPECIFY to create/add/revise/edit necessary metadata records (10 hours).
- **Total:** 2 weeks (time to select fossil list) + 40 hours/week thereafter.

Additionally, people working on the projects should be physically fit and be able to move with ease throughout the Vertebrate Paleontology (VP) room. Because of ramps and other obstacles, it will be difficult for those with limited mobility to carry or work with a large number of the fossils. Also, many of the fossils are extremely heavy and will require either: (1) moving the photography equipment to the fossil or (2) moving the fossil to the camera/lighting set up. Either situation requires that the persons involved be strong enough to move objects and avoid the obstacles in the room.

Recommendation 3: Sufficient Infrastructure

Infrastructure also remains an obstacle for full-implementation of a digitization collaboration. Since Forsyth Library, which is on FHSU's campus, is several miles away from Sternberg Museum, which is not on campus, there is an issue with IT infrastructure differences. Currently, Forsyth benefits from the high level of IT development on campus; unfortunately, Sternberg Museum's infrastructure has not been upgraded. Though there is a local company laying new fiber-optic cables in the city of Hays, it is unclear when it will actually be installed for the neighborhoods around the museum. As a result, the following items will be needed to improve infrastructure for a mass digitization project:

- Need faster network connectivity/port (not available, yet; after summer 2011).

- Need back up storage for the Forsyth Library Digital Collections Network Area Storage device (fl-nas; currently no backup system available).
- External Hard drives are a cheap alternative, but will impact the estimated 20 minutes/image time frame, further reducing ability to reach realistic benchmarks.

This especially includes the installation of a high-speed port and connection to the FHSU campus network and the purchasing of a storage backup device. Not having either of these basic infrastructure needs represents too much of a risk to data loss and recovery. A slow connection will also further slow down any progress during the optimization phases.

Recommendation 4: Sufficient Metadata Development

Metadata records need to be sufficiently cataloged by catalogers expert in the relevant metadata schema to ensure that the fossil records and digital images match as they should. Someone who is expert in the Darwin Core metadata schema should be hired to work on this project. It is beyond the expertise of the staff at Forsyth Library, and neither should they be expected to learn a new metadata scheme just for the sake of one project. Furthermore, a well-trained cataloger could be used later for archiving and cataloging the Sternberg Museum's special collection of biology, geosciences, and paleontology books.

Recommendation 5: Sufficient Time Allowed for Reaching Benchmarks

It has been estimated that each digital image taken will need an average of *11.1 minutes of total work time* to complete the whole process ranging from photographing, optimizing and archiving, cataloging and uploading.

For a full project, 11 minutes per image will translate into the following benchmarks at 28 total man-hours of work dedicated to the project per day:

- 1 week (+/- 140 combined work hours with a full, dedicated staff) = about 765 complete images per week; representing approximately .08% of the collection completed.
- 1 month = (+/- 560 combined work hours with a full, dedicated staff) = about 3060 complete images per month; representing approximately .30% of the collection completed.
- 1 year = (+/- 6,720 combined work hours with a full, dedicated staff) = about 36,700 complete images in one year; representing approximately 3.70% of the collection completed.
- 5 years = (+/- 33,600 combined work hours with a full, dedicated staff) = about 184,000 complete images in 5 years; representing approximately 18.4% of the collection completed.
- 10 years = (+/- 67,200 combined work hours with a full, dedicated staff) = 367,000 complete images in 10 years; representing approximately 37% of the collection completed.

For a small-scale project, 11 minutes per image will translate into the following benchmark at 8 total man-hours of work dedicated to the project per day:

- 1 week = (+/- 40 combined work hours with a part-time staff) = 220 complete images/week; representing approximately xx% of the collection completed.
- 1 month = (+/- 160 combined work hours with a part-time staff) = 880 complete images/month; representing approximately xx% of the collection completed.

- 1 year = (+/- 1920 combined work hours with a part-time staff) = 10,500 complete images/year; representing approximately 1% of the collection completed.
- 5 years = (+/- 9600 combined work hours with a part-time staff) = 52,500 complete images in 5 years; representing approximately 5% of the collection completed.
- 10 year = (+/- 19200 combined work hours with a part-time staff) = 105,000 complete images in 10 years; representing approximately 10% of the collection completed.

Recommendation 6: Sufficient Funding

The project viability will be enhanced greatly if funding were made available to pay for the needed labor and data backup costs. For a full-scale project, based on current rates, a full-time project manager with the digitization skills and project management skills should be paid about $50,000 per year. Catalogers and metadata specialists should also be paid in the low-mid $40K range per year. Student photographer staff should be paid regular rates (about $7.00/hour). A Web designer at ¼ rate should be paid approximately $10,000 per year. Total amount of staffing funding should be about $125,000.

For a small-scale project, funding will be much less. Approximately 40 hours per week will be allotted among 4 project members. The total amount to be spent will be roughly $30,000. Keep in mind that given the amount of funding, this will result in limited results. Additionally, another $10,000 will be needed to purchase a backup data storage device for fl-nas and any other replacement equipment.[1]

Recommendation 7: Sufficient Modeling Upon Other Institutions

Other institutions have digitized fossil records online. It is imperative that the Sternberg begin to investigate these and model their potential digitization project upon these main players in the museum world. This investigation will include a look at how other universities and institutions are displaying their collections online.

Recommendation 8: Sufficient Accounting of Existing Fossil Photographs (Digital and Film)

Currently there have been thousands of fossil photographs already taken over the past 5 – 6 years by various Sternberg professors and graduate students. Quite a few thesis manuscripts, for example, contain at least four thousand total images of vertebrate paleontology fossils from the VP room. To avoid redoing already existing work, these images will have to be accounted for and examined for their quality and their adherence to digitization best practices. In addition, they will have to be examined for their thoroughness in documenting that part of the collection. See the further reading section for the particulars about these manuscripts.

Essentially, the Sternberg staff should begin investigating what digital and analog images of fossils already exist in their collection. The museum should also contact these former students to ask for permission to either use images already housed or stored at the Sternberg (or at FHSU) or to request that any digital images in their possession be sent to the Sternberg for its use. Organizing these images will facilitate the project, allowing the museum to utilize what already exists in the development of a digital archive/digital presentation for their fossil collection. The issue will also be complicated by the fact that the images may be copyrighted by the original photographers. Though the source materials are held by the Sternberg Museum, care should be taken to ensure that any copyright laws are not broken in the use of these images.

FUTURE RESEARCH DIRECTIONS

As mentioned above, the partnership between the Sternberg and Forsyth Library would be beneficial as the two organizations collection access and preservation concerns clearly converge and their respective strengths complement each other well. Successful future research and development would be well served by clear collaborative analyses and studies regarding the partnership.

Additionally, emphasis must be put upon the development and investigation of potential grant-writing proposals. Indeed, given the immense size of the collection and its need for digital organization and preservation, a multi-year NEH grant or IMLS grant would be of great help to moving the project from a minor digitization effort to a large-scale full-on digitization project.

In addition, research into the viability of 3D rendering of the fossil record is the most important development of future fossil digitization endeavors. If someone is able to develop a simple cost-effective way for rendering fossils in 3D that is not prohibitively expensive or overly dependent on large amounts of technology (and the immense start up costs that are involved), then the 3D digitization of fossils will be much more viable on the large scale. Currently, large-scale 3D rendering does not seem possible for the Sternberg or Forsyth without a significant amount of funding.

Finally, the main issue of archeological fossil collections is the general fragmentation of the various fossil datasets, databases, and repositories. Research into a national and international linked database of the entirety of the fossil record would be the next logical step to improving the research environment for scholars. Interoperability, therefore, must be the next main area of research to focus on for the fossil record. The cliché of breaking the data silo is very much an accurate image for the state of these various digital collections.

CONCLUSION

This chapter has attempted to discuss the main results and conclusions from the Sternberg Museum/Forsyth Library Fossil Digitization Pilot program, conducted between January and March 2011. The overall conclusions of the pilot suggest that a small-scale project that digitized in 2D about 500 – 2000 fossils and incorporated previously photographed fossils found in numerous FHSU graduate theses in Geosciences would be the best way to continue the partnership between the two organizations. Essentially, no matter how one approaches this project, a large-scale endeavor will likely not succeed without sufficiently skilled labor, enough money to pay for it, and a significant amount of time—all of which should be supplied by *both* Forsyth library and the Sternberg Museum in equal amounts. Should one partner be asked to shoulder more of the burden during the project, it will likely not succeed. Even a fully funded and fully staffed project would need 5 years of intense work and an unwavering commitment to funding to make a noticeable dent in the Vertebrate Paleontology collection. In addition, both stakeholders in the project will need to invest a significant amount of money for the long-term preservation of these digital images (and all of their surrogates), resulting in ever-growing costs. Therefore, the best solution will be to lower expectations and go with a smaller, more streamlined project focusing on pre-selected fossils that have been personally prioritized by Sternberg Museum subject experts, including but not limited to: FHSU Geosciences professors, grad students and researchers (See Appendix A for full details).

Once fossils have been selected, metadata records found and matched to fossils by Sternberg staff, then Forsyth Library digitization staff can come in to photograph, optimize, archive and backup, and upload images into a content management system. The results will be smaller, but they will also be of much more use and will represent the most important part of the collection, as culled by subject specialists. A small-scale project can also be done as the pre-cursor to a much larger-scaled project, which might have a much better probability of being sufficiently.

Finally, further study into the viability and ability to use cost-effective equipment and software for the 3D rendering of fossils needs to be done. Overall, the partnership represents the mutual needs of both institutions; Forsyth Library can help with the development of digital asset management and digital collection preservation while the Sternberg Museum can provide rich source material that will allow the library's collections to grow and be better used.

REFERENCES

AnthroDatadpa. (2009). *Anthropological data digital preservation and access*. Retrieved August 11, 2011 from http://anthrodatadpa.org/addpa/home/digital-preservation-and-access-dpa

Ball State University. (2007). *Digital repository: Fossils.* Retrieved August 11, 2011 from http://libx.bsu.edu/cdm4/collection.php?CISOROOT=/FosCol

Barton., et al. (2006). Using a relational geodatabase to manage paleontological resources at Florissant fossil beds national monument: Fossils from federal lands. *New Mexico Museum of Natural History and Science Bulletin, 34.* Retrieved August 11, 2011 from http://www.nature.nps.gov/geology/paleontology/pub/fossil_conference_7/4%20Abstracts.pdf

Biodiversity Information Standards-TDWG. (2009). *Darwin core*. Retrieved August 11, 2011 from http://rs.tdwg.org/dwc/

Clark, J. T., et al. (2002). Digital archive network for anthropology. *Journal of Digital Information, 2*(4). Retrieved August 11, 2011 from http://journals.tdl.org/jodi/article/viewArticle/50/53

Dublin Core Metadata Initiative. (2011). *DCMI home*. Retrieved August 11, 2011 from http://dublincore.org/

Forsyth Library Digital Collections. (2011). *FHSU master's thesis collection*. Retrieved August 11, 2011 from http://cdm15732.contentdm.oclc.org/cdm/landingpage/collection/thesis

Fort Hays State University. (2011). *FHSU Forsyth library digital collections*. Retrieved August 11, 2011 from http://www.fhsu.edu/library/

Global Biodiversity Information Facility. (2011). *Gbif.org home page*. Retrieved August 11, 2011 from http://www.gbif.org/

MacLeod, N., Diver, P., Guralnick, R., Lazarus, D., & Malmgren, B. (2000). Computers, quantification & databases. In Lane, R. H., Steininger, F. F., Kaesler, R. L., Zeigler, W., & Lipps, J. (Eds.), *Fossils and the Future: Paleontology in the 21st Century* (pp. 191–201). Frankfurt, Germany: Senckenburg Museum.

Mallison, H., et al. (2009). Mechanical digitizing for paleontology - New and improved techniques. *Palaeontologia Electronica, 12*(2). Retrieved August 11, 2011 from http://palaeo-electronica.org/2009_2/185/index.html

Meyer., et al. (2008). *Development of an integrated paleontological database and web site of Florissant collections, taxonomy, and publications.* GSA Special Papers 435. Retrieved from http://specialpapers.gsapubs.org/content/435/159.abstract

Mueller, T. (2010). Whale evolution: Valley of the whales. *National Geographic*. Retrieved August 11, 2011 from http://ngm.nationalgeographic.com/2010/08/whale-evolution/mueller-text

National Information Standards Organization. (2011). *NISO standards: Z39.50*. Retrieved August 11, 2011 from http://www.niso.org/kst/reports/standards?step=2&gid=None&project_key%3Austring%3Aiso-8859-1=84532426495314789f843e720437a599e8db9aa7

OCLC. (2011). *CONTENTdm® digital collection management software*. Retrieved August 11, 2011 from http://www.contentdm.org/

Open Archive Initiative Protocol for Metadata Harvesting. (2008). *Open archive initiative home*. Retrieved August 11, 2011 from http://www.openarchives.org/pmh/

Paleontology Portal. (2003). *Paleontology portal home page*. Retrieved August 11, 2011 from http://www.paleoportal.org/

Reality, E. O. N. Inc. (2011). *EON reality home page*. Retrieved August 11, 2011 from http://www.eonreality.com/

Science Te Pu Ao, G. N. S. (2011). *New Zealand fossils in 3D*. Retrieved August 11, 2011 from http://www.gns.cri.nz/Home/Learning/Science-Topics/Fossils/Gallery/NZ-Fossils-in-3D

Smithsonian National Museum of Natural History. (2011) *Paleobiology collections*. Retrieved August 11, 2011 from http://paleobiology.si.edu/collections/paleoCollections.html

Specify Software Project. (2011). *Welcome to specify 6*. Retrieved August 11, 2011 from http://specifysoftware.org/content/welcome-specify-6

Sternberg Museum of Natural History. (2011). *About Sternberg museum*. Retrieved August 11, 2011 from http://sternberg.fhsu.edu/

University of Iowa. (2010). *NMITA neogene marine biota of tropical America*. Retrieved August 11, 2011 from http://nmita.geology.uiowa.edu/

University of Kansas Museum of Natural History and Biodiversity Research Center. (2006). *Division of invertebrate paleontology*. Retrieved August 11, 2011 from http://ipa.geo.ku.edu/InvertPaleo/

University of Texas-Austin. (2011). *National science foundation grant helps preserve and digitize fossil collections*. Retrieved August 11, 2011 from http://www.utexas.edu/news/2011/04/11/fossils_preserve_digitize/

US Biological Collections National Resource. (2010). *A strategic plan for establishing a network integrated collections alliance*. Retrieved August 11, 2011 from http://digbiocol.wordpress.com/2010/02/07/watch-this-space/

U.S. Geological Survey. (2011). *Paleontological resources of the USGS in Denver*. Retrieved August 11, 2011 from http://esp.cr.usgs.gov/research/fossils/index.html

Wilhite, R. (2003). Digitizing large fossil skeletal elements for three-dimensional applications. *Palaeontologia Electronica, 5*(1). Retrieved August 11, 2011 from http://palaeo-electronica.org/paleo/2002_2/scan/issue2_02.htm

Wolniewicz, P. (2009). Easily-accessible digital palaeontological databases – A new perspective for the storage of palaeontological information. *Geologos, 15*(3–4), 181–188. doi:10.2478/v10118-009-0002-1

ADDITIONAL READING

Anderson, K. (2010). Picturing the museum: Education and exhibition at the American museum of natural history. In Ng, K., & Kuksma, J. (Eds.), *Digitization in the Real World* (pp. 242–258). New York, NY: METRO.

Ball State University. (2007). *Digital repository: Fossils*. Retrieved August 11, 2011 from http://libx.bsu.edu/cdm4/collection.php?CISOROOT=/FosCol

Biodiversity Information Standards-TDWG. (2009). *Darwin core*. Retrieved August 11, 2011 from http://rs.tdwg.org/dwc/

Dalman, S. (2010). *A new carnosaur (dinosaurian: theropoda) from the upper morrison formation (late jurassic, tithonian) of Colorado*. Retrieved August 11, 2011 from http://contentcat.fhsu.edu/cdm/singleitem/collection/thesis/id/1876

Darnell, M. (2000). *Systematics of the fossil equidae (mammalia: perissodactyla), minimum quarry, Graham county, Kansas*. Retrieved August 11, 2011 from http://contentcat.fhsu.edu/cdm/singleitem/collection/thesis/id/762

Fort Hays State University. (2011). *FHSU Forsyth library digital collections*. Retrieved August 11, 2011 from http://www.fhsu.edu/library/

Garcia, W. (1999). *Teleorhinus (crocodylimorpha) from the Dakota formation (cretaceous) of Kansas, with a discussion of its paleoecology*. Retrieved August 11, 2011 from http://contentcat.fhsu.edu/cdm/singleitem/collection/thesis/id/1061

Gerhold, G. (1992). *Comparative morphology and evolution of teleoceras (mammalia: rhinocerotidae)*. Retrieved August 11, 2011 from http://contentcat.fhsu.edu/cdm/singleitem/collection/thesis/id/1073

GoMeasure3D. (2011). *GoMeasure3D home*. Retrieved August 11, 2011 from http://www.gomeasure3d.com/ImmersionMicroscribe

Ikejiri, T. (2004). *Anatomy of camarasaurus lentus (dinosauria: sauropoda) from the morisson formation (late jurassic)*. Retrieved August 11, 2011 from http://contentcat.fhsu.edu/cdm/singleitem/collection/thesis/id/1423

Mullin, T. (2006). Systematics, osteology, sexual dimorphism, age classes, and population dynamics of teleoceras fossiger from Jack Swayze quarry, Clark county, Kansas, and Minium quarry, Graham county, Kansas. Retrieved August 11, 2011 from http://contentcat.fhsu.edu/cdm/singleitem/collection/thesis/id/2096

OCLC. (2011). *CONTENTdm® digital collection management software*. Retrieved August 11, 2011 from http://www.contentdm.org/

Reality, E. O. N. Inc. (2011). *EON reality home page*. Retrieved August 11, 2011 from http://www.eonreality.com/

Science Te Pu Ao, G. N. S. (2011). *New Zealand fossils in 3D*. Retrieved August 11, 2011 from http://www.gns.cri.nz/Home/Learning/Science-Topics/Fossils/Gallery/NZ-Fossils-in-3D

Smithsonian National Museum of Natural History. (2011). *Paleobiology collections*. Retrieved August 11, 2011 from http://paleobiology.si.edu/collections/paleoCollections.html

Specify Software Project. (2011). *Welcome to specify 6*. Retrieved August 11, 2011 from http://specifysoftware.org/content/welcome-specify-6

Sternberg Museum of Natural History. (2011). *About Sternberg museum*. Retrieved August 11, 2011 from http://sternberg.fhsu.edu/

University of California-Berkeley. (2011). *CalPhotos*. Retrieved August 11, 2011 from http://calphotos.berkeley.edu/

University of Iowa. (2010). *NMITA neogene marine biota of tropical America*. Retrieved August 11, 2011 from http://nmita.geology.uiowa.edu/

University of Kansas Museum of Natural History and Biodiversity Research Center. (2006). *Division of invertebrate paleontology*. Retrieved August 11, 2011 from http://ipa.geo.ku.edu/InvertPaleo/

University of Texas-Austin. (2011). *National science foundation grant helps preserve and digitize fossil collections*. Retrieved August 11, 2011 from http://www.utexas.edu/news/2011/04/11/fossils_preserve_digitize/

U.S. Geological Survey. (2011). *Paleontological resources of the USGS in Denver*. Retrieved August 11, 2011 from http://esp.cr.usgs.gov/research/fossils/index.html

KEY TERMS AND DEFINITIONS

3D Rendering: Digital applications creating images that mimic three-dimensional experiences.

CONTENTdm: OCLC's proprietary digital content management system.

CT Scan: Computed tomography scan.

Darwin Core: Extension of Dublin Core Metadata schema tailor-made to address needs of biological sciences, paleontology and archaeology.

Data Silo: A self-contained unit of digital information, often a negative connotation; situation forces researches to search multiple collections.

Interoperability: Systems of data shared and searchable across multiple platforms.

Metadata Granularity: Specificity of metadata in a record; more granularity for an item provides a more complete description of it, though it can reduce interoperability.

Mosasaur: Large extinct marine lizards; considered to be the closest relatives of modern snakes.

SPECIFY: University of Kansas sponsored software platform for the digital content management of fossil and vertebrate paleontology collections; now on its sixth version.

ENDNOTES

1. No matter the project scale, fixed costs of $10,000 will remain due to data storage device needs and equipment maintenance/replacement.

APPENDIX

Potential Plan for Small-Scale (6 Months or Less) Project

A small-scale project is recommended for the following reasons:

- Quicker accounting of existing digitized fossil records.
- Faster creation of a useful digital project that meets user demands & expectations (within 1 year).
- Potential precursor to a much larger grant-funded project.
- Will allow partners to get acclimated to working together.
- Will allow stakeholders to work through potential workflow issues, including responsibilities, benchmarks, bottlenecks, etc.
- Less overall expense (even with larger initial cost per image estimation).

Shown in Table 1 are the basic steps to be taken for a small-scale project, along with the responsible party and time required for each step.

Table 1. Small scale fossil digitization project

STEP:	RESPONSIBLE PARTY:	TIME REQUIRED:
Step 1: determine scope: # of fossils to select: +/- 2500 fossil sample	Sternberg Mus.	2 weeks
Step 2: determine existing fossil images	Sternberg Mus.	Steps 2 -4 = 2 months
Step 3: compile existing fossil images into Access database	Sternberg Mus. Only	
Step 4: select fossils to be digitized in project	Sternberg Mus.	
Step 5: Digitize list of fossils according to best practices	Forsyth Library	Steps 5-6 = 2.5 months
Step 6: Optimize/Archive images	Forsyth Library Only	
Step 7: Append metadata from digital records to the images (via database or Specify/CONTENTdm).	Forsyth library & Sternberg Mus.	Steps 7-8 =1 month
Step 8: add fossils to Web galleries (via content management system).	Forsyth Library & Sternberg Mus.	
TOTAL TIME	***6 months***	
TOTAL COST**	***$25,400***	

Section 3

Establishing Benchmarks:

Evaluation Methodology and Practice in Digital Libraries

Chapter 8
Evaluation Constructs and Criteria for Digital Libraries:
A Document Analysis

Soohyung Joo
University of Wisconsin – Milwaukee, USA

Iris Xie
University of Wisconsin – Milwaukee, USA

ABSTRACT

The intent of this chapter is to identify constructs and criteria for Digital Library (DL) evaluation based on document analysis. Eighty-five relevant articles and five websites were reviewed to generate the evaluation constructs and criteria. The findings consist of ten constructs, including collection, information organization, interface design, system performance, effects on users, user engagement, services, preservation, sustainability/administration, and context of use with associated criteria for each dimension. In addition, this chapter discusses challenges in DL evaluation research and practices.

INTRODUCTION

In the last decade, libraries have substantially expanded their digitization efforts and contributed a number of unique digital collections in support of scholarly research, teaching, and learning. The initial development of digital collections focused on building the technical infrastructure and establishing a DL presence resulted in a number of useful digitization guidelines and best practices for creating usable and sustainable digital collections. Recommendations for undertaking periodic evaluations are also part of the guidelines for "building good digital collections" (NINCH, 2002; NISO, 2007). However, the exponential growth of DLs has not been accompanied by extensive

DOI: 10.4018/978-1-4666-2991-2.ch008

evaluation studies (Saracevic, 2004). According to Saracevic (1995), "Evaluation means assessing performances or value of system, process, product, or policy" (p. 138). DL evaluation is by no means a simple task, and is often overlooked in DL evaluation due to the nature of complex, multi-dimensional, and distributed systems of DLs (Bollen & Luce, 2002; Marchionini, 2000; Saracevic, 2004; Sumner & Marlino, 2004; Chowdhury, et al., 2006; Xie, 2006; Xie, 2008; Zhang, 2010). Currently, there are few guidelines for best practices of DL evaluation. Since DLs are new, complex, and multifaceted entities, researchers and practitioners in the field need a set of guidelines of what to evaluate, how to measure results, when to undertake evaluation, and how to incorporate results into the development process. Several researchers addressed the need for the multi-dimensional evaluation for the DL field as they identified the lack of a comprehensive and integrated evaluation framework as a major barrier to DL evaluation (Chowdhury, et al., 2006; Saracevic, 2000; Xie, 2006, 2008; Zhang, 2010).

This chapter adopts the definition of Digital Libraries (DLs) as: "representations of emergent and complex forms of digital information organization and design, consisting of multiple layers and building blocks, in various stages of development" (Matusiak, 2010, p. 15). DLs present a variety of resources created in the digital format as well as those converted from analog materials through digitization efforts, including print materials, manuscripts, images, audio, and video. The concepts of DLs are still evolving, correspond to a very complex notion, and cannot be captured by a simple definition (Bishop, Van House, & Buttenfield, 2003; Candela, et al., 2007; Greenstein, 2000).

As an initial step toward a comprehensive DL evaluation framework, this chapter reviewed a wide range of previous documents to identify evaluation constructs and associated criteria. Even though researchers suggested various evaluation constructs and criteria, there was little effort to analyze and integrate those criteria into a consolidated framework within the DL field. In this chapter, we identified 10 evaluation constructs and corresponding criteria based on the analysis of 85 previous documents and five websites related to DL evaluation. Furthermore, we discuss the limitations and challenges of previous evaluation efforts.

BACKGROUND

Researchers and DL practitioners recognize the importance of DL evaluation, and have proposed several models, frameworks, and various criteria for DL evaluation. Several practical tools and methods have been proposed to expand evaluation efforts, including DigiQUAL, eMetrics, EQUINOXISO/TSO-20938, and MIEL2 Project, but they are often limited to specific elements or services. For instance, DigiQUAL is proposed as a tool for assessing service quality (Kyrillidou & Giersch, 2005). Focusing more on vendor-provided data in academic libraries, the ARL's e-metrics project, COUNTER, and SUSHI protocols were designed for the purpose of assessing the outputs of DLs using the usage statistics (Pesch, 2007). In Europe, EQUINOX serves as a framework to assess performance of DLs based on the usage statistics (Brophy, 2001). Similarly, ISO/TSO-20983 and MIEL2 cover electronic resources in DL environments (Brophy & Wynne, 1997; Noh, 2010). The eVALUEd toolkit focuses on methodological issues (McNicol, 2004). Although all these efforts represent a step in the right direction, they fail to provide a comprehensive model for DL evaluation in a systematic way that addresses the needs of multiple evaluation constructs and criteria.

On the research side, many researchers have suggested a number of evaluation constructs, criteria, and indicators to create a comprehensive approach reflecting different components of DLs. The early DL research projects, funded by the National Science Foundation (NSF) as part of Digital Libraries Initiatives I and II, laid the groundwork by producing DL prototypes and frameworks (Borgman, et al., 2000; Buttenfield, 1999; Hill, et al., 2000; Van House, et al., 1996). Although these early projects weighed much on the development of DL prototypes, several of them undertook major evaluation efforts as part of the design cycle. For instance, Hill et al. (1997) identified six criteria, including ease of use, overall appeal, usefulness, and performance, in evaluating the Alexandria Digital Library (ADL) at the University of California, Santa Barbara. Saracevic (2000, 2004) suggested a comprehensive evaluation model and identified six classes of criteria, representing: content, technology, interface, process/service, user, and context. In Europe, DELOS is one of most comprehensive and large scale DL projects, which represent joint activities aimed at integrating and coordinating the ongoing research efforts of the major European teams working in DL area. DELOS Manifesto presents a three-tier DL framework incorporating six core components such as content, functionality, quality, policy, architecture, and user (Candela, et al., 2007). DELOS model sets up a foundation for DL research. DELOS Network of Excellence has conducted a series of research concerning the evaluation of DLs. Fuhr et al. (2001) proposed a scheme for digital library evaluation, which contains four dimensions: data/collection, system/technology, users, and usage. Tsakonas et al. (2004) further examined the interactions of DL components and proposed the following evaluation foci: usability, usefulness, and system performance. Fuhr et al. (2007) developed a DL evaluation framework based on a DELOS model and a largescale survey of DL evaluation activities. In addition, DELOS has contributed to the large test-set-based IR research of video digital libraries in TREC. For example, the TREC video track offered an evaluation test framework for IR performance of video information in digital libraries (Smeaton & Over, 2002). Xie's (2006, 2008) evaluation framework increased the focus onto users, and proposed five types of criteria: usability, collection quality, service quality, system performance efficiency, and user feedback solicitation. Recently, Zhang (2010) investigated the importance of multiple constructs of criteria including: content, technology, interface, service, user, and context using the empirical data from heterogeneous stakeholders.

Usability evaluation is another key area for research. Saracevic (2004) stated the usability evaluation studies play a role of connecting user-oriented and system-oriented usability studies. He suggested a list of specific usability criteria and attributes for DL evaluation, including content, process, format, and overall assessment. Dillon (1999) proposed a qualitative framework (TIME) for DL usability evaluation which covers user task (T), information model (I), manipulation facilities (M), and the ergonomic variables (E). Xie and Wolfram (2002) suggested organizational usability factors in state-level digital library. Based on an empirical study, they identified four contributing factors for organization usability in digital libraries, namely: access, promotion and training, content and format usage, and design. Ward and Hiller (2005) suggested usability evaluation criteria specific to library services—completion of the task, time and effort, and reaction to the product or service. Similarly, but more specifically, Jeng (2006) proposed a usability model for academic digital libraries employing four operational usability criteria—effectiveness, efficiency, satisfaction, and learnability. In addition, many other researchers conducted usability tests in DL environment (Eliasen, et al., 1997; Battleson, et al., 2001; Hammil, 2003; Blandford, et al., 2004; Joo & Lee, 2011).

In addition, Shim and Kantor (1999) adopted Data Envelopment Analysis (DEA) to evaluate DLs, and proposed an evaluation framework that focused on two main dimensions of effectiveness and efficiency. Missingham (2003) introduced the unique concept of a digital footprint representing the use of DLs through multidimensional measurement. Kim and Kim (2008) proposed 19 evaluation criteria tailored to digital collections, and validates them empirically using surveys from related stakeholders such as users, librarians and administrators. Noh (2010) suggested a set of evaluation indices for electronic resources in terms of electronic resource acquisition, electronic resource use, and electronic resource environment. Other researchers examined the DL evaluation criteria such as suitability, accuracy, costs, informativeness, timeliness, usefulness, and others (Kengeri, et al., 1999; Kenney, et al., 1998; Larsen, 2002). Most of the works in the research area investigate the DL frameworks and associated criteria, however they do not offer practical guidelines on how to gather data and implement evaluation.

DIGITAL LIBRARY EVALUATION CONSTRUCTS AND CRITERIA

As an effort to identify evaluation constructs and associated criteria pools for DL evaluation, the authors conducted a document analysis. Using keywords such as "digital library," "evaluation," "criteria," "assessment," and others in different combinations, the authors searched Google Scholar and EBSCOhost for relevant documents published primarily, but not exclusively, between 2000 to 2010. The relevance of a document was judged by the two following criteria: (1) whether the paper included any evaluation theories, framework, criteria, indicators, or measures; or (2) whether the paper included actual evaluation practices or pilot tests. The document analysis covers evaluation research associated with DLs and previous research related to evaluation. In this study, eighty-five relevant documents and five DL evaluation project websites (Equinox, DigiQUAL, LibQUAL+, eVALUEd, DELOS) were reviewed and analyzed.

All the evaluation constructs and criteria were collected and analyzed from the selected documents. Strauss and Corbin's (1990) open coding technique was applied to data analysis. For example, evaluation criteria for "user engagement" were identified by analyzing related literature in the perspectives of user usage and user involvement. After reviewing the constructs and criteria, the authors consolidated and organized them into ten constructs. Then, associated criteria for each construct were identified. The authors adopted all the criteria identified in the selected literature and the websites.

The document analysis yielded ten constructs and associated criteria, which include: collection, information organization, interface design, system performance, effects on users, user engagement, services, preservation, sustainability/administration, and context of use. In addition, associated criteria identified in previous works were also incorporated into this chapter. Table 1 presents the ten constructs and associated definitions. Table 2 shows specific evaluation criteria and corresponding objectives.

CHALLENGES IN DIGITAL LIBRARY EVALUATION

Many researchers and practitioners have expanded their efforts in digital library evaluation in the recent decade. However, there are still many challenges and problems in DL evaluation. This chapter discusses some key challenges that hinder the research and practices of evaluation in the DL community.

As discussed in Background, there are few evaluation standards and comprehensive frameworks that are directly applicable to DL fields, despite scholarly and practical efforts in the DL area. Early DL projects funded by the National Science Foundation (NSF) primarily focus on the design of DL prototypes, and do not offer direct insights and implications for DL evaluation. Several models created for DL evaluation have not been recognized and adopted by researchers and practitioners as standards. The absence of stan-

Table 1. DL evaluation constructs and definitions

Construct	Definition
Collection	Assess the quality and quantity of DL collections.
Information Organization	Assess the representation, grouping, and presentation of digital information.
Interface design	Assess the usability of DL interfaces, and the extent these interfaces support users' interaction with DLs.
System performance	Assess the efficiency, accessibility, and reliability of DLs, as well as their retrieval performance.
Effects on users	Assess the impact and value of DLs on users' accomplishment of their tasks.
Services	Assess the quality and quantity of the offered DL services.
Preservation	Assess the extent and ways of DL support for preservation.
Administration/ Sustainability	Assess administrative-related factors that affect the development of DLs; Assess whether DLs can be sustained and enhanced.
User engagement	Assess the extent and ways of usage of DLs, and the extent and ways of user involvement in the DL development.
Context	Assess the extent of DLs fitting into, responding to, following larger context—institutional, economic, legal, social, cultural—and others (Saracevic, 2004).

dards is a major obstacle to building an evaluation framework and tools in the DL area. At the same time, most of current evaluation practices are prone to focus narrowly on specific systems or particular aspects or services (e.g. DigiQUAL for service quality; Equinox for usage). A one-time evaluation of a single portion of the system, while convenient, might leave out other significant portions of the system that could lend other crucial viewpoints for decision-making (Nicholson, 2004). Several researchers note that holistic evaluation studies are conspicuously absent from the DL field, and discuss the potential benefits of comprehensive approaches (Chowdhury, et al., 2006; Xie, 2006, 2008; Zhang, 2010). Moreover, the validation of an evaluation model remains one of the most challenging tasks.

There is a gap between research and practice. As discussed above, researchers have suggested various models and criteria, but their works remain mostly conceptual or theoretical. Most of the theoretical research investigates the importance of criteria, but fails to offer detailed, practical guidelines on how to gather data, implement the analysis, and use the results of evaluation. In addition, they have not sufficiently suggested practical criteria and methodology, such as providing measureable criteria, methods to collect the data, and how to incorporate the evaluation results into the development of DLs. As a result, practitioners have adopted few of those theoretical or conceptual models into the DL fields. Researchers will need to deal with practical matters in detail to fill the gap and to create more practical evaluation tools.

Less effort was made to evaluate contextual elements surrounding digital libraries. The majority of the studies in DL evaluation adopted traditional IR criteria at a restricted level, such as precision/recall and error rate, usability criteria, or service quality criteria. Very few address how well a DL fits into or even improves people's daily work and life, via contextual criteria at higher levels, such as social, legal, and cultural aspects (Zhang, 2010). Context is another key aspect of DL evaluation, distinguished from predominant system- or user-centered evaluation framework (Adams & Bladford, 2001; Bollen & Luce, 2002). Saracevic (2004) is one of few researchers who emphasizes context criteria and suggests related measures (e.g. institutional fit, sustainability, productivity of and impact on community, members, etc.) in evaluating DLs. However, there are few practical

Table 2. DL evaluation criteria and objectives

Construct	Criterion	Objective
Collection	audience	To assess who are the main potential users of a DL.
	authority	To assess whether information provided by a DL comes from trustworthy sources.
	completeness	To assess whether a DL covers all documents in each topic area.
	cost	To assess costs to build collections in a DL.
	digitizing practices	To assess the types and methods of digitization practices conducted, as well as identifying best practices to build a DL.
	diversity	To assess whether a DL deals with a variety of issues in relation to a topic of interest.
	format flexibility	To assess whether the format of collections in a DL are compatible with a variety of software and systems for different purposes.
	quality of format	To assess the quality of a digitized item provided by a DL within its format (e.g. resolution, scanned image quality, recorded audio quality, etc.).
	size	To assess the amount of collection items provided by a DL.
	scope/coverage	To assess the range of topics that is covered by a DL.
	sufficiency	To assess whether a DL provides enough documents to satisfy a user's need.
	types of format	To assess what kinds of document formats are available in a DL.
Information Organization	accessibility to metadata	To assess how easily a user can obtain the metadata information of each item.
	appropriateness	To assess whether the organizational structure and associated categories adequately organize items in a DL.
	completeness/ comprehensiveness	To assess whether the organization structure covers all the access points of a DL.
	conformance	To assess whether metadata elements follow predefined standard and guides.
	consistency	To assess whether metadata is consistent across collections in a DL.
	controlled vocabulary	To assess the type and amount of controlled vocabularies used in a DL.
	interoperability	To assess whether metadata elements of a DL are compatible to different DLs.
	metadata accuracy	To assess how accurately metadata elements are assigned for each item.
	metadata authority	To assess whether credible metadata elements are selected for items in a DL.
	metadata elements	To assess how many metadata elements are employed to represent items in a DL.
	quality of metadata scheme	To assess the quality of metadata system selected for a DL.
Interface design	browsing function	To assess in what ways and to what extent the interface supports a user's ability to surf related items in a DL.
	consistency	To assess whether the design and layout are coherent across a DL interface.
	emotional appeal	To assess to what extent the interface of a DL is effectively attractive to users.
	help function	To assess what types of help functions are offered and how effectively they support users in their help-seeking process.
	intuitive operation	To assess how straightforward a DL interface is for a user to understand its operation, and how easily a user can learn to operate the interface.
	navigation	To assess in what ways and to what extent the interface supports a user's exploration in a DL.
	personalized page	To assess whether a DL offers personalized pages based on user profile.
	reliability	To assess the ability of a DL to perform and maintain its functions under different circumstances.

continued on following page

Table 2. Continued

Construct	Criterion	Objective
Interface design	search function	To assess what types of search functions are offered by a DL and how easy to use them.
	search results presentation	To assess the types of formats/options of search results are presented to users in a DL.
	usability	To assess the efficiency, effectiveness, and satisfactory use of a DL's interface (ISO, 1997).
	user control	To assess to what extent the DL allows users to manipulate its interface.
	view option	To assess whether and to what extent a user can customize viewing options in a DL.
	visual appeal	To assess to what extent the interface of a DL is visually attractive to users.
System performance	connectivity	To assess how stable a DL system can be connected to other information systems.
	error rate/error correction	To assess the degree of errors encountered during system operation and the ability of a DL to fix errors.
	fit-to-task	To assess to what extent a DL is adequate to perform tasks that a user requests.
	flexibility	To assess whether a DL responds to potential internal or external changes in a timely manner.
	integrated search	To assess whether a DL offers an integrated search environment for different collections within a DL.
	linkage with other DLs	To assess the identification of and in what ways a DL is linked to other related DLs.
	reliability	To assess how stable a DL's performance is over time.
	response time	To assess how quickly a DL responds to a user's request.
	retrieval effectiveness	To assess how effective the search algorithm is in a DL (e.g. recall and precision).
	server performance	To assess the ability of a server to run a DL.
	speed of page loading	To assess how quickly a DL presents a user-requested page.
	storage	To assess the size of a DL's storage capacity.
Effects on users	behavior change	To assess in what ways and to what extent a DL influences a user's behaviors.
	information literacy	To assess in what ways and to what extent a DL enhances a user's ability to find useful information for his/her tasks.
	instructional efficiency	To assess in what ways and to what extent a DL enhances user's teaching effectiveness.
	knowledge change	To assess in what ways and to what extent a DL influences a user's knowledge structure.
	learning effects	To assess in what ways and to what extent a DL influences a user's learning outcome.
	research productivity	To assess in what ways and to what extent a DL affects a user's research outputs (e.g. publications, grants, etc.).
Services	accessibility to managerial staff	To assess in what ways and to what extent a user can easily contact staff of a DL for questions, feedback, and comments.
	confidence	To assess in what ways and to what extent users have a positive attitude toward services offered by a DL.
	customized services	To assess whether a DL offers personalized services based on user profile information or user requests.
	FAQ/Q&A	To assess whether and how many FAQs or Q&A a DL provides to help users in using the DL.
	follow-up services	To assess in what ways and to what extent adequate and timely continuing services are provided to users by a DL when necessary.
	reliability	To assess how users of a DL perceive the trustworthiness of service provided.
	responsiveness	To assess the reaction time to a user's request for a DL service.

continued on following page

Table 2. Continued

Construct	Criterion	Objective
Services	service quality	To assess in what ways and to what extent DL services satisfy users' needs
	timeliness	To assess in what ways and to what extent services are offered to users in a timely manner.
	types of services	To assess the types of services provided by a DL.
	types of services for users with disabilities	To assess the types of services offered to users with disabilities.
	types of unique services	To assess the unique types of services provided by a DL compared to other related DLs.
	usefulness	To assess in what ways and to what extent DL services are useful for users to achieve their tasks.
	user education	To assess the types of user education offered by a DL.
	user satisfaction	To assess in what ways and to what extent users are satisfied with services provided by a DL.
Preservation	ability to migrate	To assess the ability of data migration for preservation.
	completeness	To assess to what extent the archiving process to preserve archived materials is complete and comprehensive.
	cost per record	To assess the average cost for archiving one record.
	data processing	To assess in what ways and to what extent data are processed for document preservation.
	incentives for archives	To assess the types and amount of incentives for performing archiving tasks.
	preservation policy	To assess whether a policy regarding preservation is developed and what is covered in the policy.
	staff dedicated to preservation	To assess how many staff members are dedicated to preservation task of a DL.
	types of archiving equipments/facilities	To assess the types of archiving equipments and facilities a DL uses for digital preservation.
	types of archiving methods	To assess the archiving methods/approaches a DL staff member has to apply in order to preserve information.
Administration /Sustainability	budget	To assess the amount and arrangement of monetary resources to efficiently manage a DL.
	fundraising/sponsor	To assess the effort of fundraising to support a DL financially.
	incentive	To assess the types of incentives provided to DL staff.
	management policy	To assess whether a well-defined policy for administration is offered by a DL.
	marketing	To assess the publicity efforts of a DL to attract potential users and inform related communities.
	planning	To assess whether strategic plans are established to create, manage, maintain, and enhance a DL.
	regular assessment	To assess whether regular, continuous evaluation is performed to maintain and enhance a DL.
	staffing	To assess the quantity and arrangement of human resources to efficiently manage a DL.
	staff training	To assess the types of, frequency of, and efficiency of training programs offered to DL staff.
User engagement	help feature use	To assess which help features are offered to users, how frequently, and in what context users try to use help-related features in a DL.
	resource use	To assess in what ways and to what extent users uses resources in a DL (item view, download, etc.)

continued on following page

Table 2. Continued

Construct	Criterion	Objective
User engagement	site visit	To assess how frequently users visit a DL website and the duration for each visit.
	user feedback	To assess the types of user comments and suggestions received by a DL, and in what ways and to what extent these comments and suggestions are incorporated into the enhancement of the DL.
	user participation channels	To assess the types of channels available to users to communicate with the staff of a DL.
Context	collaboration	To assess in what ways and to what extent stakeholders of a DL work together; To assess in what ways and to what extent stakeholders of a DL cooperate with stakeholders in another DL.
	content sharing	To assess in what ways and to what extent stakeholders of a DL are willing to share their content.
	copyrights	To assess whether a DL identifies and conforms to copyright issues.
	information ethics compliance	To assess whether a DL identifies and conforms to ethical issues related to DL creation and use.
	organizational mission	To assess in what ways and to what extent DL creation and use conform to organizational objectives.
	social impact	To assess in what ways and to what extent the use of a DL influences the society.
	targeted user community	To assess in what ways and to what extent a DL engages in targeted user groups.

attempts to evaluate the contextual elements in DL settings. Evaluating context, such as social, legal, and community is an unsolved problem due to the difficulty in measurement.

Few studies or evaluation practices attempted to employ multiple methods and data collection methods to assess components of DLs in an evaluation framework. There are few DL evaluation studies that applied multiple methods and data collection techniques at the same time. Moreover, quantitative data from surveys, transaction logs, and usage statistics, were dominantly used for a summative evaluation of DL performance or service quality. However, these quantitative data are less helpful in giving timely feedbacks about potential problems for DL design and implementation (Kaplan & Shaw, 2004). Qualitative methods, by providing findings that connect more directly with these individuals' perspectives, can increase the credibility and usefulness of evaluations (Patton, 2001).

CONCLUSION

In this chapter, we identified constructs and associated criteria for DL evaluation. Eighty-five documents and five websites in relation to DL were collected and analyzed to come up with ten constructs and associated DL evaluation criteria. This chapter presents multiple constructs of DL evaluation ranging from collection, information organization, interface design, system performance, and effects on users, services, preservation, sustainability/administration, user engagement, and context. In addition, corresponding criteria were also identified. We also discussed challenges in DL evaluation research and practices including lack of DL evaluation standards, few comprehensive evaluation models, the gap between research and practice, limited context evaluation, and few studies applying multiple research methods, in particular qualitative approaches, to their DL evaluations. These challenges call for the need for researchers to develop DL evaluation frameworks, going beyond constructs and criteria, and further exploring associated measures and data collection methods.

REFERENCES

Adams, A., & Blandford, A. (2001). Digital libraries in a clinical setting: friend or foe? Research and advanced technology for digital libraries. In *Proceedings of 5th European Conference Digital Library, ECDL 2001*. Darmstadt, Germany: ECDL.

Battleson, B., Booth, A., & Weintrop, J. (2001). Usability testing of an academic library web site: A case study. *Journal of Academic Librarianship*, *27*(3), 188–198. doi:10.1016/S0099-1333(01)00180-X

Bishop, A. P. (1995). Working towards an understanding of digital library use: A report on the user research efforts of the NSF/ARPA/NASA DLI projects. *D-Lib Magazine*. Retrieved from http://www.dlib.org/dlib/october95/10bishop.html

Bishop, A. P. Van House, N. A., & Buttenfield, B. P. (2003). *Digital library use: Social practice in design and evaluation*. Cambridge, MA: MIT Press.

Blandford, A., Keith, S., Connell, I., & Edwards, H. (2004). Analytical usability evaluation for digital libraries: A case study. In Proceedings of the 2004 Joint ACM/IEEE Conference on Digital Libraries, (pp. 27-36). ACM/IEEE.

Bollen, J., & Luce, R. (2002). Evaluation of digital library impact and user communities by analysis of usage patterns. *D-Lib Magazine*, *8*(6). Retrieved from http://www.dlib.org/dlib/june02/bollen/06bollen.html doi:10.1045/june2002-bollen

Bollen, J., & Luce, R. (2002). Evaluation of digital library impact and user communities by analysis of usage patterns. *D-Lib Magazine*, *8*(6). Retrieved from http://www.dlib.org/dlib/june02/bollen/06bollen.html doi:10.1045/june2002-bollen

Borgman, C. L., Gilliland-Swetland, A. J., Leazer, G. H., Mayer, R., Gwynn, D., Gazan, R., & Mautone, P. (2000). Evaluating digital libraries for teaching and learning in undergraduate education: A case study of the Alexandria digital earth prototype (ADEPT). *Library Trends*, *49*(2), 228–250.

Brophy, P. (2001). Electronic library performance indicators: The EQUINOX project. *Serials*, *14*(1), 5–9.

Brophy, P., & Wynne, P. M. (1997). *Management information systems and performance measurement for the electronic library: eLib supporting study*. Lancashire, UK: University of Central Lancashire, Centre for Research in Library and Information Management.

Buttenfield, B. (1999). Usability evaluation of digital libraries. *Science & Technology Libraries*, *17*(3-4), 39–59. doi:10.1300/J122v17n03_04

Candela, L., Akal, F., Avancini, H., Castelli, D., Fusco, L., & Guidetti, V. (2007). DILIGENT: Integrating digital library and grid technologies for a new earth observation research infrastructure. *International Journal on Digital Libraries*, *7*, 59–80. doi:10.1007/s00799-007-0023-8

Chowdhury, S., Landoni, M., & Gibb, F. (2006). Usability and impact of digital libraries: A review. *Online Information Review*, *30*(6), 656–680. doi:10.1108/14684520610716153

Dillon, A. (1999). TIME - A multi-leveled framework for evaluating and designing digital libraries. *International Journal on Digital Libraries*, *2*(2/3), 170–177. doi:10.1007/s007990050045

Eliasen, K., McKinstry, J., & Fraser, B. M. (1997). Navigating online menus: A quantitative experiment. *College & Research Libraries, 58*, 509–516.

Fuhr, N., Hansen, P., Mabe, M., Micsik, A., & Sølvberg, I. (2001). Digital libraries: A generic classification and evaluation scheme. *Lecture Notes in Computer Science, 2163*, 187–199. doi:10.1007/3-540-44796-2_17

Fuhr, N., Tsakonas, G., Aalberg, T., Agosti, M., Hansen, P., & Kapidakis, S. (2007). Evaluation of digital libraries. *International Journal on Digital Libraries, 8*, 21–38. doi:10.1007/s00799-007-0011-z

Greenstein, D. (2000). Digital libraries and their challenges. *Library Trends, 49*(2), 290–303.

Hammill, S. (2003). Usability testing at Florida international university libraries: What we learned. *Electronic Journal of Academic and Special Librarianship, 4*(1).

Hill, L. L., Dolin, R., Frew, J., Kemp, R. B., Larsgaard, M., & Montello, D. R. Simpson, J. (1997). User evaluation: Summary of the methodologies and results for the Alexandria digital library, University of California at Santa Barbara. In *Proceedings of 60th ASIST Annual Meeting*, (pp. 225-243, 369). Medford, NJ: Information Today.

International Standard Organization. (1997). *ISO 9241-11: Ergonomic requirements for office work with visual display terminals (VDTs), Part 11: Guidance on usability specification and measures. Technical Report*. Geneva, Switzerland: International Standard Organization.

Jeng, J. (2006). *Usability of the digital library: An evaluation model*. (Unpublished Doctoral Dissertation). Rutgers University. Hoboken, NJ.

Joo, S., & Lee, J. (2011). Measuring the usability of academic digital libraries: Instrument development and validation. *The Electronic Library, 29*(4), 523–537. doi:10.1108/02640471111156777

Kaplan, B., & Shaw, N. T. (2004). People, organizational, and social issues: Future directions in evaluation research. *Methods of Information in Medicine, 43*, 215–231.

Kengeri, R., Seals, C. D., Reddy, H. P., Harley, H. D., & Fox, E. A. (1999). Usability study of digital libraries: ACM, IEEE-CS, NCSTRL, and NDLTD. *International Journal on Digital Libraries, 2*(2/3), 157–169. doi:10.1007/s007990050044

Kenney, A. R., Sharpe, L. H., & Berger, B. (1998). Illustrated book study: Digital conversion requirements of printed illustration. In C. Nikolaou & C. Stephanidis (Eds.), *Research and Advanced Technology for Digital Libraries: Proceedings of the Second European Conference,* (pp. 279-293). Berlin, Germany: Springer.

Kim, Y. H., & Kim, H. H. (2008). Development and validation of evaluation indicators for a consortium of institutional repositories: A case study of collection. *Journal of the American Society for Information Science and Technology, 59*(8), 1282–1294. doi:10.1002/asi.20818

Kyrillidou, M., & Giersch, S. (2005). Developing the DigiQUAL protocol for digital library evaluation. In M. Marlino, T. Summer, & F. Shipman (Eds.), *Proceedings of the Fifth ACM/IEEE-CS Joint Conference on Digital Libraries,* (pp. 172-173). New York, NY: ACM Press.

Larsen, L. (2002). The DLib test suite and metrics working group: Harvesting the experience from the digital library initiative. *D-Lib Working Group on Digital Library Metrics Website*. Retrieved from http://www.dlib.org/metrics/public/papers/The_Dlib_Test_Suite_and_Metrics.pdf

Marchionini, G. (2000). Evaluating digital libraries: A longitudinal and multifaceted view. *Library Trends*, *49*(2), 304–333.

Matusiak, K. K. (2010). Use of digital resources in an academic environment: A qualitative study of students' perceptions, experiences, and digital literacy skills. (Unpublished Dissertation). University of Wisconsin – Milwaukee. Milwaukee, WI.

McNicol, S. (2004). The eVALUEd toolkit: A framework for the qualitative evaluation of electronic information services. *Vine*, *34*(4), 172–175. doi:10.1108/03055720410570957

Missingham, R. (2003). *What makes libraries relevant in the 21st century? Measuring digital collections from three perspectives. information online conference*. Retrieved from http://www.nla.gov.au/nla/staffpaper/2003/missingham2.html

Nicholson, S. (2004). A conceptual framework for the holistic measurement and cumulative evaluation of library services. *The Journal of Documentation*, *60*(2), 164–182. doi:10.1108/00220410410522043

NINCH. (2002). *The NINCH guide to good practice in the digital representation and management of cultural heritage materials*. Retrieved from http://www.nyu.edu/its/humanities/ninchguide/

NISO Framework Advisory Group. (2007). *A framework of guidance for building good digital collections* (3rd Ed.). Retrieved from http://www.niso.org/publications/rp/framework3.pdf

Noh, Y. (2010). A study on developing evaluation criteria for electronic resources in evaluation indicators of libraries. *Journal of Academic Librarianship*, *36*(1), 41–52. doi:10.1016/j.acalib.2009.11.005

Patton, M. Q. (2001). *Qualitative research and evaluation methods*. Thousand Oaks, CA: Sage Publications.

Pesch, O. (2007). Usage statistics: About COUNTER and SUSHI. *Information Services & Use*, *27*(4), 207–213.

Saracevic, T. (1995). *Evaluation of evaluation in information retrieval*. Paper Presented at the SIGIR 1995. Seattle, CA.

Saracevic, T. (2004). *Evaluation of digital libraries: An overview*. Paper presented at the DELOS Workshop on the Evaluation of Digital Libraries. Retrieved from http://www.scils.rutgers.edu/~tefko/DL_evaluation_Delos.pdf

Saracevic, T., & Covi, L. (2000). Challenges for digital library evaluation. In D. H. Kraft (Ed.), *ASIS 2000: Proceedings of the 63rd ASIS Annual Meeting*, (Vol. 37, pp. 341-350). Medford, NJ: Information Today.

Shim, W., & Kantor, P. (1999). Evaluation of digital libraries: A DEA approach. In *Proceedings of the 62nd ASIST Annual Meating*, (pp. 605-615). ASIST.

Smeaton, A., & Over, A. (2002). The TREC-2002 video track report. In E. M. Voorhees & D. K. Harman (Eds.), *The Eleventh Text REtrieval Conference* (TREC 2002). TREC.

Strauss, A., & Corbin, J. (1990). *Basics of qualitative research: Grounded theory procedures and techniques*. Newbury Park, CA: Sage Publications.

Sumner, T., & Marlino, M. (2004). Digital libraries and educational practice: A case for new models. In *Proceedings of the 2004 Joint ACM/IEEE Conference on Digital Libraries (JCDL 2004)*, (pp. 170-178). ACM/IEEE.

Tsakonas, G., Kapidakis, S., & Papatheodorou, C. (2004). Evaluation of user interaction in digital libraries. In M. Agosti & N. Fuhr (Eds.), *Notes of the DELOS WP7 Workshop on the Evaluation of Digital Libraries*. Padua, Italy: Academic Press.

Van House. N., Weil, B., & McClure, C. (1990). *Measuring academic library performance: A practical approach*. Chicago, IL: American Library Association.

Van House. N. A., Butler, M. H., Ogle, V., & Schiff, L. (1996). User-centered iterative design for digital libraries: The Cypress experience. *D-Lib Magazine, 2*. Retrieved from http://www.dlib.org/dlib/february96/02vanhouse.html

Ward, J. L., & Hiller, S. (2005). Usability testing, interface design, and portals. *Journal of Library Administration*, *43*(1), 155–171. doi:10.1300/J111v43n01_10

Xie, H. (2008). Users' evaluation of digital libraries (DLs): Their uses, their criteria, and their assessment. *Information Processing & Management*, *44*(3), 1346–1373. doi:10.1016/j.ipm.2007.10.003

Xie, I. (2006). Evaluation of digital libraries: Criteria and problems from users' perspectives. *Library & Information Science Research*, *28*(3), 433–452. doi:10.1016/j.lisr.2006.06.002

Xie, I., & Wolfram, D. (2002). State digital library usability: Contributing organizational factors. *Journal of the American Society for Information Science and Technology*, *53*(13), 1085–1097. doi:10.1002/asi.10152

Zhang, Y. (2010). Developing a holistic model for digital library evaluation. *Journal of the American Society for Information Science and Technology*, *61*(1), 88–110. doi:10.1002/asi.21220

ADDITIONAL READING

Baker, S., & Lancaster, F. W. (1991). *The measurement and evaluation of library services* (2nd ed.). Arlington, VA: Information Resources Press. doi:10.2307/40323203

Bearman, D. (2007). Digital libraries. *Annual Review of Information Science & Technology*, *41*, 223–263. doi:10.1002/aris.2007.1440410112

Bertot, J. C., Snead, J. T., Jaeger, P. T., & McClure, C. R. (2006). Functionality, usability, and accessibility: Iterative user-centered evaluation strategies for digital libraries. *Performance Measurement and Metrics*, *7*(1), 17–28. doi:10.1108/14678040610654828

Bishop, A. P. (1995). Working towards an understanding of digital library use: A report on the user research efforts of the NSF/ARPA/NASA DLI Projects. *D-Lib Magazine*. Retrieved from http://www.dlib.org/dlib/october95/10bishop.html

Bollen, J., & Luce, R. (2002). Evaluation of digital library impact and user communities by analysis of usage patterns. *D-Lib Magazine*, *8*(6). Retrieved from http://www.dlib.org/dlib/june02/bollen/06bollen.html doi:10.1045/june2002-bollen

Borgman, C. L., Gilliland-Swetland, A. J., Leazer, G. H., Mayer, R., Gwynn, D., Gazan, R., & Mautone, P. (2000). Evaluating digital libraries for teaching and learning in undergraduate education: A case study of the Alexandria digital earth prototype (ADEPT). *Library Trends*, *49*(2), 228–250.

Borlund, P. (2003). The IIR evaluation model: A framework for evaluation of interactive information retrieval systems. *Information Research*, *8*(3). Retrieved from http://informationr.net/ir/8-3/paper152.html

Brantley, P. (2008). Roles and expectations for DIGITAL libraries. *EDUCAUSE Review*, *43*(2), 30–38.

Brophy, P. (2006). *Measuring library performance: Principles and techniques*. London, UK: Facet Publishing.

Brophy, P., & Wynne, P. M. (1997). *Management information systems and performance measurement for the electronic library (MIEL2)*. Retrieved from http://www.ukoln.ac.uk/services/elib/papers/supporting/pdf/mis.pdf

Buchanan, S. (2009). Evaluating the usability and usefulness of a digital library. *Library Review*, *58*(9), 638–651. doi:10.1108/00242530910997928

Candela, L. (2007). Setting the foundations of digital libraries: The DELOS manifesto. *D-Lib Magazine*, *13*(3/4). Retrieved from http://www.dlib.org/dlib/march07/castelli/03castelli.html

Chowdhury, G. G., & Chowdhury, S. (2003). *Introduction to digital libraries*. London, UK: Facet Publishing.

Chowdhury, S., Landoni, M., & Gibb, F. (2006). Usability and impact of digital libraries: A review. *Online Information Review*, *30*(6), 656–680. doi:10.1108/14684520610716153

Comeaux, D. J. (2008). Usability studies and user-centered design in digital libraries. *Journal of Web Librarianship*, *2*(2), 457–475. doi:10.1080/19322900802190696

Cook, C., & Heath, F. (2001). Users' perceptions of library service quality: A LibQUAL+ qualitative study. *Library Trends*, *49*(4), 548–584.

Cullen, R. (2001). Perspectives on user satisfaction survey. *Library Trends*, *49*(4), 662–686.

Foo, S., Goh, D., & Na, J.-C. (2009). *Handbook of research on digital libraries: Design, development, and impact*. Hersey, PA: IGI Global.

Fox, E., & Marchionini, G. (2001). Digital libraries. *Communications of the ACM*, *44*(5), 31–32. doi:10.1145/374308.374329

Jeng, J. (2005). Usability assessment of academic digital libraries: Effectiveness, efficiency, satisfaction, and learnability. *Libri*, *55*, 96–121. doi:10.1515/LIBR.2005.96

Kani-Zabihi, E., Ghinea, G., & Chen, S. Y. (2006). Digital libraries: What do users want? *Online Information Review*, *30*(4), 396–412. doi:10.1108/14684520610686292

Kresh, D. (2007). *The whole digital library handbook*. Chicago, IL: American Library Association.

Landon, G. V. (2009). Toward digitizing all forms of documentation. *D-Lib Magazine*, *15*(3). Retrieved from http://webdoc.sub.gwdg.de/edoc/aw/d-lib/dlib/march09/landon/03landon.html doi:10.1045/march2009-landon

Lesk, M. (2004). *Understanding digital libraries*. Amsterdam, The Netherlands: Morgan-Kaufmann.

Long, H., Lage, K., & Cronin, C. (2005). The flight plan of a digital initiatives project, part 2: Usability testing in the context of user-centered design. *OCLC Systems & Services*, *21*(4), 324–345. doi:10.1108/10650750510631703

Morse, E. L. (2002). Evaluation methodologies for information management systems. *D-Lib Magazines, 8*(9). Retrieved from http://www.dlib.org/dlib/september02/morse/09morse.html

Nielson, J. (1993). *Usability engineering*. Cambridge, UK: Academic Press.

Norlin, E., & Winters, C. M. (2002). *Usability testing for library web sites*. Chicago, IL: ALA.

Reeve, T., Apedoe, X., & Woo, Y. H. (2003). Evaluating digital libraries: A user-friendly guide. *Digital Library of Information Science & Technology*. Retrieved from http://www.dpc.ucar.edu/projects/evalbook/EvaluatingDigitalLibraries.pdf

Ross, S. (2007). *Digital preservation, archival science and methodological foundations for digital libraries*. Keynote address at the 11th European Conference on Digital Libraries (ECDL). Budapest, Hungary. Retrieved from http://www.ecdl2007.org/Keynote_ECDL2007_SROSS.pdf

Scriven, M. (1991). *Evaluation thesaurus* (4th ed.). Newbury Park, CA: Sage Publications.

Tsakonas, G., & Papatheodorou, C. (2009). *Evaluation of digital libraries: An insight into useful applications and methods*. Oxford, UK: Chandos Publishing.

Van House. N. A., Butler, M. H., Ogle, V., & Schiff, L. (1996). User-centered iterative design for digital libraries: The Cypress experience. *D-Lib Magazine, 2*. Retrieved from http://www.dlib.org/dlib/february96/02vanhouse.html

Witten, I. H., Bainbridge, D., & Nichols, D. M. (2010). *How to build a digital library*. Amsterdam, The Netherlands: Morgan Kaufmann.

Xie, H., & Wolfram, D. (2002). State digital library usability: Contributing organizational factors. *Journal of the American Society for Information Science and Technology, 53*, 1085–1097. doi:10.1002/asi.10152

Xie, I. (2008). *Interactive information retrieval in digital environments*. Hershey, PA: IGI Global. doi:10.4018/978-1-59904-240-4

KEY TERMS AND DEFINITIONS

Digital Libraries: "Digital Libraries (DLs) are defined as representations of emergent and complex forms of digital information organization and design, consisting of multiple layers and building blocks, in various stages of development. DLs present a variety of resources created in the digital format as well as those converted from analog materials through digitization efforts, including print materials, manuscripts, images, audio, and video" (Matusiak, 2010, p. 15).

Digital Library Evaluation Framework: Digital library evaluation framework refers to a comprehensive evaluation structure that includes evaluation constructs, criteria, and measures to assess multiple aspects of digital libraries.

Evaluation: "Evaluation means assessing performances or value of system, process, product, or policy" (Saracevic, 1995, p. 138).

Evaluation Construct: Evaluation construct refers to a major concept or a dimension of digital libraries identified in the evaluation framework.

Evaluation Criterion: Evaluation criterion refers to a specific standard or benchmark, associated with an evaluation construct of digital libraries, on which a judgment or decision is based.

Chapter 9
Building for Success?
Evaluating Digital Libraries in the Cultural Heritage Domain

Vivien Petras
Humboldt-Universität zu Berlin, Germany

Juliane Stiller
Humboldt-Universität zu Berlin, Germany

Maria Gäde
Humboldt-Universität zu Berlin, Germany

ABSTRACT

In the cultural heritage field, heterogeneous materials and multicultural, multilingual user groups and their varying needs pose a challenge for information system design and its evaluation alike. Cultural heritage information systems can be evaluated from a system-centric or a user-centric perspective. This chapter discusses evaluation methods in digital libraries with a particular focus on cultural heritage collections and their distinctive features, interaction patterns, and challenges. It describes state-of-the-art evaluation methods illustrating them with examples from Europeana, the European portal for access to digital library, museum, and archive collections, and other projects from within the cultural heritage domain.

INTRODUCTION

The announcement of Google to digitize several big university library collections in 2005 triggered a movement in Europe to create a counter balance to the commercializing of cultural heritage. The idea of Europeana, the European portal for access to digital library, museum, and archive collections was born (Purday, 2009). Since 2009, this European cultural heritage portal provides a single access point to digital and digitized content collected by galleries, libraries, (audiovisual) archives, and museums. The content providers differ in scope, reach, and in user groups they

DOI: 10.4018/978-1-4666-2991-2.ch009

serve. Users differ in culture, language, access, and interaction requirements (Cousins, 2006). Bridging the gap between these different contexts and requirements is one of the biggest challenges for digital libraries. Evaluating these efforts and assessing when a library is "successful" is equally demanding.

Heterogeneous materials and their descriptions, multicultural and multilingual user groups and their varying needs pose a challenge for information system design and its evaluation alike. Traditional and innovative patterns (search, browse, comment) for user-system interactions cater to different user goals. Different approaches for testing the functionality and quality of individual system features, with respect to both the target audience and the target results, are necessary. Cultural heritage information systems (like all digital libraries) can be evaluated from a system-centric or a user-centric perspective. System-centric approaches have a long-standing tradition in information retrieval research and provide comparable quantitative measures for search effectiveness. However, their results are based on fixed assumptions about user-system interactions. User-centric approaches are more flexible in their assumptions. Commonly qualitative in nature, they provide deeper insights into user motivations and problems, but are also more labor-intensive and do not necessarily provide representative or comparable results for system evaluation. Some new system functionalities like personalization or collaborative features do not fit traditional use cases or evaluation set-ups. Similar to the design or implementation challenges for these features (e.g. user interface design, privacy, or data quality issues), new evaluation methods need to be developed and tested.

This chapter discusses evaluation methods in digital libraries with a particular focus on cultural heritage collections and their distinctive features and challenges. It describes state-of-the-art evaluation methods illustrating them with examples from Europeana and other projects from within the field. The chapter is organized as follows: the first section introduces general conceptual frameworks for evaluating digital library systems. The next section describes cultural heritage information systems, common system components and interaction patterns and their particular challenges. Four case study projects in the cultural heritage domain are introduced. The next sections describe first system-centric, then user-centric evaluation approaches and experimental set-ups from these case studies. The chapter concludes by discussing the challenges arising from innovative system features and interaction patterns and constraints posed by methods and project administration.

FRAMEWORKS FOR EVALUATING DIGITAL LIBRARY SYSTEMS

All evaluation efforts and experiments have to make decisions with respect to the evaluation object (elements/components to be evaluated), the evaluation aims and objectives, the evaluation context (viewpoint/framework for evaluation), the evaluation criteria and measures, and the evaluation methodology (for data collection and analysis) (Saracevic, 2000). In the research literature, reports on practical implementations of systems and their subsequent evaluations have been accompanied by discussions about general concepts, models, and frameworks that summarize work on a more theoretical level. Some of these general frameworks are described here.

Saracevic (2000, 2004) distinguishes seven approaches for digital library evaluation that address different goals or aspects:

- **The Systems-Centered Approach:** Performance, effectiveness, and efficiency.
- **The Human-Centered Approach:** Behavior, information needs, and requirements.

- **The Usability-Centered Approach:** Feature assessments, portals, mix between system- and human-centered approach.
- **The Ethnographic:** Approach: Culture and community.
- **The Anthropological Approach:** Stakeholders.
- **The Sociological Approach:** Situated actions and social settings of user communities.
- **The Economic Approach:** Costs, benefits, economic values, impacts.

Systems-centered and human-centered evaluation efforts and initiatives can be further distinguished on different levels (Saracevic, 2000). Systems-centered evaluation focuses on engineering (e.g. hardware), processing (e.g. operations), or content aspects (e.g. selection), while human-centered evaluation focuses on community, institutional or individual needs and objectives. Both systems- and human-centered evaluation also consider the interface and interactions that the system affords the users, e.g. access, search, or navigation.

Developed for a more general library evaluation, Nicholson's (2004) holistic model posits a matrix with four quadrants, which can be considered as evaluation approaches: the internal view of the library system (compliance with standards), the external (user) view of the library system (usability), the internal (library) view of use (system interactions), and the external view of use (changing knowledge states, citations).

The DELOS evaluation framework (Fuhr, et al., 2001, 2007) distinguishes three approaches (similar to Saracevic's first three): system evaluation, comprising off-line (information retrieval evaluation campaigns) and online evaluation (performance); usefulness evaluation, comprising user studies, information behavior and content-related studies and usability evaluation, including user interface related studies, task and context-oriented studies and usage studies.

Whereas Saracevic emphasizes different disciplinary approaches, Vullo (2010) describes evaluation models based on digital library components. According to her, the following types of evaluation can be distinguished:

- **The Content-Based Approach:** Data and metadata.
- **The Technical-Based Approach:** Software systems.
- **The Service-Based Approach:** Benefits.
- **The User-Based Approach:** Personal, social environments.

Xie (2008) summarizes the most often used and agreed upon evaluation criteria as system performance, collection value and interface usability. The commonly agreed DL evaluation criteria and variables are related to the usability of the interface, the value of the collection, and the system performance.

While not utilizing a particular framework per se, this chapter summarizes efforts from the two approaches, which are most prevalent in practice and occur—in different forms—in all of the cited frameworks: system-centric evaluation and user-centric evaluation. These approaches focus on system performance and effectiveness on one side and on usability and user satisfaction on the other side without claiming priority or exclusiveness. Rather, they work best in combination, which the chosen case studies will demonstrate.

Cultural Heritage Information Systems

Cultural heritage, as distinguished from natural heritage, consists of objects created by, or given meaning by, human activity. [...] In other words, things become part of cultural heritage by virtue of a human action, situated not just in time and place but, indeed, in a particular human cultural context (Bearman & Trant, 2002).

Collections of cultural heritage objects—preserved by archives, libraries, museums, and other institutions—constitute *"sites and monuments relating to natural history, ethnography, archaeology, historic monuments, as well as collections of fine and applied arts"* (International Council of Museums, 2003). Cultural heritage information systems collect, store, preserve, organize, search and display cultural heritage objects or their (metadata) representations in a digital environment. Large-scale digitization efforts in the cultural heritage domain have copied or portrayed physical objects so that they can be preserved and made available to a larger audience in a Web context. Cultural heritage information systems do not only provide access to these digitized or digital objects but also give additional information about them, in terms of *"who, where, why, how, when; and what was created, collected, discovered, described, published, and exhibited"* (Bearman & Trant, 2002).

General quality principles that cultural heritage information systems must adhere to are transparency, effectiveness, maintenance, access, user-centeredness, responsiveness, multilingualism, interoperability, management and long-term preservation (Minerva Working Group 5, 2005).

Users and Content

Cultural heritage information systems share many functions and features with information systems in other domains, however, some characteristics are particular for this domain, such as user groups, media types, and multicultural and multilingual issues.

Because of the heterogeneity of cultural heritage institutions and their objectives, it is difficult to generalize user groups into a single or even representative user typology. User types are characterized by their primary interests within the cultural heritage domain they are operating in:

- **General Users:** Interested in culture, the "informed citizen".
- **Cultural Heritage Professionals:** Content producers, collection managers.
- **Educational Users:** Researchers, teachers, students.
- **Tourist Users:** Travelers, tourist agencies, information centers.

Each user group has different skills and preferences concerning system functionalities, in particular with respect to how information should be organized, presented, and made searchable.

Cultural objects appear in many different physical forms, such as books, journals, manuscripts, letters, photographs, paintings, drawings, sculptures, buildings, music scores, music tapes, video tapes, etc. However, this multitude of object types in cultural heritage institutions is represented by just four basic media types in the digital environment: text, image, sound, and video. This does not lessen the heterogeneity of objects, just the modes of access and search available for the content. Cultural heritage information systems combine these various media types in one system and enable cross-media and object type access to this multimedia content.

Objects of any media type are described using metadata that serve as textual surrogates for the actual objects (and can then be retrieved by a text-based information retrieval algorithm). Few information systems already implement content-based retrieval algorithms (i.e. search methods that enable the searching of actual image, video, or sound features). The diversity of objects entails a variety of metadata models and standards that are applied to describe them. The aggregation and combination of differently described objects poses difficulties for information systems and can have an impact on the description power of the aggregated objects (the metadata model is commonly a much simpler model that unifies and stratifies more detailed models) and on the offered search and browsing access points. The metadata object descriptions can also contain representative views of an object, e.g. thumbnails. If a cultural heritage information system does not only provide information about objects but full access to the digital documents, the system also needs to supply software tools to open and view these documents. Tools or applications for viewing, listening or even manipulating the retrieved documents in any of the media types need to be part of the system as well.

Because of their content, cultural heritage information systems face particular challenges in balancing cultural perspectives and multilingual data in order to respect both users' and producers' sensibilities. Cultural heritage objects mirror the features of historical and contemporary societies. They carry many different cultural meanings—no matter whether they are of local, regional, national, or international importance. With cultural heritage spanning historical periods and regions and representing different societal, political, and religious aspects, the preservation issue is not only an object description issue, but also a user interaction and interface challenge.

The multilingual and multicultural background of the users of the information systems needs to be taken into account as well. If the objects organized in a cultural heritage information system are not textual themselves, their visual or audio features can be interpreted by users speaking different languages. It is therefore particularly important to overcome language barriers in the metadata descriptions (metadata descriptions are usually in the native language of the institutions providing them) so that users can find them regardless of the query or metadata language.

System Components and Interaction Patterns

According to Saracevic (2000), 21 elements or constructs of digital library systems could be individually evaluated. Instead of just enumerating this list, we will organize these constructs into three groups:

- **Content and Internal Organization:** Collections, resources, selection, gathering, holdings, organization, structure, and storage.
- **Management and Maintenance:** Availability, preservation, persistence, security, privacy, policies, legal aspects, licenses, operations, staff, costs, and economics.
- **User Access and Interaction:** Communities, links, interpretation, representation, metadata, access, interfaces, search, and services.

A simpler categorization of system components names the users, resources, the collections and services and tools (including interaction patterns) as components (Budhu & Coleman, 2002). Zhang's (2010) evaluation dimensions summarize six digital library components: content, technology, interface, service, users, and context. The DELOS working group (Fuhr, et al., 2001) distinguishes five aspects adding task and situational factors to the mix: the system and its components, interface and interactions, access and usage strategies, work tasks, and situational and contextual factors (organizational, social).

The content and collection structure and their usage of digital libraries have already been widely evaluated in traditional, physical library settings. Management and maintenance factors are discussed in organizational and legal research, which will not be reported here. This chapter focuses on system performance, user information access and interaction patterns and those approaches and methods that specialize in evaluating user-system interaction and the accompanying system features and functionalities.

Interaction patterns describe typical user actions or user information access capabilities in an information system. They can be mixed and matched variously thus representing a sequence of user interactions with an information system, i.e. a scenario. Interaction patterns constitute the basic units of use cases (Cockburn, 2001).

In cultural heritage information systems, we distinguish three essential information access or interaction patterns:

- **Search:** All interactions where users actively input a query to the system.
- **Explore and Discover:** All interactions where users navigate through the content (explore) or get information about the cultural heritage information system (discover).
- **Engage:** All interactions where users contribute content to the cultural heritage information system.

These interaction patterns do not represent clearly separated and isolated use case scenarios, but should be understood as components, which complement and alternate with each other to represent possible sequences of user interactions within a cultural heritage information system. Each interaction pattern can be differentiated by different facets or perspectives.

When using search options, the goals of the users range from finding a particular item, to finding information about a topic, or verifying the availability or existence of an object. Search scenarios involve input from the user, either by entering a query or other forms of search requests. Users of cultural heritage information systems commonly search for themes or subjects (e.g. Renaissance music), but the most often occurring search type is known-item search for a particular named entity, e.g. Eiffel tower. Another query category specific to cultural heritage information systems is the work or uniform title of a work or object, e.g. Mona Lisa, Romeo and Juliet (Stiller, et al., 2010). Since many objects are non-textual, content-based information retrieval methods are increasingly considered and implemented (Lew, et al., 2006). As is common in almost all information systems, simple search interfaces are the first access option for users, however, they are also often combined with at least one explore option.

When choosing an explore and discover interaction, users would like to fulfill a general information need by navigating, to be guided through a cultural heritage collection, or to find background information about the website or the information system. During explore and discover sequences, users might have a general information need but are not able to translate it to a specific query and thus want to navigate the system without having to input specific terms. Exploring offers multiple ways for accessing a cultural heritage collection—mostly in a topical or thematic way—and is characterized by clicking through a graphical interface. Discovering subsumes all other information categories that a cultural heritage system might provide in order to help the user navigate it. Since cultural heritage information systems contain a variety of objects, a faceted exploration or browsing interface is usually provided. Typical entities or facets offered are people, institutions, countries, subjects, media types, periods, publication dates, languages, and collections (Dekkers, et al., 2009; Fresa, 2005; Trojahn & Siciliano, 2009). Cultural heritage objects are most often described and approached through time and place categorizations—consequently, cultural heritage information systems need to offer discovery options for at least those aspects.

As a substantial part of the Web 2.0 movement, users of digital library systems are given the opportunity to contribute or edit content or engage with the system in other innovative ways (Cahill, 2009). Engage functionalities empower the user and create new virtual communities through collaborative interactions and sharing. When entering an engage interaction, users typically have the goals to improve personal information management by creating individual virtual collections for refinding, to entertain themselves, to share objects and opinions with a larger community, and to enrich and enhance the content of a cultural heritage information system. Engagement patterns usually require additional system functionalities for user management and content contributions. If user-generated content in whatever form (ratings, comments, tags, or new objects) is added to the system, questions of quality, authority and original metadata preservation become crucial. Many cultural heritage information systems now offer engage interaction functionalities. The Städel Museum (www.staedelmuseum.de) offers a rating feature; the Google Art Project (www.googleart-project.com) offers commenting facilities, and the Steve project (www.steve.museum) social tagging. Open Images (www.openbeelden.nl) and the Athenaeum (www.the-athenaeum.org) enable users to contribute their own content. Cultural heritage information systems often seek user support in identifying and describing unknown objects and provide interactions features that allow users to add new information or even upload new digital objects that will substantiate, complete or extend other objects or the collection.

Traditional system-centered evaluation focused on quantitative measures for effectiveness of search interactions (information retrieval tests where success is measured as finding relevant documents). Several cultural heritage systems have served as test cases. Explore and discover interactions have been evaluated as part of usability or user satisfaction studies, usually with a perspective on the effectiveness of the user interface. However, engage interaction patterns have not been evaluated much at all, partly due to their newness in information systems, partly because traditional evaluation criteria do not account for their particular features.

Four Case Studies: EUROPEANA, The European Library, Multimatch, and CACAO

Four case study projects developing cultural heritage information systems and their subsequent evaluation efforts will be looked at in detail. Following is a brief overview of the projects.

The Europeana portal (www.europeana.eu) is the single access point for digital objects from Europe's cultural institutions such as libraries, audio-visual archives, museums, and archives. Europeana with its partnering projects is one of the biggest initiatives in collectively offering universal access to digitized cultural heritage material in Europe and worldwide. It serves as an example for successfully unifying institutions from different countries and different scope (more than 1500 partners) in order to build a huge digital library for cultural heritage content—as of August 2011, 19 million objects are searchable. Europeana serves a wide user base from academic researchers to the general public and needs to fulfill the requirements of all these specific groups. Serving users in 28 interface languages, Europeana offers many search and browsing options for access (See Figure 1). Search results are either displayed as a table, list or on a timeline and can be refined or filtered by facets like language, country, date, provider and type. Europeana also offers virtual exhibitions. The ongoing development and improvement of semantic and multilingual features is supported by user studies and evaluation efforts targeted towards providing further insights into user behavior.

The European Library (www.theeuropeanlibrary.org) combines access to the content of 48 European national libraries. Besides bibliographic data (catalog records) and digital resources in 35 languages, TEL also offers virtual exhibitions to discover cultural heritage objects. The portal offers several access points either through searching or browsing. Generally, all national libraries' catalogs are searched; however, several themes such as "digital collections," "audio and printed music," "manuscripts," "children's literature," or "maps" can be selected for a more focused exploration. Browsing through the search results, users can directly access resources in their original settings, view bibliographic data or click on links to external services for further investigations (e.g. Google or Amazon). Launched in 2005, experiences in the development of TEL shaped the Europeana initiative (Janssen, 2007).

Figure 1. Europeana homepage and information access or interaction options

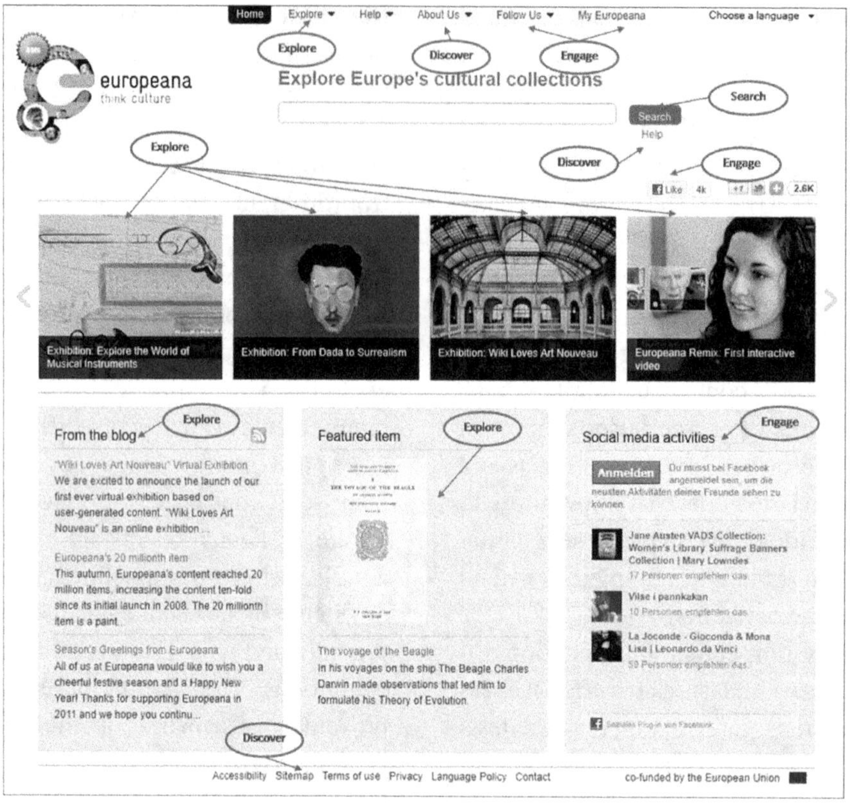

The CACAO project (www.cacaoproject.eu) built an infrastructure for cross-language access to library catalogs. Running from 2007 to 2009, the goal was to enable OPAC users to access content in different languages regardless of their query language. Natural language processing and information retrieval techniques were implemented for query and document translation (Bernardi, et al., 2009).

The Multimatch project (www.multimatch.eu) developed a search engine for multilingual and multimedia cultural heritage objects. The prototype provides free-text search matching the query language to the document languages by using machine translation and other natural language processing techniques. It also offers multimedia search and browsing functionalities for unified access to cultural materials in various forms such as video, text, and speech (Amato, et al., 2008).

SYSTEM-CENTRIC EVALUATION: INFORMATION RETRIEVAL EXPERIMENTS

System-centric evaluation of digital libraries and other information systems has been the most prevailing approach for measuring the quality of a system. System features are evaluated for their performance, output, effectiveness, and efficiency. Efficiency measures consider the engineering and processing aspects of a system (e.g. response time, storage space, uptime, or reliability). Laboratory information retrieval experiments measure the effectiveness of a search algorithm with respect to its availability to find relevant documents. Although the Cranfield paradigm (Cleverdon, 1997) dominates the experimental set-ups and has proven its value in system comparisons, different evaluation methodologies are increasingly sought.

While the laboratory setting ensures the control of the experimental design, it abstracts from real systems and posits fixed assumptions about use scenarios. The evaluation of operational systems and challenges with respect to the assumptions about user needs (stable), user-system interaction (single search input), and relevance (binary and objectively measurable) caused the development of new methods and new measures in recent years. Within the information retrieval community, a general call for more user engagement, more realistic search scenarios and the involvement of or combination with user-centric methods can be observed (Ingwersen & Järvelin, 2005).

Methods of Data Collection

The Cranfield experiments (Cleverdon, 1970) in the 1960s basically defined the experimental set-up for information retrieval evaluation for years to come. It is based on standardized test collections, queries, and provided relevance assessments for the queries. Evaluation measures the ranked results (outcome) of a search in the system. The TREC evaluation initiative and conference (Voorhees & Harman, 2005) has been the major outlet for research results in this area. Although the preparation of a standard collection of documents, the requisite number of test queries and relevance assessments of documents is a labor-intensive task, once these are prepared, the actual evaluation and comparison of systems is relatively effortless as quantitative measures can just be calculated. A major advantage of these information retrieval evaluation experiments are their reusability: once the set-up (collection, queries, assessments) is prepared, they can be used for as many rounds or experiments as necessary, enabling the standardized comparison of systems over a period of time. Often criticized for only offering a reduced, artificial insight into user-system interactions, many different search scenarios have been evaluated, dependent on collection genre (e.g. newspaper vs. patent search), collection size (e.g. Web search), or result type (e.g. routing, question-answering).

A second system-centric method for evaluation is collection- or service-related performance analysis based on logfile recordings. Logging of document ingestion rates (internal to the system), click-through rates (for full-text access) or download numbers do not express the quality of a system in itself, but can give some valuable insights into system usage in comparison with similar systems.

Measures and Metrics

Another advantage of laboratory information retrieval evaluation approaches is the multitude of quantifiable measures or metrics that have been introduced in the last 50 years. They make statistically significant comparisons between different information systems possible. Introduced during the Cranfield experiments, precision (how many documents in the result set are relevant) and recall (how many of the relevant documents are in the result set) are the most well known and used. Following, we distinguish five groups of metrics. A good overview and explanations of the example metrics can be found in Baeza-Yates and Ribeiro (2011) and Kelly (2009), a classification of their use in Demartini and Mizzaro (2006).

Measures based on precision and recall (e.g. F-measure, mean average precision MAP, geometric MAP, R-precision, precision@n) provide an overview about a system's general ability to retrieve relevant documents for a query. They are based on binary relevance assessments of the retrieved documents by trained professionals. Another group of measures focuses on the comparison of the analyzed system's performance and an ideal system's performance with respect to finding relevant documents (e.g. expected search length, average search length, sliding ratio). Since most information systems now offer a relevance-ranked result list of documents, users have adapted to expect the most relevant documents in the higher ranks and do not usually review many documents after the first result page. Therefore, measures with a stronger emphasis on the rank of a document (e.g. mean reciprocal rank MRR, ranked half-life, cumulated gain, and its variations) have become more popular, especially in Web search evaluations. To overcome assessor errors, assessor rating inconsistencies, constraints posed by binary relevance ratings or the assessments efforts (not all relevant documents might have been assessed), measures have been defined that extend the concept of binary relevance or take missing relevance ratings into account (e.g. binary preference BPREF, relative relevance, rank correlation measures, cumulated discounted gain). Finally, measures have been defined that directly involve actual user judgment of relevance and expectations (e.g. novelty ratio, coverage ratio, relative or sought recall, recall effort, interactive recall and precision, informativeness).

Application in the Cultural Heritage Domain

System-centric evaluation efforts are surprisingly rare in the cultural heritage domain. This is probably due to the fact that more attention is paid towards usability and user interface issues, as search is regarded as only one interaction pattern (and possibly not the most important one). The effectiveness and efficiency of the utilized (mostly out-of-the-box) information retrieval systems are often taken for granted and new systems rarely developed. Both TEL and Europeana use the open-source system Solr as their search solution, for example. However, supplemental system features are sometimes evaluated with these methods. Cultural heritage collections are also used in some of the information retrieval evaluation campaigns.

Cultural heritage collections are often used to evaluate the retrieval effectiveness with document types other than text. One example is the Holocaust witnesses interview collection by the Survivors of the Shoah Visual History Foundation, which was automatically transcribed by the MALACH project (Byrne, et al., 2004) and then used as a test collection for the 2005 cross-language speech retrieval track at CLEF (White, et al., 2006). The Eurovision project (Clough, et al., 2006) prepared a historic photographic collection from the St. Andrews University Library and used it for evaluation experiments (Clough & Sanderson, 2004a). The collection was also used for the ImageCLEF tracks in 2003 and 2004 (Clough & Sanderson, 2004b; Clough, et al., 2005). In later campaigns (ImageCLEF 2009-2011), an image collection comprised of Flickr images was used (Huiskes & Lew, 2008). The MediaEval Benchmarking initiative for multimedia evaluation has been assessing multimedia retrieval in different multimedia cultural heritage collections, for example video archives from the Netherlands Institute of Sound and Vision (Larson, et al., 2010). TREC Video 2001 and 2002 used a video collection with advertising, educational, industrial and amateur films from the 1930s-1970s from the Internet Archive and the Open Video Archive (Smeaton & Over, 2002). Experiments were continued within the TRECVid initiative (Smeaton, et al., 2006) using, among others, video archives from the Netherlands Institute of Sound and Vision, the BBC, and the Internet Archive in 2010 (Over, et al., 2009, 2010, 2011). The INEX Book track studied the retrieval of full texts of digitized books (Kazai & Doucet, 2007; Kazai, et al., 2010). It used book collections from Microsoft Live Search Books and the Internet Archive. In 2011, one planned task of the book track is dedicated to social search for best books using a collection from Amazon Books and LibraryThing.com. The INEX Multimedia track focused on the combination of text and image retrieval on data from the Lonely Planet Worldguide XML collection (van Zwol, et al., 2006). The Wikipedia image collection was also used (Westerveld & van Zwol, 2007; Tsikrika & Westerveld, 2008).

The European Library compiled catalog records from the Austrian, British and French national libraries and provided them for information retrieval experiments at the TEL@CLEF track in 2008 and 2009 (Agirre, et al., 2009; Ferro & Peters, 2010). The CACAO system and its translation components were evaluated with this collection (Bosca & Dini, 2009). Europeana worked with the multilingual TEL collections used at CLEF for the information retrieval evaluation of its query translation components. Another system-centric evaluation tested the semantic enrichment of documents with controlled vocabulary terms in a customized Europeana collection.

Multimatch evaluated individual components of its system with different collections and methodologies (Peters, et al., 2008). The query translation was tested with real queries taken from query logs of three cultural heritage websites, image and video search used the Corel image, and a TRECVid test collections and the speech search components were evaluated with a podcast collection.

All cited studies used a variation of the Cranfield methodology and usually several of the effectiveness metrics described above.

USER-CENTRIC EVALUATION: USABILITY AND USER SATISFACTION

User-centric evaluation approaches attempt to understand user motivations, user information needs and user behavior in information systems. Before and during development and implementation of a system, user studies typically determine typical characteristics of user groups envisioned to use the system. These user studies set the framework with respect to user requirements and desired functionalities and determine user opinions on features. After or during a system is implemented, usability studies investigate typical user behavior in a system and determine whether system functionalities work effectively for the user, the design of interfaces is appropriate for task completion and the system is easy to use. Large-scale audience surveys support information systems in determining overall opinions and perceptions of the system and do not only impact development and design of system features but also marketing and public relation efforts. Criticized for not being representative analyses, user-centric evaluation studies have increasingly employed rigid research designs and standardized methods to alleviate control and environmental issues. In comparison to system-centric evaluation efforts, user-centric evaluation studies provide a much deeper insight into user behavior and user-system interactions on an individual scale. For a single information system, a method mix of analyses is often applied.

Methods of Data Collection

All user-centric evaluation methods involve user interactions and engagement with the system directly. They differ in population size (ranging from very few to thousands of user opinions solicited), degree of interaction between observer or analyst and the user (ranging from direct interaction in an interview to indirect observation of patterns of user behavior in log files), and effort of data collection, opinion elicitation and intervention (ranging from invisible logging to direct intervention). As a general rule, more interactive, higher effort studies usually cover fewer subjects and are therefore more subjective and less representative. However, they also provide more detail and insight into user behavior. For a brief and concise overview of the most common methods and measures, Kelly (2009) is a good starting point.

We distinguish between three groups of user-centric evaluation methods. Methods that do not intervene with the user's interaction and observe user behavior through indirect representations (e.g. A/B testing, transaction or click-stream log file analysis) are able to study large parts or the whole user population over a predetermined period of time. Because they observe user behavior from a distance and through representations (logged systems actions), they cannot provide detailed insight into the how's and why's of user behavior. However, due to their coverage and relatively low effort implementation, they are popular tools for initial analyses and overviews of user-system interactions. Large-scale opinion polls, surveys and post-system interaction questionnaires enable the system developers and evaluators to ask direct questions of the user population. Due to their size, they provide a good overview of large parts of the population and can be analyzed with statistical tools. Usually short in duration, they do not intervene much with a user's interaction with the system. Since they are presented to many users automatically, questions have to be predetermined, standardized, understandable, and relatively simple. While they can solicit user opinions on look and feel of the system and some of the user motivations, the lack of direct interaction with the observer means that the potential for misunderstandings or miscommunication is higher. Because questions need to be able to cover the whole surveyed user population, detailed insights into specific user actions are not necessarily possible. Direct user studies (e.g. focus groups, interviews, task-based observations, think aloud protocols) provide the best insights into user behavior and motivation. They are usually targeted towards a small, carefully selected user sample and allow direct observation and intervention of all aspects of user behavior and motivations. Often based in a laboratory setting to control for disturbances, they might create an artificial environment, can be obtrusive (e.g. observation) and ask users to behave in a non-natural way (e.g. to think aloud while processing a task). Usually time-consuming and labor-intensive, these studies can elicit the most direct and most detailed user feedback and are the only methods, where miscommunication and misunderstanding can be avoided. However, careful preparation and selection of study method, questions, and user sample are required in order to avoid biases in the outcomes.

Measures and Metrics

In contrast to the many quantitative measures developed in system-centric evaluation efforts, user-centric evaluation does not use as many standardized measures, because the outcomes of the evaluation studies are not often quantifiable. User perceptions and opinions might be expressed on a scale from favorable to not favorable but it is difficult to state user satisfaction in comparison with other systems.

We distinguish between three groups of measures that are analyzed in user-centric evaluation studies. To describe the interactions of users with a system, there are frequency measures that can be used to give a general overview of the usage of a system (e.g. number of queries per search session, number of results viewed, number of documents saved). They do not provide a real understanding of the usefulness of the system for its users or their satisfaction of it, but they show broad patterns of interaction. The most common measures in user-centric evaluation attempt to describe the degree of usefulness or usability of a system. Ease of use measures how efficiently and how appropriately users are enabled to accomplish their tasks with a particular system. These measures are usually task-based. As a specific type of usability measures, concepts like ease of learning, mental effort or cognitive load analyze how much effort it takes a user to use and handle the system correctly or appropriately. Finally, measures like satisfaction or preference (when two or more systems are compared) provide an overview of user's attitudes, whereas new measures like flow or engagement (O'Brien, et al., 2008) attempt to measure aspects of the user experience like aesthetic appeal, interest, and affect.

Application in the Cultural Heritage Domain

Many projects in the cultural heritage domain use a plethora of methods in order to tease out user perceptions and user requirements of a system—both in the development and production phases. Usually, several rounds of evaluations are performed in order to test different prototypes or study changing user behavior and opinions. Earlier examples are Cornell University's Human-Computer Interaction Group's list of methods and discussion of challenges in user-centric evaluation, aggregated from five cultural heritage initiatives, including the Making of America project and the Global Digital Museum (Jones, et al., 1999) and Marchionini's description of the evaluation efforts for the Perseus Digital Library, which started with its inception in 1989 and included interviews, observations, document analysis, transaction log analysis and learning analysis (Marchionini, 2000).

General research on user needs or user behavior in the cultural heritage domain is rare (see Amin, et al., 2008, for an exception). Most of the time, the prototype or developed system is the basis for analysis (e.g. Marlow, et al., 2007). Following, the four case study projects CACAO, Multimatch, TEL, and Europeana and their evaluation efforts are described. Table 1 summarizes both system-centric and user-centric evaluation methods used in these four case studies.

Multimatch

Multimatch first conducted a detailed user requirements analysis where different user types were identified. They finished about a hundred interviews with domain experts in order to collect user needs. A brief log file analysis of two cultural heritage portals and a document analysis completed the requirements stage (Minelli, et al., 2006). Scenarios that describe typical user tasks were developed and representatives from cultural heritage institutions and consumers were aggregated in user groups. An evaluation plan for both user- and system-centric evaluation outlined all further steps (Multimatch, 2006a). The Multimatch site underwent a heuristic usability inspection by a usability expert. In the first stage of the project, users were shown mock-ups of the interface for evaluation. The final prototype was tested in field trials at three cultural heritage institutions (Multimatch, 2006b). Based on various scenario-based tasks, task completion ratios were measured. Other subjective measures gathered through questionnaires and face-to-face interviews related to the general user satisfaction (e.g. system complexity, speed, coverage of results, ease of use). Because the field trials were held in a controlled environment with predetermined tasks, a last user test was performed: a link to the Multimatch system was put on a cultural heritage portal when certain search criteria were fulfilled (e.g. query was cultural heritage-related). All user actions that started by clicking on this link were logged and analyzed for index coverage, query and result numbers as well as response times. The user-centric assessments were accompanied with a throughout information retrieval evaluation of the individual system components thus providing data about user satisfaction and system effectiveness.

CACAO

CACAO set clear validation aims for its evaluation efforts—both with respect to user satisfaction (goal: deduplication of parallel multilingual querying decreasing user frustration) and technical adequacy (goal: increased F-measure and translation coverage increasing system effectiveness). In order to measure user satisfaction, various methods were applied: (online) questionnaires and interviews to survey users about their general impressions, task-based observations to measure concrete system features and Web log analysis to unobtrusively observe interactions with the system. For the task-based tests and post-test interviews, typical use cases were defined (Bosca, et al., 2009a). The interface design of the system was tested with unsupervised and task-based tests, subsequent log file analysis and an expert review (Bernardi, et al., 2008). A second round of testing

Table 1. Cultural heritage information system case studies and their evaluation methods and criteria

Evaluation approach	Multimatch	CACAO	The European Library	Europeana
System-centric	Retrieval effectiveness experiments (several collections) Logfile analysis (response times, user, query, result numbers)	Retrieval effectiveness experiments within TEL@CLEF	TEL@CLEF track (provided test collections) Logfile analysis (user, query, result numbers)	Logfile analysis (user, query, result numbers)
User-centric	User requirements analysis (user types) Interviews (user needs) Document analysis Logfile analysis (user requirements) Scenario development Usability inspection Field trials: lab tests, questionnaires, interviews (user satisfaction)	Online question-naires Interviews Use case development Task-based observation (user satisfaction) Logfile analysis (user interactions) Usability review	Logfile analyses (user interaction, query categori-zation, user success) Questionnaires (user satisfaction)	Online surveys (user impressions) Focus groups Task-based lab tests (user satisfaction) Eye-tracking (user interaction, usability) Test panels (user satisfaction) Usability review Logfile analysis (user interaction, success) A/B testing (usability)

with task-based questionnaires was performed after the final prototype was completed (Bosca, et al., 2009b). CACAO also tested the technical effectiveness with standard information retrieval experiments using the TEL@CLEF collection and utilized TEL log file data in order to evaluate user-based translation strategies (Bosca & Dini, 2010)—an interesting combination of a user-centric tool used for system-centric evaluation.

The European Library (TEL)

TEL was built in a series of consecutive research projects adding and improving system components and functionality with each project. Each project was correlated with evaluation efforts, usually assessing particular system components or aspects. Due to obsolescence and disappearance of past project websites and documentation, an interesting problem is illustrated: a precise timeline and complete list of evaluation or assessments efforts for the than 10-year period since TEL's inception is difficult to impossible to compile. Log files were analyzed early in the project phases to identify usage habits and patterns in order to enhance the usability of the portal, to derive best practices for search interfaces and to be able to provide personalized services to the users (Angelaki, 2008). Later, TEL provided log files for investigation in the LogCLEF initiative aimed at analyzing and classifying queries as input for multilingual information systems (Mandl, et al., 2010a, 2010b). This released the data for analysis by different groups and different perspectives. Besides further log file analysis (Agosti, et al., 2009a), user studies at different national libraries and research institutions (mostly with questionnaires) complemented the analysis of users, their perceptions and system functionalities (Agosti, et al., 2008).

Europeana

Europeana, even more so than TEL, draws from a project cluster, the Europeana group (group.europeana.eu), to drive development and improvements of system functionalities. Most of its user-centric evaluation efforts are concentrated in two core projects (Europeana v1.0 and Europeana-Connect) and overseen and guided by the central Europeana office in The Hague, Netherlands and a "users" working group. Since the beginning of the projects in 2009, a number of activities ranging from large-scale online surveys gathering general opinions to focus groups, test panels, and log file analysis were undertaken. A Europeana personas catalog (Rasmussen, et al., 2009) and usability guidelines for conducting user tests (Guldbæk & Petersen, 2011) were developed and a user test panel was formed. Large online user surveys in 2009 and 2011, reaching an audience of 3200 and 5200 users respectively, provided user feedback on general questions such as user characteristics (profession, residency, language), usage frequencies, reasons for use and new features (IRN Research, 2009, 2011). A much smaller user survey gathered information on language preferences for interface and system interactions (Agosti, et al., 2009b). A website navigation review based on the Nielsen heuristics for usability testing was performed in 2009 (Saulnier & Viaud, 2009). A large scale user study comprising six focus groups in four countries and a media lab was tasked to provide detailed qualitative analyses of user behavior (based on predetermined tasks) (Dobreva & Chowdhury, 2010; Dobreva, et al., 2010). The task-based observations in the media labs also used eye tracking in order to get more detailed insights into user foci on the Europeana interface (Sykes, et al., 2010). More specific user testing was also done for particular components, for example, a task-based observation study with post-interaction questionnaires for the mobile interfaces. Another methodology used extensively for observing user interactions in Europeana is log file analysis. While server transaction logs are regularly analyzed, a click-stream logger with a particular focus on language-dependent interactions was also developed (Gäde, et al., 2010) and the query logs further analyzed for query term recommendation (Ceccarelli, et al., 2011). The development team also uses A/B testing software to assess the perception of specific interface elements online. A small user test panel of 17 selected users is used to gather first feedback on proposed changes in the interface or new system features. Setting up a permanent user test panel like this serves as the first instance to assess new development ideas and helps save efforts and costs in case of misguided development or evaluation set-ups. In 2011, a new Europeana version of the production system was released. Again, an expert heuristic evaluation and cognitive walkthroughs of paper prototypes were performed in order to assess the usability of the new prototype. This description of different assessment rounds and tests shows another issue in evaluation: as long as a system changes and is further developed, evaluation is also an ongoing effort. As user perceptions and audiences can change, even basic assumptions about user groups and associated information needs need to be questioned repeatedly.

CHALLENGES IN EVALUATION AND FUTURE RESEARCH

When evaluating an information system, both system-centric and user-centric evaluation approaches are necessary to be able to form a balanced view of the quality of the system. Applying appropriate evaluation methods presupposes expertise in different disciplinary research traditions. Interdisciplinary teams contributing their methods and tools have to be formed in order to plan overarching evaluation frameworks and execute them according to varying system development phases and changing institutional environments. A confounding factor of combining information retrieval effectiveness experiments with user studies is the discrepancies in outcomes and conclusions that can be observed when comparing results from these different methods. Several studies have found that user satisfaction does not necessarily correlate with system effectiveness as measured in a TREC-style evaluation (Hersh, et al., 2000; Turpin & Scholer, 2006). User might even change their behavior in order to accommodate bad retrieval results from a system (Smith & Kantor, 2008).

Many new measures have been developed in order to focus more on user needs and user perception of system effectiveness, however, a clear relation has not been determined (Mandl, 2008).

Other challenges and opportunities for further research in the evaluation of cultural heritage system can be grouped into:

- Challenges posed by innovative system features and non-traditional content,
- Challenges posed by unexpected user types and behavior,
- Challenges posed by evaluation methods, and
- Challenges posted by administrative and other project constraints.

Due to the diversity of material, the visual discovery options and flexible access requirements expected in cultural heritage information systems (Roffia, et al., 2011), functionalities such as time line and map-based browsing, virtual exhibitions and discovery through social features are equally important as searching in this context (Minerva Working Group 5, 2008). To determine the reach and scope of these functionalities, different and sometimes new evaluation methods have to be employed (see, for example, Trant, 2009).

Cultural heritage information systems attempt to fulfill the information needs from school children to serious academic researchers. A very common user type is the "tourist" or "information flaneur" (Dörk, et al., 2011), who approaches an information system out simple of curiosity and expects to be entertained or to explore an information space through serendipitous wandering. This does not fit the mold of traditional user types and consequently puts different requirements to the system. How the entertainment or serendipity value of a system can be determined, is a focus of future research.

Although many different and innovative information access options are now offered by systems that are more appropriate for the presentation of cultural heritage content, users find it difficult or sometimes inconvenient to learn or use them. Convenience (Connaway, et al., 2011) and user expectations shaped by Web search patterns (simple search boxes) also impact evaluation of system features and their outcomes.

The limitations of individual evaluation methods are well known and can be found in the literature. Two important considerations for evaluations in the cultural heritage domain are the availability and willingness of test subjects for user-centric studies and the difficulties to develop standard test collections and create relevance assessments for system-centric approaches. Due to the variety of users, finding a representative user sample is labor-intensive and time-consuming and—in the case of multicultural and multilingual cultural heritage systems—crosses country and language borders. An information tourist is, by its very nature, an ephemeral user type—gathering a group for usability testing is a difficult challenge. Traditional information retrieval test collections have been built over many years and often with institutional support (e.g. NIST for TREC). Building a cultural heritage collection often not only deals with many different content types, but also with many different rights owners. Clearing (rights) and cleaning (format) cultural heritage data for standard, comparative evaluation initiatives has been proven a complicated undertaking. Particular cases in point are log files, which pose privacy and data security issues (Agosti, et al., 2011).

A dynamically changing system environment (e.g. new prototype features, obsolescence of other system functionalities) requires permanent evaluation efforts. In a short-term project-based development landscape, cultural heritage information systems face challenges of constancy (in evaluation planning, overview and execution) and documentation. Valuable lessons are lost because projects are ended without proper documentation or publication of results or personal or even institutional responsibilities change. While this is not a phenomenon strictly limited to the cultural heritage domain, the varied environment and many innovative developments in user-system interactions and features merit a concentrated effort in bundling and exchanging experiences.

ACKNOWLEDGMENT

Work on this chapter was partly supported by PROMISE (Participative Research labOratory for Multimedia and Multilingual Information Systems Evaluation). Advancing the Evaluation and Benchmarking of Multimedia and Multilingual Information Systems. Network of Excellence co-funded by the 7th Framework Program of the European Commission, grant agreement no. 258191. We would like to thank Madlen Frieseke for research assistance.

REFERENCES

Agirre, E., Di Nunzio, G., Ferro, N., Mandl, T., & Peters, C. (2009). CLEF 2008: Ad hoc track overview. *Lecture Notes in Computer Science*, *5706*, 15–37. doi:10.1007/978-3-642-04447-2_2

Agosti, M., Bergamin, G., Crivellari, F., Nunzio, G. M. D., Ferro, N., Ioannidis, Y., et al. (2008). *D5.1: Report on user requirements of the target library services - TELplus project.* Retrieved August, 2011 from http://www.theeuropeanlibrary.org/portal/organisation/cooperation/telplus/documents/TELplus_D5.1_31122008.pdf

Agosti, M., Crivellari, F., Deambrosis, G., Ferro, N., Gäde, M., Petras, V., et al. (2009). *D2.1.1: Report on user preferences and information retrieval scenarios for multilingual access in Europeana - EuropeanaConnect-project.* Retrieved August, 2011 from http://www.europeanaconnect.eu/documents/D2.1.1_eConnect_Report_User_Preferences_MLIA_v1.0_20091222.zip

Agosti, M., Crivellari, F., & Di Nunzio, G. (2011). Web log analysis: a review of a decade of studies about information acquisition, inspection and interpretation of user interaction. *Data Mining and Knowledge Discovery*, *24*(3), 663–696. doi:10.1007/s10618-011-0228-8

Agosti, M., Crivellari, F., Di Nunzio, G. M., Ioannidis, Y., Stamatogiannakis, L., Triantafillidi, M.-L., & Vayanou, M. (2009a). *D5.2: Report on search engines and HTTP log analysis - TELplus project.* Retrieved August 2011 from http://www.theeuropeanlibrary.org/portal/organisation/cooperation/telplus/documents/TELplus_D5.2_15102009.pdf

Amato, G., Cigarrán, J., Gonzalo, J., Peters, C., & Savino, P. (2007). MultiMatch – Multilingual/multimedia access to cultural heritage. *Lecture Notes in Computer Science*, *4675*, 505–508. doi:10.1007/978-3-540-74851-9_53

Amin, A., Van Ossenbruggen, J., Hardman, L., & Van Nispen, A. (2008). Understanding cultural heritage experts' information seeking needs. In *Proceedings of the 8th ACM/IEEE-CS Joint Conference on Digital libraries, JCDL 2008,* (pp. 39-47). New York, NY: ACM Press.

Angelaki, G. (2008). *D1.2: Final report on usability developments in the European library - EDL project.* Retrieved August 2011 from http://www.theeuropeanlibrary.org/portal/organisation/cooperation/archive/edlproject/downloads/EDLprojectD1.2Rep_usage_usability.pdf

Baeza-Yates, R., & Ribeiro-Neto, B. (2011). *Modern information retrieval: The concepts and technology behind search* (2nd ed.). New York, NY: Addison Wesley.

Bearman, D., & Trant, J. (2002). *Issues in structuring knowledge and services for universal access to online science and culture.* Paper presented at the Nobel Symposium (NS 120): Virtual Museums and Public Understanding of Science and Culture. Retrieved August, 2011 from http://nobelprize.org/ nobel_organizations/nobelfoundation/symposia/interdisciplinary/ns120/lectures/bearman.pdf

Bernardi, R., Balestrieri, M., & Bosca, A. (2009). *CACAO system: An overview.* Paper presented at the Workshop on Advanced Technologies for Digital Libraries. Retrieved August, 2011 from http://www.cacaoproject.eu/fileadmin/media/AT4DL/paper-01.pdf

Bernardi, R., Buoso, P., Schiller, A., & Gobbetti, D. (2008). *D4.1: Simple interface (with report of usability and accessibility) - CACAO project.* Retrieved August, 2011 from http://www.cacaoproject.eu/fileadmin/media/Deliverables/CACAO_D4.1.pdf

Bosca, A., & Dini, L. (2009). Query expansion via library classification system. *Lecture Notes in Computer Science, 5706,* 42–49. doi:10.1007/978-3-642-04447-2_4

Bosca, A., & Dini, L. (2010). User logs as a means to enrich and refine translation dictionaries. *Lecture Notes in Computer Science, 6241,* 544–551. doi:10.1007/978-3-642-15754-7_67

Bosca, A., Djebbari, E., Grzesiak, Ł., Levergood, B., Mazurek, J., Siciliano, L., et al. (2009a). *D6.2: Second validation report (technical adequacy + user satisfaction) - Cacao project.* Retrieved August 2011 from http://www.cacaoproject.eu/fileadmin/media/Deliverables/CACAO_D6.2.pdf

Bosca, A., Grzesiak, Ł., & Mazurek, J. (2009b). *D6.3: Final validation report (technical adequacy+user satisfaction) - CACAO project.* Retrieved August 2011 from http://www.cacaoproject.eu/fileadmin/media/Deliverables/CACAO_D6.3.pdf

Budhu, M., & Coleman, A. (2002). The design and evaluation of interactivities in a digital library. *D-Lib Magazine, 8*(11). doi:10.1045/november2002-coleman

Byrne, W., Doermann, D., Franz, M., Gustman, S., Hajic, J., & Oard, D. (2004). Automatic recognition of spontaneous multilingual oral history archives. *IEEE Transactions on Speech and Audio Processing, 12*(4), 420–435. doi:10.1109/TSA.2004.828702

Cahill, K. (2009). *User-generated content and its impact on web-based library services.* Oxford, UK: Chandos. doi:10.1533/9781780630083

Ceccarelli, D., Gordea, S., Lucchese, C., Nardini, F. M., & Tolomei, G. (2011). *Improving Europeana search experience using query logs.* Paper presented at the Theories and Practice of Digital Libraries Conference. Berlin, Germany. Retrieved August, 2011 from http://miles.isti.cnr.it/~nardini/wp-content/uploads/2011/06/tpdl2011.pdf

Cleverdon, C. (1997). The Cranfield tests on index language devices. In Jones, K. S., & Willett, P. (Eds.), *Readings in Information Retrieval.* San Francisco, CA: Morgan Kaufmann. doi:10.1108/eb050097

Cleverdon, C. W. (1970). *The effect of variations in relevance assessments in comparative experimental tests of index languages*. Cranfield, UK: Cranfield Institute of Technology.

Clough, P., Müller, H., & Sanderson, M. (2005). The CLEF 2004 cross language image retrieval track. *Lecture Notes in Computer Science*, *3491*, 597–613. doi:10.1007/11519645_59

Clough, P., & Sanderson, M. (2004a). The effects of relevance feedback in cross language image retrieval. In McDonald & Tait (Eds.), *Advances in Information Retrieval: Proceedings of the 26th European Conference on IR Research (ECIR 2004),* (pp. 238-252). Sunderland, UK: ECIR.

Clough, P., & Sanderson, M. (2004b). The CLEF 2003 cross language image retrieval track. *Lecture Notes in Computer Science*, *3237*, 127–147. doi:10.1007/978-3-540-30222-3_56

Clough, P., Sanderson, M., & Reid, N. (2006). The Eurovision St Andrews collection of photographs. *ACM SIGIR Forum, 40*(1), 21-30.

Cockburn, A. (2001). *Writing effective use cases*. Boston, MA: Addison-Wesley.

Connaway, L. S., Dickey, T. J., & Radford, M. L. (2011). If it is too inconvenient I'm not going after it: Convenience as a critical factor in information-seeking behaviors. *Library & Information Science Research*, *33*(3), 179–190. doi:10.1016/j.lisr.2010.12.002

Cousins, J. (2006). The European library - Pushing the boundaries of usability. *The Electronic Library*, *24*(4), 434–444. doi:10.1108/02640470610689142

Dekkers, M., Gradmann, S., & Meghini, C. (2009). *Europeana outline functional specification: For development of an operational European digital library: D 2.5 – Europeana thematic network project*. Retrieved August, 2011 from http://www.version1.europeana.eu/web/europeana-project/technicaldocuments/

Demartini, G., & Mizzaro, S. (2006). A classification of IR effectiveness metrics. *Lecture Notes in Computer Science*, *3936*, 488–491. doi:10.1007/11735106_48

Dobreva, M., & Chowdhury, S. (2010). A user-centric evaluation of the Europeana digital library. *Lecture Notes in Computer Science*, *6102*, 148–157. doi:10.1007/978-3-642-13654-2_19

Dobreva, M., McCulloch, E., Birrell, D., Unal, Y., & Feliciati, P. (2010). Digital natives and specialised digital libraries: A study of Europeana users. *Communications in Computer and Information Science*, *96*, 45–60. doi:10.1007/978-3-642-16032-5_5

Dörk, M., Carpendale, S., & Williamson, C. (2011). The information flaneur: A fresh look at information seeking. In *Proceedings of the 2011 Annual Conference on Human Factors in Computing Systems, CHI 2011,* (pp. 1215-1224). Vancouver, Canada: ACM Press.

Ferro, N., & Peters, C. (2010). CLEF 2009 ad hoc track overview: TEL & Persian tasks. *Lecture Notes in Computer Science*, *6241*, 13–35. doi:10.1007/978-3-642-15754-7_2

Fresa, A. (2005). *MICHAEL: Multilingual inventory of cultural heritage in Europe*. Paper presented at the EVA. Retrieved August, 2011 from http://www.michael-culture.eu/documents/fresaeva05.pdf

Fuhr, N., Hansen, P., Mabe, M., Micsik, A., & Sølvberg, I. (2001). Digital libraries: A generic classification and evaluation scheme. *Lecture Notes in Computer Science*, *2163*, 187–199. doi:10.1007/3-540-44796-2_17

Fuhr, N., Tsakonas, G., Aalberg, T., Agosti, M., Hansen, P., & Kapidakis, S. (2007). Evaluation of digital libraries. *International Journal on Digital Libraries*, *8*(1), 27–38. doi:10.1007/s00799-007-0011-z

Gäde, M., Petras, V., & Stiller, J. (2010). Which log for which information? Gathering multilingual data from different log file types. *Lecture Notes in Computer Science, 6360*, 70–81. doi:10.1007/978-3-642-15998-5_9

Guldbæk, K., & Petersen, G. (2011). *D3.2.3: Recommendations for conducting user tests: User involvement – A toolbox: How to involve users in development processes in Europeana - EuropeanaConnect project.* Retrieved August 2011 from http://www.europeanaconnect.eu/documents/D3.2.3_eConnect_usability_guidelines_v1.0_KB-DK.pdf

Hersh, W., Turpin, A., Price, S., Chan, B., Kramer, D., Sacherek, L., et al. (2000). Do batch and user evaluations give the same results? In *Proceedings of the 23rd Annual International ACM SIGIR Conference on Research and Development in Information Retrieval,* (pp. 17-24). Athens, Greece: ACM Press.

Huiskes, M. J., & Lew, M. S. (2008). The MIR flickr retrieval evaluation. In *Proceedings of the 1st ACM International Conference on Multimedia Information Retrieval,* (pp. 39-43). New York, NY: ACM.

Ingwersen, P., & Järvelin, K. (2005). *The turn - Integration of information seeking and retrieval in context.* Dordrecht, The Netherlands: Springer.

International Council of Museums. (2003). *Scope definition of the CIDOC conceptual reference model.* Retrieved August, 2011 from http://www.cidoc-crm.org/scope.html

Janssen, O. D. (2007). Building the European digital library - An insider's point of view. In H. A. Thompson (Ed.), *ACRL 13th National Conference Proceedings.* Retrieved August 2011 from http://www.ala.org/ala/mgrps/divs/acrl/events/national/baltimore/papers/46.pdf

Jones, M. L. W., Gay, G. K., & Rieger, R. H. (1999). Project soup: Comparing evaluations of digital collection efforts. *D-Lib Magazine, 5*(11). Retrieved August 2011 from http://www.dlib.org/dlib/november99/11jones.html

Kazai, G., & Doucet, A. (2007). Overview of the INEX 2007 book search track. *ACM SIGIR Forum, 42*(1).

Kazai, G., Koolen, M., Doucet, A., & Landoni, M. (2010). Overview of the INEX 2010 book track: At the mercy of crowdsourcing. In Shlomo, G., Kamps, J., Schenkel, R., & Trotman, A. (Eds.), *INEX 2010 Workshop Pre-Proceedings.* Huize Bergen, The Netherlands: INEX.

Kelly, D. (2009). Methods for evaluating interactive information retrieval systems with users. *Foundations and Trends in Information Retrieval, 3*(1-2), 1–224.

Larson, M., Newman, E., & Jones, G. (2010). Overview of VideoCLEF 2009: New perspectives on speech-based multimedia content enrichment. *Lecture Notes in Computer Science, 6242*, 354–368. doi:10.1007/978-3-642-15751-6_46

Lew, M. S., Sebe, N., & Djeraba, C. (2006). Content-based multimedia information retrieval: State of the art and challenges. *ACM Transactions on Multimedia Computing, Communications, and Applications, 2*(1).

Mandl, T. (2008). Recent developments in the evaluation of information retrieval systems: Moving towards diversity and practical relevance. *Informatica, 32*, 27–38.

Mandl, T., Agosti, M., Di Nunzio, G. M., Yeh, A., Mani, I., & Doran, C. (2010a). LogCLEF 2009: The CLEF 2009 multilingual logfile analysis track overview. *Lecture Notes in Computer Science, 6241*, 508–517. doi:10.1007/978-3-642-15754-7_62

Mandl, T., Di Nunzio, G. M., & Schulz, J. M. (2010b). LogCLEF 2010: The CLEF 2010 multilingual logfile analysis track overview. *Lecture Notes in Computer Science*, 6360.

Marchionini, G. (2000). Evaluating digital libraries: A longitudinal and multifaceted view. *Library Trends*, *49*(2), 304–333.

Marlow, J., Clough, P. D., & Dance, K. (2007). Multilingual needs of cultural heritage web site visitors: A case study of tate online. In J. Trant & D. Bearman (Eds.), *Proceedings of International Cultural Heritage Informatics Meeting (ICHIM 2007)*. Toronto, Canada: ICHIM.

Minelli, S., Del Secco, I., & Naldi, G. (2006). *D1.2: User requirements analysis - Multimatch-project*. Retrieved August 2011 from http://www.multimatch.org/docs/publicdels/D1.2Final.pdf

Minerva Working Group 5 (Ed.). (2005). *Quality principles for cultural websites: A handbook*. Retrieved August, 2011 from http://www.minervaeurope.org/publications/qualitycommentary/qualitycommentary050314final.pdf

Minerva Working Group 5 (Ed.). (2008). *Handbook on cultural web user interaction*. Retrieved August 2011 from http://www.minervaeurope.org/publications/Handbookwebuserinteraction.pdf

Multimatch. (2006a). *D7.1: Evaluation methodology - Multimatch project*. Retrieved August 2011 from http://www.multimatch.eu/docs/publicdels/7.1-final.pdf

Multimatch. (2006b). *D7.4: Results of field trials - Multimatch project*. Retrieved August 2011 from http://www.multimatch.eu/docs/publicdels/D7.4_FINAL.pdf

Nicholson, S. (2004). A conceptual framework for the holistic measurement and cumulative evaluation of library services. *The Journal of Documentation*, *60*(2), 164–182. doi:10.1108/00220410410522043

O'Brien, H. L., Toms, E. G., Kelloway, E. K., & Kelley, E. (2008). Developing and evaluating a reliable measure of user engagement. *Proceedings of the American Society for Information Science and Technology*, *45*(1), 1–10. doi:10.1002/meet.2008.1450450258

Over, P., Awad, G., Fiscus, J., Antonishek, B., Michel, M., Smeaton, A. F., et al. (2011). TrecVid 2010 – Goals, tasks, data, evaluation mechanisms and metrics. *TRECVid Workshop Notebook Papers*. Retrieved August 2011 from http://www-nlpir.nist.gov/projects/tvpubs/tv10.papers/tv10overview.pdf

Over, P., Awad, G., Fiscus, J., Michel, M., Smeaton, A. F., & Kraaij, W. (2010). TrecVid 2009 – Goals, tasks, data, evaluation mechanisms and metrics. *TRECVid Workshop Notebook Papers*. Retrieved August 2011 from http://www-nlpir.nist.gov/projects/tvpubs/tv9.papers/tv9overview.pdf

Over, P., Awad, G., Rose, T., Fiscus, J., Kraaij, W., & Smeaton, A. F. (2009). TrecVid 2008 – Goals, tasks, data, evaluation mechanisms and metrics. *TRECVid Workshop Notebook Papers*. Retrieved August 2011 from http://www-nlpir.nist.gov/projects/tvpubs/tv8.papers/tv8overview.pdf

Peters, C., Bruno, E., Carmichael, J., Clough, P., Jones, G., Larson, M., et al. (2006). *D7.3 evaluation of second prototype - Multimatch project*. Retrieved August, 2011 from http://www.multimatch.info/docs/publicdels/7.3.pdf

Purday, J. (2009). Think culture: Europeana.eu from concept to construction. *The Electronic Library*, *27*(6), 919–937. doi:10.1108/02640470911004039

Rasmussen, K. G., Iversen, R., & Petersen, G. (2009). *M3.2.3: Personas catalogue - EuropeanaConnect project*. Retrieved August 2011 from http://www.europeanaconnect.eu/documents/M3.2.3_eConnect_PersonasCatalogue_v1.0_20091228.pdf

Research, I. R. N. (2009). *EUROPEANA - Online visitor survey.* Retrieved August 2011 from http://www.version1.europeana.eu/c/document_library/get_file?uuid=df49b382-aa16-497f-8405-948b532dc0d7&groupId=10602

Research, I. R. N. (2011). *EUROPEANA - Online visitor survey.* Retrieved August 2011 from http://www.version1.europeana.eu/c/document_library/get_file?uuid=334beac7-7fc2-4a4e-ba23-4dcc1450382d&groupId=10602

Roffia, L., Bartolini, S., & Manzaroli, D. (2011). Requirements on system design to increase understanding and visibility of cultural heritage. In *Handbook of Research on Technologies and Cultural Heritage: Applications and Environments* (pp. 259–284). Hershey, PA: IGI Global. doi:10.4018/978-1-60960-044-0.ch013

Saracevic, T. (2000). Digital library evaluation: Toward an evolution on concepts. *Library Trends, 49*(2), 350–369.

Saracevic, T. (2004). *Evaluation of digital libraries: An overview.* Paper presented at the DELOS WP7 Workshop on the Evaluation of Digital Libraries. Padua, Italy.

Saulnier, A., & Viaud, M.-L. (2009). *Evaluation report of the usability of the Europeana web site.* Retrieved August 2011 from http://www.version1.europeana.eu/c/document_library/get_file?uuid=ae1d74de-29c1-463c-887e-a6bc6ee0ed7a&groupId=10602

Smeaton, A., & Over, P. (2002). The TREC-2002 video track report. In *Proceedings of the Eleventh Text Retrieval Conference, TREC 2002.* NIST.

Smeaton, A. F., Over, P., & Kraaij, W. (2006). Evaluation campaigns and TRECVid. In *Proceedings of the 8th ACM International Workshop on Multimedia Information Retrieval,* (pp. 321-330). Santa Barbara, CA: ACM Press.

Smith, C. L., & Kantor, P. B. (2008). User adaptation: Good results from poor systems. In *Proceedings of the 31st Annual International ACM SIGIR Conference on Research and Development in Information Retrieval,* (pp. 147-154). New York, NY: ACM Press.

Stiller, J., Gäde, M., & Petras, V. (2010). *Ambiguity of queries and the challenges for query language detection.* Paper presented at the CLEF 2010 LABs and Workshops. Retrieved August, 2011 from http://clef2010.org/resources/proceedings/clef2010labs_submission_41.pdf

Sykes, J., Dobreva, M., Birrell, D., McCulloch, E., Ruthven, I., & Yurdagül, Ü. (2010). A new focus on end users: Eye-tracking analysis for digital libraries. *Lecture Notes in Computer Science, 6273,* 510–513. doi:10.1007/978-3-642-15464-5_69

Trant, J. (2009). Tagging, folksonomy and art museums: Early experiments and ongoing research. *Journal of Digital Information, 10*(1). Retrieved August 2011 from http://journals.tdl.org/jodi/article/view/270

Trojahn, C., & Siciliano, L. (2009). *User requirements for advanced features: D7.4 - CACAO project.* Retrieved August 2011 from http://www.cacaoproject.eu/fileadmin/media/Deliverables/CACAO_D7.4.pdf

Tsikrika, T., & Westerveld, T. (2008). The INEX 2007 multimedia track. *Lecture Notes in Computer Science, 4862,* 440–453. doi:10.1007/978-3-540-85902-4_37

Turpin, A., & Scholer, F. (2006). User performance versus precision measures for simple search tasks. In *Proceedings of the 29th Annual International ACM SIGIR Conference on Research and Development in Information Retrieval,* (pp. 11-18). New York, NY: ACM Press.

van Zwol, R., Kazai, G., & Lalmas, M. (2006). INEX 2005 multimedia track. *Lecture Notes in Computer Science*, *3977*, 497–510.

Voorhees, E., & Harman, D. K. (2005). *TREC: Experiment and evaluation in information retrieval.* Cambridge, MA: MIT Press.

Vullo, G. (2010). A global approach to digital library evaluation. *The Library Quarterly*, *20*(2), 169–178.

Westerveld, T., & van Zwol, R. (2007). The INEX 2006 multimedia track. *Lecture Notes in Computer Science*, *4518*, 331–344. doi:10.1007/978-3-540-73888-6_33

White, R. W., Oard, D. W., Jones, G. J. F., Soergel, D., & Huang, X. (2006). Overview of the CLEF-2005 cross-language speech retrieval track. *Lecture Notes in Computer Science*, *4022*, 744–759. doi:10.1007/11878773_82

Xie, H. (2008). Users' evaluation of digital libraries: Their uses, their criteria, and their assessment. *Information Processing & Management*, *44*(3), 1346–1373. doi:10.1016/j.ipm.2007.10.003

Zhang, Y. (2010). Developing a holistic model for digital library evaluation. *Journal of the American Society for Information Science and Technology*, *61*(1), 88–110. doi:10.1002/asi.21220

KEY TERMS AND DEFINITIONS

Cultural Heritage Information System: Information systems that collect, store, preserve, organize, search and display cultural heritage objects or their (metadata) representations in a digital environment.

Evaluation Approach: Broad disciplinary or component-based perspective or theory of evaluation.

Evaluation Measure: Instrument that allows assessing a given evaluation criterion in a standardized, precise, and repeatable way.

Interaction Pattern: Typical user actions or user information access capabilities in an information system. They can be mixed and matched variously thus representing a sequence of user interactions with an information system, i.e. a scenario.

System-Centric Evaluation: Mostly quantitative evaluation of system features with respect to their performance, output, effectiveness, and efficiency.

User-Centric Evaluation: Mostly qualitative evaluation of user-system interactions to understand user motivations, user information needs and user behavior on a specific information system.

Chapter 10
A Cognitive Task Analysis Approach for Usability Evaluation of Digital Libraries

Ping Li
City University of New York, USA

ABSTRACT

This chapter focuses on the usability evaluation of Digital Libraries (DL). The research literature in this area is reviewed. The strengths and weaknesses of the traditional evaluation techniques are discussed. A Cognitive Task Analysis (CTA) approach is proposed based on its applicability for the iterative and formative usability evaluation of digital libraries. The theoretical framework and features of CTA are explained. The advantages of the proposed approach for the usability evaluation of digital libraries are elucidated and the procedure of carrying out this type of evaluation is detailed. Future directions for DL usability evaluation, especially for the purpose of iterative design process, are recommended.

INTRODUCTION

Digital Libraries (DL) have been a topic of great interest of both research and practice for many years. They "serve communities of people and are created and maintained by and for people" (Marchionini, Plaisant, & Komlodi, 2003, p. 119). Compared to the ongoing effort in digital library research and practice, evaluation of digital libraries did not keep pace, especially in the first period of digital library development (Saracevic, 2000; Chowdhury, Landoni, & Gibb, 2006).

Digital libraries are extensions and augmentations of physical libraries (Marchionini & Fox, 1999). They are developed to serve the informational needs of users. Therefore, it is important to

DOI: 10.4018/978-1-4666-2991-2.ch010

evaluate both existing digital libraries and those still in developmental stages (Van House, Butler, Ogle, & Schiff, 1996). Evaluation is a research activity, aiming at assessing the extent to which a digital library meets its objectives and offering suggestions for improvements (Chowdhury & Chowdhury, 2003). It is a judgment of worth and "has both theoretical and practical impact in information science" (Marchionini, 2000, p. 312). Among all the evaluations of digital libraries, a great amount of effort focuses on the usability. "Usability is a multidimensional construct that can be examined from various perspectives" (Jeng, 2005a, p. 96). Different approaches have been adopted for the purpose of evaluating DL's usability (Jeng, 2005a, p. 99). Many of them are traditional summative evaluation approaches, aiming at how a developed digital library meets a set of pre-defined goals. Yet these approaches often have limitations. This book chapter discusses the theoretical framework of Cognitive Task Analysis (CTA), its features, the proposed procedures of carrying out this kind of evaluation, and the advantages of this approach for the evaluation of digital library usability.

BACKGROUND

The evaluation of digital libraries is a challenging task because of the complicated technology, rich content and variety of users who are involved (Borgman, Leazer, Gilliland-Swetland, & Gazan, 2000; Saracevic & Covi, 2000). While various sets of criteria have been developed for the evaluation of digital libraries, the most recognized ones are derived from evaluation criteria for traditional libraries, Information Retrieval (IR) system performance, and human-computer interaction (Chowdhury & Chowdhury, 2003; Marchionini, 2000; Saracevic, 2000; Saracevic & Covi, 2000). In the past years, DL evaluation research has been conducted on different aspects and can be summarized mainly into such categories as 1) general DL evaluation framework and evaluation criteria, 2) specific DL evaluation framework and evaluation criteria, 3) usability studies, and 4) evaluation studies on other aspects (Xie, 2008, p. 1348).

Among the categories of DL evaluation research, there has been continued interest in usability since the beginning of this century (Jeng, 2005a, p. 100). Usability is a multidimensional construct, and people usually hold the belief that "there is no uniform definition of usability" (Joo, & Lee, 2011, p. 524). It may mean different things to different people and many previous studies in different areas have mentioned various attributes of usability (e.g. Shackel, 1991; Nielson, 1993; International Standards Organization, 1997; Shneiderman, 1998; Kengeri, Seals, Harley, Reddy, & Fox, 1999; Brink, Gergle, & Wood, 2002; Guenther, 2003). Among these various usability attributes, effectiveness, efficiency, subjective satisfaction, and learnability are most commonly applied in different studies (Joo & Lee, 2011, p. 525). Effectiveness refers to the completeness at which users achieve specified goals; efficiency can be understood as the resources used in completing a task; and subjective satisfaction is positive attitudes toward using the system (International Standards Organization, 1997). Learnability, according to Nielson (1993), is easiness with which casual users learn a system. In the field of digital libraries, different categories of usability criteria were developed for the evaluation purpose (e.g. Saracevic, 2004; Ward & Hiller, 2005; Xie, 2008). One set of usability criteria of digital libraries was proposed by Jeng (2005b), including effectiveness, efficiency, satisfaction, and learnability.

People have been employing various approaches in evaluating usability, many of which are traditional techniques. Questionnaire is one of the techniques often used for usability assessment. One such assessment was carried out by the National Taiwan University Library. In this study, one thousand, seven hundred and eighty-four users were surveyed via questionnaires and some usability problems were identified as a result (Lan, 2001).

In 2002, Adams and Blandford did a research that had the purpose of finding out the perceived effectiveness of traditional and digital libraries as clinical resources and the impact of clinician status on their access to information. They performed focus groups and in-depth interviews of seventy-three hospital clinicians. The conclusion was that digital library technology had the strength of providing remote access to materials, but the system's usability was poor and it was time-consuming to access information.

Aiming at understanding the purpose of digital libraries, Theng, Mohd-Nasir, and Thimbleby (2000) investigated the usability of the ACM Digital Library, the Networked Computer Science Technical Reference Library, and the New Zealand Digital Library. They used questionnaires and heuristic evaluation for the assessment purpose. The research results revealed the importance of mental models and of traditional library support.

Sumner, Khoo, Recker, and Marlino (2003) studied usability of National Science Digital Library (NSDL) and the Digital Library for Earth System Education (DLESE). The data collection technique was a series of five focus groups. Via this technique, the researchers aimed at determining the participants' expectations and requirements for the design of educational digital collections for classroom use. It was discovered that content quality, advertising, bias, and design impacted the participants' perceptions.

Quijano-Solis and Novelo-Pena (2005) evaluated the usability of a monolingual multinational digital library from the University of Alicante in Spain. They used two questionnaires to solicit the thirty-five librarian participants' perceptions of what a digital library should have. The survey results showed that respondents had used digital libraries mostly in their own fields. It was noted that additional surveys need to be conducted to further identify their understanding of the search features of the digital library.

Some researchers adopted formal usability testing technique to assess the usability of digital libraries. Hartson, Shivakumar, and Pérez-Quinones (2004), for instance, evaluated the design and functionality of Networked Computer Science Technical Reference Library (NCSTRL) via the usability inspection method. They found NCSTRL's design was functionally oriented. They also noticed that the use of terms was designer-centered rather than user-centered.

Long, Lage, and Cronin (2005) conducted a usability testing as a part of a user-centered redesign. The evaluation encompassed three stages: a requirements analysis, a heuristic evaluation, and user testing. The usability testing revealed the needs of the project's target user group and the issues with the interface.

A number of studies used triangulation of data for the evaluation purpose. One such study evaluated the University of Illinois DeLIver service. The researchers employed a mixture of data collection techniques, including transaction log analysis, surveys, interviews, focus groups, and formal usability testing to measure accessibility (Bishop, 1998; Neumann & Bishop, 2000). The evaluation process allowed the evaluators to pursue the different social issues surrounding digital library use as well as dealing with specific usability issues.

In 2002, Dorward, Reinke, and Recker performed an assessment of Instructional Architect, which was to increase the utility of National Science Digital Library (NSDL) resources for classroom teachers. They used both formal usability testing and focus group techniques for the evaluation of interface design and contents.

One other example of data triangulation is the usability study of the University of Arizona Library Web site, SABIO. The techniques employed include heuristic evaluation, walk-through, card sorting, and formal usability testing (Dickstein & Mills, 2000). Heuristic evaluation was adopted to systematically inspect user interface; walk-through technique was used for the exploration of user problems in the prototype stage; card-sorting method was employed for the assessment of organization and menu structure; and formal usability testing was conducted to investigate users' use of the site.

Norberg, Vassiliadis, Ferguson, and Smith (2005) conducted a series of usability tests and focus groups to investigate users' interactions with a digital library's interface. They followed an iterative design process that included the development and testing of prototypes by representative users and stakeholders. They found that users' interaction with a digital library was task-oriented and context dependent.

Jeng (2005a, 2005b) proposed an evaluation model for the usability of digital libraries. Based on the evaluation model, a set of instruments were designed. The instruments included a pretest questionnaire collecting participants' demographic data, a list of tasks including nine questions representative of typical uses of the digital library, and a post-test questionnaire that examined participants' satisfaction levels regarding the ease of use, organization of information, clear labeling, visual appearance, contents, and error corrections of the digital library. The participants were also asked to rank their satisfaction with the system after each task and to write down comments (Jeng, 2005b).

Tsakonas and Papatheodorou (2008) sought to find which DL interaction attributes affected most significantly E-LIS usefulness and usability. Two data collection tools were used. One was an online questionnaire survey and inferential statistical analysis was conducted to define the attributes. The other tool was regression analysis, which aimed at finding out their predictive strength and the impact of the system's functionalities.

MAIN FOCUS OF THE CHAPTER

Limitations of Traditional Evaluation Approaches

Traditional usability evaluation approaches such as questionnaires, interviews and focus groups are usually employed for summative evaluation with the objective of assessing how completed information systems meet pre-defined goals. While they are useful for the elicitation of certain categories of information (e.g. subject demographics and the reported satisfaction levels with the system), they may not be able to reveal how a system fits into the context of actual use. They may not be able to identify new or emergent issues that researchers have not previously thought of. Besides, by asking users to rate an information system after the actual use, the results are subject to the difficulty that users may encounter in recalling their experience with the system. In many cases, both experienced and inexperienced users may not be aware of what they actually do. This can result in their inadequate or inaccurate reflections on the usability of the information system (Kushniruk & Patel, 2004, p. 58).

Another problem related to the use of questionnaire, interview, or focus group for the usability evaluation is that these techniques, if used alone, may be insufficient for revealing how people actually use a system. They may need to be complemented by other evaluation techniques (Kushniruk & Patel, 2004, pp. 58-59). Thus, new evaluation approaches need to be developed to avoid the disadvantages.

Cognitive and Usability Engineering Evaluation Methods

In the past two decades, cognitive and usability engineering approaches have been adopted for the evaluation of information technology. These approaches have been formulated from an interdisciplinary perspective. They are drawn from a number of fields including cognitive psychology, computer science, systems engineering, and usability engineering (Kushniruk & Patel, 2004, p. 56).

Different from traditional summative evaluation techniques, cognitive and usability engineering methods are often used in the iterative evaluation of information systems during their development. The objective of this type of evaluation is to improve the design of information systems and to ensure that the systems work effectively. It gathers information about the actual process of system usage by representative users who perform representative tasks. With these techniques, researchers can characterize how easily a user is able to perform a task. They can assess how a user is proficient in using a system and find out the problems he or she has in interacting with the system. The results of this type of assessment can be used either to improve the features of the system before the completion of its development, or to assess the impact of the fully developed system.

Cognitive Task Analysis

One type of the cognitive approaches is Cognitive Task Analysis (CTA), which integrates the ideas from the field of systems engineering and cognitive research. It is "a family of methods and tools for gaining access to the mental processes that organize and give meaning to observable behavior" (Applied Research Associates, Inc., 2011). CTA methods can be useful tools for the identification of operator dynamic goal sets, factual knowledge stores, mental strategies, critical decisions, and situation awareness requirements. These identified factors can form a basis for both new human-machine interface design and for critiquing existing interfaces, processes, and systems (Kaber, Segall, Green, Entzian, & Junginger, 2006, p. 237).

Cognitive Task Analysis (CTA) has been adopted for the designing of new system interfaces, for cognitive engineering of human-machine systems, for the development of expert systems, for operator selection, and for training purposes (Wei & Salvendy, 2004). It focuses on the characterization of the participants' decision making and reasoning skills, as well as information processing needs while they perform information processing tasks. It has a Hierarchical Task Analysis (HTA) structure and its top-level goal or objective is established by a set of tasks or operations (van Westrenen, 2011, p. 31).

Various CTA approaches have been developed for research purposes. One such approach is Goal-Directed Task Analysis (GDTA). Endsley et al. (2003a, 2003b), for instance, adopted a Situation Awareness-Oriented Design for new systems. The goal of this design was to support operators in achieving and maintaining good Situation Awareness (SA). To achieve the purpose, a GDTA was created for the analysis of SA requirements, which were translated to a system design by SA-oriented design principles. The system was then evaluated using SA measurement tools and changes were made as necessary.

One other CTA approach was employed by Hajdukiewicz, Vicente, Doyle, Milgram, and Burns (2001). It was the Abstraction Hierarchy (AH) modeling approach that provided a framework for the support of integrated medical informatics design. This approach is especially useful for the defining of new interface content operations.

Saitwal, Feng, Walji, Patel, and Zhang (2010) utilized GOMS (Goals, Operators, Methods, and Selection rules) approach to evaluate the Armed Forces Health Longitudinal Technology Application (AHLTA) user interface by classifying each step of a given task into Mental (Internal) or Physical (External) operators.

"Compared to other methods for system design and assessment, CTA is superior for its predominance in analyzing both physical and mental procedures in a task" (Saitwal, Feng, Walji, Patel, & Zhang, 2010, p. 502). The various CTA methodologies put emphasis on understanding the processes involved in complex decision making and reasoning. They take into account and characterize the effects of experience and prior knowledge on decision processes. In addition, they can identify problems people of varying levels of expertise may have in decision making and reasoning (Kushniruk, 2001, p. 371).

Proposed Cognitive Task Analysis Approach for the Evaluation of DL Usability

Cognitive task analysis, based on its strengths, should be applicable for the usability evaluation of digital libraries. One variation of cognitive task analysis approach can be adapted from what was proposed by Means and Gott (1988) as the basis for the development of intelligent tutoring systems. This approach develops a task hierarchy that describes and catalogs the individual work activities or tasks that take place in an organization (with or without the aid of information technology). When tasks are identified, subjects with varying levels of expertise will be observed as they perform selected tasks of interest. One important feature of this approach is to characterize how user variation affects the task and the occurrence of potential problems characteristic of different types of subjects. This technique should be able to achieve a better understanding of human information needs in the development of systems (Vicente, 1999).

The proposed evaluation approach consists of eight phases. The first phase is to develop a good evaluation plan, which is the basis for the whole evaluation process. At this stage, the objectives of the DL usability evaluation should be identified. Since the evaluation is focused on the usability of digital libraries, the objectives can be formulated based on the four operational usability criteria of digital libraries proposed by Jeng (2005b), that is, effectiveness, efficiency, satisfaction, and learnability.

The second phase of this evaluation process is to select participants who should be representative of the end users of the digital library under study. To make sure different levels of participants are included for the evaluation, purposive sampling technique may be adopted. Consideration should be given to such dimensions as the participants' educational background and levels, their familiarity with digital libraries, online information retrieval skills, as well as their demographic information.

The third phase is to select representative tasks. This step should be based on the study objectives, combined with the consideration of participants' informational needs for their daily life, work, and study purposes. Tasks can include finding the call number of a book, locating a journal, finding some visual material, finding overdue information, etc.

The fourth step is to develop a background questionnaire. This data collection instrument can be given either before or after a participant's actual interaction with the digital library under evaluation. The questionnaire can be used to obtain the participants' demographic and historical information, e.g. their previous experience with digital libraries. This type of historical information can be helpful to the evaluators' understanding of the participants' behavior and performance during the evaluation (Kushniruk, Patel, Patel, & Cimino, 2001).

The fifth phase is to collect data. Before the actual data collection, the researcher needs to select the evaluation environment, that is, where the evaluation is to be conducted and what facilities should be set up for the data collection (e.g. launching the Adobe Captivate software installed on the computer to record participants' activities on the screen and their thought processes). The evaluation environment should be the same for all the participants. When everything is settled, participants are asked to perform the selected tasks while interacting with the digital library. They are instructed to "think aloud" during the interaction as well. In other words, participants are expected to speak out whatever they are looking at, thinking, doing, and feeling when they complete the selected tasks.

The sixth step is the data analysis. Both the participants' activities on the screen and their think-aloud protocols are to be transcribed and reviewed carefully. A coding scheme is to be developed based on the evaluation objectives and operational definitions of the evaluation criteria. For instance, to assess the effectiveness of the digital library, the coding categories should include such observations as whether the digital library system as a whole can provide information and functionality effectively, the ratio of a participant's successful information searches to the total number of his or her searches. For efficiency, it can be coded by the length of time it takes a participant to complete the tasks. Satisfaction can be coded based on participants' thinking-aloud data regarding their perceptions of ease of use of the system, their satisfaction levels with the system's structure, layout, organization of information, understandability of terminology, visual appearance, authority and accuracy of information, as well as error correction. Learnability, relates to how soon a participant learns to perform tasks and how many tasks are correctly completed (Jeng, 2005b). To guarantee the reliability of the coded data, two blind codings should be conducted and they should be checked for disagreements when completed.

The seventh phase is the interpretation of the data. This stage should be based on the objectives of the evaluation. "The findings should be interpreted for what they mean, within the context of the theoretical frame work" (Kushniruk & Patel, 2004, p. 66). The process should start with the elucidation of meaning from the coded data. The person who exams the data should ask himself or herself such questions as "What does this mean?" and "What does this tell me about the nature of the phenomenon of interest?" With these questions in mind, he or she should work back and forth between the data and his or her own perspectives and understandings to make sense of the data.

The eighth and also the final stage is the iterative input into design. The usability evaluation should be an iterative process. The evaluation results should be shared with the developers of the digital library, based on which changes should be made to the designing of the digital library. After the change is implemented, evaluation should be repeated to determine how the changes affect the digital library's usability.

FUTURE RESEARCH DIRECTIONS

While increasing attention has been paid to the evaluation of digital libraries in the past decade, this type of effort cannot parallel the effort devoted to the digital library development. In addition, traditional evaluation techniques are still predominant in spite of the increasing adoption of cognitive and usability testing methods. Cognitive task analysis approaches have their advantages in evaluating digital libraries, especially for the sake of iterative designing and improvement process.

The proposed cognitive task analysis approach is to be carried out in the actual usability evaluation of digital libraries. Challenges can be anticipated in each of the evaluation phases. In the conduct of actual usability evaluations of digital libraries, revisions and modifications of specific aspects of this proposed evaluation approach will be expected.

Digital library evaluation is a very complex and demanding undertaking. It encompasses various dimensions and levels. More research effort needs to be made to find effective digital library evaluation approaches and criteria. In addition, the evaluation of digital libraries should be iterative and on an ongoing basis. The developers of digital libraries should constantly look for ways to assess and improve the systems.

CONCLUSION

This book chapter reviews the evaluation methods of digital library usability in the research literature and proposes a cognitive task analysis approach for the usability evaluation purpose. Compared to the traditional summative evaluation techniques, the proposed approach that emerges from cognitive science and usability engineering has its strengths, especially for the iterative designing purposes. While it is not ideal to use this approach exclusively for the usability evaluation of digital libraries, it should be beneficial to complement other evaluation approaches with this proposed one.

REFERENCES

Adams, A., & Blandford, A. (2002). Acceptability of medical digital libraries. *Health Informatics Journal*, *8*(2), 58–66. doi:10.1177/146045820200800202

Applied Research Associates, Inc. (2011). *Cognitive task analysis.* Retrieved November 22, 2011 from http://www.ara.com/Capabilities/c_cognitive_science.htm

Bishop, A. P. (1998). Logins and bailouts: Measuring access, use, and success in digital libraries. *Journal of Electronic Publishing*, *4*(2). Retrieved from http://quod.lib.umich.edu/j/jep/3336451.0004.207?rgn=main;view=fulltext

Borgman, C. L., Leazer, G. H., Gilliland-Swetland, A. J., & Gazan, R. (2000). Evaluating digital libraries for teaching and learning in undergraduate education: A case study of the Alexandria digital earth prototype (ADEPT). *Library Trends*, *49*, 228–250.

Brink, T., Gergle, D., & Wood, S. D. (2002). *Designing web sites that work: Usability for the web.* San Francisco, CA: Morgan Kaufmann.

Chowdhury, G. G., & Chowdhury, S. (2003). *Introduction to digital libraries.* London, UK: Facet Publishing.

Chowdhury, S., Landoni, M., & Gibb, F. (2006). Usability and impact of digital libraries: A review. *Online Information Review*, *30*(6), 656–680. doi:10.1108/14684520610716153

Dickstein, R., & Mills, V. (2000). Usability testing at the University of Arizona library: How to let the users in on the design. *Information Technology and Libraries*, *19*(3), 144–151.

Dorward, J., Reinke, D., & Recker, M. (2002). An evaluation model for a digital library services tool. In *Proceedings of the Second ACM/IEEE-CS Joint Conference on Digital Libraries,* (pp. 322-323). New York, NY: ACM Press.

Endsley, M. R., Bolstad, C. A., Jones, D. G., & Riley, J. M. (2003a). Situation awareness oriented design: From user's cognitive requirements to creating effective supporting technologies. In *Proceedings of the 47th Annual Meeting of the Human Factors & Ergonomics Society,* (pp. 268–272). Santa Monica, CA: Human Factors & Ergonomics Society.

Endsley, M. R., Bolte, B., & Jones, D. G. (2003b). *Designing for situation awareness: An approach to human-centered design.* London, UK: Taylor & Francis.

Guenther, K. (2003). Assessing web site usability. *Online*, *27*, 65–68.

Hajdukiewicz, J. R., Vicente, K. J., Doyle, D. J., Milgram, P., & Burns, C. M. (2001). Modeling a medical environment: An ontology for integrated medical informatics design. *International Journal of Medical Informatics*, *62*, 79–99. doi:10.1016/S1386-5056(01)00128-9

Hartson, H. R., Shivakumar, P., & Perez-Quinones, M. A. (2004). Usability inspection of digital libraries: A case study. *International Journal on Digital Libraries*, *4*(2), 108–123. doi:10.1007/s00799-003-0074-4

International Standard Organization. (1997). *ISO 9241-11: Ergonomic requirements for office work with visual display terminals (VDTs), part 11: Guidance on usability specification and measures, technical report.* Geneva, Switzerland: International Standard Organization.

Jeng, J. (2005a). Usability assessment of academic digital libraries: Effectiveness, efficiency, satisfaction, and learnability. *Libri*, *55*(2/3), 96–121.

Jeng, J. (2005b). What is usability in the context of the digital library and how can it be measured? *Information Technology and Libraries*, *24*(2), 47–56.

Joo, S., & Lee, J. Y. (2011). Measuring the usability of academic digital libraries: Instrument development and validation. *The Electronic Library*, *29*(4), 523–537. doi:10.1108/02640471111156777

Kaber, D. B., Segall, N., Green, R. S., Entzian, K., & Junginger, S. (2006). Using multiple cognitive task analysis methods for supervisory control interface design in high-throughput biological screening processes. *Cognition Technology and Work*, *8*(4), 237–252. doi:10.1007/s10111-006-0029-9

Kengeri, R., Seals, C. D., Harley, H. D., Reddy, H. P., & Fox, E. A. (1999). Usability study of digital libraries: ACM, IEEE-CS, NCSTRL, NDLTD. *International Journal on Digital Libraries*, *2*, 157–169. doi:10.1007/s007990050044

Kushniruk, A. W. (2001). Analysis of complex decision-making processes in health care: Cognitive approaches to health informatics. *Journal of Biomedical Informatics*, *34*(5), 365–376. doi:10.1006/jbin.2001.1021

Kushniruk, A. W., Patel, C., Patel, V. L., & Cimino, J. J. (2001). Televaluation of information systems: An integrative approach to design and evaluation of web-based systems. *International Journal of Medical Informatics*, *61*(1), 45–70. doi:10.1016/S1386-5056(00)00133-7

Kushniruk, A. W., & Patel, V. L. (2004). Cognitive and usability engineering methods for the evaluation of clinical information systems. *Journal of Biomedical Informatics*, *37*(1), 56–76. doi:10.1016/j.jbi.2004.01.003

Lan, S. H. (2001). A study of usability evaluation of information architecture of the university library web site: A case study of National Taiwan University library web site. *Bulletin of the Library Association of China*, *67*, 139–154.

Long, H., Lage, K., & Cronin, C. (2005). The flight plan of a digital initiatives project, part 2: Usability testing in the context of user-centered design. *OCLC Systems & Services*, *21*(4), 324–345. doi:10.1108/10650750510631703

Marchionini, G. (2000). Evaluating digital libraries: A longitudinal and multifaceted view. *Library Trends*, *49*(2), 304–333.

Marchionini, G., & Fox, E. (1999). Progress toward digital libraries: Augmentation through integration. *Information Processing & Management*, *35*(3), 219–225.

Marchionini, G., Plaisant, C., & Komlodi, A. (2003). The people in digital libraries: Multifaceted approaches to assessing needs and impact. In A. P. Bishop, N. A. Van House, & B. P. Buttenfield (Eds.), *Digital Library Use: Social Practice in Design and Evaluation*, (pp. 119-160). Cambridge, MA: The MIT Press.

Means, B., & Gott, S. (1988). Cognitive task analysis as a basis for tutor development: Articulating abstract knowledge representations. In Psotka, J., Massey, L., & Mutter, S. (Eds.), *Intelligent Tutoring Systems: Lessons Learned* (pp. 35–57). Hillsdale, NJ: Lawrence Erlbaum.

Neumann, L. J., & Bishop, A. P. (2000). From usability to use: Measuring success of testbeds in the real world. In H. Susan & T. Michael (Eds.), *Successes and Failures of Digital Libraries: Proceedings of the 35th Annual Clinic on Library Applications of Data Processing*, (pp. 58-69). Urbana-Champaign, IL: University of Illinois at Urbana-Champaign.

Nielson, J. (1993). *Usability engineering*. Cambridge, MA: Academic Press.

Norberg, L. R., Vassiliadis, K., Ferguson, J., & Smith, N. (2005). Sustainable design for multiple audiences: The usability study and iterative redesign of the documenting the American south digital library. *OCLC Systems & Services*, *21*(4), 285–299. doi:10.1108/10650750510629625

Quijano-Solis, A., & Novelo-Pena, R. (2005). Evaluating a monolingual multinational digital library by using usability: An exploratory approach from a developing country. *The International Information & Library Review*, *37*(4), 329–336. doi:10.1016/j.iilr.2005.09.002

Saitwal, H., Feng, X., Walji, M., Patel, V., & Zhang, J. (2010). Assessing performance of an electronic health record (EHR) using cognitive task analysis. *International Journal of Medical Informatics*, *79*, 501–506. doi:10.1016/j.ijmedinf.2010.04.001

Saracevic, T. (2000). Digital library evaluation: Toward an evolution of concepts. *Library Trends*, *49*(2), 350–369.

Saracevic, T. (2004). *Evaluation of digital libraries: An overview*. Retrieved from http://comminfo.rutgers.edu/~tefko/DL_evaluation_Delos.pdf

Saracevic, T., & Covi, L. (2000). Challenges for digital library evaluation. *Proceedings of the American Society for Information Science*, *37*, 341–350.

Shackel, B. (1991). Usability – Context, framework, definition, design and evaluation. In Shackel, B., & Richardson, S. (Eds.), *Human Factors for Informatics Usability* (pp. 21–37). Cambridge, MA: Cambridge University Press. doi:10.1016/j.intcom.2009.04.007

Shneiderman, B. (1998). *Designing the user interface: Strategies for effective human-computer interaction*. Reading, MA: Addison-Wesley Publishing. doi:10.1145/25065.950626

Sumner, T., Khoo, M., Recker, M., & Marlino, M. (2003). Understanding educator perceptions of "quality" in digital libraries. In *Proceedings of the 3rd ACM/IEEE-CS Joint Conference on Digital Libraries*, (pp. 269-279). New York, NY: ACM Press.

Theng, Y. L., Mohd-Nasir, N., & Thimbleby, H. (2000). Purpose and usability of digital libraries. In *Proceedings of the Fifth ACM Conference on Digital Libraries*, (pp. 238-239). New York, NY: ACM Press.

Tsakonas, G., & Papatheodorou, C. (2008). Exploring usefulness and usability in the evaluation of open access digital libraries. *Information Processing & Management*, *44*, 1234–1250. doi:10.1016/j.ipm.2007.07.008

Van House. N. A., Butler, M. H., Ogle, V., & Schiff, L. (1996). User-centered iterative design for digital libraries: The Cypress experience. *D-Lib Magazine*, *2*(2). Retrieved from www.dlib.org/dlib/february96/02vanhouse.html

van Westrenen, F. (2011). Cognitive work analysis and the design of user interfaces. *Cognition Technology and Work*, *13*(1), 31–42. doi:10.1007/s10111-010-0153-4

Vicente, K. J. (1999). *Cognitive work analysis: Toward safe, productive and healthy computer-based work*. New York, NY: Lawrence Erlbaum. doi:10.1109/TPC.2002.808348

Ward, J. L., & Hiller, S. (2005). Usability testing, interface design and portals. *Journal of Library Administration*, *43*(1), 155–171. doi:10.1300/J111v43n01_10

Wei, J., & Salvendy, G. (2004). The cognitive task analysis methods for job and task design: Review and reappraisal. *Behaviour & Information Technology*, *23*(4), 273–299. doi:10.1080/01449290410001673036

Xie, H. I. (2008). Users' evaluation of digital libraries (DLs): Their uses, their criteria, and their assessment. *Information Processing & Management*, *44*, 1346–1373. doi:10.1016/j.ipm.2007.10.003

ADDITIONAL READING

Barnard, P., & May, J. (2000). Towards a theory-based form of cognitive task analysis of broad scope and applicability. In Schraagen, J. M., Chipman, S. F., & Shalin, V. L. (Eds.), *Cognitive Task Analysis* (pp. 147–163). Mahwah, NJ: Lawrence Erlbaum.

Blandford, A., Buchanan, G., & Jones, M. (2004). Usability of digital libraries. *International Journal on Digital Libraries*, *4*(2), 69–70. doi:10.1007/s00799-003-0070-8

Buttenfield, B. (1999). Usability evaluation of digital libraries. *Science & Technology Libraries*, *17*(3/4), 39–59. doi:10.1300/J122v17n03_04

Campbell, N. (2001). *Usability assessment of library-related web sites: Methods and case studies*. Chicago, IL: American Library Association.

Chipman, S. F., Schraagen, J. M., & Shalin, V. L. (2000). Introduction to cognitive task analysis. In Schraagen, J. M., Chipman, S. F., & Shalin, V. L. (Eds.), *Cognitive Task Analysis* (pp. 3–23). Mahwah, NJ: Lawrence Erlbaum.

Chowdhury, S., Landoni, M., & Gibb, F. (2006). Usability and impact of digital libraries: A review. *Online Information Review*, *30*(6), 656–680. doi:10.1108/14684520610716153

Crandall, B., Klein, G. A., & Hoffman, R. R. (2006). *Working minds: A practitioner's guide to cognitive task analysis*. Cambridge, MA: MIT Press.

Ferreira, S. M., & Pithan, D. N. (2005). Usability of digital libraries: A study based on the areas of information science and human-computer Interaction. *OCLC Systems & Services*, *21*(4), 311–323. doi:10.1108/10650750510631695

Frokjaer, E., Hertzum, M., & Hornbaek, K. (2000). Measuring usability: Are effectiveness, efficiency, and satisfaction really correlated? In *Proceedings of the CHI2000 Conference on Human Factors in Computing Systems,* (pp. 345-352). New York, NY: ACM Press.

Gordon, S. E., & Gill, R. T. (1997). Cognitive task analysis. In Zsambok, C. E., & Klein, G. (Eds.), *Naturalistic Decision Making* (pp. 131–140). Mahwah, NJ: Lawrence Erlbaum.

Hartson, H. R., & Shivakumar, P., & Pe'rez-Quin˜ones, M. A. (2004). Usability inspection of digital libraries: A case study. *International Journal on Digital Libraries*, *4*(2), 108–123. doi:10.1007/s00799-003-0074-4

Hornbæk, K. (2006). Current practice in measuring usability: Challenges to usability studies and research. *International Journal of Human-Computer Studies*, *64*(2), 79–102. doi:10.1016/j.ijhcs.2005.06.002

Jeng, J. (2005a). Usability assessment of academic digital libraries: Effectiveness, efficiency, satisfaction, and learnability. *Libri*, *55*(2/3), 96–121.

Jeng, J. (2005b). What is usability in the context of the digital library and how can it be measured? *Information Technology and Libraries, 24*(2), 47–56.

John, B., & Kieras, D. (1996). Using GOMS for user interface design and evaluation: Which technique? *ACM Transactions on Computer-Human Interaction, 3*(4), 287–319. doi:10.1145/235833.236050

Kengeri, R., Seals, C. D., Reddy, H. P., Harley, H. D., & Fox, E. A. (1999). Usability study of digital libraries: ACM, IEEE-CS, NCSTRL, and NDLTD. *International Journal on Digital Libraries, 2*(2/3), 157–169. doi:10.1007/s007990050044

May, J., & Barnard, P. J. (2004). Cognitive task analysis in interacting cognitive subsystems. In Diaper, D., & Stanton, N. (Eds.), *The Handbook of Task Analysis for Human–Computer Interaction* (*Vol. 1*, pp. 291–325). Mahwah, NJ: Lawrence Erlbaum.

McCray, A. T., & Gallagher, M. E. (2001). Principles for digital library development. *Communications of the ACM, 44*(5), 49–54. doi:10.1145/374308.374339

Means, B., & Gott, S. (1988). Cognitive task analysis as a basis for tutor development: Articulating abstract knowledge representations. In Psotka, J., Massey, L., & Mutter, S. (Eds.), *Intelligent Tutoring Systems: Lessons Learned* (pp. 35–57). Hillsdale, NJ: Lawrence Erlbaum.

Militello, L., & Hutton, R. (2000). Applied cognitive task analysis (ACTA): A practitioner's toolkit for understanding cognitive task demands. In Annett, J., & Stanton, N. (Eds.), *Task Analysis* (pp. 90–113). London, UK: Taylor & Francis.

Saracevic, T., & Covi, L. (2000). Challenges for digital library evaluation. *Proceedings of the American Society for Information Science, 37*, 341–350.

Shackel, B. (1991). Usability – Context, framework, definition, design and evaluation. In Shackel, B., & Richardson, S. J. (Eds.), *Human Factors for Informatics Usability* (pp. 21–37). Cambridge, UK: Cambridge University Press. doi:10.1016/j.intcom.2009.04.007

Theng, Y. L., Mohd-Nasir, N., & Thimbleby, H. (2000). Purpose and usability of digital libraries. In *Proceedings of the Fifth ACM Conference on Digital Libraries,* (pp. 238-239). New York, NY: ACM Press.

Tsakonas, G., & Papatheodorou, C. (2008). Exploring usefulness and usability in the evaluation of open access digital libraries. *Information Processing & Management, 44*(3), 1234–1250. doi:10.1016/j.ipm.2007.07.008

Wixon, D. (2003). Evaluating usability methods: Why the current literature fails the practitioner. *Interaction, 10*(4), 28–34. doi:10.1145/838830.838870

Zabihi, E. K., Ghinea, G., & Chen, S. Y. (2006). Digital libraries: What do users want? *Online Information Review*, *30*(4), 395–412. doi:10.1108/14684520610686292

KEY TERMS AND DEFINITIONS

Cognitive Task Analysis: A family of methods that assess the cognitive processes underlying the performance of tasks and the cognitive skills that are needed for the adept responses to complex situations.

Digital Library: A library whose collections are stored in digital formats (as opposed to print or microform) and accessible either locally or remotely via computer networks.

Effectiveness: A criterion that is often used to assess the usability of a digital library. It refers to the accuracy and completeness with which specified groups of users perform specified tasks when using the digital library.

Efficiency: A criterion that is often used to assess the usability of a digital library. It refers to the length of time it takes specified groups of users to perform specified tasks when using the digital library after they have been introduced to its design.

Learnability: A criterion that is often used to assess the usability of a digital library. It refers to the easiness with which specified groups of users learn to perform specified tasks via the digital library.

Satisfaction: A criterion that is often used to assess the usability of a digital library. It refers to the positive attitudes held by specified groups of users towards the digital library based on their experience with it.

Usability: A quality attribute that is used for the assessment of the extent to which a product (e.g. a digital library) can be used by specified groups of users to achieve specified goals.

Section 4
The Social Construction of Digital Library Technology

Chapter 11
Documenting the Untold Stories of Feminist Activists at Welfare Rights Initiative:
A Digital Oral History Archive Project

Cynthia Tobar
City University of New York, USA

ABSTRACT

The authors document the process as they undertake the pre-planning, creation, and initial steps towards the construction of a born digital oral history project. The goal with this project is to retool the concept of a digital exhibit as not solely an educational tool aimed at scholarly researchers but also to reach out to a wider audience of community activists interested in examining the history of grassroots activism and the role of grassroots activist organizations in policymaking. Themes include: approaches to user-centered digital library design, lessons learned, and challenges ahead; for whom are digital libraries being created, and for what purpose? digital libraries for individuals, communities, and societies; digital collection building, collection development policy, and content management; techniques for creating collections.

INTRODUCTION

I will create a digital oral history archive documenting the Welfare Rights Initiative (WRI), a grassroots student activist and community leadership training organization located at Hunter College. The WRI was founded to aid student welfare recipients in becoming agents of social change and to actively involve them with policymaking. I will examine, via these oral history interviews, social movement activity at the level of grassroots organization as exemplified by the WRI. I believe this social justice organization exemplifies not only grassroots efforts in New York City, but also the history of working-class feminist activism in the United States.

DOI: 10.4018/978-1-4666-2991-2.ch011

An oral narrative of an individual's experience in a feminist grassroots organization provides us with new insights to the origins of advocacy. It documents the singular historical importance of fundamental organizing and working-class feminist activism. These narratives help us to better understand what political and social conditions are needed in order for a grassroots community organization to succeed despite race, class, and gender tensions within its ranks.

This digital oral history archive will be targeted at researchers, students, activists, and historians. It will function as a tool to enhance research and teaching in social protest movements and feminist activism. Additionally, this project seeks to fill gaps in the historical research available on said topic and to capture the experiences of its founders and participants. These oral history interviews will investigate broad questions such as: What effect has WRI had on workforce development and social policy for welfare recipients in New York City? What are the major barriers to implementing policies for the poor and how have changing national attitudes shaped the welfare reform agenda? How does this examination help us define working-class feminist activism?

This project will document WRI's progression from a student and faculty-led grassroots movement to its present incarnation as a student advocacy organization. WRI seeks to serve underserved populations citywide, primarily women and girls, via its outreach programs that are designed to encourage those who are economically disadvantaged to study and obtain higher education and/or job training. This oral history project will give a platform to those who generally have little voice in the public debate on welfare reform: former and/or current welfare recipients- WRI's founders and membership base. It will provide students and scholars of social movements a positive working example of how women from various backgrounds can band together and enact social change.

BACKGROUND

Previous welfare regulations made it relatively easy for recipients to go to college. However, in 1995, New York City instituted the Work Experience Program (WEP), which required welfare recipients to perform unpaid labor for the city. WEP was created in tandem with the 1996 federal welfare reform legislation turning welfare funds and jurisdiction primarily over to individual states. Hundreds of thousands of people were removed from the welfare rolls with no guarantee of employment training or education. At CUNY, enrollment of welfare recipients fell from 28,000 to 10,000 (Golden, 1999) as students dropped out to fulfill their workfare obligations. WRI aims to help students on public assistance throughout the CUNY system remain in college despite time-consuming, dead-end workfare requirements as well as other roadblocks the system puts in their way. (Weikart, 2005)

Digital Oral History Projects

For the digital framework of the project, this proposal is modeled after the Bracero History Archive (http://braceroarchive.org/), a project of the Center for History and New Media at George Mason University. This online digital oral history archive collects and makes available the oral histories and artifacts pertaining to the Bracero program, which was a Mexican guest agricultural worker initiative that spanned the years 1942-1964. It uses Omeka, an open source collection management system that offers feature-rich digital exhibition tools, which will be a possible program under consideration for this project.

A similar documentary project in 2006, undertaken by Tamar Carroll (College of the Holy Cross), focused on documenting the National Congress of Neighborhood Women (NCNW). Taking the form of an electronic resource and providing an in-depth introduction, primary documents, and oral history interviews, Carroll chronicled how working-class women were able to form cross-racial partnerships to work for women's empowerment. The one drawback, however, is that it is only accessible via the "Women and Social Movements in the United States, 1600-2000" database which is available only to paid subscribers via Alexander Street Press.

There have been oral history projects that have focused on working-class feminist grassroots organizations and activists, such as the New York City Women Community Activists Oral History Project (Carroll, 2004), and documentary projects that have aimed at collecting primary source material specific to welfare programs in the United States, such as *Welfare in the United States: A History with Documents, 1935-1996* (Nadasen, 2009). However, this would be the first attempt to transform this type of research into in a free digital archive, a Web-based oral history that will incorporate multiple voices, reach diverse audiences, and encourage popular participation in presenting and preserving the history of the Welfare Rights Initiative.

Scope of Project

After conducting background research in secondary literature and available primary sources, I will conduct an initial series of 10-15 interviews that will cover the history, formation, and current infrastructure of Welfare Rights Initiative. As the project progresses, initial interviewees can be expected to yield additional contacts that will broaden and deepen the scope until a comprehensive narrative history takes shape. The interviews will be recorded and transcribed according to Oral History Association guidelines. Signed release forms will be secured from each interviewee, and, following transcription of each interview, the digital files, transcripts, valuable papers, photographs, and other ephemera that are generated by the interview process will be collected, catalogued, and preserved. After I have collected and cataloged the oral history interviews, I will begin work on a Web-based oral history project online using an open source Web publishing software program that will access an open source database for these oral history interviews, where researchers can listen to audio clips and read the corresponding interview transcripts.

USER-CENTERED DIGITAL LIBRARY DESIGN

The goal of this project is to provide a Web-based oral history archive online using an open source Web publishing software program that will access an open source database for these oral history interviews, where researchers can listen to audio clips and read the corresponding interview transcripts. I want this site to be easy for visitors to use and easy for me to administer. I will be able to add interviews quickly and easily without having to learn any complex programming languages.

Design/Site Layout

The website needs to be visually captivating, dynamic, interactive, and easy-to-use as it is targeted also to activists outside of academia and not just to scholars. Visitors will be able to play audio, examine supplemental images, and read text through a comfortable interface. I want the site to be easy to use so that listening to these interviews and hearing these unique stories becomes a pleasure. Technology has made our collective attention span unpresidentedly brief. Subsequently, perfect clarity and usability have now become manditory. This site must load almost instantly, navigation must be intuitive, and any barriers to entry must be eliminated, less visitors storm away in frustration.

I expect to go through many rounds of visual design for this site. The conclusion of this stage in the design process culminates with mockups of all site pages. These mockups set the template for programming to be done by a professional Web consultant. My site will consist of a homepage, an About page, a Bibliography, a chronology/timeline which will outline WRI's legislative and advocacy campaigns, and links to the interviews.

The first step in the design process, now completed, was the development a site layout that identified all site sections and content. To organize the content for my prospective website, I first listed the content topics or types of information that the site was likely to contain. I grouped these items into categories using index cards on a tabletop, with one topic per card. This method of card sorting provided a useful way in which to build the structure for the site. I decided what to put on the home page and labeled the home page categories by visually arranging and sorting the cards. This ensured that I organized information on the site in a way that will be logical to the site's users.

Once I was done analysing the data via card sorting, I generated a site layout that contained all my site's sections, pages, and subpages. I then submitted the layout to my programmer to inspect and consult on (See Figure 1).

Once the layout was further refined, I worked with my website consultant on developing a visual mockup or "wireframe" that will define all site functionality. Figure 2 is one of the preliminary versions as of the writing of this chapter.

The website will be built so that I can easily add new pages and manage existing ones while possessing little technical background. Interviews will be easily searchable by the use of a navigational horizontal bar that will be searchable by subject terms (See Figure 3).

Publishing new content must be accomplished in a few clicks so I can focus on generating content and not on techncial managment. The site will be fast, efficient, and ready for future upgrades and expansions.

Figure 1. Site layout

SITE SECTIONS

ABOUT
- About **
- Acknowledgements **
- Metadata **
- Transcript Usage **
- Contact **

TIMELINE/CHRONOLOGY
- List of WRI's legislative and advocacy campaigns in chronological order.

LISTEN
Audio files sortable by:
- Category/Subject*
- List of all interviewees in alphabetical order.

READ TRANSCRIPTS
PDF files, which will open in a window, are sortable by:
- Last name of interviewees
- List of all interviewees in alphabetical order.

BIBLIOGRAPHY***
- List of related readings on welfare rights activism.

GET INVOLVED
- Donate Now **
- Volunteer **
- Social Media **

HOMEPAGE
- "Featured Items" (large box to showcase special interviews with rotating images) **
- "Recent News" (small box) **
- Sidebar

INTERVIEW TEMPLATE
- Title
- Interviewee
- Date of Birth
- Place of Birth
– Affiliation
- Interview date
- Extent [Need to be able to put in length of transcript pages and time length of audio]
- Resource type [Text; Sound]
- Format [Application/PDF; Audio/MP3]
- Subject [Agencies, Organizations, Laws and Legislation, Key Individuals, Subject] *
- Rights
- Reproduction Policies
- Digital ID
- Main image

Transcripts

The best way to learn all that is contained in an oral history transcript is to read it from beginning to end. Unlike books and articles that are organized around themes or chronology, oral histories often move back and forth through time and contain information about the same event in various parts of the transcript. Transcripts will be lightly edited for readability. Name spellings, dates and other material will be fact-checked. Then transcripts will be annotated to help readers understand specialized material, with explanatory references placed in brackets. Project participants will be given the opportunity to review their transcripts and make

Figure 2. Preliminary wireframe mockup 1

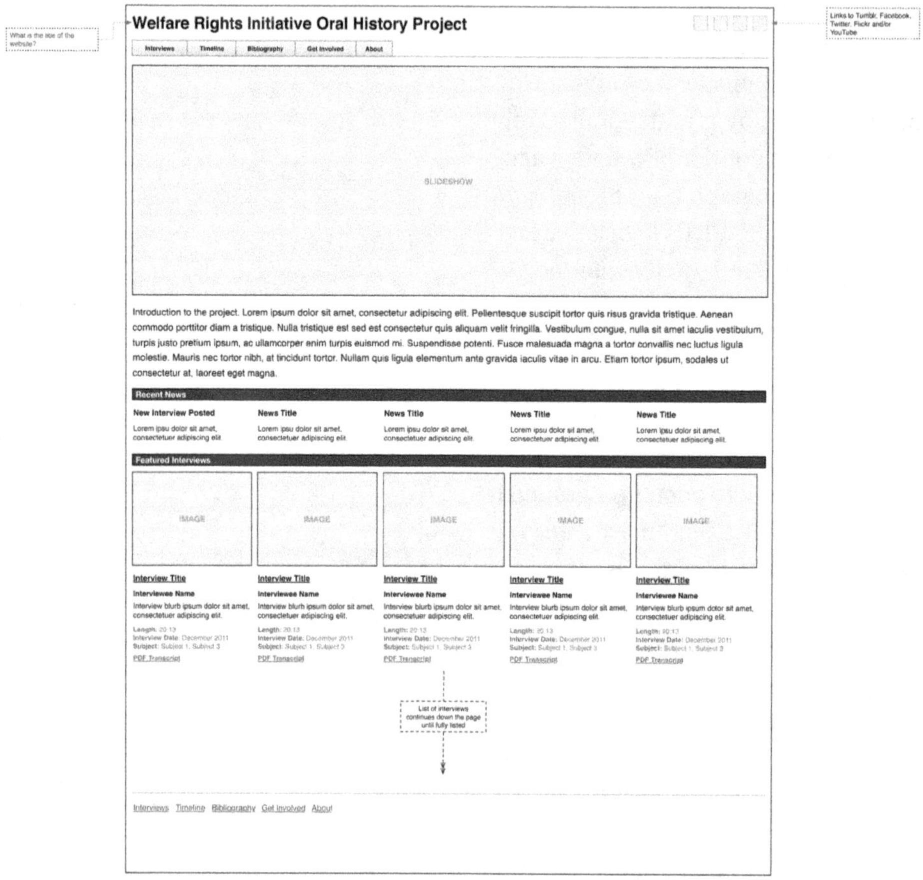

Figure 3. Preliminary mockup 2 of wireframe

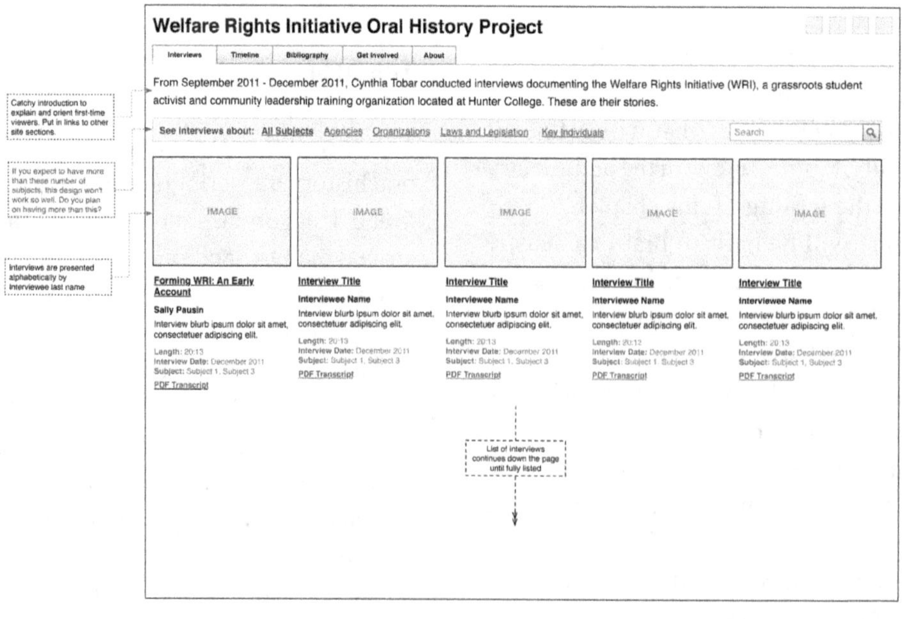

corrections of fact. For the most part, such corrections should be minor. Due to editing, transcripts will not always exactly match audio. In cases when interviewees add explanatory passages, this material will be bracketed. Each transcript will begin with a table of contents describing major themes. Each transcript will be loaded as a single-item PDF and full-text searching enabled.

Content Management System: Expression Engine

Expression Engine is proprietary content management system developed by Ellis Labs, which provides more of a user-centric perspective to exhibit and site design and less required programmer knowledge of PHP. As I began planning this archive, I wanted a CMS that would offer me the flexibility to add the metadata fields I needed for each of my records. As a result, with Expression Engine I can focus my efforts on designing the more crucial aspect of the public visitor's interface. By avoiding bulkier systems, I can craft a powerful user experience that allows researchers to focus on actually listening to the interviews.

According to its online documentation, Expression Engine is built on a open source PHP framework, CodeIgniter and runs on MySQL. In addition, the open-source capabilities of this CMS mean that users can add to and create extensions for their own sites. However, because Expression Engine is a commercial product, real resources are dedicated to writing quality documentation for ExpressionEngine. Consequently, there is a very active forum with a technical support staff employed by Ellis Labs and a wiki that contains useful ExpressionEngine tips and tricks. Many sites outside Ellis Labs also run tutorials, podcasts, and other information around Expression Engine.

Basic Workflow

Once I log on to the admin interface, I begin by creating a entry/channel for each type of content, such as Timeline or Interview (See Figure 4). Then a group is created, with custom fields for each entry; for example, the "News" channel might have: date, title, brief, link, article. After assigning the custom field groups to the entry, users can start entering content (See Figure 5).

The templates can use one's own valid, semantic, lean mean mark- up. No lengthy CSS rules are required. It can extend to manage any design, and is not constrained to header, columns, and footers. The URL structure is built around templates, and one can save and edit templates as well. As I learn more about using Expression Engine and its interface, I hope to learn more about its functionality and assess if it truly is the best fit for this digital oral history archive.

Figure 4. Expression engine administrative interface

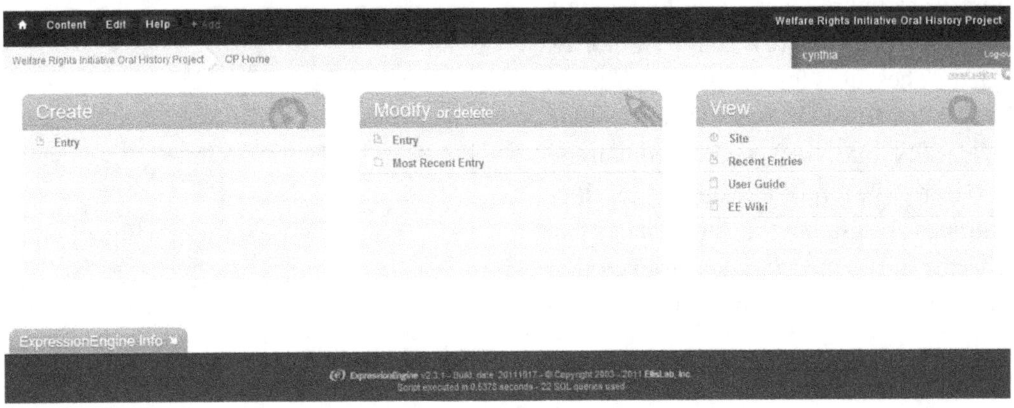

Figure 5. Expression engine's interface for creating an interview entry

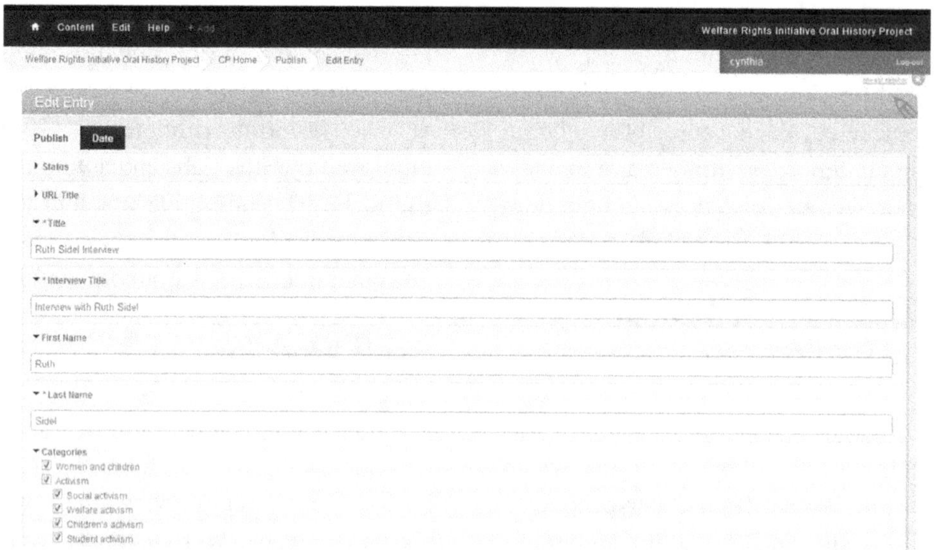

Metadata Standards

Individual records in the collection will provide detailed information about each project participant and interview. Unique identifying information—subject name, date of interview, and interviewer name—will be at the top of each record. Most participants will provide descriptions of their current or past activity within WRI. Project participants often use abbreviations and acronyms when speaking about the various organizations related to the WRI. Institutions were also reorganized and/or renamed over time. Metadata was created using qualified Dublin Core (See Figure 6). Controlled vocabulary was selected from several sources such as the Library of Congress Thesaurus for Graphic Materials, Library of Congress Name Authority, and the Getty Thesaurus for Geographic Names. These fields also function as a collection-wide index to identify interview records containing the same descriptive terms; one aim as development continues is to set up the site so users can click on terms in the metadata to retrieve other transcripts in which the same theme is discussed (See Figure 7).

FUTURE DIRECTIONS

One future consideration for the site will be to implement Schema.org. This joint effort from Google, Bing and Yahoo! to create and support a common vocabulary for structured data markup on Web pages, by and for Web developers and Webmasters, will improve how sites appear in

Figure 6. Metadata crosswalk for Dublin core

Metadata fields	Dublin Core markup
Title	<dc:title>Oral history interview with Dillonna Lewis, 2011 August 8.</dc:title>
Interviewee	<dc:creator> Lewis, Dillonna. Interviewee.</dc:creator> <dc:creator>Tobar, Cynthia. Interviewer.</dc:creator>
Interview date	<dc:date>2011</dc:date>
Resource type [text; Sound]	<dc:type xsi:type="dcterms:DCMIType">Sound</dc:type>
Format [Application/PDF; Audio/MP3]	<dc:format>1 sound recording (ca. 82 min.): digital. Transcript (ca. 16 p.): digital.</dc:format>
Subject [Agencies, Organizations, Laws and Legislation, Key Individuals, Subject]	<dc:subject xsi:type="dcterms:LCSH">Welfare reform.</dc:subject>
Digital ID	<dc:identifier>00.01<dc:identifier>
Description	<dc:description>As Welfare Rights Initiative (WRI) Co-Executive Director, Dillonna Lewis shares responsibility for overall governance, funding, programming development and leadership. Dillonna supervises and trains staff, interns and undergraduate students to operate and evaluate WRI's programs. She develops curriculum and instructs WRI's (two-semester, credit-bearing) Community Leadership training program at Hunter College.</dc:description>

Figure 7. Preliminary mockup of sample interview record as displayed on site

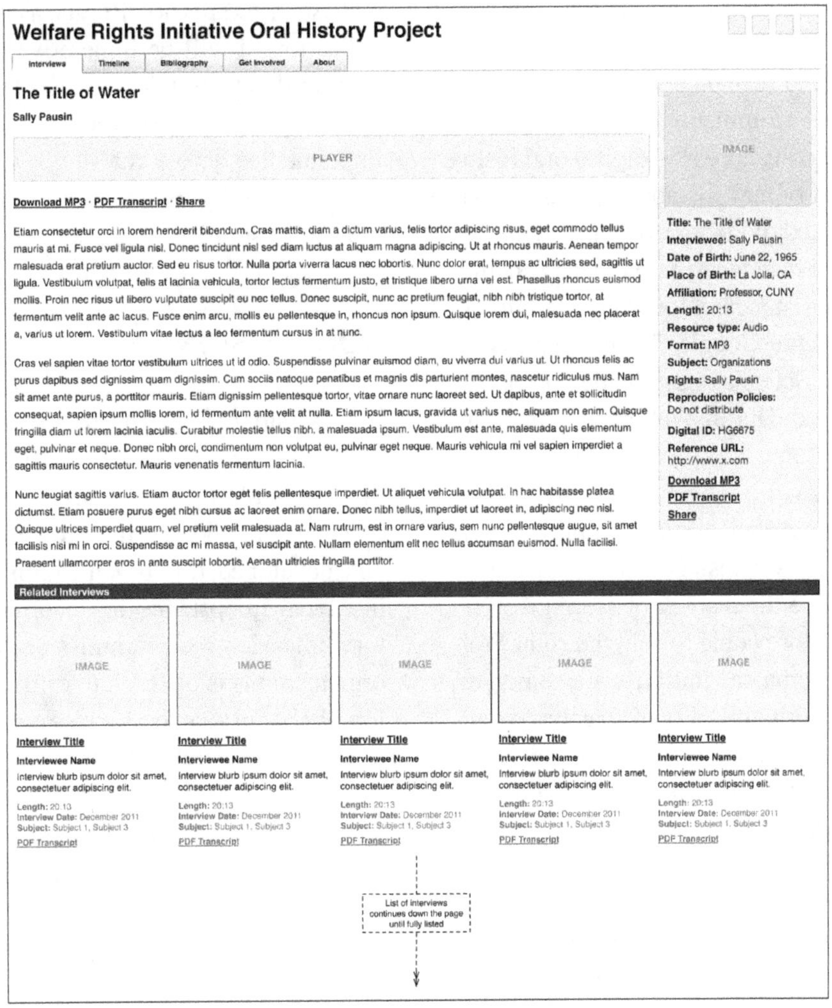

major search engines. This schema aims to be a one-stop resource for Webmasters looking to add markup to their pages, sets a common set of schemas for various types of multimedia (movies, music) supported across various search engines, and provide richer search results.

Oral histories present a non-linear path between primordial, archived collections and constructed, selective, and linear histories. The overlooked perspectives contained in these oral narratives via transcripts, which are also available online alongside the audio file, gain access to a wider audience through this Web-based archive. By combining oral histories and promoting its use via digital technologies, the underrepresented in the community take an active role in framing the historical record.

Search Engine Optimization (SEO) is becoming increasingly important to the success of a website. Search engine optimization means ensuring that Web pages are accessible to search engines and are focused in ways that help improve the likelihood of being found via semantic markup language, based on the schemas provided by schema.org. Comprehensive SEO and meta tag management, along with implementation of

Google Analytics that will provide me with a free Web statistics tracking system, will also be key in tracking where visitors are going on the site.

The new role of metadata and Semantic Web technologies have an immense impact on resource discovery, increasing access to digital oral histories. In the spirit of new metadata standards that explore distributed, collaborative approaches to "finding stuff," I decided to implement Schema.org, a microdata standard for Web markup. A collaboration of the Google, Yahoo!, and Bing search engines, Schema.org provides a way to include structured data in Web pages. Since its introduction in June 2011, the Schema.org vocabulary has grown to cover descriptive terms for content such as movies, music, organizations, locations, and news items. The goal of Schema.org is "to improve the display of search results, making it easier for people to find the right Web pages." The Schema.org initiative has emerged as a focal point for publishers of structured data in Web pages, and this standard has been applied to the WRI Oral History Project site. The goal will be to develop a crosswalk to map these schema.org terms to Dublin Core fields for each interview record.

I also plan to provide cross-referencing and searchable access in and across audio interviews that scholars and researchers can conveniently study, as well as to analyze if the user-centric interface can offer the most worthwhile access to this digital collection. Future considerations will involve digital preservation efforts for these born digital interviews, as well as to digitally archive the project site. Currently, I am also exploring options such as using the Internet Archive's Archive-It service, which allows subscribers to archive website content, which is hosted and stored by the Internet Archive.

After I go through the basic implementation and use of Expression Engine as the CMS for my collection, it will be imperative to set priorities for usability testing for the site. The focus will be on testing interfaces and concepts that are broadly implemented across the site. I will also analyze the accessibility, functionality, and aesthetics of the site's usability.

CONCLUSION

It is essential to capture the first-person memories of grassroots feminist activism, in the case of WRI within CUNY, and in New York City in particular, before the women who founded and developed this organization move on. The historical importance of documenting oral history interviews of feminist activist grassroots organizations is difficult to estimate. CUNY has long been influenced by a strong activist spirit; a spirit that is prevalent amongst its faculty and student body. CUNY is emblematic of dramatic demographic, social, economic, technological, and political shifts in New York and across the nation that have fundamentally altered both the nature of social welfare and workforce development. The future aim of this project will be to expand the number of interviews to additional WRI participants, as well as other social justice grassroots organizations in New York City to the digital archive, which will be funded by outside grant monies.

REFERENCES

Bracero History Archive. (2010). *Website.* Retrieved December 2, 2010 from http://bracero-archive.org/

Carroll, T. W. (2006). *How did working-class feminists meet the challenges of working across differences? The national congress of neighborhood women, 1974-2006*. Binghamton, NY: State University of New York.

Carroll, T. W. (2007). *Grassroots feminism: Direct action organizing and coalition building in New York City, 1955-1995*. (PhD Thesis). University of Michigan. Ann Arbor, MI.

Carroll. T. W. (2004). *New York City women community activists oral history project*. Retrieved from http://qe2aproxy.mun.ca/login?url=http://www.aspresolver.com/aspresolver.asp?WASM;S10020421

Nadasen, P. (2005). *Welfare warriors: The welfare rights movement in the United States*. New York, NY: Routledge.

Weikart, L. (2005). The era of meanness: Welfare reform and barriers to a college degree. *Affilia*, *20*(4), 416–433. doi:10.1177/0886109905279802

ADDITIONAL READING

Knight, K. (2011). *Usability testing with card sorting*. Retrieved August 22, 2011, from http://sixrevisions.com/usabilityaccessibility/card-sorting/

Kucsma, J., Reiss, K., & Sidman, A. (2010). Using omeka to build digital collections: The METRO case study. *D-Lib Magazine*, *16*(3-4), 3–4.

Omeka. (2009a). *Documentation - Omeka how to*. Retrieved September 22, 2009, from http://omeka.org/codex/Documentation

Omeka. (2009b). *Home*. Retrieved September 22, 2009, from http://omeka.org/

Omeka. (2010). *Web publishing for archives & museums*. Retrieved December 2, 2010, from http://omeka.org/

Racki, K. (2011). *The expression engine 2 client guide is here*. [Web log]. Retrieved from http://headspacedesign.ca/blog/entry/the-expressionengine-2-client-guide-is-here/

Chapter 12
Creating an Online Image Database:
Illustrating a Hands-On Approach to Experiential Learning

Claudia A. Perry
City University of New York, USA

Walter E. Valero
City University of New York, USA

ABSTRACT

The concept of experiential learning is particularly useful when students are required to create database entries as part of an ongoing, real-life, online experience. A METRO grant in 2005 resulted in an opportunity to use students to create a CONTENTdm database, which, with the continued software support from METRO, has continued and evolved until the present. This case study chapter describes the experience of both faculty and students in the Queens College Graduate School of Library and Information Studies course entitled "Introduction to Digital Imaging." Sections include a review of related literature, the background, technical issues, and implications for teaching, project procedures and workflow, successes and lessons learned, challenges, next steps, and emerging trends. Of particular interest is the use of out of copyright postcards and the metadata that has resulted from intensive student study and evaluation of the data contained on these cards. Those contemplating a digitization project of their own will be able to learn much about best practices, project planning, management, and the advantages/disadvantages of the CONTENTdm software.

INTRODUCTION

Experiential learning is an ideal pedagogical approach to teaching many subjects in a Master's program. Actual practice combined with a theoretical underpinning can be applied in a number of courses in any MLS curriculum. Past experience has shown that the tensions between these two constructs are artificial, and that an ideal situation can result when both are employed. This is particularly evident when one begins to teach, or talk about teaching, the planning, creation, management, and maintenance of an active, Internet-based, online database.

DOI: 10.4018/978-1-4666-2991-2.ch012

In 2005, the Queens College (QC) Graduate School of Library and Information Studies (GSLIS) and the QC Rosenthal Library received a grant from METRO, the Manhattan based Metropolitan New York Library Council (2012), to digitize a portion of the Queens College archives (see http://qcpages.qc.edu/GSLIS/digitization.html) (METRO is one of nine regional library councils serving libraries and residents of New York State; support for digital projects has been a high priority for much of the past decade). This, admittedly over-ambitious project, was an eye opener for all concerned. In the *Introduction to Digital Imaging* course, developed by Professor Perry, students and the instructor found that the variety of material designated for digitization (text, photographs, letters, magazine covers, slides, etc.) created an overly complex technological and teaching environment.

Although a new Mac teaching lab had been established in 2003 in time for the first iteration of the course, subsequent modifications added to the difficulties, given the necessity to troubleshoot/tweak hardware and software updates/changes. In addition, from the METRO feedback to the final report, and from a pedagogical standpoint, it became obvious that digitizing a single medium was best for the teaching/learning process. Course objectives were simplified to enhance the theoretical aspects of the course and awareness of essential standards/best practices, along with incorporating a real life database project that included hands-on work.

This chapter has the following objectives:

1. To document, analyze and summarize how the development of a graduate library course, which introduces the concepts of digital image capture and data creation and storage, has evolved.
2. To demonstrate how the experiential learning model is well suited for the teaching of the concepts and skills required in digital librarianship.
3. To identify pedagogy that enhances the teaching of technological concepts and skills integral to the design of digital libraries.
4. To illustrate how user-centered/student-centered feedback is critical to the evaluation and assessment strategies of digital librarianship.

BACKGROUND

According to the ERIC Thesaurus, experiential learning is "learning by doing" (http://www.eric.ed.gov/ERICWebPortal/thesaurus/thesaurus.jsp). It is closely related to—and an example of—active learning ("learning in which the learner is the principal driving force, with the instructor[if one is present] as facilitator of the process…"). A similar concept is that of service learning ("learning through community service [or public service in a public sphere] usually integrated with regular instruction in school or college"). Schools of Library and Information Science (LIS) have long offered experiential and service learning in terms of field work, practicums, or internships, in order to offer a balance between theory and practice. Ball (2008) provides a thorough review of the literature on practicums and service learning since the time of Dewey, then addresses these trends historically within LIS education. Interestingly, she notes tremendous shifts in the degree to which fieldwork has been required, from the founding of formal library school education through changes over the decades. In light of recent controversy regarding the success of LIS education in meeting the needs of the profession, Ball suggests the importance of further investigation of the value of experiential and service learning in the field at this time.

Currum (2011) describes an alternative approach to experiential learning beyond that of fieldwork or internships, based on the question-answering components of the ipl2. Formed by a merger of the Internet Public Library (IPL) and

Librarians Internet Index (LII) websites, ipl2 is hosted by Drexel University's College of Information Science and Technology and numerous other partner and participating universities (http://ipl2.org/div/about/). Currum discusses the advantages and challenges of implementing experiential learning opportunities, especially given the rapid changes in technology within LIS. The author then describes the specific ways in which use of the question answering service in the ipl2 can help students achieve some of the ALA core competencies for reference and user services that might be difficult in a typical classroom setting without the use of experiential learning.

Others stress the importance of experiential learning when working within digital librarianship, as well. Lin and Abels (2010) trace the evolution of Digital Library (DL) education through a series of publications beginning with the 1999 survey by Spink and Cool. Lin and Abels note not only that DL should now be considered an integrated part of LIS education, but also the need to provide a balance of theory and practice, including hands-on work. They describe the development of a digital library lab at Drexel University, based on the consortial IPL and following a number of key principles. The evolving IPL Digital Lab has been used to support student hands-on learning activities in assignments as various as metadata evaluation, collaborative interface design, and also digital reference, much like the examples described by Currum (2011).

Dahlstrom and Doracic (2009) emphasize recent calls for teaching of the conversion and digitization of Cultural Heritage (CH) materials by a number of authors. They then relate their own experiences with digitization education at the Swedish School of Library and Information Science (SSLIS), along with an overview of developments in other Nordic countries. Of particular value in this chapter is the thorough assessment of challenges in terms of the "emergence, process and evaluation of the CH digitization courses" ("Challenges" section). Some, though not all of these challenges, apply to the current case study. However, it is clear that further discussion of these challenges (and successes) will contribute substantively to collective progress in digitization education in a global setting.

Evolution of the Waterways Project

This background and literature review thus sets the context for the evolution of the Queens College GSLIS experience with digitization education.

FROM INDEPENDENT STUDY TO FULL COURSE

Following then-student Walter Valero's successful immersion in the METRO funded grant initiative in Spring 2005, he was looking for a potential focus for the required research requirement that is part of the GSLIS curriculum (GSLIS 709: Research in Library and Information Studies (LIS)). In consultation with Professor Thomas Surprenant, Valero decided to use the latter's collection of early 20th century Erie Canal postcards as the basis for his content analysis project. The project was completed in Fall 2005. At the time, the postcard collection totaled over 500 cards, which made selection of the 103 to be examined for content analysis a relatively easy task. Scanning the postcards into TIFF files, a skill gained in *Digital Imaging*, allowed him to zoom in on card details, aiding his ability to discern the finer points for his analysis. His final paper included numerous postcard images that illustrated key points that directly supported the content analysis.

Once Valero had completed the research project, it was a logical next step to use the digitized images and knowledge gained in their analysis to create a coherent online digital collection. In consultation with Perry and Surprenant, Valero devised an Independent Study project for Spring 2006. The Independent Study incorporated JPEG derivatives of the scanned postcard images, including metadata and key documentation. All were incorporated into the online database that he created.

As compared to the archival materials digitized in the METRO grant project in 2005, the choice of the postcard medium was soon shown to be a major improvement. Due to the vagaries of course scheduling, *Digital Imaging* was not offered in Spring 2006. This provided time for a pilot project to unfold as a possible alternative model for future course sessions, and allowed for collaborative experimentation. What worked and what needed additional attention in a more formal class setting were identified and adjusted.

It became clear that postcards could serve as an ideal choice of medium in a teaching/learning environment, because they are information rich, usually of uniform size and, in the case of this collection, not subject to copyright since they were produced prior to 1923. A literature search for possible digital collection software resulted in the selection of Greenstone, an open-source product (New Zealand Digital Library Project, 2005-2007). This software, created by a UNESCO/University of New Zealand collaboration, is designed to be used by computer and software novices. Greenstone is a template style database program that utilizes Dublin Core as its default metadata schema. The simple interface allows users to create, input, and maintain a database with relative ease. While it is fairly easy for program savvy users to tweak the program, it is still quite limited in its capabilities. This is a major strength of the software, but it is also a detriment for those who want to move very far beyond the standard template and/or for those who lack the requisite technical skills.

"Wednesdays with Walter" was born when the three participants in the Independent Study got together to plan and implement the revised approach to *Digital Imaging*. In Spring 2006, the group met weekly to discuss scope, controlled vocabulary, database structure and search features, among other issues. Additional essential steps were the development of relevant project documentation, in the context of existing best practices and the historical background relating to the New York State canal system. The resulting online "Waterways of New York" postcard collection was hosted on a Queens College server supported by the QC Office of Converging Technologies (see http://gsdl.qc.cuny.edu/gsdl/cgi-bin/library.exe?site=localhost&a=p&p=about&c=canalsof&ct=1&qto=3&l=en&w=utf-8).

As the semester progressed, the advantages of post cards as a choice of format for future class use became increasingly apparent. Other aspects of the pilot seemed somewhat less applicable to the classroom setting. Among these were the use of the Greenstone digital collection software, and independent development of a project-specific controlled vocabulary. To lessen the workload on all course participants, and given METRO's willingness to continue to provide access to CONTENTdm (CDM) (OCLC, 2010), it was decided to use this platform, instead of Greenstone, for the expansion of the Waterways Project. The choice of CDM guided the selection of Dublin Core as the metadata schema, and the Library of Congress' *Thesaurus of Graphic Materials* (TGM), (Library of Congress, 2007) adjusted for local needs, as the basis of a controlled vocabulary. File naming conventions and digitization specifications were identified following TASI (now JISC Digital Media, 2008), and California Digital Library guidelines (now revised as BCR's CDP Digital Imaging Best Practices, 2008).

It was decided early on that members of each class would act as "consultants" or as an informal "Advisory Council" to give the students hands-on experience in providing ongoing project-based feedback. In this role, students were encouraged to comment on the conduct/structure of the class and, more importantly, on all aspects of the digitization development process and project itself. As a result, many changes were made, and continue to be made, due to ongoing, sometimes quite vociferous, student input. Students with strong cataloging experience insisted on adherence to standard cataloging conventions, which substantially enhanced both the class and the content of the database itself. Other student suggestions included an expanded emphasis on architecture, dress, and activities of daily living that went far beyond the initial emphasis on canals and water-based transportation. Student efforts to research noted architectural sites or famous disasters resulted in the addition of a "References" metadata field, with hyperlinks to additional information. Thus, the "consultants" have been an essential underpinning to mutual learning and the evolving quality of the entire enterprise. Such formative assessment, promoting student attainment through direct feedback in the teaching/learning process, allows students to take control of their own learning. It is easily the most important element in *Digital Imaging*.

EVOLVING SCOPE AND PURPOSE OF THE PROJECT

As is perhaps inevitable in a real-life project embedded in a student-learning environment, the intended scope and purpose of the "Waterways" project have evolved over time, in accordance with the input of our Advisory Councils. Initially, given the focus of Surprenant's postcard collection, materials relating to the Erie Canal and other waterways of New York, the emphasis was on maritime topics. As noted above, student interest in non-maritime elements of the cards expanded the scope of the thesaurus terminology and card descriptions. As Valero observed during the course of his independent study, "the postcards spoke to me and I listened. But I still had to know what look and listen for." Similarly, the analyses of the backs of the postcards proved to be at least as interesting to project participants as the images themselves. Transcription of postcard messages, addresses, analysis of stamps, stamp boxes, postmarks and trademarks all became increasingly important elements of the analytical process as participants learned from the materials and the materials challenged them. In addition, the scope of the collecting of postcards was extended from an initial focus primarily on Erie Canal postcards, to those of the Barge Canal, Champlain Canal, Delaware and Hudson Canal, the Hudson River and New York Harbor, among other waterways. In large part this was due to the need to provide sufficient materials for students to digitize, but also due to the continuing availability of interesting and relevant postcards offered for sale on eBay (a primary source for additions to the analogue collection). With one exception, the course has been offered every semester since 2005, often in multiple sections, and nearly always with substantial waiting lists. At present, the database contains over 1,750 images (http://cdm128401.cdmhost.com/cdm/search/collection/qcgslis_f06).

Clearly, it is essential that class readings and discussions emphasize the importance of planning a project from the beginning, considering such issues as audience, scope, budget, timeframe, software, hardware, and preservation issues. However, an advantage of a long-term evolving project is that initial expectations can be adjusted, with accompanying discussion of how these changes need to consider the nature of potential audiences and the subject matter and other characteristics of the materials analyzed.

TEACHING/LEARNING METHODOLOGIES

Table 1 illustrates the various steps in the process of creating the database and other hands-on activities used to reinforce the learning process.

HANDLING AND QUALITY CONTROL OF STUDENT METADATA

As noted above, students input copies of their JPEG files and their metadata into Excel templates as part of established workflow procedures. These templates already include data in fields that are

Table 1. Creating the waterways database

Process	Hardware	Software	Support With Handout and Faculty Assistance
Scan postcard fronts and backs (TIFFs) to create archival masters	Epson 8800 Scanner	Silverfast AI	Yes (see as BCR's CDP Digital Imaging Best Practices, 2008 for determining specs)
Create derivative files from TIFFs (JPEGs)	Mac or PC	Photoshop	Yes
Check file size, adherence to digital specifications, record height and width of JPEGS in pixels per inch	Mac or PC	Photoshop Bridge	Yes (see as BCR's CDP Digital Imaging Best Practices, 2008 for determining specs)
Insert JPEGS into Excel template, add metadata	Mac or PC	Excel	Thesaurus, Project documentation/Handouts, consultation with faculty
Quality Control partners review metadata and digital specs, add corrections (one card at a time)	Mac or PC	Excel, Photoshop Bridge	As above
Faculty reviews metadata on initial card, provides additional feedback [Process continues for subsequent cards for both partners and faculty]	Mac or PC	Excel	As above
Create CDM template, input recurring metadata fields (e.g. dig. specs), select autoimport options, test with imported images)	PC	CONTENTdm (CDM client software is PC-compliant only)	Lab Handouts, faculty assistance
Import JPEG images, copy/paste metadata from Excel files	PC	CONTENTdm	Lab Handouts, faculty assistance and review (one card at a time)
Students upload reviewed images and metadata to Administrative interface	PC	CONTENTdm	Lab Handouts, faculty assistance and review (one card at a time)
Faculty reviews uploaded files; perform minor corrections as needed, uploads to "Live" database; if errors are substantial, deletes files and informs student of need to redo work.	Mac or PC	CONTENTdm Administrative interface	
Faculty indexes databases so files display live	Mac or PC	CONTENTdm Administrative interface	
Students save backup files (TIFFs, JPEGs, Excel) on CD and external drives, print out Excel files for future reference	Mac or PC	Excel	
Students are provided with an pre-designed XML schema, and shown how to import this schema into an Excel file to illustrate the ease of conversion	Mac or PC	Excel	Yes
Students are provided with instructions on how to set-up a hosted server & with instructions on how to upload their JPEG image file(s) and XML file(s) onto their hosted server & then shown how to display the content using a pre-designed HTML file.	Mac or PC	Hosted Server	Yes

consistent across the project, such as digital specifications, format, rights management etc. Students enter only that information that is specific to their individual cards, such as title, creator, description, subjects, and date (original and digital). This approach serves multiple purposes. Quality control partners can email each other copies of the files, comment and make corrections (in another color or row), then forward the file to the faculty member (with a copy to their partner), for additional review and commentary. This creates a progressive record of the status of the metadata, essential to assessing student work at this step in the process. It also produces an archival record of changes to the thesaurus and other metadata conventions over time. In addition, it reduces time spent using the

CDM client interface, as students can simply cut-and-paste their corrected metadata into the CDM template. This has been especially important at times when CDM crashed unexpectedly during data input, a not infrequent occurrence over the years, and especially before we had regular access to the PC OS in our teaching lab (The CDM client software only is available on a PC; we now are equipped with dual-boot Mac/PC computers). In recent iterations of the course, the instructor has posted screen-shots of Excel templates with edits and corrections on the Blackboard Course Management System (CMS) class website. This has spurred student efforts to be more consistent in their handling of metadata issues.

Early on it was determined that, for well done metadata input, it took approximately 15 minutes per card (front and back) for faculty to conduct quality control on student submissions. While this cuts down on errors, faculty review of poor work can require as much as an hour or more per card, especially for initial submissions. Thus, at a minimum, given 14-15 students with three cards each, faculty time on quality control at this stage easily exceeds ten hours. In reality, multiple submissions of each card may be required, and students do not always adhere to set deadlines for card submissions or return of partners' work. Thus, faculty may have limited time to review student submissions prior to a scheduled class. This can cause substantial disruption to the course schedule, not to mention high levels of stress and inevitable oversights of errors. It has not been exceptional for faculty to spend over 25 hours per semester on this stage of quality control, and an additional 25+ hours reviewing files uploaded to CDM's administrative interface. This has been especially true when new sub-collections of the Waterways Project were introduced (e.g. Barge Canal cards as compared to Erie Canal cards). For example, in one course section in Spring 2010, out of a total of 84 images with associated metadata uploaded to CDM, only seven were free of mistakes or omissions, while 77 included errors. See Figure 1.

Examples of input errors included the following: (1) date digital missing or incorrect format, (2) missing or incorrect source (e.g. Barge canal vs. Erie Canal sub-collection), (3) misspelled title, incorrect file name (e.g. e0273ac1—this is NOT an incorrect example) in title field, title copied and pasted twice, (4) duplicate subject headings, failure to appropriately capitalize TGM terms, (5) missing date original, (6) using letter "o" instead of number "0" in resource identifier field. These errors were introduced despite extensive quality control on the metadata submitted to both the quality control partner and the faculty. The importance of some elements (e.g. file name in title field) relates more to administrative oversight and approval of uploaded files by faculty than to ultimate usability, but it illustrates the complexities of managing an ongoing project over many years. More serious errors (not reported above) reflect oversights in the CDM template setup. It appears that error rates vary depending on student preparedness and commitment. As time has gone on, and more students hear positive feedback about the course, less experienced or less technically adept students are more likely to enroll than in earlier years. An additional difficulty is that strong students tend to choose each other as partners, and the converse, which can exacerbate the challenges for this component of the project.

Figure 1. Errors in CDM final uploads, Spring 2010

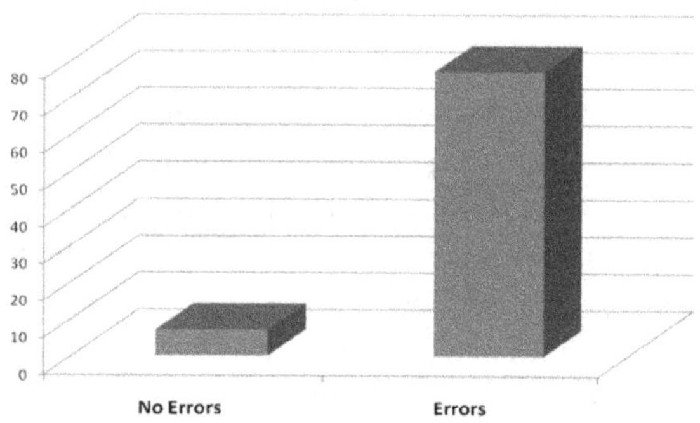

It also became apparent that "ownership" was a significant issue for both students and faculty. Early on, it was decided that, unless students wished to use only their initials, their names would be associated with each record that they created for the database. The vast majority of students recognize that providing employers, and potential employers, with access to practical examples of their work can be extremely valuable. Students have taken substantial pride in searching their names in Google and finding their records displayed in the database. Beginning in Spring 2009, listing the names of quality control partners as part of the Digitization Team was instituted as the role of quality control became ever more essential and demanding.

While Microsoft Excel provides a viable solution for storing metadata when creating an online image database it may not necessarily be the best option for transporting or migrating metadata. This is where Extensible Markup Language (XML) can be utilized as an alternative solution to store metadata. According to Banerjee (2002) XML "is extremely useful because it simplifies the transfer of information from one system or program to another" (http://www.infotoday.com/cilmag/sep02/Banerjee.htm). Because it provides a standard for defining containers that store information, XML is an ideal alternative solution to include as part of an online image database's long-term digital preservation/sustainability plan, especially when most digital asset management platforms and/or systems available in the marketplace are proprietary in nature. Therefore, the inclusion of a basic exercise in XML that demonstrates its effectiveness in storing and transporting metadata is most essential when introducing to students the concept of preservation for digital materials.

CASE STUDY ANALYSIS

Students also are required to write a case study that examines a selected, well-documented, faculty-approved online digital collection, and evaluate it using the practical experience gained in their hands-on work along with what was learned in the readings, lectures and class discussions. The assignment was designed to emphasize such areas as: project goals and objectives, planning, materials selection, technology/software, metadata and digitization standards, funding and maintenance of effort, copyright, staffing, collaboration, documentation, evaluation and quality control, storage, and long-term digital preservation and management strategies (Credit is due to Professor Karen F. Gracey for her course LIS 2674: Digital Preservation, at the University of Pittsburgh School of Information Sciences, from which this assignment was adapted). Required class presentations summarizing highlights afford a greatly expanded look at the current state of the art of digitization, as well as changes over time. Since this is a rapidly evolving field, students and faculty gain a tremendous amount of perspective and understanding from the individual case study analyses, and the opportunity to view key characteristics of a range of other projects. This is valuable in terms of seeing close-up the tremendous changes that have taken place in the field in a remarkably short span of time. Students also are impressed with the quality and extent of their own metadata contributions, compared to some other, often nationally prominent collections. Lastly, it is tremendously rewarding to hear the ways in which students will highlight points from key readings, class lectures, or other students' case studies or experiences in their presentations, a practice that the faculty endeavor to model throughout the semester.

A more recent innovation, introduced by Prof. Valero, is the inclusion of peer feedback in the grading process regarding student presentations of their case studies. This component contributes to the real-world model of teamwork and peer mentoring that students are likely to encounter when they enter the workforce. It also provides a means for students to celebrate their colleagues' successes, and expands the range of feedback beyond that provided by a single instructor. This is not dissimilar to findings that student blogging or group work in wikis reinforces student attention on the quality of their work (e.g. see Lapp, Shea, & Wolsey, 2011; Robertson, 2011). Related studies include a fairly recent focus on the impact of student peer evaluations on student learning (Girard, Pinar, & Trapp, 2011; Lavy & Yadin, 2010). Topping (1998) provides a expanded literature review that also could prove helpful to explore earlier work using this approach.

OVERALL DISTRIBUTION AND ASSESSMENT OF COURSE REQUIREMENTS

Objectives and Activities

At the end of the course students will be able to:

Objective 1: Describe the role and place of digital imaging in Library and Information Studies (LIS).

Objective 2: Describe major problems and challenges associated with digital imaging.

Activity: Class Participation; Case Study.

Objective 3: Describe the principles and criteria used in selecting materials for conversion to digital format.

Activity: Class Participation; Tech Review Sheet, Case Study.

Objective 4: Analyze major digitization projects and how they are being run.

Activity: Case Study.

Objective 5: Apply standards and best practices to digitization projects.

Activity: Class participation; Tech Review Sheet, CONTENTdm Project, Metadata and Quality Control, Hosted Server and XML Conversion Assignments.

Objective 6: Deduce project and workflow planning techniques essential for managing and oversight of digital initiatives.

Activity: Class participation; CONTENTdm Project, Class participation; CONTENTdm Project, Metadata and Quality Control, Hosted Server and XML Conversion Assignments.

Objective 7: Produce metadata that ensures the long-term reusability of digital materials.

Activity: Class participation; CONTENTdm Project, Class participation; CONTENTdm Project, Metadata and Quality Control, Hosted Server and XML Conversion Assignments.

Table 2 provides a summary of the relative proportion of credit allocated to students for various components of the course. This balance has shifted over time in response to perceptions of time and effort spent in various activities. In particular, coursework relating to project activities

Table 2. Summary of the relative proportion of credit allocated to students

Assignments/Activities	Percentage	Objectives Met
Technical Review Sheet Assignment	10%	3, 5
Metadata and Quality Control	15%	5, 6, 7
CONTENTdm Project	20%	5, 6, 7
Hosted Server and XML Conversion Assignments	10%	5, 6, 7
Class Participation/In-Class Labs/Case Study Presentation	15%	1, 2, 3, 5, 6, 7
Case Study	30%	1, 2, 3, 4, 5
Total:	**100%**	

(scanning, metadata, quality control, final upload) has been adjusted regularly to reflect changing challenges in the nature of the course, the complexity of the postcards, and the characteristics of project activities.

The Technical Review Assignment was introduced as an alternative mechanism for students to demonstrate familiarity with key technical concepts that will be applied in the lab and project implementation. Rather than listening to lectures on these admittedly dry, but essential topics, after completing relevant assigned readings, students respond to a series of questions regarding the meaning and application of such topics as file formats, file naming conventions, color space, file compression, and decisions related to digital specifications. Contrary to faculty expectations, student written mid-semester feedback on this graded exercise has been extremely positive. While there is some inevitable delay between exposure to hands-on lab work, and grasp of these technical concepts, by the seventh week nearly all students manage to connect the theoretical with the practical in a most rewarding way. Students also are encouraged assist one another during and outside of class, since many vary greatly in their skills in software/hardware, metadata aptitude, and relevant experience. By the end of a typical semester, extremely strong bonds have been formed. As a result, *Digital Imaging* alumni are among the school's strongest supporters, and alums frequently remain in regular contact with the faculty as well as each other. Email connections and social networking sites sustain these relationships, as do informal social gatherings. Ironically, this bond exists even with students/alums who have not taken the course, but who sense the value of networking and connections among those with related interests.

ROLE OF THE COURSE WITHIN THE LARGER GSLIS CURRICULUM

No course within a curriculum exists in a vacuum, and this is especially true in the rapidly evolving area of Library and Information Science (LIS) education. From its initial introduction in Fall 2003, *Introduction to Digital Imaging* has attracted numerous students with an interest in archives and preservation. A certificate program in *Archives, Records Management, and Preservation*, including a required internship, was formally approved in July 2003. Since that time, a substantial proportion of students enrolled in the course have either earned a certificate, or taken substantial coursework related to archives. Further, those enrolled in *Digital Imaging* often bring substantive experience and backgrounds in related fields, ranging from publishing, studio/digital arts, and graphic design, to the management of photo or audio archives, to cite just a few. The expertise, experience, and insights these individuals bring to the course make an invaluable contribution to the learning experience for faculty and students alike.

Student interest, tracking of employment trends, and perceptions of curricular need led to discussions of possible additional certificate programs in the GSLIS in early 2008. Among those considered were certificates in Web management/design and digital librarianship/digitization. Due to a variety of factors, these certificates remain in planning mode, but may be considered in the future. In parallel, adjustments were being considered to the Archives Certificate program to include a greater digital emphasis. An Institute of Museum and Library Services (IMLS) planning grant was awarded in August 2008 with the goal of revising the Archives curriculum. These efforts resulted in an improved *Certificate in Archives and Preservation of Cultural Materials*, formally approved in Fall 2009. The revised certificate includes new courses in *Digital Preservation*; *Archival Appraisal, Arrangement and Access*; as well as revisions to previously required classes.

Introduction to Digital Imaging, *Introduction to Metadata/XML*, and *Digital Libraries* are among the courses recommended for the program, in some cases suggested as pre- or co-requisites.

In general, these changes reflect an increasing focus on the role of technology as an "area of emphasis" in the GSLIS program, and in the sorts of skills frequently featured in recent job postings. Additional course offerings range from *Web Programming in Libraries* to *Design and Construction of Bibliographic Databases*, to a new emphasis on Web 2.0 technologies in previously existing courses. All of these courses are heavily involved in experiential, hands-on learning. Further, the changes and additions to the curriculum encourage students to develop a much more detailed appreciation of all phases in the life cycle of materials than ever could be achieved within a single, stand-alone course. Just in the context of digital curation, these range from selection and the process of soliciting archival materials from donors, through preparation of finding aids, digitization, creation of metadata, building and maintaining collections, and planning for long term preservation and archiving of digital objects.

Student interest in technology and independent, hands-on practice are represented in a range of individually designed independent studies, as well as innovative projects in the *Research in Library and Information Studies* (LBSCI 709) course. Independent study students have conducted extensive quality control to update the existing metadata in the Waterways project, and created valuable documentation on procedures and practices. In Spring 2010, Scott Voth, a graduate of the *Digital Imaging* course, migrated a substantial portion of the Waterways collection to the open source Web-publishing platform Omeka (Center for History and New Media, 2007-2010), as a key element in his capstone research project in 709 (See http://www.pcnyw.net/omeka/). This work, like many other student projects and internships, draws heavily on the range of theoretical and practical skills gained throughout the program. In particular, it encourages students to demonstrate their skills in independent, experiential learning that bring together the best of their master's education, previous experience, and extra-curricular activities. The authors will be working with this alumnus in migrating our CDM database to Omeka as the preferred platform for our collection in early 2012.

CHALLENGES AND RECOMMENDATIONS

The above narrative seeks to point out the many positive aspects of experiences with a digital library course project integrated into an LIS program. However, it would be inappropriate not to mention the many challenges inherent in such an initiative. With declining university budgets, there is increased pressure to expand class sizes nearly everywhere. Project-based courses like *Digital Imaging* simply cannot be adequately taught with large numbers of students, especially in an environment with no teaching or lab assistants to provide support either inside or outside the classroom. The department limits the class size in *Digital Imaging* to 15, and even that places extensive time demands on the faculty. The often grim realities of teaching with technology also must be acknowledged. Not a semester has gone by without some major technology glitch, ranging from computers upgraded the first week of class (and resulting delays in lab availability) through unexpected software upgrades the two weeks prior to the end of the semester (in this case, of CDM). In many semesters, such incidents have been ongoing and have required great effort to resolve.

In an ideal educational world, the availability of lab assistants, teaching assistants, and information technology support attuned to the nuances of the academic schedule would substantially reduce the stresses associated with a course like this. Those planning similar initiatives would be well advised to request such support in advance, if at all feasible. The existence of a supportive cadre of like-minded faculty, whether inside or outside one's department, either adjunct or full-time, for sharing tips on teaching and learning with technology, can be of tremendous help. Involvement with campus colleagues, through the QC Center for Teaching and Learning on such initiatives as ePortfolio implementation and the mentoring of faculty teaching hybrid/blended courses (partly online), has expanded the network of faculty technology gurus with varying levels of expertise. Such engagement can provide mutual support and essential collaborative learning opportunities. In addition, of course, ongoing networking with practicing colleagues in the field, including former students and fellow LIS educators and practitioners, cannot be underestimated.

Yet additional issues affecting a commuting, primarily part-time master's program are the inherent incompatibilities between the challenges of course scheduling, the realities of students' work and family/life responsibilities, and the constraints of a 36-credit program. It is not uncommon for GSLIS students to travel 3 hours round-trip to attend class, while working full-time. This encourages creativity in ensuring that class time is used as constructively as possible, and activities that can be handled outside of school are maximized. It also poses substantial sequencing challenges, especially in digital library and digital curation curricula. One can suggest, but usually not require, key pre- or co-requisites that would provide the optimal learning experience for all concerned. Increasingly we find graduates returning for a sixth year certificate, simply to enroll in essential courses that were closed due to over-enrollment or unavailable during their scheduled time earning their degree.

Lastly, it is important to note that key aspects of a course such as *Digital Imaging* certainly can be implemented in microcosm. Group consultation and problem solving, hands-on work with partners, peer-review, a strong emphasis on student-initiated learning, collaboration, and leadership in the conduct of a course all are possible even without a central, project focal point. Perhaps the most essential characteristics required of participating faculty are the capacity to accept the role of "guide-on-the-side," who will learn as much or more from their students as their students learn from them.

FUTURE AND EMERGING TRENDS

In light of the stated objectives of this chapter, and in the context of the broader theme of digital librarianship, a number of trends can be identified.

As is true of the rapid pace of change within digital librarianship, and especially education for digitization, adjustments to the ways in which students and practitioners learn about digital image capture and data creation and storage are inevitable, but other values and practices will endure. McNemeny (2007) proposes that "the notion of digital content creation needs to be more firmly perceived by the library community as an essential skill for all new entrants to the profession rather than an occasionally desirable one" (p. 537). He references the example of LIS students working with community organizations to digitize historic images of local importance as part of digitization course (Burton & McNemeny, 2005), an intriguing approach that potentially can benefit both students and smaller cultural heritage organizations. However, he also emphasizes the continuing importance of collaboration, strategic leadership, and cognizance of the best practices in the field (p. 539). Certainly, these have long been the hallmarks of success in the development of digital librarianship globally within recent decades, and will continue to be essential to the field while facing emerging challenges.

Work by Bastian, Harvey, Mahard, and Plum (2010) and Long (2011) similarly explores the importance of collaboration and experiential learning within DL education, This is especially true as the disparate disciplines involved with the digitization increasingly converge. Cultural heritage institutions, including archives, museums, libraries, digital repositories, electronic records managers, and digital preservationists must share their expertise within and among these respective professional communities, but also with educators, in order to adequately prepare practitioners for the needs of the future. Social networking technologies are likely to facilitate interaction among these different groups, but cultural norms and linguistic differences also will pose challenges to effective interaction. And equally important, it will be essential to adequately document, evaluate and assess alternative models for addressing the challenges of DL education.

The challenges of dealing with both born-digital and those analog materials yet to be digitized are indeed extensive. These authors note the need for future and current practitioners to integrate traditional theory and practice seamlessly with information technology skills in order to address problems that perhaps have not yet even been envisioned. They also address the need to inculcate within the broad realm of LIS an appreciation of the value of information no matter the formats in which they may exist. What will happen to those items NOT born digital; as more and more new items are born digital what will happen to those that have yet to be digitized? What technologies will become available in the future? And who will decide what content is important or not?

The issue of metadata is but one topic on which one might focus. In considering approaches to the handling of metadata, both within the educational setting and in practice, the following are but a few of the questions to consider: (1) Which schema to choose and why? (2) How much data/metadata to include? (3) Should one focus on what is obvious, prominent, and overt? Or on the less prominent and obscure? (4) What role should inference play? (5) How does one proceed in the absence of a subject expert? (6) How might the practices of large cultural heritages institutions best be adapted for smaller, local institutions and learning communities with more limited skills and budgets? (7) How might social tagging be used in various contexts to augment the creation of metadata by information professionals?

These and other challenges too numerous to mention suggest that active tracking and careful analysis not just of trends within the digitization library community, but also examples within education for digital librarianship will become if anything increasingly important in the years to come.

CONCLUSION

The evolution of the *Digital Imaging* course over the last nine years has been a challenging learning experience for all concerned. Primary conclusions concern the ways in which students' roles as key players in the decision-making, implementation, and practical development of an online digital database, strongly reinforce their theoretical and practical learning. In many ways, the faculty have tried to model the structure of a project work group in the field, exactly the sort of work environment that most librarians and information specialists will enter in the future. The issues likely to be encountered include, but are not limited to, project planning and management, identifying and troubleshooting technical problems, dealing with recalcitrant hardware/software and networking issues, working collaboratively under deadline, correcting errors and inconsistencies in documentation, dealing with a changing project scope, staying current with evolving trends and best practices, and providing useful but supportive feedback to others. Such feedback in the course involves not just informal and ongoing consultation, but also written quality control comments, and anonymous mid-semester and end-of-term written course evaluations by students. Based on all these elements, the course, the students, and the faculty are in a constant process of formative assessment, with the goal to prepare our students appropriately for the very challenging work environment in which they will find themselves. A secondary goal is to ensure that the course remains a valid teaching/learning tool.

Without the requisite theoretical framework, students could hardly engage on a project of this sort. Course activities, readings and activities are carefully structured to build progressively towards a greater mastery of required skills and decision-making abilities. Equally important are efforts to encourage and reinforce a model of problem-solving and active learning, by exploring various avenues to find needed information, and making connections among seemingly disparate elements. In creating metadata, students frequently research the geography and historical context of the images on the cards, the publishers, and the information to be gained by close examination of trademarks and stamp boxes. In their case studies, students are encouraged to contact key personnel when documentation is lacking. The response, more often than not, has been incredibly positive, with some contacts requesting copies of the finished paper. In this way, students become intimately engaged in the professional community of which they will soon be a part.

The challenges of staying current while teaching a very time-intensive course are undeniable. Nonetheless, it is essential for dedicated educators to remain alert to mechanisms for incorporating promising teaching/learning approaches within the structure of their courses. These may include experiential or service learning, reflection, peer evaluation, use of social networking technologies, and hybrid/blended learning (party online, partly face-to-face) (In the QC setting exclusively online courses are not at this point deemed viable, but it is important to note that other programs have had success in this area, a point worthy of further investigation). Developments that may make hybrid/blended learning more feasible in the GSLIS environment include the expanding availability of freely-available open-source Web-publishing software like Omeka, or free software facilitating the creation of screenshots and videos to enhance visual learning outside of the classroom setting, such as Jing (http://www.techsmith.com/jing.html). Further innovations to consider include incorporating learning modules on setting up a free-hosted server, and instructions on how to upload their JPEG image file(s) and XML file(s) onto their hosted server and how to display the content using a pre-designed HTML file. As noted previously, this process affords students the knowledge and experience of having an alternative approach to generically storing and displaying data in the absence of a particular software such as CDM.

This chapter has stressed the many advantages to be gained by collaboration within and among the disparate disciplines involved in digitization among cultural heritage institutions and many other fields. However, collaborating with innovative educators within and outside higher education and professional communities of practice can provide valuable insights as well. Shifts in recent decades, from the "sage-on-the-stage" model to student-centered learning (e.g. King, 1993) are increasingly embraced at Centers for Teaching and Learning throughout academe. They can serve as a valuable resource for DL educators grappling with the challenges ahead.

REFERENCES

Ball, M. A. (2008). Practicums and service learning in LIS education. *Journal of Education for Library and Information Science*, *51*(4), 241–250.

Banerjee, K. (2002). How does XML help libraries. *Computers in Libraries*, *22*(8). Retrieved from http://www.infotoday.com/cilmag/sep02/Banerjee.htm

Bastion, J., Harvey, R., Mahard, M., & Plum, T. (2010). Building a virtual archives and preservation laboratory at Simmons College: A case study in collaboratative construction. *Journal of Education for Library and Information Science*, *49*(1), 70–82.

BCR's CDP Digital Imaging Best Practices Working Group. (2008). *BCR's CDP digital imaging best practices version 2.0*. Retrieved from http://www.lyrasis.org/Products-and-Services/Digital-and-Preservation-Services/Digital-Toolbox/~/media/Files/Lyrasis/Products%20and%20Services/Digital%20Services/digital%20imaging%20bp.ashx

Burton, P. F., & McMenemy, D. (2005). Future librarians digitizing the past. *Information Scotland, 3*(5). Retrieved from http:///www.slainte.org.ul/publications/serial/infoscot/vol3(5)article5.htm

Currum, S. (2011). Experiential learning: Reducing the real-world divide between libraries and library schools. *The Reference Librarian*, *52*, 300–307. doi:10.1080/02763877.2011.585282

Dahlstrom, M., & Doracic, A. (2009). Digitization education: Courses take and lessons learned. *D-Lib Magazine*, *15*(3/4). Retrieved from http://www.dlib.org/dlib/march09/dahlstrom/03dahlstrom.html

Digital Media, J. I. S. C. (2008). *Choosing a file name*. Retrieved from http://www.jiscdigitalmedia.ac.uk/crossmedia/advice/choosing-a-file-name/

Frank, R. (2010). *Comparing the ALA core competencies to New York librarian job postings and New York Library school curricula: An analysis with a job seeker's toolkit for the new MLIS graduate. Unpublished Research Project*. Flushing, NY: Queens College, CUNY.

George Mason University. (2011). *Omeka*. Retrieved September 10, 2011, from http://omeka.org/

Girard, T., Pina, M., & Trapp, P. (2011). An exploratory study of class presentations and peer evaluations: Do students perceive the benefits? *Academy of Educational Leadership Journal*, *15*(1), 77–94.

King, A. (1993). From sage on the stage to guide on the side. *College Teaching*, *41*(1), 30–35. Retrieved from http://www.jstor.org/stable/27558571 doi:10.1080/87567555.1993.9926781

Lapp, D., Shea, A., & Wolsey, T. D. (2011). Blogging and audience awareness. *Journal of Education*, *191*(1), 33–44.

Lavy, I., & Yadin, A. (2010). Team-based peer-review as a form of formative assessment—The casae of a systems anlaysis and design workshop. *Journal of Information Systems Education*, *21*(1), 85–98.

Library of Congress. (2007). *Thesaurus for graphic materials I*. Retrieved September 10, 2011, from http://www.loc.gov/rr/print/tgm1/

Lin & Abels. (2010). Digital library education lab. *Journal of Education for Library and Information Science*, *51*(2), 120–124.

Long, C. (2011). Developing and implementing a master of archival studies program: A collaborative effort of a state university, a state archives, and the national archives and records administration. *Journal of Education for Library and Information Science*, *52*(2), 120–124.

McMenemy, D. (2007). Less conversation, more action: Putting digital content creation at the heart of modern librarianship. *Library Review*, *56*(7), 537–541. doi:10.1108/00242530710775926

Metropolitan New York Library Council. (2010). *Website*. Retrieved June 29, 2010, from http://www.metro.org/

New Zealand Digital Library Project. (2007). *Greenstone digital library software*. Retrieved September 10, 2011, from http://www.greenstone.org/

OCLC. (2011). *CONTENTdm digital collection management software*. Retrieved from http://www.contentdm.org/

Robertson, J. (2011). The educational affordances of blogs for self-directed learning. *Computers & Education*, *57*(2), 1628–1644. doi:10.1016/j.compedu.2011.03.003

Spink, A., & Cool, C. (1999). Education for digital libraries. *D-Lib Magazine*, *5*(8).

ADDITIONAL READING

Besser, H. (2003). *Introduction to imaging*. Retrieved from http://www.getty.edu/research/publications/electronic_publications/index.html

California Digital Library. (2011). *Resources*. Retrieved from http://www.cdlib.org/services/dsc/contribute/resources.html

Canadian Heritage Information Network. (2009). *CHIN's professional exchange: Digital information*. Retrieved from http://www.pro.rcip-chin.gc.ca/index-eng.jsp?Ne=8109&N=8109

Carignan, Y., Evander, J., Gueguen, G., Hanlon, A., Murray, K., Roper, J., et al. (2006). *Best practice guidelines for digital collections at University of Maryland libraries*. Retrieved from http://www.lib.umd.edu/dcr/publications/best_practice.pdf

Cole, T. W. (2002). Creating a framework of guidance for building good digital collections. *First Monday*, *7*(5).

Cornell University Library. (2003). *Moving theory into practice: Digital imaging tutorial*. Retrieved from http://www.library.cornell.edu/preservation/tutorial/contents.html

Cornell University Library. (2007). *Digital preservation management: Implementing short-term strategies for long-term problems*. Retrieved from http://www.dpworkshop.org/dpm-eng/eng_index.html

CreativeCommons.org. (2012). *Website*. Retrieved from http://creativecommons.org/

Deegan, M., & Tanner, S. (2002). *Digital futures: Strategies for the information age*. New York, NY: Neal-Schuman.

Digital Media, J. I. S. C. (2011). *Cross-media advice: Managing a project*. Retrieved from http://www.jiscdigitalmedia.ac.uk/crossmedia/docs/category/managing-a-project

Hirtle, P. (2011). *Copyright term and the public domain in the United States*. Retrieved from http://www.copyright.cornell.edu/training/Hirtle_Public_Domain.htm

Hughes, L. (2003). *The price of digitization: New cost models for cultural and educational institutions: A digitization symposium presented by NINCH and Innodata*. Retrieved from http://www.ninch.org/forum/price.report.html

Humanities Advanced Technology and Information Institute, University of Glasgow, and the National Initiative for a Networked Cultural Heritage. (2002). *The NINCH guide to good practice in the digital representation and management of cultural heritage materials*. Retrieved from http://www.nyu.edu/its/humanities/ninchguide/

Liblicense. (2008). CLIR/DLF model license. In *Licensing Digital Materials: A Resource for Librarians*. Retrieved from http://www.library.yale.edu/~llicense/modlic.shtml

Library of Congress. (2011). *National digital information infrastructure & preservation program.* Retrieved November 1, 2011, from http://www.digitalpreservation.gov/index.html

Library of Congress. (2012). *Digital library standards*. Retrieved from http://www.loc.gov/library/digitalstandards.html

National Information Standards Organization. (2004). *Understanding metadata*. Bethesda, MD: National Information Standards Organization (NISO) Press. Retrieved from http://www.niso.org/standards/resources/UnderstandingMetadata.pdf

National Information Standards Organization. (2008). *Framework of guidance for building good digital collections* (3rd ed.). Retrieved from http://framework.niso.org/

National Library of Australia. (2011). PADI: *Gateway to international digital preservation resources and to ICADS IFLA-DCNL alliance for digital strategies*. Retrieved November 1, 2011 from http://www.nla.gov.au/padi/

North Carolina, E. C. H. O. (2007). *NC ECHO guidelines for digitization, 2007 revised edition.* Retrieved from http://www.ncecho.org/dig/dig-guidelines.shtml

Northeast Document Conservation Center. (2000). *Handbook for digital projects: A management tool for preservation and access*. Andover, MA: NEDCC. Retrieved from http://www.nedcc.org/resources/pubs.php

Refsnes Data. (2011). *XML tutorial.* Retrieved from http://www.w3schools.com/Xml/default.asp

Smith, A. (2001). *Strategies for building digitized collections*. Retrieved from http://www.clir.org/pubs/reports/pub101/contents.html

Smithsonian Institution. (2011). *Greetings from the Smithsonian: A postcard history of the Smithsonian institution.* Retrieved September 10, 2011, from http://siarchives.si.edu/history/exhibits/postcard/index.htm

University of Colorado Digital Library. (2009). *Digitization best practices, version 1.0.* Retrieved from https://www.cu.edu/digitallibrary/cudldigitizationbp.pdf

University of Washington Libraries. (2011). *Metadata guidelines for CONTENT collections.* Retrieved from http://www.lib.washington.edu/msd/pubcat/mig/advice/

Vince, P., & Emery, M. D. (2005). *Scanning best practices: The Claremont colleges digital library.* Retrieved from http://www.uni.edu/fabos/seminar/tools/CCDLScanningBestPractices.pdf

Chapter 13
Enterprise 2.0 in a Digital Library:
Implementations and Outcomes

Adam Sofronijevic
University of Belgrade, Serbia

ABSTRACT

The chapter presents the concept of Enterprise 2.0 in a library environment. This concept describes the use of Web 2.0 tools and approaches by organizations in order to foster internal functions, e.g. communication, collaboration, innovativeness. Various aspects of this concept are tackled including implementation of Web 2.0 technologies for business purposes in a library. Importance of intrapreneurship for implementation of Enterprise 2.0 is suggested. Short theoretical reviews on both intrapreneusrhip and Enterprise 2.0 are followed by some general conclusions on the relationship between these two concepts based on the research results gathered in libraries in Serbia. Results from the ongoing European study on awareness and implementation of Enterprise 2.0 are also presented. The chapter is a valuable companion for anyone interested in the practical aspects of Enterprise 2.0 implementation in a library and presents an addition to librarianship theory by introducing a new idea on the relation between Enterprise 2.0 implementation and intrapreneurship.

INTRODUCTION

Collaboration and communication is always technology dependant. A radical change in communication technology occurs rarely, and when it does, it presents organizations with great opportunity to improve their business performance, but also poses a great risk of losing competitive advantage if they do not implement these new technologies in time frame defined by the competition. Sometime such a radical change can bring new players into an industry creating unexpected competition. All

DOI: 10.4018/978-1-4666-2991-2.ch013

of this happened during the last few years with the rise of Web 2.0 technologies. The industry of information creation with librarianship as one of its more prominent sectors is one in which Web 2.0 technologies did create unexpected competition empowering users and making them information creators by placing at their disposal abundant data resources. Organizations from investment intensive industries have started to implement Web 2.0 technologies in order to foster communication and collaboration both with users and among employees. Similarly to other management concepts, this practice was soon described and defined theoretically and the pace of the implementation surged. Today various concepts describe implementation of Web 2.0 technologies for purposes of improvement of communication and collaboration with users, Banking 2.0, Government 2.0, and Education 2.0 are some of the more prominent examples. In librarianship concept of Library 2.0 is well defined and described. Usage of Web 2.0 technologies for business purposes in libraries is not so well described and this chapter aims at filling a part of this blank.

In a complex and fast changing environment in order to survive businesses need to adapt. Nonprofit nature and government related funding have placed libraries in somewhat comfortable position. This has been compromised by the financial crisis and globalization processes. The rising competition has often eluded definitions given by librarians themselves. The pace of Web 2.0 development suggests that in the few years' time enough Internet users will have a know how to retrieve and post online almost every book that was ever printed. Is copyright enough of an obstacle to make people turn to libraries again in such a situation? Libraries must face such challenges and adapt in order to survive. In addition, even if most of library managers do not feel the pressure yet, they should act now, for other industries examples thought us that it is about the pace of the change and not about the level of change achieved.

Building on the research conducted in Serbian libraries in 2007 and 2009 and on the ongoing research of European libraries, various aspects of Enterprise 2.0 implementation in the library environment will be presented as well as outcomes evaluation strategies and methods. Author's theory on relationship between intrapreneurship and Enterprise 2.0 implementation is described. This relationship is of utmost importance for efficient implementation of new technologies in libraries. Enterprise 2.0 implementation via intrapreneurship is discussed on basis of previously published theory, data collected by author, and the best practices cases of various European libraries.

Intrapreneurship is the practice of entrepreneurial skills and approaches within an organization applied by employees. This concept is very well studied and described in many industries, but librarianship theory almost never deals with cases of intrarpeneurship in libraries though one might met them very often. Therefore any application of this concept in libraries so far has been based on intuitive decision making by intrapreneurs and managers alike.

Enterprise 2.0 describes the use of Web 2.0 tools and approaches by organizations in order to foster internal functions e.g. communication, collaboration, innovativeness. In libraries this concept describes the use of Web 2.0 tools by librarians for communication and collaboration with other librarians. It should not be confused with user oriented implementation of Web 2.0 tools, i.e. Library 2.0. Librarianship theory is lagging behind the practice in this field too. Data presented show that many libraries have already implemented Enterprise 2.0, while almost no mention of this can be found in theory on libraries.

Both concepts are of utmost importance for digital libraries. By dealing with them and relationship that exist between them chapter adds missing pieces to contemporary librarianship theory. Specific contribution of the chapter is that it presents solution to the specific and growing problem of declining efficiency in implementation of new technology solutions in libraries. Libraries seems to leg behind in the race to implementation new technologies arising in the fast changing ICT field. Chapter looks into possible solutions for this.

ENTERPRISE 2.0 AND INTRAPRENEURSHIP

Enterprise 2.0 concept was defined by Andrew McAfee of MIT Sloan School of Management in milestone paper "Enterprise 2.0: The dawn of emergent collaboration" in 2006 (McAfee, 2006). It has been promoted since by McAfee and growing number of evangelists via traditional means of academic communication and even more via publishing venues provided by Web 2.0 technologies. Enterprise 2.0 conference (www.e2conf.com), the main venue for meeting and discussing new trends in this field, prides itself with specific system for paper selection based on fusion of community voting and more traditional expert review. This might be very illustrative of Enterprise 2.0 when compared to traditional double blind review process. Enterprise 2.0 flattens the organizational structure providing better chances for ideas coming from the organizational bottom. When implemented properly it empowers employees at all levels taking away information dominance of any specific group. In essence Enterprise 2.0 describes the use of Web 2.0 technologies for fostering internal functions of an organization e.g. communication, collaboration, innovativeness. In libraries Enterprise 2.0 describes the use of Web 2.0 technologies by librarians for fostering communication and collaboration with librarians and other employees. It should not be confused with Library 2.0 a concept that describes the use of Web 2.0 technologies in a library for fostering communication and collaboration between patrons and librarians. On the other hand these two concepts have a lot in common sine the underlying technologies are the same Web 2.0 technologies and therefore knowledge and experience gained in implementation of one might be valuable for the useage of other.

In order to understand better how Enterprise 2.0 functions we will use concept of weak ties described by (Granovetter, 1973) as did McAfee (2009). The relationship between employees who often work closely is defined as a strong tie. On the other hand, the relationship between employees that know of each other existence and have a means to contact each other and collaborate is defined as a weak tie. The absence of the weak tie connecting certain employees is defined as a structural hole. The main aim of Enterprise 2.0 implementation is to bridge structural gaps in an organization. Various Web 2.0 technologies are inherently suitable for creation of weak ties i.e. among employees separated by geographical or organizational boundaries. Besides this Web 2.0 technologies can significantly improve collaboration among employees how collaborate closely. Enhancing quality of strong ties collaboration is important for medium and small organizations and most libraries do fall in these categories. Many technologies have been used in the past to underlay the processes of collaboration and communication in organizations. Enterprise 2.0 differs from all of these in two points: it is easy to use and it does not amend certain structure, working process or prescribed outputs for employees using it. In order to implement it properly one must always bear in mind that different Web 2.0 technologies provide for different functions, but some similarities do exist and nature of the relationship for which we are using technology to enhance collaboration must be always accounted for (McAfee, 2009, position 740). For instance wiki technology can be used to bridge structural gaps as McAfee shows via example of Intellipedia, a Wikipedia-like tool of US intelligence community (McAfee, 2009, position 960). The outcomes of Enterprise 2.0 implementation can differ depending on several factors. Management needs to provide crucial backup for replacing traditional workflow with the one originating from the use of novel technologies. Successful implementation can be achieved in only on of the organizational units providing benefits for only a small number of employees. Technologies implemented may include just the ones fostering strong ties collaboration. Because of this, although many parameters regarding Enterprise 2.0 can be quantified and measured McAfee advocates that no quantitative ROI analysis should be implemented as a tool to approve of or assess Enterprise 2.0 implementation (McAfee, 2009, postion 1652). Idea is that intangible assets such as knowledge, innovativeness or work satisfaction that are advanced by Enterprise 2.0 seldom have a direct impact on measures mostly used in the process of quantitative ROI analysis. Therefore other means of evaluation, mostly qualitative needs to be employed.

Most important characteristics of Enterprise 2.0 i.e. Web 2.0 technologies implemented for business purposes are described by mnemonics SLATE and FLATNESSES that have been described by McAfee (2006) and Hinchcliffe (2007). By SLATE McAfee defines: Search as a capability of the technology to provide easy access to data; Links as manmade relations between objects that allow for a broader pattern to emerge when numerous objects are linked; Authoring as an surge in numbers of content providers enabled by the easy and free venue provided by technology; Tags as means for employee made structure (folksonomy) that renders useless any imposed structure (taxonomy); Extensions as intelligent-like behavior of technology that provides for automated suggestions that save time and finally; Signals as possibility fir aggregation of various sources of data that are updated frequently, again saving time for employees. By FLATNESSES Hinchcliffe defines same six characteristics as McAfee with addition of four new that should emphasize the following aspects of Enterprise 2.0: Social, Freeform, Emergent, and Network oriented.

Various authors also provide important input that builds theoretical basis of Enterprise 2.0 concept. Jedd (2008) presents technologies that fall into Enterprise 2.0 definition and the ones that do not. Wiki technology when implemented for internal use of employees as in the example of internal wiki page used for accumulating and discussing changes in procedures in an organization that is used and created by employees represent an example of Enterprise 2.0 implementation. Other examples of Enterprise 2.0 usages include employees and managers use of blog technology to write about and discuss internally everyday operations of an organization or when a folksonomy exists created by tagging objects in internal database of an organization by employees. Often Enterprise 2.0 manifests as social networking either through proprietary social networks in huge organizations or via the public ones, with both being used for creation of weak ties bringing together employees that previously did not know of each other existence or were separated by geographical or organizational boundaries. On the other hand, Enterprise 2.0 does not include the use of email, existence of the taxonomy created and controlled by few experts, traditional systems for document management, information portals with no collaborative elements, traditional intranet. Kohler-Kruner (2009) advocates the importance of continuous education for successful Enterprise 2.0 implementation. Several obstacles have been identified as crucial for success of Enterprise 2.0 implementation in an organization: organizational culture that is complex and time-consuming to change, business strategy that defines the sheer need for Enterprise 2.0 implementation, and technology strategy that defines possibilities for certain Web 2.0 technology usage in a given timeframe having in mind previously used technologies.

Often author present concrete examples of Web 2.0 usage for business purposes and then describe broader conclusions. (Leader-Chivee, Hamilton, & Cowan, 2008) describe the use of social networks in recruitment process. Via this example they describe the possibilities for cutting on expenses in a HR department and further this issue with a research result claiming that 74% of organizations that did implement Enterprise 2.0 decided on this path in order to cut spending. Fanning (2009) goes with similar process presenting first a workflow on new PDF standard development enhanced by Enterprise 2.0 implementation. The conclusions revolve around efficiency increase, expenses decrease, and time saved. In general, these are the exact results of a successful Enterprise 2.0 implementation. Results of the research conducted during Enterprise 2.0 conference in 2009 reveals some of the issues that hamper implementation and some of the advantages as seen by the organizations that are successfully using Web 2.0 technologies for business purposes (Enterprise 2.0 Conference, 2009). The resistance to change was the main obstacle for implementation for 52.3% of respondents while 42.1% identified the difficult assessment of return on investment for Enterprise 2.0 implementation. Web 2.0 technologies availability and characteristics, growing need for business application to become more social and organizational culture that allows for organizations to exploit all advantages of Web 2.0 technologies were identified as a driving force behind Enterprise 2.0 surge. While almost 67% of respondents expect rise in the budgets for Enterprise 2.0 implementation in the following year some negative comments were attached to issues of security and integration with older technologies. The characteristics of Enterprise 2.0 that were mentioned most frequently are as follows: flattening the organizational structure, flexibility, user driven, bottom up, distributed, transparent, simple.

In order to implement Enterprise 2.0 in most efficient and low cost manner management of any library will need the help of employees that are intrapreneurial. In order to understand this better we will present a short review of intrapreneurship concept. Intrapreneurship is the practice of entrepreneurial skills and approaches within an organization applied by employees (Pinchot, 1985). The concept is very well founded in theory with researches being conducted in various countries (Menzel, 2008; Ulijn & Menzel, 2004; Zampetakis & Moustakis, 2007) and across many industries (Wunderer, 2001; Thomas & Augustyn, 2007; Manimala, Jose, & Thomas, 2006). Intrapreneurship provides a shortcut to achieving business goals in times of economic crisis when only limited funding is available for most organizations. This should be even truer for libraries—a non-for-profit organizations always in a need for investment following the needs of patrons, but short on funding to implement it. Authors that influenced intrapreneurship theory heavily Antoncic and Hisrich (2001, 2003) showed that intrapreneurship when existent in an organization leads to growth and profitability which in case of libraries may translate to higher level of stakeholders satisfaction and funding increase. Some factors that affect the levels of intrapreneurial activities in an organization originate in the organization itself. Others are products of the environment. In order to foster intrapreneurship management of an organization needs to manipulate factors it can have influence upon: communication between employees, formal control, organizational values, empowerment of employees and information gathering. Managers also need to know environmental factors that might be out of their scope of influence and add them up in order to have a precise forecast of intrapreneurial activities in their organization.

Antoncic and Hisrich (2001) introduces the dimensions of intrapreneurship and present a consistent concept. Eight dimensions of intrapreneurship encompass various aspects of intrapreneurial activities that might be observed in organizations: New ventures – creation of new autonomous unit within existing organization or new firm from within the existing one presents the first dimension of intrapreneurship; New business – the second one encompass all various forms of entering into new business that is related to current products or markets; The third one is perhaps most intrapreneurial – product/service innovativeness. Creation of new products and services is often related to entrepreneurial activities and therefore this attribute. This also goes with process innovativeness—innovation in production/service procedures and techniques, but this by its own virtue is perceived as an activity that is performed within an existing organization. Risk taking is also one of the dimensions of intrapreneurship that is most commonly associated with entrepreneurship. It stands for quickness in taking bold action and committing resources in the pursuit of new opportunities. Self-renewal describes quickening pace on reaching for established aims of the organization by new means and includes strategy reformulation, reorganization, and organizational change. Proactivness stands for pioneering, initiative taking, and other approaches that involve active stance of an organization towards its environment and changes in it. The last dimension of intrapreneurship according to Antoncic and Hisrich is competitive aggressiveness—aggressive stance towards competitors.

Many authors provided input for intrapreneurship concept theory building. By summarizing some of their ideas, we will get to know the concept better and ideas on it may crystallize further. If an employee in an organization try to exploit possibilities no meter what resources he/she control then he/she might be called intrapreneur (Stevenson & Jarillo, 1990). Intrapreneurship may lead to the creation of the new organization on behalf of an existing one (Sharma & Chrisman, 1999) or it can manifest itself as the spirit of entrepreneurship in an organization that already exists (Hisrich & Peters, 1998). An intrapreneur have the motivation to innovate and refresh the way of doing business (Sharma & Chrisman, 1999) and the work on the new things by parting with old ways for sake of exploiting opportunities presented (Vesper, 1990). Behavioral intentions and behaviors that are related to departures from the customary ways of doing business in the existing organizations is one important aspect of intrapreneurship (Antoncic & Hisrich, 2003). One early name for what will be later branded as intrapreneurship was corporate entrepreneurship. Zahra (1991, 1993) established the connection between the high level of entrepreneurial activities in a company and favorable financial outcome. Together with Jefrey Covin he explored the influence of business context on the success of entrepreneurial activities in a company (Zahra & Covin, 1995). Covin and Slevin surveyed the connection between the organizational structure and intrapreneurship (Slevin & Covin, 1989), and came up with the 'Entrescale' – insturment for measuring the level of intrapreneurial activities (Slevin & Covin, 1986). They also defined the model of intrapreneurial behavior of a company (Slevin & Covin, 1991). Kuratko and Montagno (1989) analyzed the relationship between the level of innovation implemented and the organizational culture. Together with Hornsby (Kuratko, Montagno, & Hornsby, 1990) they developed an instrument for testing the effects of organizational culture on innovation and intrapreneurship implemented in an organization.

ENTERPRISE 2.0 IMPLEMENTATION IN LIBRARIES

The problem with Enterprise 2.0 implementation is not the cost of the technology or the time consumed by the training employees need in order to use it. The problem is more sophisticated one. Enterprise 2.0 is the first communication technology that does not come alone. It brings with it the whole social aspect. Underlying Web 2.0 technologies have affected the needs and expectations of its users in a way that reach far beyond the organizational limits. The complexity of this goes further. Besides employees, who need to use these technologies in order to further their organizational goals, the users of their services, the final judges of these goals, also have the needs and expectations that are thoroughly changed by these same technologies. In addition, the same goes for the managers who need to make decisions in regards to Enterprise 2.0 implementation. As the plot thickens, the data from the field is needed more than ever. In addition, here the librarianship community runs into a problem since as of first half of 2011 no significant data on Enterprise 2.0 implementation in libraries is available. Enterprise 2.0 is not widely discussed in librarianship theory as well at the moment, although many libraries do profit from their usage in this area. This is not unusual having in mind experiences from other industries. Theoretical work on concept that would describe Web 2.0 technologies implementation for business purposes has been hampered by organizations' unwillingness to provide information for academics in order to keep this sensitive area of business operations as closed as possible at first. Because of this Enterprise 2.0 concept describing this area of Web 2.0 implementation is relatively new and originates from investment intensive for profit industries. By providing some data on European libraries in general and some more specific data on Serbian libraries this chapter sheds some light on complex situation that Enterprise 2.0 implementation poses for a library practitioner. It further provides a hint to the existence of the relationship between Enterprise 2.0 implementation and intrapreneurship that might be a very useful tool for library managers willing to embark upon usage of Web 2.0 tools for business purposes.

Awareness and State of Implementation of Enterprise 2.0 in European Libraries

The survey of awareness and implementation of Enterprise 2.0 in European libraries conducted by author started in December 2010 and at the moment is ongoing. Some results illustrative enough of general trends will be presented along with case studies. The survey has several phases, the first one being the online research conducted via the Surveymonkey online survey tool. We present here the results gathered from one collector that was active from December 2010 until the end of February 2011. The link to the collector along with the cover letter has been distributed via mailing lists and provided for 175 filled questionnaires. The online questionnaire contained 8 questions that were directly connected to Enterprise 2.0 concept. This part of the survey showed that high level of awareness does exist among librarians in Europe on Enterprise 2.0 issue. On the other hand, implementation of Enterprise 2.0 is sketchy with some examples of high-level implementation and more instances of no Web 2.0 technologies implemented for business purposes at all. Numerous initiatives and ideas on what should be implemented, when and how exist and are at various stages of progress. In many libraries, just a general idea of the need for implementation exists.

Three quarters of respondents share various degree of understanding of Enterprise 2.0 concept and the possibilities it provides for upgrading library business performance. At the top of this group, 25% of respondents are well aware of the concept with their organization already benefiting from using it. The remaining quarter of all respondents has no clear understanding of what Enterprise 2.0 is or what it can do. In confirmation with this the next question revealed that in 71% of cases some of Web 2.0 technologies has been used for furthering collaboration between employees or in other professional applications not connected with users directly. Again 25% of respondents claimed that their institution is using more than one Web 2.0 technology for these purposes. Social networks are at the top with two thirds of respondents using them, the second most favored technology—the RSS is used by 55% respondents. Blogs are following closely with 52% while wikis and social video sharing sites like Youtube are positioned good at 43% and 40% respectively. Social bookmarking sites like Delicious, Forums, online collaboration tools like Google apps and social photo sharing sites like Flickr are all used by quarter to 30% of respondents. This shows a great richness in usage of Web 2.0 technologies in libraries of Europe. It might be instructive to discuss the answers of those respondents not using Web 2.0 technologies in their libraries for business purposes. Most common reason, with 40% of respondents blaming no implementation on it is unknown costs associated with maintenance and training. The next one is no support from senior management that was important for 36% of respondents. The resistance to change, the lack of budget, problems when integrating with existing technologies and lack of product knowledge were all reasons for approximately 30% of respondents compounding more than 100% because usually several reasons were picked by respondents for omission of Enterprise 2.0 implementation. It is a bit surprising that only 18% of respondents named security concerns and 13% difficulties in measuring return on investment as the challenges to contemplating Enterprise 2.0 implementation.

The reasons respondents find Enterprise 2.0 useful in a library are different with almost all of suggested answers gaining some level of approval. Respondents' top choice was increase of individual's knowledge with 48%, followed by three almost equally prized qualities: improves creativity, harnesses collective knowledge, and stimulates team building and better internal collaboration all at around 40%. Solutions to problem provision and improvement of cross-functional/interdepartmental collaboration followed closely with 35%. The last two qualities gaining any significant threshold are sparking innovation and providing timely access to key individuals at 28% and 21% respectively. With this, European librarians' notion of Enterprise 2.0 qualities is complete presenting an overall picture of diverse and informed insight.

Enterprise 2.0 seems to be adopted at various levels at different European libraries. 30% of respondents claim that it has been adopted across the whole library at their institution, 17% opted for team adoption and 10% for departmental one. Surprisingly 23% of respondents chose the individual level of adoption. This needs further clarifying in next phases of research. It needs to be established if such a big number of respondents was referring to individuals from different organizational units using Web 2.0 technologies to collaborate among them or there was a misunderstanding of the whole concept. On the other hand, individual employees have been designated as main driving force behind Enterprise 2.0 usage in European libraries with 47% of respondents opting for them. Another 35% of respondents claim that working groups are driving the usage and 22% chose IT department. Only 16% respondents designated department heads and 18% library directors as main drivers of Enterprise 2.0 usage in their libraries. Having this in mind it is not difficult to comprehend importance of intrapreneurship in Enterprise 2.0 implementation, since vast majority of respondents marked employees in one way or another as responsible for Enterprise 2.0 usage. Another clue to importance of intrapreneurship for Enterprise 2.0 implementation can be revealed when looking at answers to organizational resources committed to implementation. Only 2% of respondents claim that their library has Enterprise 2.0 implementation budget. Just 6% marked defined Enterprise 2.0 strategy and further 9% opted for Enterprise 2.0 implementation plan. Department/employees/employee formally responsible for Enterprise2.0 implementation is present at 21% of respondents' institutions. The fact that 67% or two thirds of respondents coming from European libraries claim that their library has nothing of above mentioned suggest even stronger the role of intrapreneurship. It is a classical intrapreneurial situation in which employees further an activity even without proper resources at their disposal, claiming the risk of failure and hope for the prize in case of success solely for themselves. We may very well see that in many libraries in Europe Enterprise 2.0 implementation is well under way and that Web 2.0 technologies are used quite often for business purposes. On the other hand, all this is achieved without apparent resources being put in use by the organization. The only viable solution for this riddle is intrapreneurship.

The Relationship between Enterprise 2.0 Implementation and Intrapreneurship

Relationship between intrapreneurship and Enterprise 2.0 implementation should present a valuable shortcut for library managers willing to embark upon Web 2.0 usage for business purposes in their library. This relationship will be therefore described in some detail in order to provide further ideas and insights in possibilities for practice use. The implementation of Enterprise 2.0 technologies in a library can be approached top-down with top management prescribing ideas and means for implementing them. Enterprise 2.0 implementation can be performed bottom-up by intrapreneurial librarians starting the process, providing ideas, betting on the success without needed resources at first and gaining the support of the top management at later stages. Performed this way Enterprise 2.0 implementation proves to be far superior to top down approach. Enterprise 2.0 implementation is described as a three-stage process by (McAfee, 2009). Each of the three phases of implementation of Enterprise 2.0 can be defined also within the framework of intrapreneurship dimensions as defined by (Antoncic & Hisrich, 2001). The first phase that is decision making on aims, scope and techniques of Enterprise 2.0 implementation comprises of risk taking, pioneering activities that renews communication processes and collaboration methods. The second phase is formation of a working group responsible for roll up of Enterprise 2.0. This may be described in the framework of Antoncic and Hisrich's theory as a classical new venture operation. The third phase is the period after initiation of technology and initial adoption. This phase brings in the long-term success or failure of the project. In terms of Antoncic and Hisrich's conceptual frame, it brings changes in educational processes for library staff foremost in lifelong learning processes. It also brings the risk for intrapreneurs responsible for its execution. The main risk being non-adoption on part of certain employees, for various reasons ranging from real problems in using new technology to possible personal issues if a history exists between certain employees and intrapreneurs. In addition, some intrapreneurs might be at risk of being labeled as promoters of Enterprise 2.0 and consequently blamed for all the problems arising from implementation of Enterprise 2.0 technologies and creation of competing working processes. This phase is obviously risk taking for those involved in Enterprise 2.0 technologies rollout and promotion, requires of them to be proactive in problem solving, innovative in creating new educational possibilities for other employees and competitive aggressive when competing/promoting for attention of employees in new working processes.

Organizational prerequisites of intrapreneurship defined by Antoncic and Hisrich (2001) are fostering the implementation of Enterprise 2.0. Library management has certain methods at its disposal for fostering intrapreneurship with most of the resulting effects being known in general terms. Network effects will start to manifest as soon as management starts to foster communication. This will probably be followed by further improvement in communication quality and quantity. Control and selection of ideas is essential in making intrapreneurship efficient tool for Enterprise 2.0 implementation. Separating ideas and proposals in organized manner with clearly stated reasons and propositions known in advance might seem as a lot of work but since Enterprise 2.0 can be implemented in a vast number of different ways, it is essential for filtering out the optimal solution for a given situation. Information gathering is a key building block in any intrapreneurial activity aiming at implementation of Enterprise 2.0, since the technologies are especially dynamic and require constant monitoring by intrapreneurs. In order to stay on top of things intrapreneurs need to be well informed on possibilities and other issues regarding each proposition they suggest. If not the risk taken by them is not acceptable. Luckily for librarian intrapreneurs information creation is the essence of their profession. Organizational support is very important as with almost all successful cases of implementation top management has demonstrated direct support by adopting the novel technology at an early phase. Besides this top management needs to play an active role in promotion of novel technologies and this can be achieved only by active content creation and presentation of this content through channels created by these technologies. If the organizational culture promotes individualism and competitiveness, then intrapreneurial activities on implementation of Enterprise 2.0 will be favored because Enterprise 2.0 technology flattens the organizational structure and thus promotes individual visibility and success. On the other hand, it allows for a much greater level of competitiveness inside the organization since it removes all barriers to information flow and allows concurrent ideas and plans to be equally valued.

Additional arguments for the existence of the relationship between intrapreneurship and Enterprise 2.0 implementation can be found if we analyze the motivation of intrapreneurs for their activities in the context of both concepts. Intrapreneurs who act in order to implement technologies that improve collaboration of librarians connected by strong ties certainly are motivated by the idea that is decisive motivator for every intrapreneur—that such activities will increase productivity and efficiency. From the perspective of other concept, some aspects of these activities can be defined as dimensions of intrapreneurship. Service innovativeness and/or process innovativeness are two possibilities depending on nature of problems that are solved by introduction of Web 2.0 technologies. If they solve the problem that has already been tackled by means of previous technologies then activities of Enterprise 2.0 implementation bring process innovativeness dimension of intrapreneurship, but if they represent answer to a completely novel problem not addressed before then they may be labeled as service innovativeness dimension of intrapreneurship. The next one, proactivness, is defined by willingness to solve the problems in collaboration of closely netted colleagues by implementation of Web 2.0 technologies. Self-renewal is evident as organizational change is made through new ways of communication and collaboration introduced with Enterprise 2.0 implementation. Finally, risk taking is evident since tampering with the ways in which one collaborates with close colleagues brings repercussions that are felt on daily basis in the future. The motivations of intrapreneurs who act in order to implement technologies that improve collaboration of librarians connected by weak ties or bring possibilities for structural holes bridging are certainly more intense. If a structural hole is bridged, most of the social capital created will be captured by the one who did it; therefore, intrapreneurs and technology evangelists will have considerable advantage over other colleagues in this field. However, this can also backfire since the social capital created might be also a negative one if the relationship established proves to bear negative connotations for the organization. Again we have dimensions of intrapreneurship embedded in activities of Enterprise 2.0 implementation, risk taking have already being described. Innovativeness lies in providing new possibilities in establishing and enhancing collaboration across organizational and geographical boundaries. While proactivness and self-renewal bear mostly the same explanations as in the case of Enterprise 2.0 implementation activates aiming for strong ties new dimension of intrapreneurship can be described for activities that aim for weak ties. Fostering interactions between previously unrelated colleagues brings with it inherent possibilities for new ventures—dimension of intrapreneurship that allows creation of new autonomous unit within existing organization or new firm from within the existing one. This aspect of Web 2.0 technology implementation in a library aiming at structural holes bridging might be very interesting in the context of changes of organizational structure. Most libraries still have some form of functional organizational structure and aim at changing this to some more project-friendly form like matrix form. This always brings to the table the question of collaboration between employees of previous functional organizational units that might not know each other. An important role for Enterprise 2.0 might be foreseen in this area.

These theoretical contemplations are based on hard evidence that emerged during researching intrapreneurship and Enterprise 2.0 implementation in Serbian libraries in 2007 and 2009. The results of both researches and two cases from ongoing research of awareness and state of implementation of enterprise 2.0 in European libraries will be presented in the following text.

Original instrument for exploring intrapreneurship in libraries of Serbia has been developed by the author. A new instrument was needed for the research of intrapreneurship in librarianship because of the very complex nature of this industry. Contemporary instruments that influenced author the most are instruments of Heinonen and Korvela (2012) and Hil (2003). Authors' original questionnaire consists of seven groups of statements each numbering ten statements. These groups of statements follow the theoretical framework defined by Antoncic and Hisrich (2001). Four groups are dealing with important prerequisites of intrapreneurship: organizational culture, personal qualities of employees, formal organization and management. Central group explores intrapreneurial activities of employees and the last two are about outcomes of intrapreneurship where results are summarized through patrons' and employees' satisfaction. Due to difficulties in obtaining relevant patrons' opinion, it is indirectly given through employees' opinion on patrons' satisfaction and attitudes. Questionnaire required that respondents show the level of their agreement or disagreement with given statements. Likert scaling applied to questionnaire offered respondents five possible answers: strongly disagree, disagree, neutral, agree, strongly agree. This scale was later quantified for statistical analysis with values reaching from 1 to 5, strongly agree being 5. SPSS 13.0 software tool for statistical data analysis was used.

The research was conducted in August 2007 and 42 participants from 10 institutions in 5 different cities took part. In May 2009, the research was conducted again and 45 participants from same institutions took part.

The existence of intraprenurial activities was proved during both research periods with high mean values of the statements acknowledging intrapreneurial activates. Correlations connecting statements describing the prerequisites of intrapreneurship and statements describing intrapreneurial activities and correlations connecting statements that describe intrapreneurial activities and the results of intraprenurial activities have been found. Finding of these correlations was important for proving that the model proposed in Antoncic and Hisrich (2001) is viable in a library environment too. With this confirmed we are able to recommend measures that should be taken by library management to foster intrapreneurship in any library.

Statements from the group regarding the organizational culture have high mean values mostly around 3.5 in both research periods. The organizational culture is generally favorable for intrapreneurship in Serbian libraries. The library management can upgrade the rules and regulations of libraries to make them more suitable for intrapreneurial activities. Statements from the group regarding self-evaluation of employees have very high mean values, above 4, except of one where again the rules and regulations of a library may be more suitable for intrapreneurs. In this group of statements, some progress can be noticed as a result of managerial actions when comparing results from 2007 and 2009. The area of rules and regulations is the only one that is not favorable for intrapreneurial activities. Very high proportion of "no opinion" answers indicates that employees do have an awareness problem or are not interested in rules and regulations of their libraries. When it comes to judging managers, employees do have good opinion of them. Mean values for statements of this group are grouped around 3.5 in both research periods. On top of this, they show a rising trend. This is in line with results that can be observed in other groups of statements and is in relations to managerial activities on fostering intrapreneurship that have been started after the first round of research in 2007. The existence of intrapreneurial activists is proved by high mean values in the group of statements related to the intraprenurial activities. The most important result coming from this area is the positive trend showing that an increase in managerial activities that foster intrapreneurship leads to significant improvement of these activities. Statements regarding employee and patron satisfaction are high and have a positive trend. The important thing to notice is that mean values of these statements do not show such a big increase as statements from the group describing intrapreneurial activities. From this we can conclude that even that in both areas a positive managerial activity does exist, it is harder to create an increase in the output of the working process than to upgrade the working process itself.

Examples of correlations between statements regarding prerequisites of intrapreneurship and those and statements regarding intrapreneurial activities and their aftermaths will be presented. Pearson chi-Square test shows the correlation of .017 between the statements "In my organization emphasis is on group work and group achievement of work aims" representing intrapreneurship prerequisites and the statement "During working hours scheduled to perform regular work duties I try to think about new ways to perform existing tasks more efficiently" representing intrapreneurial activities. This represents regular value less then 0.05 so the correlation holds. In the same way a correlation of .006 was found between the statements "During the working time provided for performing regular job duties I collect information that we can use to improve existing operations" representing intrapreneurial activities and the statement "Executives value my personal engagement intended to improve work processes even if it were unsuccessful efforts that take place during working hours" representing results of intrapreneurship.

The research showed the existence of intrapreneurial activities: employees propose changes in existing work processes or implementation of new services, employees gather information not related to librarianship that might be useful to them for invention of work process changes or new services during official work hours, employees improve their professional work skills and knowledge during official work hours.

Enterprise 2.0 research in Serbian libraries was conducted in 2007 in order to reveal levels of awareness and usage of Web 2.0 technologies for business purposes by librarians. Data was gathered by means of original questionnaire consisting of three parts. The first part aimed at gathering personal data in order to provide for possible correlations between particular demographic characteristics in librarians and data gathered in other two parts of the questionnaire. The second part was aimed at gathering data on general awareness and usage of Web 2.0 technologies as a prerequisite for their usage in business purpose. This part consisted of 8 questions that, like the ones in the third part of the questionnaire, combined open and closed question style for enhanced reliability. The third part was about gathering data on actual awareness and possible usage of Web 2.0 technologies for business purposes and consisted of 12 questions. The research was conducted in line with ideas about providing additional information for respondents described in the part of the chapter regarding intrapreneurship research. This yielded 42 valid fully filled questionnaires. SPSS software tool was also used for statistical analysis.

It was surprising that no correlation was found between the data from the first part and the second and the third parts of the questionnaire. It shows that Web 2.0 usage is not limited by sex, age, work experience, or educational level of respondents. This is not surprising having in mind the open and easy to use nature of these technologies. The only barrier for their usage might be elementary skills in using basic personal computer and Internet technology, which is not an issue for librarians. We can conclude that everyone employed in a library might be a user of Web 2.0 technologies and might use them for both private and business purposes.

The second and the third parts of the questionnaire revealed that some librarians did use Web 2.0 technologies and even have experimented with their use for business purposes. Their numbers have been relatively small but a certain degree of awareness of Web 2.0 technologies existed in Serbian libraries in 2007, which lead to a degree of use for business purposes in 2009. Web 2.0 service that attracted most attention of respondents was Youtube with 55% of them browsing and watching video materials via Youtube. The next one was some expression of blog or forum technology with 23% of respondents read a blog or a forum. It is important to notice that almost half of respondent that used these technologies, almost 10% had a username in one of the forums allowing them to create content. 14% of respondents used an instant messaging client. Everything so far was related to private use of Web 2.0 technology. Business usage was detected in small numbers with percentages lower than 5% for each question related to this subject. The only question that provided more positive answers was the one regarding librarians awareness of user-created content regarding the library where they work, 9.5% of respondents confirmed that they knew about the existence of such content. The important result is that 97% of respondents were ready and willing to be educated in using Web 2.0 technologies and the same percentage thought it was a good idea that the library should have a Web 2.0 platform.

Following this quantitative research a qualitative case study of Enterprise 2.0 implementation was executed in 2009 at the University library in Belgrade. It was one of the institutions whose employees took part in previous research. With 100 employees, an organizational unit that provides services for IT and development and organizational culture that is favorable for intrapreneurship it was an obvious choice among Serbian libraries. The Enterprise 2.0 implementation in this institution is mostly oriented towards providing better solutions for collaboration of closely linked colleagues, i.e. those connected by strong ties. Implementation is not spread across the entire organization but focused mostly in the departments of scientific information and IT support, digitization and development. Before describing details of Enterprise 2.0 implementation, it is important to notice that almost all employees have Facebook accounts, a lot of them have Twitter or Linkedin accounts and that the usage of Web 2.0 technologies for private purposes is wide. It is also very important to observe the existence of Web 2.0 services for patrons, i.e. Library 2.0 services that have been employed on a large scale via the Facebook, Twitter, and Youtube portals. More than 11,000 patrons have been networked via Facebook service. These two elements grounded basis for business usage of Web 2.0 technologies that librarians were familiar with and that were already used for collaboration with patrons. Several Web 2.0 technologies have been put in use for business purposes in University library in Belgrade. The Google apps platform was activated and unilib.rs domain name is used for its services. Gmail with this proprietary domain was used in order to enhance the existing e-mail service providing for instant messaging function. Google calendars are used by 20 employees who use this service in order to collaborate more closely. Sms text messaging was activated in order to alert employees of calendar changes. Employees gain access to work shift schedules through a specially designed calendar and special events calendar is also maintained, which has proved to be highly efficient since different employees are responsible for planning and execution of different types of special events. In the past many problems arose from inefficient communications that even led to cancellation of some events due to overbooking of available space. The Google Docs application is used to a lesser extent at the moment but wider adoption is expected soon. Blog and forum technologies are used for internal communication between closely linked employees who used to exchange a great number of e-mail messages on a daily basis. This has proved to be very useful because the volume of internal e-mail in organizational units that adopted this technology has decreased by almost 60% providing for more efficient and easier internal collaboration.

As one can deduce from analysis of quantitative data presented intrapreneurship is indeed instrumental in Enterprise 2.0 implementation. In order to focus this notion we will wrap up again aspects of presented research data that imply importance of intrapreneurship for implementation of Enterprise 2.0 in libraries. In the case of University library in Belgrade data from the research conducted in 2007 and 2009 show that intrapreneural activities have been noticed and the overall organizational environment was favorable for intrapreneurship. In addition, a positive trend was detected in both intrapreneural activities and organizational environment factors that resulted from managerial activities intended to foster intrapreneurship. These activities were sparked by the research on intrapreneurship in 2007 when library management was informed of possibilities intrapreneurship offered for library output upgrade and informed on activities and techniques that will foster intrapreneurship. Enterprise 2.0 awareness and usage research conducted in 2007 showed that employees were aware of Web 2.0 technologies and that some of them were using them for private purposes. Some experiments in using these technologies for business purposes were noticed but they were present with really small numbers of employees. Then in 2009 further qualitative research reviled the existence of elements of Enterprise 2.0 implementation which was consistent with increase in intrapreneurial activities. In the case of University library in Belgrade we can conclude that the fostering of intrapreneurship led to Enterprise 2.0 implementation that otherwise would be most difficult to achieve.

In order to further complement these quantitative data, we will present two case studies from ongoing research of Enterprise 2.0 implementation in European libraries. The first case is the one of a library in Italy that we will call library 1. This is a university library situated in the region of Italy that has one of the highest GDP per capita in Europe. The institution is well provided for, budgeting for acquisition, mostly of electronically resources, being in the range of over 1 million Euros. The library provides for an academic population of around 20.000. The staff numbers around 30 providing for some 6000 active patrons. It has three geographically dispersed location, the central one and two smaller outposts. The new management of the library was appointed in 2004 and since then intrapreneurship has been gradually fostered, mostly intuitively. Library director and department heads were available for employees and their ideas. Strict rules and regulations were implemented but employees were left with possibility of coming forward with their own ideas on how to improve working processes and introduce the new ones. Although a non-successful undertaking is considered as a personal failure in the context of national culture, the spirit of entrepreneurship is relatively strong in Italy, the fact being of no small importance for some employees deciding to take the risk of pursuing the projects of their own in the library environment. The management of the library pursued the policy of life ling learning and fostering of education of employees leaving to department heads to balance the time spent for this and other working processes. In such an environment a range of intrapreneurial activities have been detected. Some of them were quite complex involving collaboration with university staff members and other experts from outside of the library. Others were more simple with just one employee pursuing service upgrade on his own initiative in her area of work and expertise. In library 1 there exists the awareness among both employees and management on Enterprise 2.0 possibilities for upgrading library operations. Most employees and members of the library management use Web 2.0 technologies for private purposes, mostly public social networks, video and photo sharing services and wiki and blog technology enabled sites. Management of the library is in a dilemma on return on investment on Enterprise 2.0 implementation and therefore no consistent top down approach is possible. Some employee initiatives have led to implementation of some elements of Enterprise 2.0 A wiki page designated for collaboration of employees have been kick started and regularly updated by an employee. She also started Library 2.0 services on public social sites Twitter and Facebook. Other employees sometime create content at the wiki page, but the input of the management is nonexistent in this area. Therefore, most employees do not have an impression that collaboration by content creation is something valued in this library and they stay passive users most of the time. The same employee started the internal blog but it is engulfed with the same problems. Management does not actively participate by content creation and most of the other employees prefer to put their time into other working processes judging they are more valued by the library management. There are employees who value the efforts of their intrapreneurial colleague and their additional help and participation keeps the implementation of wiki and blog technology alive. In the case of library 1 the general environment was favorable for intrapreneurship which was partly mirrored in organizational environment where some of the elements fostering intrapreneurial activities could be defined. Because of this, some intrapreneurial activities were detected and these ultimately lead to Enterprise 2.0 implementation. Wiki and blog technologies were applied to foster communication of employees but insufficient participation of library management and their laissez-faire attitude induced by the doubts about Enterprise 2.0 implementation return on investment projections made these intrapreneurial activities not as successful as they might have been. In this case, we can see how intrapreneurship even when not fostered by managerial activities leads to initial Enterprise 2.0 implementation. Activities of intrapreneurs can provide for this but without at least some managerial backing it is hard to expect that Enterprise 2.0 will be used in optimal way.

The second case is the one of a national library of an ex-communist country that we will refer to as Library 2.0. It is a big institution for librarianship industry standards with around 300 employees. It has sufficient budgeting and librarianship is still a relatively respected employment in this environment. As a national library it has a lot of responsibilities and a vast range of working processes and working groups performing different tasks. Its IT department is sufficiently equipped with both human and IT resources. The organizational culture is not favorable for intrapreneurship since it is still burdened with the legacy of communist past that suppressed entrepreneurship in general. Organizational structure has three or in same organizational units even four levels. The management style is not favorable for intrapreneurship. Employees could not access the managers easily and all new ideas and initiatives had to be initially presented in a very formal way in writing. Lifelong learning processes were very strictly predefined with little changes soon becoming obsolete. Onsite research showed no signs of intraprenurial activates and employees were very reserved when asked about possibilities for their own initiative. Library management showed no awareness of possibilities that may be gained by intrapreneurial activities of employees. In Library

2.0, there were no instances of implementation of Enterprise 2.0. Employees have not shown any initiative in this direction although many of them do use public social networking sites for private purposes. There was also no top down initiative coming from the library management. On the other hand, this library has a very well developed Library 2.0 service for patrons via Facebook. Thousands of patrons are networked and considerable human resources have been committed in providing content for patrons through this venue. An onsite investigation of reasons for ignoring possibilities of Web 2.0 for business purposes revealed that management and employees share the same belief that it is not an option since not much has been written and discussed about this issue in the library community of their country and internationally. It seems that they wait for a go ahead of some imaginary authority i.e. a wider acceptance of Enterprise 2.0 in wider librarianship community shown through articles, conference papers and other forms of dissemination of positive experiences, as was the case with Library 2.0. When asked about the reason not to contact colleagues on professional and business meters via public social networks the main reason for not doing so was the feeling it was not appropriate and that social networking sites were for private purposes and not for mixing of private and professional aspects of one's life. Again, this was influenced by general organizational culture rooted in traditional slow changing attitudes towards new technologies and various possibilities of its employment. In the case of Library 2.0, neither general environment nor the organizational one was favorable for intrapreneurship. The managerial style and organizational culture were not suited for intrapreneurs and therefore it comes as no surprise that no intrapreneurial activities were detected. One might have expected to witness Enterprise 2.0 implementation in an environment with enough human and material resources especially in IT. The presence of quality Library 2.0 service might further these expectations, but it must be remembered that this came top down not the other way around. But no Enterprise 2.0 implementation happen probably because of the combined effect of lack of intrapreneurial activities and organizational culture that was not prone to accepting easy new technology and new roles of the technology previously used for other purposes.

Based on these two case studies and in conjunction with quantitative data gained by research of Enterprise 2.0 awareness and usage in libraries of Europe and intrapreneurship and Enterprise 2.0 implementation research in Serbian libraries, that was presented previously, one can conclude that there is a relationship between intrapreneurship and Enterprise 2.0 implementation. Some concrete guidelines can be deduced building on these evidences. These mostly regard managerial activities that should be conducted in order to further intrapreneurial possibilities. Managers should provide opportunities for efficient and up-to-date lifelong learning with emphasis on bottom up approach i.e. it should be expected of employees to work on their own education and information gathering about the possibilities on how to improve business operations of the library. This should be combined with logistical support the library provided for disseminating the results of this ongoing educational process at international congresses, via journal articles etc. Library managers should provide time and space for intrapreneurs to explain their ideas, making the organizational structure more flat, even at first only by personal decisions of managers and not by changing rules and regulations of the organization that might take some time. Managers should be improving the area of rules and regulations in a library giving the employees more clearer picture of this area and changing the rules to suit intraprenurial activities more. It is the most difficult task since the fast changing of the rules leads to confusion and provides opportunities for cheating and all kind of misbehavior. Therefore one must realize that this area is slow to change and no fast solutions can be expected here. The first step in this area might be the documentation of criteria for accepting/rejecting intrapreneurial initiatives. These should be grounded in basic organizational documents e.g. Mission and Vision statement, etc. and in the reality of both human and financial resources of the organization. Managers in a library should start working in direction of changing organizational culture in order for it to be more favorable for intrapreneurs. This also takes time and effort that does not seem to pay off, so managers need to be persistent and patient in this area. Combination of techniques always yields best results. Combination of awards and punishments with both in soft and hard categories might be the best combination for the beginning of the process. In addition, perhaps the most importantly the education for members of management of the library on intrapreneurship should be available. It should provide them with guidance on how to approach and deal with intrapreneurial employees they are directly responsible for.

If Enterprise 2.0 implementation initiatives are detected coming from intrapreneurial employees the managers of a library should take a certain course of action in order to explore this. They should be providing psychological and moral help to intrapreneurs that promote Enterprise 2.0 implementation. It is important that library management show other employees that it value this initiative. Library managers should discuss plans and activities of Enterprise 2.0 implementation with intrapreneurs, but making it clear that they have the leading role in the project. This often calls for compromise, but organizational aims should come first at all times. Intrapreneurs could be carried away sometimes and project might become a goal of its own for them. Management should avoid the trap of dismissing a good idea for sake of bad initial planning. Instead, library management needs to make intrapreneurs work for achieving organizational goals by making their personal goals converge with those of the organization. Library management should take active part in Enterprise 2.0 implementation by content creation via Web 2.0 technologies provided. The virtual space of Enterprise 2.0 software should be made an important place by delegating information and power to this place. Other employees need to feel that this is the place to be. They need to know that their input and initiatives will be noticed more easily and quicker by the management if expressed via Enterprise 2.0. They should feel the urge to prove their qualities once again to the management in this new environment. This can only be achieved by everyday presence of management at virtual spaces designated by Web 2.0 technology put to use for business purposes by intrapreneurs. This presence can be visible, genuine, and verifiable only by constant creation of content. A library directors' internal blog might be an ideal start for Enterprise 2.0 implementation. Ideas on library business might be disseminated easily to all employees in this way and their feedback discussed even more easily. This flattens the organizational structure enormously sparking creativity and making decision-making process more transparent. Library management needs to know that most of the resistance to the changes described will come from its own ranks, most usually from ranks of middle management. In smaller libraries it can be those not in an official position but who made it their job to manipulate internal information flow and benefit from it. Library management need to have a strategy in place to overcome such resistance and this might be the tipping point of the whole project of Enterprise 2.0 implementation in a library. If middle management resistance is not overcome and if they are not persuaded to collaborate on it the whole project might collapse. If the Enterprise 2.0 implementation initially works, library managers need to decide on timing of switching from old working processes to the new ones. For instance, a decision should be made in one instance on switching to compulsive use of forum technology for internal communication and banning internal email messages altogether. This should not come too soon since there will be always a group of employees not completely familiar with the new technology or reluctant to use it for any number of reasons. If the timing is not right this group might be still big enough to blame intrapreneurs for their misfortunes and the whole thing might backfire resulting in intrapreneurs retreating from future intrapreneurial activities.

By adopting knowledge on intrapreneurship and Enterprise 2.0 concepts and their relationship, and by implementing favorable conditions for intrapreneurial activities in libraries, library managers can fill the gap in management skills and style that divides them from other industries that have already done this. More importantly, they can exploit intrinsic potentials of librarianship to its full extent creating a significant sustainable competitive advantage for their library by implementing Enterprise 2.0 in it.

FURTHER RESEARCH OF ENTERPRISE 2.0 IN THE LIBRARY ENVIRONMENT

Importance of successful Enterprise 2.0 implementation in a library should now be obvious and some elements of this process know. However, it is important to stress the need for further research in this field since its dynamism is unparalleled. It is of utmost importance for research community and librarianship theory and practice that data on state of Enterprise 2.0 implementation in libraries worldwide exist and are updated regularly. We have described a sketchy nature of current state of Enterprise 2.0 implementation in European libraries, so it is not hard to imagine how important it is to know exact state of this process in a certain region or a country in order to be able to assess the needs for investments in technology or training. This stands of course for all various kinds of data regarding libraries as well as other industries, but the need for current data regarding Enterprise 2.0 is the most urgent since it is and will be more and more the driving force behind any future change in libraries. And in a changing environment, having in mind the globalization processes and in a time of economic crisis changes are the only thing that are guaranteed in a libraries' future.

The data and theoretical concepts presented in this chapter build a basis for future research. The relationship between Enterprise 2.0 implementation and intrapreneurship needs to be verified in as many different library environments as possible, including different library types, within different cultural and economic environments. In addition, intrapreneurship in libraries needs to be researched further since it provides an important tool for library managers to improve library business outcomes and to cope with information flood that is surging on a daily basis. Guidelines provided in this chapter on how to foster intrapreneurship and by this speed up the process of Enterprise 2.0 implementation need to be verified by further surveys that will check the status of ongoing managerial activities in this area and confirm their validity and effectiveness. Only by providing further hard evidence will library research community be able to make viable more precise guidelines for library management on what managerial activities are needed in domain of intrapreneurship fostering. In addition, one always needs to have in mind that besides organizational factors influencing intrapreneurship managers need to factor in environmental factor that do vary drastically in different cultural and economic environments. Because of this, any research of intrapreneurship in libraries in new environment is more than welcomed and needed to complement presented results.

The one single most needed thing when one thinks of researching the mentioned concepts is furthering collaboration among interested parties. We have emphasized the need for the research activities in different cultural and economic environments, in different regions and countries. What we really need in librarianship research community today is more collaboration of researchers from different parts of the world. Only by obtaining comprehensive research results from different parts of a sketchy world, we can hope that more general rules and concepts might emerge. In addition, we need those in order to optimize our operations and in order to viably propose managers on how to optimize the business activities in a library. Also furthering of collaboration between researchers and librarians is needed. Both groups need to understand the needs and potentials of one another and by this virtue the opportunities that might arise from mutual beneficial collaboration.

CONCLUSION

Using Web 2.0 technologies for achieving the business aims of a library, i.e. the implementation of Enterprise 2.0, offers the most balanced approach of costs vs. benefits in a library environment. The nature of these technologies and the challenges that their adoption poses to any management system are considerable. By using certain techniques proposed in the chapter which emerged as best practice cases library management can speed up the adoption of new technologies and maximize the likelihood they will be productive. Considerable effort has been committed to obtaining data on this issue in for-profit industries, but the implementation of Enterprise 2.0 is a novel challenge in the public sector. Librarians still have little understanding in this area, although they are in dire need of improving their intra-organizational communication and collaboration. The presented materials are therefore important not only for introducing this novel problem into librarianship theory but also for providing some solutions that are discovered in the research process as cases of best practice or by means of comparing different practices and styles of implementation.

In the area of creation of basis for continuous efficient updating of library services chapter advocates for implementation of possibilities for collaboration and interactivity among library staff which is fundamental in allowing a library to cope with the fast changing, global environment. Enterprise 2.0 implementation in a library is therefore essential for efficient operations of a library. Enterprise 2.0 implementation in a digital library leads to better alignment of services with patrons' needs and expectations.

REFERENCES

Antoncic, B., & Hisrich, R. (2001). Intrapreneurship: Construct refinement and cross-cultural validation. *Journal of Business Venturing*, *16*, 495–527. doi:10.1016/S0883-9026(99)00054-3

Antoncic, B., & Hisrich, R. (2003). Clarifying the intrapreneurship concept. *Journal of Small Business and Enterprise Development*, *10*, 7–24. doi:10.1108/14626000310461187

Enterprise 2.0 Conference. (2009). *Enterprise 2.0: What, why and how*. Retrieved May 15, 2011, from www.e2conf.com/whitepaper

Fanning, B. (2009). Of wikis, blogs, and tweets: The use of enterprise 2.0 in standards development. *Infonomics*. Retrieved July 15, 2011, from http://www.aiim.org/infonomics/wikis-blogs-tweets-standards-development.aspx

Granovetter, M. (1973). The strength of weak ties. *American Journal of Sociology*, *78*, 1360–1380. doi:10.1086/225469

Heinonen, J., & Korvela, K. (2011). *How about measuring intrapreneurship?* Retrieved May 15, 2011, from http://labsel.pesarosviluppo.it/Modules/ContentManagment/Uploaded/CMItemAttachments/How%20about%20measuring%20intrapreneurship.pdf

Hil, M. (2003). *The development of an instrument to measure intrapreneurship: Entrepreneurship within the corporate settings*. (Unpublished Master Thesis). Rhodes University. Grahamstown, South Africa. Retrieved May 15, 2011, from http://eprints.ru.ac.za/210/01/hill-ma-thesis.pdf

Hinchcliffe, D. (2007). *The state of enterprise 2.0*. Retrieved May 15, 2011, from http://blogs.zdnet.com/Hinchcliffe/?p=143

Hisrich, R., & Peters, M. (1998). *Entrepreneurship: Starting, developing and managing a new enterprise*. Chicago, IL: Irwin Publishing Ltd.

Hornsby, J., Naffziger, D., Kuratko, D., & Montagno, R. (1993). An interactive model of the corporate entrepreneurship process. *Entrepreneurship. Theory into Practice*, *17*(2), 29–37.

Jedd, M. (2008). Enterprise 2.0. *Infonomics*. Retrieved March 12, 2011, from www.aiim.org/infonomics/enterprise-2.0.aspx

Kohler-Kruner, H. (2009). Best practices for implementing enterprise 2.0. *Infonomics*. Retrieved May 15, 2011, from http://www.aiim.org/infonomics/implementing-enterprise-20.aspx

Kuratko, D., & Montagno, R. (1989). Intrapreneurship: Developing innovation in the corporate culture. *Training and Development Journal*, *43*, 83–85.

Kuratko, D., Montagno, R., & Hornsby, J. (1990). Developing an intrapreneurial assessment instrument for an effective corporate entrepreneurial environment. *Strategic Management Journal*, *11*, 49–58.

Leader-Chivee, L., Hamilton, B., & Cowan, E. (2008). Networking the way to success: Online social networks for workplace and competitive advantage. *People and Strategy*, *32*, 41–46.

Manimala, M., Jose, P., & Thomas, K. (2006). Innovation and intrapreneurship: Insights from public sector. *Vikalpa*, *31*, 49–60.

McAfee, A. (2006). Enterprise 2.0: The dawn of emergant colalboration. *MIT Sloan Management Review*, *47*, 21–28.

McAfee, A. (2009). *Enterprise 2.0: New collaborative tools for your organization's toughest challenges*. Cambridge, MA: Harvard Business School Press.

Menzel, H. C. (2008). *Intrapreneurship-conductive culture in industrial R&D: The design of a simulation game to create awareness and provide insight*. (Unpublished Doctoral Dissertation). Technische Universiteit. Eindhoven, The Netherlands. Retrieved May 15, 2011, from http://alexandria.tue.nl/extra2/200810440.pdf

Pinchot, G. (1985). *Intrapreneuring: Why you don't have to leave the corporation to become an entrepreneur*. New York, NY: Harper & Row.

Sharma, P., & Chrisman, J. (1999). Toward a reconcilation of the definitonal issues in the field of corporate entrepreneurship. *Entrepreneurship Theory and Practice*, *23*, 11–28.

Slevin, D., & Covin, J. (1986). The development and testing of an organizational-level entrepreneurship scale. In Ronstadt, R. (Ed.), *Frontiers of Enterpreneurship Research* (pp. 628–639). Wellesley, MA: Babson College.

Slevin, D., & Covin, J. (1989). Juggling entrepreneurial style and organization structure – How to get your act together. *MIT Sloan Management Review*, *31*, 43–53.

Slevin, D., & Covin, J. (1991). A conceptual model of entrepreneurship as firm behavior. *Entrepreneurship Theory and Practice*, *16*, 7–25.

Stevenson, H., & Jarillo, J. (1990). A paradigm of entrepreneurship: Entrepreneurial management. *Strategic Management Journal*, *11*, 17–27.

Thomas, R., & Augustyn, M. (2007). *Tourism in the new Europe: Perspectives on SME policies and practices*. Amsterdam, The Netherlands: Elsevier.

Ulijn, J., & Menzel, H. (2004). *Conceptualizing and measuring intrapreneurship: A French vs. an Anglo-Germanic way of paradigming*. Paper presented to the Second Summer University of European Entrepreneurship Research. Enschede, The Netherlands. Retrieved May 15, 2011, from www.utwente.nl/nikos/archief/esu2004/papers/menzelulijn.pdf

Vesper, K. (1990). *New venture strategies*. Englewood Cliffs, CA: Prentice-Hall.

Wunderer, R. (2001). Employees as co-intrapreneurs – A transformation concept. *Leadership and Organization Development Journal*, *22*, 193–211. doi:10.1108/EUM0000000005676

Zahra, S. (1991). Predictors and financial outcomes of corporate enrepreneurship: An exploratory study. *Journal of Business Venturing*, *6*, 259–285. doi:10.1016/0883-9026(91)90019-A

Zahra, S. (1993). Envirnoment, corporate enrepreneurship and financial outcomes: A taxonomic approach. *Journal of Business Venturing*, *8*, 319–340. doi:10.1016/0883-9026(93)90003-N

Zahra, S., & Covin, J. (1995). Contextual influences on the corporate enrepreneurship – Performance relationship: A longitudinal analysis. *Journal of Business Venturing*, *10*, 43–58. doi:10.1016/0883-9026(94)00004-E

Zampetakis, L., & Moustakis, V. (2007). Entrepreneurial behaviour in the Greek public sector. *International Journal of Entrepreneurial Behaviour & Research*, *13*, 19–38. doi:10.1108/13552550710725165

ADDITIONAL READING

Bernal, J. (2010). *Web 2.0 and social networking for the enterprise*. Pearson Place, NJ: IBM Press.

Collins, P. (2002). *Virtual and networked organizations*. Oxford, UK: John Wiley & Sons Inc.

Cook, N. (2008). *Enterprise 2.0*. Aldersot, UK: Gower Publishing.

Emory, M., & Craig, E. M. (2007). Changing paradigms: Managed learning environments and web 2.0. *Campus-Wide Information Systems*, *24*(3), 152–161. doi:10.1108/10650740710762185

Gorman, G. E. (2006). What does "online" mean in 2006? *Online Information Review*, *30*(5), 481–484. doi:10.1108/14684520610713822

Granovetter, M. (2001). *The sociology of economic life*. Boulder, CO: Westview Press.

Habib, M. (2006). *Toward academic library 2.0: Development and application of a library 2.0 methodology*. (Unpublished Master Thesis). University of North Carolina. Chapel Hill, NC. Retrieved May 15, 2011, from http://mchabib.com/masterspaper.pdf

Harford, T. (2005). *Undercover economist*. Oxford, UK: Oxford University Press.

Harford. (2012). *Website*. Retrieved from http://timharford.com/

Hofstede, G., & Hofstede, G. J. (2005). *Cultures and organizations*. New York, NY: McGraw-Hill.

Kaplan, R., & Norton, D. (2004). *Strategy maps*. Boston, MA: Harvard Business School Publishing.

Logan, D., King, J., & Fischer-Wright, H. (2008). *Tribal leadership*. New York, NY: Harper Collins.

McAfee. (2012). *Website*. Retrieved from http://andrewmcafee.org/

Morris, M. R., & Teevan, J. (2010). *Collaborative search*. San Rafael, CA: Morgan & Claypool.

Net, Z. D. (2012). *Website*. Retrieved from http://www.zdnet.com/blog/hinchcliffe

Newman, A., & Thomas, J. (2009). *Enterprise 2.0 implementation*. New York, NY: McGraw-Hill.

Paroutis, S., & Saleh, A. A. (2009). Determinants of knowledge sharing using web 2.0 technologies. *Journal of Knowledge Management*, *13*(4), 52–63. doi:10.1108/13673270910971824

Porta, M., House, B., Buckley, L., & Blitz, A. (2008). Value 2.0: Eight new rules for creating and capturing value from innovative technologies. *Strategy and Leadership*, *31*(6), 448–483.

Scott. (2012). *Website.* Retrieved from http://dontapscott.com/

Simon, N. (2010). *The participatory museum.* Santa Cruz, CA: Museum 2.0.

Sofronijevic, A., Milicevic, V., & Ilic, B. (2011). Enhancing library business performance by implementation of enterprise 2.0 via intrapreneurship: The case of a serbian library. *Journal of Academic Librarianship, 37*(4), 358–362. doi:10.1016/j.acalib.2011.04.010

Surowiecki, J. (2004). *The wisdom of crowds.* New York, NY: Doubleday.

Tapscott, D., & Williams, D. (2010). *Macrowikinomics.* New York, NY: Portfolio Penguin.

Wyld, C. D. (2008). Management 2.0: A primer on blogging for executives. *Management Research News, 31*(6), 448–483. doi:10.1108/01409170810876044

Yoong, P. (2009). *Leadership in the digital enterprise: Issues and challenges.* Hershey, PA: IGI Global. doi:10.4018/978-1-60566-958-8

Compilation of References

Adams, A., & Blandford, A. (2001). Digital libraries in a clinical setting: friend or foe? Research and advanced technology for digital libraries. In *Proceedings of 5th European Conference Digital Library, ECDL 2001*. Darmstadt, Germany: ECDL.

Adams, A., & Blandford, A. (2002). Acceptability of medical digital libraries. *Health Informatics Journal*, *8*(2), 58–66. doi:10.1177/146045820200800202

Agirre, E., Di Nunzio, G., Ferro, N., Mandl, T., & Peters, C. (2009). CLEF 2008: Ad hoc track overview. *Lecture Notes in Computer Science*, *5706*, 15–37. doi:10.1007/978-3-642-04447-2_2

Agosti, M., Bergamin, G., Crivellari, F., Nunzio, G. M. D., Ferro, N., Ioannidis, Y., et al. (2008). *D5.1: Report on user requirements of the target library services - TEL-plus project.* Retrieved August, 2011 from http://www.theeuropeanlibrary.org/portal/organisation/cooperation/telplus/documents/TELplus_D5.1_31122008.pdf

Agosti, M., Crivellari, F., Deambrosis, G., Ferro, N., Gäde, M., Petras, V., et al. (2009). *D2.1.1: Report on user preferences and information retrieval scenarios for multilingual access in Europeana - EuropeanaConnect-project.* Retrieved August, 2011 from http://www.europeanaconnect.eu/documents/D2.1.1_eConnect_Report_User_Preferences_MLIA_v1.0_20091222.zip

Agosti, M., Crivellari, F., Di Nunzio, G. M., Ioannidis, Y., Stamatogiannakis, L., Triantafillidi, M.-L., & Vayanou, M. (2009). *D5.2: Report on search engines and HTTP log analysis - TELplus project.* Retrieved August 2011 from http://www.theeuropeanlibrary.org/portal/organisation/cooperation/telplus/documents/TEL-plus_D5.2_15102009.pdf

Agosti, M., Crivellari, F., & Di Nunzio, G. (2011). Web log analysis: a review of a decade of studies about information acquisition, inspection and interpretation of user interaction. *Data Mining and Knowledge Discovery*, *24*(3), 663–696. doi:10.1007/s10618-011-0228-8

Allan, R. (2009). *Virtual research environments: From portals to science gateways.* Oxford, UK: Chandos Publishing.

Amato, G., Cigarrán, J., Gonzalo, J., Peters, C., & Savino, P. (2007). MultiMatch – Multilingual/multimedia access to cultural heritage. *Lecture Notes in Computer Science*, *4675*, 505–508. doi:10.1007/978-3-540-74851-9_53

Amin, A., Van Ossenbruggen, J., Hardman, L., & Van Nispen, A. (2008). Understanding cultural heritage experts' information seeking needs. In *Proceedings of the 8th ACM/IEEE-CS Joint Conference on Digital libraries, JCDL 2008,* (pp. 39-47). New York, NY: ACM Press.

Anderson, C. G., & Maxwell, D. C. (2004). *Starting a digitization center.* Oxford, UK: Chandos Publishing. doi:10.1533/9781780630663

Angelaki, G. (2008). *D1.2: Final report on usability developments in the European library - EDL project.* Retrieved August 2011 from http://www.theeuropeanlibrary.org/portal/organisation/cooperation/archive/edlproject/downloads/EDLprojectD1.2Rep_usage_usability.pdf

AnthroDatadpa. (2009). *Anthropological data digital preservation and access.* Retrieved August 11, 2011 from http://anthrodatadpa.org/addpa/home/digital-preservation-and-access-dpa

Antoncic, B., & Hisrich, R. (2001). Intrapreneurship: Construct refinement and cross-cultural validation. *Journal of Business Venturing*, *16*, 495–527. doi:10.1016/S0883-9026(99)00054-3

Antoncic, B., & Hisrich, R. (2003). Clarifying the intrapreneurship concept. *Journal of Small Business and Enterprise Development*, *10*, 7–24. doi:10.1108/14626000310461187

Applied Research Associates, Inc. (2011). *Cognitive task analysis*. Retrieved November 22, 2011 from http://www.ara.com/Capabilities/c_cognitive_science.htm

Arms, W. Y. (2000). *Digital libraries*. Cambridge, MA: MIT Press.

Assante, M., Pagano, P., Candela, L., De Faveri, F., & Lelii, L. (2011). An approach to virtual research environment user interfaces dynamic construction. In *Proceedings of Research and Advanced Technology for Digital Libraries - International Conference on Theory and Practice of Digital Libraries, TPDL 2011*, (pp. 101-109). Berlin, Germany: Springer.

Assante, M., Candela, L., Castelli, D., Frosini, L., Lelii, L., & Manghi, P. (2008). An extensible virtual digital libraries generator. *Lecture Notes in Computer Science*, *5173*, 122–134. doi:10.1007/978-3-540-87599-4_14

Audio Description Illinois. (2009). *Website*. Retrieved February 13, 2011 from http://www.alsaudioillinois.net/

Audio Description Project. (2011). *What is audio description?* Retreived August 11, 2011 from http://www.acb.org/adp/ad.html

Baeza-Yates, R., & Ribeiro-Neto, B. (2011). *Modern information retrieval: The concepts and technology behind search* (2nd ed.). New York, NY: Addison Wesley.

Ball State University. (2007). *Digital repository: Fossils*. Retrieved August 11, 2011 from http://libx.bsu.edu/cdm4/collection.php?CISOROOT=/FosCol

Ball, M. A. (2008). Practicums and service learning in LIS education. *Journal of Education for Library and Information Science*, *51*(4), 241–250.

Bandy, J. (2009). Mining protein-protein interactions from published literature using linguamatics I2E. *Protein Networks and Pathway Analysis*, *563*, 3–13. doi:10.1007/978-1-60761-175-2_1

Banerjee, K. (2002). How does XML help libraries. *Computers in Libraries*, *22*(8). Retrieved from http://www.infotoday.com/cilmag/sep02/Banerjee.htm

Barton., et al. (2006). Using a relational geodatabase to manage paleontological resources at Florissant fossil beds national monument: Fossils from federal lands. *New Mexico Museum of Natural History and Science Bulletin, 34*. Retrieved August 11, 2011 from http://www.nature.nps.gov/geology/paleontology/pub/fossil_conference_7/4%20Abstracts.pdf

Bastion, J., Harvey, R., Mahard, M., & Plum, T. (2010). Building a virtual archives and preservation laboratory at Simmons College: A case study in collaboratative construction. *Journal of Education for Library and Information Science*, *49*(1), 70–82.

Battleson, B., Booth, A., & Weintrop, J. (2001). Usability testing of an academic library web site: A case study. *Journal of Academic Librarianship*, *27*(3), 188–198. doi:10.1016/S0099-1333(01)00180-X

BCR's CDP Digital Imaging Best Practices Working Group. (2008). *BCR's CDP digital imaging best practices version 2.0*. Retrieved from http://www.lyrasis.org/Products-and-Services/Digital-and-Preservation-Services/Digital-Toolbox/~/media/Files/Lyrasis/Products%20and%20Services/Digital%20Services/digital%20imaging%20bp.ashx

Bearman, D., & Trant, J. (2002). *Issues in structuring knowledge and services for universal access to online science and culture*. Paper presented at the Nobel Symposium (NS 120): Virtual Museums and Public Understanding of Science and Culture. Retrieved August, 2011 from http://nobelprize.org/ nobel_organizations/nobelfoundation/symposia/interdisciplinary/ns120/lectures/bearman.pdf

Beisler, A., & Willis, G. (2009). Beyond theory: Preparing Dublin core metadata for OAI-PMH harvesting. *Journal of Library Metadata*, *9*(1/2), 65–97. doi:10.1080/19386380903095099

Bell, S. J., & Shank, J. D. (2007). *Academic librarianship by design: A blended librarian's guide to the tools and technique*. Chicago, IL: ALA.

Bernardi, R., Balestrieri, M., & Bosca, A. (2009). *CACAO system: An overview*. Paper presented at the Workshop on Advanced Technologies for Digital Libraries. Retrieved August, 2011 from http://www.cacaoproject.eu/fileadmin/media/AT4DL/paper-01.pdf

Bernardi, R., Buoso, P., Schiller, A., & Gobbetti, D. (2008). *D4.1: Simple interface (with report of usability and accessibility) - CACAO project*. Retrieved August, 2011 from http://www.cacaoproject.eu/fileadmin/media/Deliverables/CACAO_D4.1.pdf

Biodiversity Information Standards-TDWG. (2009). *Darwin core*. Retrieved August 11, 2011 from http://rs.tdwg.org/dwc/

Bishop, A. P. (1995). Working towards an understanding of digital library use: A report on the user research efforts of the NSF/ARPA/NASA DLI projects. *D-Lib Magazine*. Retrieved from http://www.dlib.org/dlib/october95/10bishop.html

Bishop, A. P. Van House, N. A., & Buttenfield, B. P. (2003). *Digital library use: Social practice in design and evaluation*. Cambridge, MA: MIT Press.

Bishop, A. P. (1998). Logins and bailouts: Measuring access, use, and success in digital libraries. *Journal of Electronic Publishing*, *4*(2). Retrieved from http://quod.lib.umich.edu/j/jep/3336451.0004.207?rgn=main;view=fulltext

Black, E. L. (2007). Web 2.0 and library 2.0: What librarians need to know. In Courney, N. (Ed.), *Library 2.0 and Beyond: Innovative Technologies and Tomorrow's Users* (pp. 1–14). Westport, CT: Libraries Unlimited.

Blandford, A., Keith, S., Connell, I., & Edwards, H. (2004). Analytical usability evaluation for digital libraries: A case study. In Proceedings of the 2004 Joint ACM/IEEE Conference on Digital Libraries, (pp. 27-36). ACM/IEEE.

Blanke, T., Candela, L., Hedges, M., Priddy, M., & Simeoni, F. (2010). Deploying general-purpose virtual research environments for humanities research. *Philosophical Transactions of the Royal Society A*, *368*, 3813–3828. doi:10.1098/rsta.2010.0167

Bollen, J., & Luce, R. (2002). Evaluation of digital library impact and user communities by analysis of usage patterns. *D-Lib Magazine*, *8*(6). Retrieved from http://www.dlib.org/dlib/june02/bollen/06bollen.htmldoi:10.1045/june2002-bollen

Borgman, C. (1999). What are digital libraries? Competing visions. *Information Processing & Management*, *35*(3), 227–243.

Borgman, C. (2000). *From Gutenberg to the global information infrastructure: Access to information in the networked world*. Cambridge, MA: The MIT Press.

Borgman, C. (2007). *Scholarship in the digital age: Information, infrastructure, and the internet*. Cambridge, MA: MIT Press.

Borgman, C. L., Gilliland-Swetland, A. J., Leazer, G. H., Mayer, R., Gwynn, D., Gazan, R., & Mautone, P. (2000). Evaluating digital libraries for teaching and learning in undergraduate education: A case study of the Alexandria digital earth prototype (ADEPT). *Library Trends*, *49*(2), 228–250.

Bosca, A., Djebbari, E., Grzesiak, Ł., Levergood, B., Mazurek, J., Siciliano, L., et al. (2009). *D6.2: Second validation report (technical adequacy + user satisfaction) - Cacao project*. Retrieved August 2011 from http://www.cacaoproject.eu/fileadmin/media/Deliverables/CACAO_D6.2.pdf

Bosca, A., Grzesiak, Ł., & Mazurek, J. (2009). *D6.3: Final validation report (technical adequacy+user satisfaction) - CACAO project*. Retrieved August 2011 from http://www.cacaoproject.eu/fileadmin/media/Deliverables/CACAO_D6.3.pdf

Bosca, A., & Dini, L. (2009). Query expansion via library classification system. *Lecture Notes in Computer Science*, *5706*, 42–49. doi:10.1007/978-3-642-04447-2_4

Bosca, A., & Dini, L. (2010). User logs as a means to enrich and refine translation dictionaries. *Lecture Notes in Computer Science*, *6241*, 544–551. doi:10.1007/978-3-642-15754-7_67

Boss, R. W. (2009). Digital asset management systems. *Tech Notes*. Retrieved August 10, 2011 from http://www.ala.org/ala/mgrps/divs/pla/tools/technotes/DigitalAssetManageme.pdf

Boyns, R. (1999). Archivists and family historians: Local authority record repositories and the family history user group. *Journal of the Society of Archivists*, *20*(1), 61–74. doi:10.1080/003798199103730

Bracero History Archive. (2010). *Website*. Retrieved December 2, 2010 from http://braceroarchive.org/

Brink, T., Gergle, D., & Wood, S. D. (2002). *Designing web sites that work: Usability for the web*. San Francisco, CA: Morgan Kaufmann.

Brophy, P. (2001). Electronic library performance indicators: The EQUINOX project. *Serials*, *14*(1), 5–9.

Brophy, P., & Wynne, P. M. (1997). *Management information systems and performance measurement for the electronic library: eLib supporting study*. Lancashire, UK: University of Central Lancashire, Centre for Research in Library and Information Management.

Bruce, T., & Hillmann, D. (2004). The continuum of metadata quality: Defining, expressing, exploiting. In Hillmann, D., & Westbrooks, E. (Eds.), *Metadata in Practice* (pp. 238–256). Chicago, IL: American Library Association.

Budhu, M., & Coleman, A. (2002). The design and evaluation of interactivities in a digital library. *D-Lib Magazine*, *8*(11). doi:10.1045/november2002-coleman

Burton, P. F., & McMenemy, D. (2005). Future librarians digitizing the past. *Information Scotland*, *3*(5). Retrieved from http:///www.slainte.org.ul/publications/serial/infoscot/vol3(5)article5.htm

Bush, V. (1945). As we may think. *The Atlantic Monthly*. Retrieved from http://www.theatlantic.com/doc/194507/bush

Buttenfield, B. (1999). Usability evaluation of digital libraries. *Science & Technology Libraries*, *17*(3-4), 39–59. doi:10.1300/J122v17n03_04

Butterworth, R. (2006). Information seeking and retrieval as a leisure activity. In A. Blandford & J. Gow (Eds.), *First International Workshop, DL-CUBA 2006, JCDL 2006, Digital Libraries in the Context of Users' Broader Activities*, (pp. 29-32). Chapel Hill, NC: JCDL. Retrieved August 11, 2011 from http://citeseerx.ist.psu.edu/viewdoc/download?doi=10.1.1.96.8745&rep=rep1&type=pdf#page=43

Byrne, W., Doermann, D., Franz, M., Gustman, S., Hajic, J., & Oard, D. (2004). Automatic recognition of spontaneous multilingual oral history archives. *IEEE Transactions on Speech and Audio Processing*, *12*(4), 420–435. doi:10.1109/TSA.2004.828702

Cahill, K. (2009). *User-generated content and its impact on web-based library services*. Oxford, UK: Chandos. doi:10.1533/9781780630083

Candela, L., Athanasopoulos, G., Castelli, D., El Raheb, K., Innocenti, P., Ioannidis, Y., et al. (2011). *The digital library reference model*. D3.2b DL.org Project Deliverable.

Candela, L., Castelli, D., Manghi, P., & Pagano, P. (2007). Enabling services in knowledge infrastructures: The driver experience. In *Proceedings of the Third Italian Research Conference on Digital Library Systems, IRCDL 2007*, (pp. 71-77). Padova, Italy: DELOS.

Candela, L., Castelli, D., Pagano, P., & Simi, M. (2005). From heterogeneous information spaces to virtual documents. In *Proceedings of Digital Libraries: Implementing Strategies and Sharing Experiences, 8th International Conference on Asian Digital Libraries, ICADL 2005*. Bangkok, Thailand: Springer.

Candela, L., Akal, F., Avancini, H., Castelli, D., Fusco, L., & Guidetti, V. (2007). Diligent: Integrating digital library and grid technologies for a new earth observation research infrastructure. *International Journal on Digital Libraries*, *7*(1-2), 59–80. doi:10.1007/s00799-007-0023-8

Candela, L., Akal, F., Avancini, H., Castelli, D., Fusco, L., & Guidetti, V. (2007). DILIGENT: Integrating digital library and grid technologies for a new earth observation research infrastructure. *International Journal on Digital Libraries*, *7*, 59–80. doi:10.1007/s00799-007-0023-8

Candela, L., Castelli, D., & Pagano, P. (2009). On-demand virtual research environments and the changing roles of librarians. *Library Hi Tech, 27*(2), 239–251. doi:10.1108/07378830910968191

Candela, L., Castelli, D., & Pagano, P. (2010). Making virtual research environments in the cloud a reality: The gCube approach. *ERCIM News, 83*, 32–33.

Candela, L., Castelli, D., & Pagano, P. (2011). History, evolution and impact of digital libraries. In Iglezakis, I., Synodinou, T.-E., & Kapidakis, S. (Eds.), *E-Publishing and Digital Libraries: Legal and Organizational Issues* (pp. 1–30). Hershey, PA: IGI Global.

Carroll, T. W. (2007). *Grassroots feminism: Direct action organizing and coalition building in New York City, 1955-1995*. (PhD Thesis). University of Michigan. Ann Arbor, MI.

Carroll. T. W. (2004). *New York City women community activists oral history project*. Retrieved from http://qe2aproxy.mun.ca/login?url=http://www.aspresolver.com/aspresolver.asp?WASM;S10020421

Carroll, T. W. (2006). *How did working-class feminists meet the challenges of working across differences? The national congress of neighborhood women, 1974-2006*. Binghamton, NY: State University of New York.

Carusi, A., & Reimer, T. (2010). Virtual research environment collaborative landscape study. *JISC*. Retrieved from http://www.jisc.ac.uk/media/documents/publications/vrelandscapereport.pdf

Casey, M. (2005). *Working towards a definition of library 2.0*. Retrieved August 5, 2009 from http://www.librarycrunch.com/2005/10/working_towards_a_definition_o.html

Casey, M., & Savastinuk, L. C. (2006). Library 2.0. *Library Journal, 131*(14), 40–42.

CDC. (2004). *Vision impairment*. Retrieved February 1, 2011 from http://www.cdc.gov/ncbddd/dd/ddvi.htm

Ceccarelli, D., Gordea, S., Lucchese, C., Nardini, F. M., & Tolomei, G. (2011). *Improving Europeana search experience using query logs*. Paper presented at the Theories and Practice of Digital Libraries Conference. Berlin, Germany. Retrieved August, 2011 from http://miles.isti.cnr.it/~nardini/wp-content/uploads/2011/06/tpdl2011.pdf

Cherry, J., & Duff, W. (2002). Studying digital library users over time: A follow-up survey of early Canadiana online. *Information Research, 7*(2). Retrieved August 16, 2011 from http://informationr.net/ir/7-2/paper123.html

Chowdhury, G. G., & Chowdhury, S. (2003). *Introduction to digital libraries*. London, UK: Facet Publishing.

Chowdhury, S., Landoni, M., & Gibb, F. (2006). Usability and impact of digital libraries: A review. *Online Information Review, 30*(6), 656–680. doi:10.1108/14684520610716153

Clark, J. T., et al. (2002). Digital archive network for anthropology. *Journal of Digital Information, 2*(4). Retrieved August 11, 2011 from http://journals.tdl.org/jodi/article/viewArticle/50/53

Clark, M. (2006). Notable New Yorkers. *Columbia University Libraries Oral History Research Office*. Retrieved August 1, 2011 from http://www.columbia.edu/cu/lweb/digital/collections/nny/index.html

Cleverdon, C. (1997). The Cranfield tests on index language devices. In Jones, K. S., & Willett, P. (Eds.), *Readings in Information Retrieval*. San Francisco, CA: Morgan Kaufmann. doi:10.1108/eb050097

Cleverdon, C. W. (1970). *The effect of variations in relevance assessments in comparative experimental tests of index languages*. Cranfield, UK: Cranfield Institute of Technology.

Clough, P., & Sanderson, M. (2004). The effects of relevance feedback in cross language image retrieval. In McDonald & Tait (Eds.), *Advances in Information Retrieval: Proceedings of the 26th European Conference on IR Research (ECIR 2004)*, (pp. 238-252). Sunderland, UK: ECIR.

Clough, P., Sanderson, M., & Reid, N. (2006). The Eurovision St Andrews collection of photographs. *ACM SIGIR Forum, 40*(1), 21-30.

Clough, P., Müller, H., & Sanderson, M. (2005). The CLEF 2004 cross language image retrieval track. *Lecture Notes in Computer Science, 3491*, 597–613. doi:10.1007/11519645_59

Cockburn, A. (2001). *Writing effective use cases*. Boston, MA: Addison-Wesley.

Connaway, L. S., Dickey, T. J., & Radford, M. L. (2011). If it is too inconvenient I'm not going after it: Convenience as a critical factor in information-seeking behaviors. *Library & Information Science Research, 33*(3), 179–190. doi:10.1016/j.lisr.2010.12.002

Cottin, M., & Faria, R. (2008). *The black book of colors*. Toronto, Canada: Groundwood Books.

Cousins, J. (2006). The European library - Pushing the boundaries of usability. *The Electronic Library, 24*(4), 434–444. doi:10.1108/02640470610689142

Coyle, K. (2005). Understanding metadata and its purpose. *Journal of Academic Librarianship, 31*(2), 160–163. doi:10.1016/j.acalib.2004.12.010

Crawford, W. (2006). Library 2.0 and "library 2.0". *Cites and Insights, 6*(2), 1–32.

Creswell, J. W. (2005). *Educational research: Planning, conducting, and evaluating quantitative and qualitative research* (2nd ed.). Upper Saddle River, NJ: Merrill.

Currier, S. (2002). INSPIRAL: Digital library services and online learning environments: Issues for integration. In Brophy, P., Fisher, S., & Clarke, Z. (Eds.), *Libraries without Walls 4: The Delivery of Library Services to Distant Users* (pp. 50–61). London, UK: Facet Publishing.

Currum, S. (2011). Experiential learning: Reducing the real-world divide between libraries and library schools. *The Reference Librarian, 52*, 300–307. doi:10.1080/02763877.2011.585282

Cyberinfrastructure Council. (2007). *Cyberinfrastructure vision for the 21st century discovery*. Washington, DC: National Science Foundation.

Dahlstrom, M., & Doracic, A. (2009). Digitization education: Courses take and lessons learned. *D-Lib Magazine, 15*(3/4). Retrieved from http://www.dlib.org/dlib/march09/dahlstrom/03dahlstrom.html

Dekkers, M., Gradmann, S., & Meghini, C. (2009). *Europeana outline functional specification: For development of an operational European digital library: D 2.5 – Europeana thematic network project*. Retrieved August, 2011 from http://www.version1.europeana.eu/web/europeana-project/technicaldocuments/

Demartini, G., & Mizzaro, S. (2006). A classification of IR effectiveness metrics. *Lecture Notes in Computer Science, 3936*, 488–491. doi:10.1007/11735106_48

Dickstein, R., & Mills, V. (2000). Usability testing at the University of Arizona library: How to let the users in on the design. *Information Technology and Libraries, 19*(3), 144–151.

DiConsiglio, J. (2010). *Connecting to collections: A report to the nation*. Retrieved from http://www.imls.gov/resources/year.shtm.

Digital Library Federation. (1998). *A working definition of digital library*. Retrieved March 29, 2008 from www.diglib.org/about/dldefinition.htm

Digital Media, J. I. S. C. (2008). *Choosing a file name*. Retrieved from http://www.jiscdigitalmedia.ac.uk/crossmedia/advice/choosing-a-file-name/

Dillon, A. (1999). TIME - A multi-leveled framework for evaluating and designing digital libraries. *International Journal on Digital Libraries, 2*(2/3), 170–177. doi:10.1007/s007990050045

Dimitrakos, T., Martrat, J., & Wesner, S. (Eds.). (2010). *Service oriented infrastructures and cloud service platforms for the enterprise*. Berlin, Germany: Springer. doi:10.1007/978-3-642-04086-3

Dobreva, M., & Chowdhury, S. (2010). A user-centric evaluation of the Europeana digital library. *Lecture Notes in Computer Science, 6102*, 148–157. doi:10.1007/978-3-642-13654-2_19

Dobreva, M., McCulloch, E., Birrell, D., Unal, Y., & Feliciati, P. (2010). Digital natives and specialised digital libraries: A study of Europeana users. *Communications in Computer and Information Science, 96*, 45–60. doi:10.1007/978-3-642-16032-5_5

Donald, C. Davidson Library Special Collections. (2011). *Cylinder preservation and digitization project*. Retrieved July 29, 2011 from http://cylinders.library.ucsb.edu/

Dörk, M., Carpendale, S., & Williamson, C. (2011). The information flaneur: A fresh look at information seeking. In *Proceedings of the 2011 Annual Conference on Human Factors in Computing Systems, CHI 2011,* (pp. 1215-1224). Vancouver, Canada: ACM Press.

Dorward, J., Reinke, D., & Recker, M. (2002). An evaluation model for a digital library services tool. In *Proceedings of the Second ACM/IEEE-CS Joint Conference on Digital Libraries,* (pp. 322-323). New York, NY: ACM Press.

Drake, P. J. (2001). *Findings from the Fullerton genealogy study.* Retrieved August 11, 2011 from http://psych.fullerton.edu/genealogy/

Dublin Core Metadata Initiative. (2004). *DCMI glossary.* Retrieved from http://dublincore.org/documents/usageguide/glossary.shtml

Dublin Core Metadata Initiative. (2011). *DCMI home.* Retrieved August 11, 2011 from http://dublincore.org/

Duff, W. M., & Johnson, C. A. (2003). Where is the list with all the names? Information-seeking behavior of genealogists. *The American Archivist, 66*(1), 79–95.

EAC-CPF. (2012) *Welcome to the EAC-CPF homepage.* Retrieved from http://eac.staatsbibliothek-berlin.de

e-Infrastructure Reflection Group. (2010). *Blue paper.* E-IRG.

Eliasen, K., McKinstry, J., & Fraser, B. M. (1997). Navigating online menus: A quantitative experiment. *College & Research Libraries, 58,* 509–516.

Ellis, F. (1991). *A picture is worth a thousand words for blind and visually impaired persons too!: An introduction to audiodescription.* New York, NY: American Foundation for the Blind.

Endsley, M. R., Bolstad, C. A., Jones, D. G., & Riley, J. M. (2003). Situation awareness oriented design: From user's cognitive requirements to creating effective supporting technologies. In *Proceedings of the 47th Annual Meeting of the Human Factors & Ergonomics Society,* (pp. 268–272). Santa Monica, CA: Human Factors & Ergonomics Society.

Endsley, M. R., Bolte, B., & Jones, D. G. (2003). *Designing for situation awareness: An approach to human-centered design.* London, UK: Taylor & Francis.

Enterprise 2.0 Conference. (2009). *Enterprise 2.0: What, why and how.* Retrieved May 15, 2011, from www.e2conf.com/whitepaper

European Parliament Council. (2007). *Directive 2007/2/EC of the European parliament and of the council of 14 March 2007 establishing an Infrastructure for spatial information in the European community (INSPIRE).* Brussels, Belgium: European Parliament.

European Strategy Forum on Research Infrastructures. (2010). *Strategy report on research infrastructures.* Brussels, Belgium: Publications Office of the European Union.

Europeana. (2008). *Website.* Retrieved from http://www.europeana.eu

Fanning, B. (2009). Of wikis, blogs, and tweets: The use of enterprise 2.0 in standards development. *Infonomics.* Retrieved July 15, 2011, from http://www.aiim.org/infonomics/wikis-blogs-tweets-standards-development.aspx

Fear, K. (2010). User understanding of metadata in digital image collections: Or, what exactly do you mean by "coverage"? *The American Archivist, 73,* 26–60.

Fernandez, J. D., Martinez-Prieto, M. A., de la Fuente, P., Vegas, J., & Adiego, J. (2008). Agile DL: Building a DELOS-conformed digital library using agile software development. In B. Christensen-Dalsgaard, D. Castelli, B. A. Jurik, & J. Lippincott (Eds.), *Research and Advanced Technology for Digital Libraries, 12th European Conference, ECDL 2008,* (pp. 398-399). Berlin, Germany: Springer-Verlag.

Ferro, N., & Peters, C. (2010). CLEF 2009 ad hoc track overview: TEL & Persian tasks. *Lecture Notes in Computer Science, 6241,* 13–35. doi:10.1007/978-3-642-15754-7_2

Forsyth Library Digital Collections. (2011). *FHSU master's thesis collection.* Retrieved August 11, 2011 from http://cdm15732.contentdm.oclc.org/cdm/landingpage/collection/thesis

Fort Hays State University. (2011). *FHSU Forsyth library digital collections.* Retrieved August 11, 2011 from http://www.fhsu.edu/library/

Foster, I., Zhao, Y., Raicu, I., & Lu, S. (2008). Cloud computing and grid computing 360-degree compared. In *Proceedings of Grid Computing Environments Workshop, 2008, GCE 2008.* GCE.

Foster, I., & Kesselman, C. (1998). *The grid: Blueprint for a new computing infrastructure*. San Francisco, CA: Morgan Kaufmann.

Frank, R. (2010). *Comparing the ALA core competencies to New York librarian job postings and New York Library school curricula: An analysis with a job seeker's toolkit for the new MLIS graduate. Unpublished Research Project*. Flushing, NY: Queens College, CUNY.

Fresa, A. (2005). *MICHAEL: Multilingual inventory of cultural heritage in Europe*. Paper presented at the EVA. Retrieved August, 2011 from http://www.michael-culture.eu/documents/fresaeva05.pdf

Fuhr, N., Hansen, P., Mabe, M., Micsik, A., & Sølvberg, I. (2001). Digital libraries: A generic classification and evaluation scheme. *Lecture Notes in Computer Science*, *2163*, 187–199. doi:10.1007/3-540-44796-2_17

Fuhr, N., Tsakonas, G., Aalberg, T., Agosti, M., Hansen, P., & Kapidakis, S. (2007). Evaluation of digital libraries. *International Journal on Digital Libraries*, *8*(1), 27–38. doi:10.1007/s00799-007-0011-z

Fulton, C. (2009). The pleasure principle: The power of positive affect in information seeking. *Aslib Proceedings*, *61*(3), 245–261. doi:10.1108/00012530910959808

Gäde, M., Petras, V., & Stiller, J. (2010). Which log for which information? Gathering multilingual data from different log file types. *Lecture Notes in Computer Science*, *6360*, 70–81. doi:10.1007/978-3-642-15998-5_9

Gallop-Gerdman, G. (2000). We are family. *American Demographics*, *22*(9), 24.

Gapen, D. K. (1993). The virtual library: Knowledge, society and the librarian. In Saunders, L. M. (Ed.), *The Virtual Library: Vision and Realities* (pp. 1–14). Westport, CT: Meckler.

Garrison, D. R., & Kanuka, H. (2004). Blended learning: Uncovering its transformative potential in higher education. *The Internet and Higher Education*, *7*(2), 95–105. doi:10.1016/j.iheduc.2004.02.001

Generations Network. (2005). *Americans' fascination with family history is rapidly growing*. Retrieved August 11, 2011 from http://corporate.ancestry.com/press/press-releases/view/?id=406

George Mason University. (2011). *Omeka*. Retrieved September 10, 2011, from http://omeka.org/

Gerber, B., & Guay, D. (Eds.). (2006). *Reaching and teaching: Students with special needs through art*. Reston, VA: National Art Education Association.

Girard, T., Pina, M., & Trapp, P. (2011). An exploratory study of class presentations and peer evaluations: Do students perceive the benefits? *Academy of Educational Leadership Journal*, *15*(1), 77–94.

Global Biodiversity Information Facility. (2011). *Gbif.org home page*. Retrieved August 11, 2011 from http://www.gbif.org/

Granovetter, M. (1973). The strength of weak ties. *American Journal of Sociology*, *78*, 1360–1380. doi:10.1086/225469

Greenberg, J. (2011). *Keynote*. Paper presented at the Webwise 2011. Baltimore, MD. Retrieved from http://www.tvworldwide.com/events/webwise/110309/globe_show/default_go_archive.cfm?gsid=1585&type=flv&test=0&live=0

Greenstein, D. (2000). Digital libraries and their challenges. *Library Trends*, *49*(2), 290–303.

Guenther, K. (2003). Assessing web site usability. *Online*, *27*, 65–68.

Guldbæk, K., & Petersen, G. (2011). *D3.2.3: Recommendations for conducting user tests: User involvement – A toolbox: How to involve users in development processes in Europeana - EuropeanaConnect project*. Retrieved August 2011 from http://www.europeanaconnect.eu/documents/D3.2.3_eConnect_usability_guidelines_v1.0_KB-DK.pdf

Hagedorn, K. (2003). OAIster: A "no dead ends" OAI service provider. *Library Hi Tech*, *21*(2), 170–181. doi:10.1108/07378830310479811

Hajdukiewicz, J. R., Vicente, K. J., Doyle, D. J., Milgram, P., & Burns, C. M. (2001). Modeling a medical environment: An ontology for integrated medical informatics design. *International Journal of Medical Informatics*, *62*, 79–99. doi:10.1016/S1386-5056(01)00128-9

Hammill, S. (2003). Usability testing at Florida international university libraries: What we learned. *Electronic Journal of Academic and Special Librarianship*, *4*(1).

Han, M. J., Cho, C., Cole, T. W., & Jackson, A. S. (2009). Metadata for special collections in CONTENTdm: How to improve interoperability of unique fields through OAI-PMH. *Journal of Library Metadata*, *9*(3), 213–238. Retrieved from http://hdl.handle.net/2142/15415. doi:10.1080/19386380903405124

Harrison, L. D., et al. (2001). A lexical approach to text mining for the integration of genomic information. In C. Wu (Eds.), *Proceedings of the Atlantic Symposium on Computational Biology and Genome Information Systems & Technology*. Durham, NC: IEEE.

Harrison, L. D., & Lacerna, L. (1992). Reducing barriers to the utilization of literature at Hoffmann-La Roche. *Drug Information Journal*, *26*(3), 433–443. doi:10.1177/009286159202600317

Hartson, H. R., Shivakumar, P., & Perez-Quinones, M. A. (2004). Usability inspection of digital libraries: A case study. *International Journal on Digital Libraries*, *4*(2), 108–123. doi:10.1007/s00799-003-0074-4

Hawkins, S. (2005). Beyond the digital divide: Issues of access and economics. *Canadian Journal of Information and Library Science*, *29*(2), 171–189.

Hearst, M. A., Divoli, A., Guturu, H., Ksikes, A., Nakov, P., Wooldridge, A., & Ye, J. (2007). BioText search engine: Beyond abstract search. *Bioinformatics (Oxford, England)*, *23*(16), 2196–2197. doi:10.1093/bioinformatics/btm301

Heinonen, J., & Korvela, K. (2011). *How about measuring intrapreneurship?* Retrieved May 15, 2011, from http://labsel.pesarosviluppo.it/Modules/ContentManagment/Uploaded/CMItemAttachments/How%20about%20measuring%20intrapreneurship.pdf

Herold, P. (2004). Teams and teamwork. In Barnes, S. J. (Ed.), *Becoming a Digital Library* (pp. 117–142). New York, NY: Marcel Dekker.

Hersh, W., Turpin, A., Price, S., Chan, B., Kramer, D., Sacherek, L., et al. (2000). Do batch and user evaluations give the same results? In *Proceedings of the 23rd Annual International ACM SIGIR Conference on Research and Development in Information Retrieval,* (pp. 17-24). Athens, Greece: ACM Press.

Hey, T., Tansley, S., & Tolle, K. (2009). *The fourth paradigm - Data-intensive scientific discovery*. New York, NY: Microsoft Research.

Hil, M. (2003). *The development of an instrument to measure intrapreneurship: Entrepreneurship within the corporate settings*. (Unpublished Master Thesis). Rhodes University. Grahamstown, South Africa. Retrieved May 15, 2011, from http://eprints.ru.ac.za/210/01/hill-mathesis.pdf

Hill, L. L., Dolin, R., Frew, J., Kemp, R. B., Larsgaard, M., & Montello, D. R. Simpson, J. (1997). User evaluation: Summary of the methodologies and results for the Alexandria digital library, University of California at Santa Barbara. In *Proceedings of 60th ASIST Annual Meeting*, (pp. 225-243, 369). Medford, NJ: Information Today.

Hillmann, D. (2005). Using Dublin core. *Dublin Core Metatdata Inititative*. Retrieved from http://dublincore.org/documents/usageguide/elements.shtml

Hinchcliffe, D. (2007). *The state of enterprise 2.0.* Retrieved May 15, 2011, from http://blogs.zdnet.com/Hinchcliffe/?p=143

Hisrich, R., & Peters, M. (1998). *Entrepreneurship: Starting, developing and managing a new enterprise*. Chicago, IL: Irwin Publishing Ltd.

Hornsby, J., Naffziger, D., Kuratko, D., & Montagno, R. (1993). An interactive model of the corporate entrepreneurship process. *Entrepreneurship. Theory into Practice*, *17*(2), 29–37.

Howe, K. (2011). *Session #3: Tapping into science: Promoting collections for use in teaching, learning and research.* Paper presented at the Webwise 2011. Baltimore, MD. Retrieved from http://www.tvworldwide.com/events/webwise/110309/globe_show/default_go_archive.cfm?gsid=1576&type=flv&test=0&live=0

Huiskes, M. J., & Lew, M. S. (2008). The MIR flickr retrieval evaluation. In *Proceedings of the 1st ACM International Conference on Multimedia Information Retrieval,* (pp. 39-43). New York, NY: ACM.

Iatropoulou, K., Lebesis, A., Manghi, P., Manola, N., & Mikulicic, M. (2010). On constructing repository infrastructures - The D-NET software toolkit. In *Proceedings of the International Conference on Open Repositories.* Open Repositories.

Illinois General Assembly. (2007). *Illinois information technology accessibility act.* Retrieved February 14, 2011 from http://ilga.gov/legislation/publicacts/95/PDF/095-0307.pdf

Ingwersen, P., & Järvelin, K. (2005). *The turn - Integration of information seeking and retrieval in context*. Dordrecht, The Netherlands: Springer.

International Council of Museums. (2003). *Scope definition of the CIDOC conceptual reference model*. Retrieved August, 2011 from http://www.cidoc-crm.org/scope.html

International Standard Organization. (1997). *ISO 9241-11: Ergonomic requirements for office work with visual display terminals (VDTs), Part 11: Guidance on usability specification and measures. Technical Report*. Geneva, Switzerland: International Standard Organization.

Jackson, A. S., Han, M. J., Groetsch, K., Mustafoff, M., & Cole, T. W. (2008). Dublin core metadata harvested through OAI-PMH. *Journal of Library Metadata, 8*(1), 5–21. Retrieved from http://hdl.handle.net/2142/9091. doi:10.1300/J517v08n01_02

Janssen, O. D. (2007). Building the European digital library - An insider's point of view. In H. A. Thompson (Ed.), *ACRL 13th National Conference Proceedings*. Retrieved August 2011 from http://www.ala.org/ala/mgrps/divs/acrl/events/national/baltimore/papers/46.pdf

Jansson, E. (2010). *DSpace manakin UI: Case study of value and costs*. Retrieved August 11, 2011 from http://hdl.handle.net/10090/12618

Jedd, M. (2008). Enterprise 2.0. *Infonomics*. Retrieved March 12, 2011, from www.aiim.org/infonomics/enterprise-2.0.aspx

Jeng, J. (2006). *Usability of the digital library: An evaluation model*. (Unpublished Doctoral Dissertation). Rutgers University. Hoboken, NJ.

Jeng, J. (2005). Usability assessment of academic digital libraries: Effectiveness, efficiency, satisfaction, and learnability. *Libri, 55*(2/3), 96–121.

Jeng, J. (2005). What is usability in the context of the digital library and how can it be measured? *Information Technology and Libraries, 24*(2), 47–56.

Johnson, K., & Magusin, E. (2005). *Exploring the digital library: A guide for online teaching and learning*. San Francisco, CA: Jossey-Bass.

Joint Information Systems Committee. (2006). *e-Infrastructure briefing paper.* New York, NY: JISC.

Joint, N. (2006). Common principles in managing digital libraries and managing VLEs. *Library Review, 55*(4), 232–236. doi:10.1108/00242530610660771

Jones, M. L. W., Gay, G. K., & Rieger, R. H. (1999). Project soup: Comparing evaluations of digital collection efforts. *D-Lib Magazine, 5*(11). Retrieved August 2011 from http://www.dlib.org/dlib/november99/11jones.html

Joo, S., & Lee, J. (2011). Measuring the usability of academic digital libraries: Instrument development and validation. *The Electronic Library, 29*(4), 523–537. doi:10.1108/02640471111156777

Kaber, D. B., Segall, N., Green, R. S., Entzian, K., & Junginger, S. (2006). Using multiple cognitive task analysis methods for supervisory control interface design in high-throughput biological screening processes. *Cognition Technology and Work, 8*(4), 237–252. doi:10.1007/s10111-006-0029-9

Kahn, R. E., & Cerf, V. G. (1988). *The digital library project volume 1: The world of knowbots (draft): An open architecture for a digital library system and a plan for its development*. Retrieved February 9, 2009 from http://www.cnri.reston.va.us/kahn-cerf-88.pdf

Kaplan, B., & Shaw, N. T. (2004). People, organizational, and social issues: Future directions in evaluation research. *Methods of Information in Medicine, 43*, 215–231.

Kaske, N. (2004). The ubiquitous library is here. *Libraries and the Academy, 4*(2), 291–297. doi:10.1353/pla.2004.0030

Kazai, G., & Doucet, A. (2007). Overview of the INEX 2007 book search track. *ACM SIGIR Forum, 42*(1).

Kazai, G., Koolen, M., Doucet, A., & Landoni, M. (2010). Overview of the INEX 2010 book track: At the mercy of crowdsourcing. In Shlomo, G., Kamps, J., Schenkel, R., & Trotman, A. (Eds.), *INEX 2010 Workshop Pre-Proceedings*. Huize Bergen, The Netherlands: INEX.

Kelly, D. (2009). Methods for evaluating interactive information retrieval systems with users. *Foundations and Trends in Information Retrieval, 3*(1-2), 1–224.

Kengeri, R., Seals, C. D., Harley, H. D., Reddy, H. P., & Fox, E. A. (1999). Usability study of digital libraries: ACM, IEEE-CS, NCSTRL, NDLTD. *International Journal on Digital Libraries, 2*, 157–169. doi:10.1007/s007990050044

Kenney, A. R., Sharpe, L. H., & Berger, B. (1998). Illustrated book study: Digital conversion requirements of printed illustration. In C. Nikolaou & C. Stephanidis (Eds.), *Research and Advanced Technology for Digital Libraries: Proceedings of the Second European Conference,* (pp. 279-293). Berlin, Germany: Springer.

Kim, Y. H., & Kim, H. H. (2008). Development and validation of evaluation indicators for a consortium of institutional repositories: A case study of collection. *Journal of the American Society for Information Science andTechnology, 59*(8), 1282–1294. doi:10.1002/asi.20818

Kim, Y., Ahronheim, J., Suzuka, K., King, L. E., Bruell, D., Miller, R., & Johnson, L. (2007). Enterprise digital asset management system pilot: Lessons learned. *Information Technology & Libraries, 26*(4), 4–16.

King, A. (1993). From sage on the stage to guide on the side. *College Teaching, 41*(1), 30–35. Retrieved from http://www.jstor.org/stable/27558571d oi:10.1080/87567555.1993.9926781

Kohler-Kruner, H. (2009). Best practices for implementing enterprise 2.0. *Infonomics*. Retrieved May 15, 2011, from http://www.aiim.org/infonomics/implementing-enterprise-20.aspx

Kuglin, H. (2004). *Granny hunting: The information seeking behaviour of genealogists in open access libraries: A quantitative study*. Paper presented at the Lianza Conference 2004. Auckland, Australia. Retrieved April 14, 2010 from http://www.lianza.org.nz/library/files/store_018/Granny_Hunting_Kuglin.pdf

Kuratko, D., & Montagno, R. (1989). Intrapreneurship: Developing innovation in the corporate culture. *Training and Development Journal, 43*, 83–85.

Kuratko, D., Montagno, R., & Hornsby, J. (1990). Developing an intrapreneurial assessment instrument for an effective corporate entrepreneurial environment. *Strategic Management Journal, 11*, 49–58.

Kurth, M., Ruddy, D., & Rupp, N. (2004). Repurposing MARC metadata: Using digital project experience to develop a metadata management design. *Library Hi Tech, 22*(2), 153–165. Retrieved from http://proquest.umi.com.queens.ezproxy.cuny.edu:2048/pqdlink?did=679670391&Fmt=7&clientId=13031&RQT=309&VName=PQDd oi:10.1108/07378830410524585

Kushniruk, A. W. (2001). Analysis of complex decision-making processes in health care: Cognitive approaches to health informatics. *Journal of Biomedical Informatics, 34*(5), 365–376. doi:10.1006/jbin.2001.1021

Kushniruk, A. W., Patel, C., Patel, V. L., & Cimino, J. J. (2001). Televaluation of information systems: An integrative approach to design and evaluation of web-based systems. *International Journal of Medical Informatics, 61*(1), 45–70. doi:10.1016/S1386-5056(00)00133-7

Kushniruk, A. W., & Patel, V. L. (2004). Cognitive and usability engineering methods for the evaluation of clinical information systems. *Journal of Biomedical Informatics, 37*(1), 56–76. doi:10.1016/j.jbi.2004.01.003

Kyrillidou, M., & Giersch, S. (2005). Developing the DigiQUAL protocol for digital library evaluation. In M. Marlino, T. Summer, & F. Shipman (Eds.), *Proceedings of the Fifth ACM/IEEE-CS Joint Conference on Digital Libraries,* (pp. 172-173). New York, NY: ACM Press.

Lagoze, C., & Van de Sompel, H. (2001). The open archives initiative: Building a low-barrier interoperability framework. In *Proceedings of the ACM/IEEE Joint Conference on Digtial Libraries,* (pp. 54-62). ACM/IEEE. Retrieved from http://www.openarchives.org/documents/papers.html

Lagoze, C., Krafft, D., Cornwell, T., Dushay, N., Eckstrom, D., & Saylor, J. (2006). Metadata aggregation and "automated digital libraries": A retrospective on the NSDL experience. In *Proceedings of the 6th ACM/IEEE-CS Joint Conference on Digital Libraries,* (pp. 230-239). ACM/IEEE.

Lancaster, F. W. (1986). Why vocabulary control? In *Vocabulary Control for Information Retrieval* (2nd ed., pp. 1–4). Arlington, VA: Information Resources Press.

Lan, S. H. (2001). A study of usability evaluation of information architecture of the university library web site: A case study of National Taiwan University library web site. *Bulletin of the Library Association of China, 67*, 139–154.

Lapp, D., Shea, A., & Wolsey, T. D. (2011). Blogging and audience awareness. *Journal of Education, 191*(1), 33–44.

Larsen, L. (2002). The DLib test suite and metrics working group: Harvesting the experience from the digital library initiative. *D-Lib Working Group on Digital Library Metrics Website*. Retrieved from http://www.dlib.org/metrics/public/papers/The_Dlib_Test_Suite_and_Metrics.pdf

Larson, M., Newman, E., & Jones, G. (2010). Overview of VideoCLEF 2009: New perspectives on speech-based multimedia content enrichment. *Lecture Notes in Computer Science*, *6242*, 354–368. doi:10.1007/978-3-642-15751-6_46

Latham, K. F. (2010). Medium rare: Exploring archives and their conversion from original to digital part one: Lessons from the history of print media. *LIBRES: Library & Information Science Research Electronic Journal*, *20*(2), 1–14.

Lave, J., & Wenger, E. (1991). *Situated learning: Legitimate peripheral participation*. Cambridge, UK: Cambridge University Press. doi:10.1017/CBO9780511815355

Lavy, I., & Yadin, A. (2010). Team-based peer-review as a form of formative assessment—The casae of a systems anlaysis and design workshop. *Journal of Information Systems Education*, *21*(1), 85–98.

Leader-Chivee, L., Hamilton, B., & Cowan, E. (2008). Networking the way to success: Online social networks for workplace and competitive advantage. *People and Strategy*, *32*, 41–46.

Lee, S. H. (Ed.). (1997). *Economics of digital information: Collection, storage and delivery*. New York, NY: Haworth Press.

Lerner, F. (1998). *The stories of libraries: From the invention of writing to the computer age*. New York, NY: Continuum.

Lew, M. S., Sebe, N., & Djeraba, C. (2006). Content-based multimedia information retrieval: State of the art and challenges. *ACM Transactions on Multimedia Computing, Communications, and Applications, 2*(1).

Library of Congress. (2006). *Encoded archival description tag library, version 2002: Appendix d: Index by element name*. Retrieved from http://www.loc.gov/ead/tglib/appendix_d.html

Library of Congress. (2007). *Thesaurus for graphic materials I*. Retrieved September 10, 2011, from http://www.loc.gov/rr/print/tgm1/

Library of Congress. (2010). *Outline of elements and attributes in MODS version 3.4*. Retrieved from http://www.loc.gov/standards/mods/mods-outline.html

Licklider, J. (1965). *Libraries of the future*. Cambridge, MA: The MIT Press.

Lin & Abels. (2010). Digital library education lab. *Journal of Education for Library and Information Science*, *51*(2), 120–124.

Lonbom, K. C. (2010). Drawing on imagination: Children's art in the academic library. *Art Documentation*, *29*(1), 11–15.

Long, C. (2011). Developing and implementing a master of archival studies program: A collaborative effort of a state university, a state archives, and the national archives and records administration. *Journal of Education for Library and Information Science*, *52*(2), 120–124.

Long, H., Lage, K., & Cronin, C. (2005). The flight plan of a digital initiatives project, part 2: Usability testing in the context of user-centered design. *OCLC Systems & Services*, *21*(4), 324–345. doi:10.1108/10650750510631703

Lyons, C., & Peters, T. (2008). Audio description Illinois: Workshop outline. *Audio Description Illinois*. Retrieved July 15, 2011 from http://www.alsaudioillinois.net/workshops.cfm

Macaulay Library and Cornell Lab of Ornithology. (2006). Online archive: The world's largest archive of animal sounds and videos. *Macaulay Library*. Retrieved July 29, 2011 from http://macaulaylibrary.org/index.do

MacLeod, N., Diver, P., Guralnick, R., Lazarus, D., & Malmgren, B. (2000). Computers, quantification & databases. In Lane, R. H., Steininger, F. F., Kaesler, R. L., Zeigler, W., & Lipps, J. (Eds.), *Fossils and the Future: Paleontology in the 21st Century* (pp. 191–201). Frankfurt, Germany: Senckenburg Museum.

Mallison, H., et al. (2009). Mechanical digitizing for paleontology - New and improved techniques. *Palaeontologia Electronica, 12*(2). Retrieved August 11, 2011 from http://palaeo-electronica.org/2009_2/185/index.html

Mandl, T. (2008). Recent developments in the evaluation of information retrieval systems: Moving towards diversity and practical relevance. *Informatica, 32*, 27–38.

Mandl, T., Agosti, M., Di Nunzio, G. M., Yeh, A., Mani, I., & Doran, C. (2010). LogCLEF 2009: The CLEF 2009 multilingual logfile analysis track overview. *Lecture Notes in Computer Science, 6241*, 508–517. doi:10.1007/978-3-642-15754-7_62

Mandl, T., Di Nunzio, G. M., & Schulz, J. M. (2010). LogCLEF 2010: The CLEF 2010 multilingual logfile analysis track overview. *Lecture Notes in Computer Science*, 6360.

Manghi, P., Mikulicic, M., Candela, L., Artini, M., & Bardi, A. (2010). General-purpose digital library content laboratory systems. In *Proceedings of Research and Advanced Technology for Digital Libraries, 14th European Conference, ECDL 2010,* (pp. 14-21). Springer.

Manghi, P., Mikulicic, M., Candela, L., Castelli, D., & Pagano, P. (2010). Realizing and maintaining aggregative digital library systems: D-NET software toolkit and OAIster system. *D-Lib Magazine, 16*(3/4). doi:10.1045/march2010-manghi

Manimala, M., Jose, P., & Thomas, K. (2006). Innovation and intrapreneurship: Insights from public sector. *Vikalpa, 31*, 49–60.

Marchionini, G., Plaisant, C., & Komlodi, A. (2003). The people in digital libraries: Multifaceted approaches to assessing needs and impact. In A. P. Bishop, N. A. Van House, & B. P. Buttenfield (Eds.), *Digital Library Use: Social Practice in Design and Evaluation,* (pp. 119-160). Cambridge, MA: The MIT Press.

Marchionini, G. (2000). Evaluating digital libraries: A longitudinal and multifaceted view. *Library Trends, 49*(2), 304–333.

Marchionini, G., & Fox, E. (1999). Progress toward digital libraries: Augmentation through integration. *Information Processing & Management, 35*(3), 219–225.

Marchionini, G., & Maurer, H. (1995). The roles of digital libraries in teaching and learning. *Communications of the ACM, 38*(4), 67–76. doi:10.1145/205323.205345

Marchionini, G., Plaisant, C., & Komlodi, A. (2003). The people in digital libraries: Multifaceted approaches to assessing needs and impact. In Bishop, A., Buttenfield, B., & VanHouse, N. (Eds.), *Digital Library Use: Social Practice in Design and Evaluation* (pp. 119–160). Cambridge, MA: MIT Press.

Marlow, J., Clough, P. D., & Dance, K. (2007). Multilingual needs of cultural heritage web site visitors: A case study of tate online. In J. Trant & D. Bearman (Eds.), *Proceedings of International Cultural Heritage Informatics Meeting (ICHIM 2007).* Toronto, Canada: ICHIM.

Matusiak, K. K. (2010). Use of digital resources in an academic environment: A qualitative study of students' perceptions, experiences, and digital literacy skills. (Unpublished Dissertation). University of Wisconsin – Milwaukee. Milwaukee, WI.

Matuskiak, K. (2006). Information seeking behavior in digital image collections: A cognitive approach. *Journal of Academic Librarianship, 32*(5), 479–488. doi:10.1016/j.acalib.2006.05.009

McAfee, A. (2006). Enterprise 2.0: The dawn of emergant colalboration. *MIT Sloan Management Review, 47*, 21–28.

McAfee, A. (2009). *Enterprise 2.0: New collaborative tools for your organization's toughest challenges.* Cambridge, MA: Harvard Business School Press.

McGinnis, R. (2003). Museum programs: Metropolitan Museum of Art. In Levent, N., & Axel, E. (Eds.), *Art beyond Sight* (pp. 454–457). New York, NY: AFB Press.

McLean, N., & Lynch, C. (2004). *Interoperability between library information services and learning environments - Bridging the caps.* Retrieved from http://www.estandard.no/tilgjengelig/CNIandIMS_2004.pdf

McMenemy, D. (2007). Less conversation, more action: Putting digital content creation at the heart of modern librarianship. *Library Review, 56*(7), 537–541. doi:10.1108/00242530710775926

McNicol, S. (2004). The eVALUEd toolkit: A framework for the qualitative evaluation of electronic information services. *Vine, 34*(4), 172–175. doi:10.1108/03055720410570957

Means, B., & Gott, S. (1988). Cognitive task analysis as a basis for tutor development: Articulating abstract knowledge representations. In Psotka, J., Massey, L., & Mutter, S. (Eds.), *Intelligent Tutoring Systems: Lessons Learned* (pp. 35–57). Hillsdale, NJ: Lawrence Erlbaum.

Menzel, H. C. (2008). *Intrapreneurship-conductive culture in industrial R&D: The design of a simulation game to create awareness and provide insight.* (Unpublished Doctoral Dissertation). Technische Universiteit. Eindhoven, The Netherlands. Retrieved May 15, 2011, from http://alexandria.tue.nl/extra2/200810440.pdf

Metropolitan Museum of Art. (2011). *Programs for visitors with disabilities.* Retrieved August 1, 2011, from http://www.metmuseum.org/events/visitorsdisabilities/blind

Metropolitan New York Library Council. (2010). *Website.* Retrieved June 29, 2010, from http://www.metro.org/

Meyer., et al. (2008). *Development of an integrated paleontological database and web site of Florissant collections, taxonomy, and publications.* GSA Special Papers 435. Retrieved from http://specialpapers.gsapubs.org/content/435/159.abstract

Miles, M. B., & Huberman, A. M. (1994). *Qualitative data analysis: An expended sourcebook.* Thousand Oaks, CA: Sage.

Millington, P., & Nixon, W. J. (2007). EPrints 3 pre-launch briefing. *Ariadne*, 50.

Mills, E. S. (2007). *Evidence explained: Citing history sources from artifacts to cyberspace.* Baltimore, MD: Genealogical Publishing Company.

Minelli, S., Del Secco, I., & Naldi, G. (2006). *D1.2: User requirements analysis - Multimatch-project.* Retrieved August 2011 from http://www.multimatch.org/docs/publicdels/D1.2Final.pdf

Minerva Working Group 5 (Ed.). (2005). *Quality principles for cultural websites: A handbook.* Retrieved August, 2011 from http://www.minervaeurope.org/publications/qualitycommentary/qualitycommentary050314final.pdf

Minerva Working Group 5 (Ed.). (2008). *Handbook on cultural web user interaction.* Retrieved August 2011 from http://www.minervaeurope.org/publications/Handbookwebuserinteraction.pdf

Missingham, R. (2003). *What makes libraries relevant in the 21st century? Measuring digital collections from three perspectives. information online conference.* Retrieved from http://www.nla.gov.au/nla/staffpaper/2003/missingham2.html

Moore, M. (2006). Foreword. In Bonk, C., & Graham, C. (Eds.), *The Handbook of Blended Learning: Global Perspectives, Local Designs.* San Francisco, CA: John Wiley and Sons.

Mueller, T. (2010). Whale evolution: Valley of the whales. *National Geographic.* Retrieved August 11, 2011 from http://ngm.nationalgeographic.com/2010/08/whale-evolution/mueller-text

Multimatch. (2006). *D7.1: Evaluation methodology - Multimatch project.* Retrieved August 2011 from http://www.multimatch.eu/docs/publicdels/7.1-final.pdf

Multimatch. (2006). *D7.4: Results of field trials - Multimatch project.* Retrieved August 2011 from http://www.multimatch.eu/docs/publicdels/D7.4_FINAL.pdf

Nadasen, P. (2005). *Welfare warriors: The welfare rights movement in the United States.* New York, NY: Routledge.

National Information Standards Organization. (2011). *NISO standards: Z39.50.* Retrieved August 11, 2011 from http://www.niso.org/kst/reports/standards?step=2&gid=None&project_key%3Austring%3Aiso-8859-1=84532426495314789f843e720437a599e8db9aa7

Nelson, S. (2003). A professional artist and curator who is blind. In Levent, N., & Axel, E. (Eds.), *Art beyond Sight* (pp. 28–30). New York, NY: AFB Press.

Neumann, L. J., & Bishop, A. P. (2000). From usability to use: Measuring success of testbeds in the real world. In H. Susan & T. Michael (Eds.), *Successes and Failures of Digital Libraries: Proceedings of the 35th Annual Clinic on Library Applications of Data Processing,* (pp. 58-69). Urbana-Champaign, IL: University of Illinois at Urbana-Champaign.

New Zealand Digital Library Project. (2007). *Greenstone digital library software.* Retrieved September 10, 2011, from http://www.greenstone.org/

Nicholson, S. (2004). A conceptual framework for the holistic measurement and cumulative evaluation of library services. *The Journal of Documentation*, *60*(2), 164–182. doi:10.1108/00220410410522043

Nielsen, J. (2000). *Why you only need to test with 5 users.* Retrieved August 12, 2011 from http://www.useit.com/alertbox/20000319.html

Nielson, J. (1993). *Usability engineering.* Cambridge, MA: Academic Press.

NINCH. (2002). *The NINCH guide to good practice in the digital representation and management of cultural heritage materials.* Retrieved from http://www.nyu.edu/its/humanities/ninchguide/

NISO Framework Advisory Group. (2007). *A framework of guidance for building good digital collections* (3rd Ed.). Retrieved from http://www.niso.org/publications/rp/framework3.pdf

Noh, Y. (2010). A study on developing evaluation criteria for electronic resources in evaluation indicators of libraries. *Journal of Academic Librarianship*, *36*(1), 41–52. doi:10.1016/j.acalib.2009.11.005

Norasieh, M. A., & Fadzilah, A. (2011). *Synchronous and asynchronous interaction between librarians and library customers: Where are we heading?* Paper presented at the meeting of the Seminar Kebangsaan Perpustakaan Akademik (National Academic Libraries Seminar). Kelantan, Malaysia.

Norasieh, M. A., & Gerbic, P. (2010). Exploring the use of digital library services in blended learning environments: A Malaysian higher education perspective. In L. G. Chova, D. M. Belenguer, & I. C. Torres (Eds.), *Proceedings of the International Conference of Education, Research and Innovation,* (pp. 1782-1792). Valencia, Spain: International Association of Technology, Education, and Development (IATED).

Norberg, L. R., Vassiliadis, K., Ferguson, J., & Smith, N. (2005). Sustainable design for multiple audiences: The usability study and iterative redesign of the documenting the American south digital library. *OCLC Systems & Services*, *21*(4), 285–299. doi:10.1108/10650750510629625

O'Brien, H. L., Toms, E. G., Kelloway, E. K., & Kelley, E. (2008). Developing and evaluating a reliable measure of user engagement. *Proceedings of the American Society for Information Science and Technology*, *45*(1), 1–10. doi:10.1002/meet.2008.1450450258

Ochs, M. A., & Saylor, J. M. (2004). Resources for the digital library. In Barnes, S. J. (Ed.), *Becoming a Digital Library* (pp. 49–80). New York, NY: Marcel Dekker.

OCLC. (2010). *Best practices for CONTENTdm and other OAI-PMH compliant repositories: Creating shareable metadata.* Retrieved from http://www.oclc.org

OCLC. (2011). *CONTENTdm digital collection management software.* Retrieved from http://www.contentdm.org/

OCLC. (2011). *WorldCat digital collection gateway: Overview.* Retrieved from http://www.oclc.org/gateway/overview/default.htm

Open Archive Initiative Protocol for Metadata Harvesting. (2008). *Open archive initiative home.* Retrieved August 11, 2011 from http://www.openarchives.org/pmh/

Over, P., Awad, G., Fiscus, J., Antonishek, B., Michel, M., Smeaton, A. F., et al. (2011). TrecVid 2010 – Goals, tasks, data, evaluation mechanisms and metrics. *TRECVid Workshop Notebook Papers.* Retrieved August 2011 from http://www-nlpir.nist.gov/projects/tvpubs/tv10.papers/tv10overview.pdf

Over, P., Awad, G., Fiscus, J., Michel, M., Smeaton, A. F., & Kraaij, W. (2010). TrecVid 2009 – Goals, tasks, data, evaluation mechanisms and metrics. *TRECVid Workshop Notebook Papers.* Retrieved August 2011 from http://www-nlpir.nist.gov/projects/tvpubs/tv9.papers/tv9overview.pdf

Over, P., Awad, G., Rose, T., Fiscus, J., Kraaij, W., & Smeaton, A. F. (2009). TrecVid 2008 – Goals, tasks, data, evaluation mechanisms and metrics. *TRECVid Workshop Notebook Papers.* Retrieved August 2011 from http://www-nlpir.nist.gov/projects/tvpubs/tv8.papers/tv8overview.pdf

Paleontology Portal. (2003). *Paleontology portal home page.* Retrieved August 11, 2011 from http://www.paleoportal.org/

Park, J. (2009). Metadata quality in digital repositories: A survey of the current state of the art. *Cataloging & Classification Quarterly*, *47*, 213–238. doi:10.1080/01639370902737240

Patton, M. Q. (2001). *Qualitative research and evaluation methods*. Thousand Oaks, CA: Sage Publications.

Payette, S., & Lagoze, C. (1998). Flexible and extensible digital object and repository architecture (FEDORA). In *Proceedings of Research and Advanced Technology for Digital Libraries, Second European Conference, ECDL 1998,* (pp. 41-59). Heraklion, Greece: Springer.

Pesch, O. (2007). Usage statistics: About COUNTER and SUSHI. *Information Services & Use*, *27*(4), 207–213.

Peters, C., Bruno, E., Carmichael, J., Clough, P., Jones, G., Larson, M., et al. (2006). *D7.3 evaluation of second prototype - Multimatch project.* Retrieved August, 2011 from http://www.multimatch.info/docs/publicdels/7.3.pdf

Peters, T., & Bell, L. (2006). Audio description adds value to digital images. *Computers in Libraries*, *26*(4), 26–28.

Pieper, D., & Summann, F. (2006). Bielefeld academic search engine (BASE): An end-user oriented institutional repository search service. *Library Hi Tech*, *24*(4), 614–619. doi:10.1108/07378830610715473

Pinchot, G. (1985). *Intrapreneuring: Why you don't have to leave the corporation to become an entrepreneur*. New York, NY: Harper & Row.

Purday, J. (2009). Think culture: Europeana.eu from concept to construction. *The Electronic Library*, *27*(6), 919–937. doi:10.1108/02640470911004039

Quijano-Solis, A., & Novelo-Pena, R. (2005). Evaluating a monolingual multinational digital library by using usability: An exploratory approach from a developing country. *The International Information & Library Review*, *37*(4), 329–336. doi:10.1016/j.iilr.2005.09.002

Rasmussen, K. G., Iversen, R., & Petersen, G. (2009). *M3.2.3: Personas catalogue - EuropeanaConnect project.* Retrieved August 2011 from http://www.europeanaconnect.eu/documents/M3.2.3_eConnect_PersonasCatalogue_v1.0_20091228.pdf

Reality, E. O. N. Inc. (2011). *EON reality home page*. Retrieved August 11, 2011 from http://www.eonreality.com/

Reese, T. (2009). Automated metadata harvesting: Low-barrier MARC record generation from OAI-PMH repository stores using MarcEdit. *Library Resources & Technical Services*, *53*(2), 121–134.

Research, I. R. N. (2011). *EUROPEANA - Online visitor survey.* Retrieved August 2011 from http://www.version1.europeana.eu/c/document_library/get_file?uuid=334beac7-7fc2-4a4e-ba23-4dcc1450382d&groupId=10602

Riley, J., Chapman, J., Shreeves, S., Akerman, L., & Landis, W. (2008). Promoting shareability: Metadata activities of the DLF aquifer initiative. *Journal of Library Metadata*, *8*(3), 221–247. doi:10.1080/19386380802397083

Riley, J., & Shepherd, K. (2009). A brave new world: Archivists and shareable descriptive metadata. *The American Archivist*, *72*, 91–112.

Robertson, J. (2011). The educational affordances of blogs for self-directed learning. *Computers & Education*, *57*(2), 1628–1644. doi:10.1016/j.compedu.2011.03.003

Roberts, S., & Davey, J. (2002). VLEs and information services: Redefining distance learning and the role of information services within the virtual learning environment. In *Libraries without Walls 4: The Delivery of Library Services to Distant Users* (pp. 73–84). London, UK: Facet Publishing.

Roel, E. (2005). The MOSC project: Using the OAI-PMH to bridge metadata cultural differences across museums, archives, and libraries. *Information Technology and Libraries*. Retrieved from http://www.ala.org/lita/ital/sites/ala.org.lita.ital/files/content/24/1/roel.pdf

Roffia, L., Bartolini, S., & Manzaroli, D. (2011). Requirements on system design to increase understanding and visibility of cultural heritage. In *Handbook of Research on Technologies and Cultural Heritage: Applications and Environments* (pp. 259–284). Hershey, PA: IGI Global. doi:10.4018/978-1-60960-044-0.ch013

Rose, D. H., Harbor, W. S., Johnston, C. S., Daley, S. G., & Abarbanell, L. (2008). Universal design for learning in postsecondary education: Reflections on principles and their application. In *Universal Design in Higher Education*. Cambridge, MA: Harvard Education Press.

Rowlands, I., & Bawden, D. (1999). Digital libraries: A conceptual framework. *Libri*, *49*(4), 192–202. doi:10.1515/libr.1999.49.4.192

Royal National Institute of the Blind. (2003). *The talking images research: Museums, galleries and heritage sites: Improving access for blind and partially sighted people*. Retrieved August 1, 2011 from http://www.rnib.org.uk/professionals/solutionsforbusiness/leisure/museumsgalleries/Pages/talking_images.aspx

Ruiz, B., Pajares, J. L., Utray, F., & Moreno, L. (2011). Design for all in multimedia guides for museums. *Computers in Human Behavior*, *27*, 1408–1415. doi:10.1016/j.chb.2010.07.044

Saitwal, H., Feng, X., Walji, M., Patel, V., & Zhang, J. (2010). Assessing performance of an electronic health record (EHR) using cognitive task analysis. *International Journal of Medical Informatics*, *79*, 501–506. doi:10.1016/j.ijmedinf.2010.04.001

Salo, D. (2008). Innkeeper at the roach motel. *Library Trends*, *57*(2), 98–123. doi:10.1353/lib.0.0031

Saracevic, T. (1995). *Evaluation of evaluation in information retrieval*. Paper Presented at the SIGIR 1995. Seattle, CA.

Saracevic, T. (2004). *Evaluation of digital libraries: An overview*. Paper presented at the DELOS WP7 Workshop on the Evaluation of Digital Libraries. Padua, Italy.

Saracevic, T. (2000). Digital library evaluation: Toward an evolution of concepts. *Library Trends*, *49*(2), 350–369.

Saulnier, A., & Viaud, M.-L. (2009). *Evaluation report of the usability of the Europeana web site*. Retrieved August 2011 from http://www.version1.europeana.eu/c/document_library/get_file?uuid=ae1d74de-29c1-463c-887e-a6bc6ee0ed7a&groupId=10602

Science Te Pu Ao, G. N. S. (2011). *New Zealand fossils in 3D*. Retrieved August 11, 2011 from http://www.gns.cri.nz/Home/Learning/Science-Topics/Fossils/Gallery/NZ-Fossils-in-3D

Secker, J. (2004). *Electronic resources in the virtual learning environment: A guide for librarians*. Oxford, UK: Chandos. doi:10.1533/9781780630700

Shackel, B. (1991). Usability – Context, framework, definition, design and evaluation. In Shackel, B., & Richardson, S. (Eds.), *Human Factors for Informatics Usability* (pp. 21–37). Cambridge, MA: Cambridge University Press. doi:10.1016/j.intcom.2009.04.007

Sharifabadi, S. R. (2006). How digital libraries can support e-learning. *The Electronic Library*, *24*(3), 389–401. doi:10.1108/02640470610671231

Sharma, P., & Chrisman, J. (1999). Toward a reconcilation of the definitonal issues in the field of corporate entrepreneurship. *Entrepreneurship Theory and Practice*, *23*, 11–28.

Shim, W., & Kantor, P. (1999). Evaluation of digital libraries: A DEA approach. In *Proceedings of the 62nd ASIST Annual Meating*, (pp. 605-615). ASIST.

Shneiderman, B. (1998). *Designing the user interface: Strategies for effective human-computer interaction*. Reading, MA: Addison-Wesley Publishing. doi:10.1145/25065.950626

Shreeves, S. L., Riley, J., & Milewicz, L. (2006). Moving toward shareable metadata. *First Monday*, *11*(8), 1–9. Retrieved from http://firstmonday.org/issues/issue11_8/shreeves/index.html

Skinner, J. (2010). Does greater specialization imply greater satisfaction? Amateur genealogists and resource use at the state historical society of Iowa libraries. *Libri: International Journal of Libraries & Information Services*, *60*(1), 27–37.

Slevin, D., & Covin, J. (1986). The development and testing of an organizational-level entrepreneurship scale. In Ronstadt, R. (Ed.), *Frontiers of Enterpreneurship Research* (pp. 628–639). Wellesley, MA: Babson College.

Slevin, D., & Covin, J. (1989). Juggling entrepreneurial style and organization structure – How to get your act together. *MIT Sloan Management Review*, *31*, 43–53.

Slevin, D., & Covin, J. (1991). A conceptual model of entrepreneurship as firm behavior. *Entrepreneurship Theory and Practice*, *16*, 7–25.

Smeaton, A. F., Over, P., & Kraaij, W. (2006). Evaluation campaigns and TRECVid. In *Proceedings of the 8th ACM International Workshop on Multimedia Information Retrieval,* (pp. 321-330). Santa Barbara, CA: ACM Press.

Smeaton, A., & Over, P. (2002). The TREC-2002 video track report. In *Proceedings of the Eleventh Text Retrieval Conference, TREC 2002.* NIST.

Smith, C. L., & Kantor, P. B. (2008). User adaptation: Good results from poor systems. In *Proceedings of the 31st Annual International ACM SIGIR Conference on Research and Development in Information Retrieval,* (pp. 147-154). New York, NY: ACM Press.

Smith, M., Barton, M., Bass, M., Branschofsky, M., McClellan, G., & Stuve, D. (2003). DSpace - An open source dynamic digital repository. *D-Lib Magazine, 9*(1). doi:10.1045/january2003-smith

Smithsonian National Museum of Natural History. (2011) *Paleobiology collections.* Retrieved August 11, 2011 from http://paleobiology.si.edu/collections/paleoCollections.html

Snyder, J. (2008). Audio description: The visual made verbal. J. Cintas (Ed.), *The Didactics of Audiovisual Translation,* (192-197). Philadelphia, PA: John Benjamins Publishing Company.

Society of American Archivists. (2011). *SAA council adopts EAC-CPF standard, calls for member comments on draft code of ethics and proposed constitutional amendments.* Retrieved from http://www2.archivists.org/news/2011/saa-council-adopts-eac-cpf-standard-calls-for-member-comments-on-draft-code-of-ethics-and-

Specify Software Project. (2011). *Welcome to specify 6.* Retrieved August 11, 2011 from http://specifysoftware.org/content/welcome-specify-6

Spink, A., & Cool, C. (1999). Education for digital libraries. *D-Lib Magazine, 5*(8).

Spool, J. (2005). *Looking back on 16 years of paper prototyping.* Retrieved August 15, 2011 from http://www.uie.com/articles/looking_back_on_paper_prototyping/

Stacey, E., & Gerbic, P. (2007). Teaching for blended learning - Research perspectives from on campus and distance students. *Education and Information Technologies, 12*(3), 165–174. doi:10.1007/s10639-007-9037-5

Stacey, E., & Gerbic, P. (2009). Introduction to blended learning practice. In Stacey, E., & Gerbic, P. (Eds.), *Effective Blended Learning Practices: Evidence-Based Perspectives in ICT-Facilitated Education.* Hershey, PA: IGI Global. doi:10.4018/978-1-60566-296-1.ch001

Sternberg Museum of Natural History. (2011). *About Sternberg museum.* Retrieved August 11, 2011 from http://sternberg.fhsu.edu/

Stevenson, H., & Jarillo, J. (1990). A paradigm of entrepreneurship: Entrepreneurial management. *Strategic Management Journal, 11,* 17–27.

Stiller, J., Gäde, M., & Petras, V. (2010). *Ambiguity of queries and the challenges for query language detection.* Paper presented at the CLEF 2010 LABs and Workshops. Retrieved August, 2011 from http://clef2010.org/resources/proceedings/clef2010labs_submission_41.pdf

Strauss, A., & Corbin, J. (1990). *Basics of qualitative research: Grounded theory procedures and techniques.* Newbury Park, CA: Sage Publications.

Suleman, H., & Fox, E. (2001). The open archives initiative: Realizing simple and effective digital library interoperability. *Journal of Library Administration, 35*(1/2), 125–145.

Sumner, T., & Marlino, M. (2004). Digital libraries and educational practice: A case for new models. In *Proceedings of the 2004 Joint ACM/IEEE Conference on Digital Libraries (JCDL 2004),* (pp. 170-178). ACM/IEEE.

Sumner, T., Khoo, M., Recker, M., & Marlino, M. (2003). Understanding educator perceptions of "quality" in digital libraries. In *Proceedings of the 3rd ACM/IEEE-CS Joint Conference on Digital Libraries,* (pp. 269-279). New York, NY: ACM Press.

Swanson, D. R. (1986). Fish oil, Raynaud's syndrome, and undiscovered public knowledge. *Perspectives in Biology and Medicine, 30*(1), 7–18.

Sykes, J., Dobreva, M., Birrell, D., McCulloch, E., Ruthven, I., & Yurdagül, Ü. (2010). A new focus on end users: Eye-tracking analysis for digital libraries. *Lecture Notes in Computer Science, 6273,* 510–513. doi:10.1007/978-3-642-15464-5_69

Taylor, M. (2008). *Genealogy research process.* Retrieved August 15, 2011 from http://www.thinkgenealogy.com/wp-content/uploads/genealogy-research-map.pdf

Taylor, R. S. (1991). Information use environments. In Dervin, B., & Voight, M. J. (Eds.), *Progress in Communication Science (Vol. 10)*. Norwood, NJ: Ablex Publishing.

Tedd, L. A., & Large, J. A. (2005). *Digital libraries: Principles and practice in a global environment*. Munchen, Germany: Saur, K.G.

Thanos, C. (2011). *Global research data infrastructures: The GRDI2020 vision*. GRDI2020.

Theng, Y. L., Mohd-Nasir, N., & Thimbleby, H. (2000). Purpose and usability of digital libraries. In *Proceedings of the Fifth ACM Conference on Digital Libraries,* (pp. 238-239). New York, NY: ACM Press.

Thomas, R., & Augustyn, M. (2007). *Tourism in the new Europe: Perspectives on SME policies and practices*. Amsterdam, The Netherlands: Elsevier.

Tillett, B. B. (2003). AACR2 and metadata: Library opportunities in the global semantic web. *Electronic Cataloging: AACR2 and Metadata for Serials and Monographs, 36*(3/4), 101-119.

Trant, J. (2009). Tagging, folksonomy and art museums: Early experiments and ongoing research. *Journal of Digital Information, 10*(1). Retrieved August 2011 from http://journals.tdl.org/jodi/article/view/270

Trojahn, C., & Siciliano, L. (2009). *User requirements for advanced features: D7.4 - CACAO project*. Retrieved August 2011 from http://www.cacaoproject.eu/fileadmin/media/Deliverables/CACAO_D7.4.pdf

Tsakonas, G., Kapidakis, S., & Papatheodorou, C. (2004). Evaluation of user interaction in digital libraries. In M. Agosti & N. Fuhr (Eds.), *Notes of the DELOS WP7 Workshop on the Evaluation of Digital Libraries*. Padua, Italy: Academic Press.

Tsakonas, G., & Papatheodorou, C. (2008). Exploring usefulness and usability in the evaluation of open access digital libraries. *Information Processing & Management, 44*, 1234–1250. doi:10.1016/j.ipm.2007.07.008

Tsikrika, T., & Westerveld, T. (2008). The INEX 2007 multimedia track. *Lecture Notes in Computer Science, 4862*, 440–453. doi:10.1007/978-3-540-85902-4_37

Turpin, A., & Scholer, F. (2006). User performance versus precision measures for simple search tasks. In *Proceedings of the 29th Annual International ACM SIGIR Conference on Research and Development in Information Retrieval,* (pp. 11-18). New York, NY: ACM Press.

U.S. Geological Survey. (2011). *Paleontological resources of the USGS in Denver*. Retrieved August 11, 2011 from http://esp.cr.usgs.gov/research/fossils/index.html

Udo, J., & Fels, D. (2010). The rogue poster-children of universal design: Closed captioning and audio description. *Journal of Engineering Design, 21*(2-3), 207–221. doi:10.1080/09544820903310691

Ulijn, J., & Menzel, H. (2004). *Conceptualizing and measuring intrapreneurship: A French vs. an Anglo-Germanic way of paradigming*. Paper presented to the Second Summer University of European Entrepreneurship Research. Enschede, The Netherlands. Retrieved May 15, 2011, from www.utwente.nl/nikos/archief/esu2004/papers/menzelulijn.pdf

University of Chicago. (2003). *The Chicago manual of style*. Chicago, IL: University of Chicago Press.

University of Iowa. (2010). *NMITA neogene marine biota of tropical America*. Retrieved August 11, 2011 from http://nmita.geology.uiowa.edu/

University of Kansas Museum of Natural History and Biodiversity Research Center. (2006). *Division of invertebrate paleontology*. Retrieved August 11, 2011 from http://ipa.geo.ku.edu/InvertPaleo/

University of Michigan – Digital Library Production Service. (2012). *Website*. Retrieved from http://www.dlxs.org

University of Texas-Austin. (2011). *National science foundation grant helps preserve and digitize fossil collections*. Retrieved August 11, 2011 from http://www.utexas.edu/news/2011/04/11/fossils_preserve_digitize/

US Biological Collections National Resource. (2010). *A strategic plan for establishing a network integrated collections alliance*. Retrieved August 11, 2011 from http://digbiocol.wordpress.com/2010/02/07/watch-this-space/

Uzwyshyn, R. (2008). Repurposing open source software for agile digital image library development: The University of West Florida libraries model. *D-Lib Magazine, 14*(9/10). Retrieved August 12, 2011 from http://www.dlib.org/dlib/september08/uzwyshyn/09uzwyshyn.html

Van House. N. A., Butler, M. H., Ogle, V., & Schiff, L. (1996). User-centered iterative design for digital libraries: The cypress experience. *D-Lib Magazine, 2*(2). Retrieved August 11, 2011 from http://www.dlib.org/dlib/february96/02vanhouse.html

Van House. N., Weil, B., & McClure, C. (1990). *Measuring academic library performance: A practical approach*. Chicago, IL: American Library Association.

van Westrenen, F. (2011). Cognitive work analysis and the design of user interfaces. *Cognition Technology and Work, 13*(1), 31–42. doi:10.1007/s10111-010-0153-4

van Zwol, R., Kazai, G., & Lalmas, M. (2006). INEX 2005 multimedia track. *Lecture Notes in Computer Science, 3977*, 497–510.

Vellay, S. G. P. (2009). Interactive text mining with pipeline pilot: A bibliographic web-based tool for PubMed. *Infectious Disorders Drug Targets, 9*(3), 366–374. doi:10.2174/1871526510909030366

Vesper, K. (1990). *New venture strategies*. Englewood Cliffs, CA: Prentice-Hall.

Vicente, K. J. (1999). *Cognitive work analysis: Toward safe, productive and healthy computer-based work*. New York, NY: Lawrence Erlbaum. doi:10.1109/TPC.2002.808348

Visual Resources Association. (2007). *VRA core 4.0 outline*. Retrieved from http://www.loc.gov/standards/vracore/VRA_Core4_Outline.pdf

Voorhees, E., & Harman, D. K. (2005). *TREC: Experiment and evaluation in information retrieval*. Cambridge, MA: MIT Press.

Vullo, G. (2010). A global approach to digital library evaluation. *The Library Quarterly, 20*(2), 169–178.

Ward, J. L., & Hiller, S. (2005). Usability testing, interface design and portals. *Journal of Library Administration, 43*(1), 155–171. doi:10.1300/J111v43n01_10

Warschauer, M. (2003). *Technology and social inclusion: Rethinking the digital divide*. Cambridge, MA: MIT Press.

Wei, J., & Salvendy, G. (2004). The cognitive task analysis methods for job and task design: Review and reappraisal. *Behaviour & Information Technology, 23*(4), 273–299. doi:10.1080/01449290410001673036

Weikart, L. (2005). The era of meanness: Welfare reform and barriers to a college degree. *Affilia, 20*(4), 416–433. doi:10.1177/0886109905279802

Wenger, E. (1998). *Communities of practice: Learning, meaning and identity*. Cambridge, UK: Cambridge University Press.

Westerveld, T., & van Zwol, R. (2007). The INEX 2006 multimedia track. *Lecture Notes in Computer Science, 4518*, 331–344. doi:10.1007/978-3-540-73888-6_33

White, R. W., Oard, D. W., Jones, G. J. F., Soergel, D., & Huang, X. (2006). Overview of the CLEF-2005 cross-language speech retrieval track. *Lecture Notes in Computer Science, 4022*, 744–759. doi:10.1007/11878773_82

Wilhite, R. (2003). Digitizing large fossil skeletal elements for three-dimensional applications. *Palaeontologia Electronica, 5*(1). Retrieved August 11, 2011 from http://palaeo-electronica.org/paleo/2002_2/scan/issue2_02.htm

Witten, I. H., Bainbridge, D., & Boddie, S. J. (2001). Greenstone - Open-source digital library software. *D-Lib Magazine, 7*(10). doi:10.1045/october2001-witten

Wolniewicz, P. (2009). Easily-accessible digital palaeontological databases – A new perspective for the storage of palaeontological information. *Geologos, 15*(3–4), 181–188. doi:10.2478/v10118-009-0002-1

Wong, D. (2006). Fulltime students' and working adults' perceptions of e-learning in Malaysia. *Asian Journal of Distance Education, 4*(1), 67–84.

Wunderer, R. (2001). Employees as co-intrapreneurs – A transformation concept. *Leadership and Organization Development Journal, 22*, 193–211. doi:10.1108/EUM0000000005676

Xie, H. (2008). Users' evaluation of digital libraries: Their uses, their criteria, and their assessment. *Information Processing & Management, 44*(3), 1346–1373. doi:10.1016/j.ipm.2007.10.003

Xie, I. (2006). Evaluation of digital libraries: Criteria and problems from users' perspectives. *Library & Information Science Research, 28*(3), 433–452. doi:10.1016/j.lisr.2006.06.002

Xie, I., & Wolfram, D. (2002). State digital library usability: Contributing organizational factors. *Journal of the American Society for Information Science and Technology, 53*(13), 1085–1097. doi:10.1002/asi.10152

Yakel, E. (2004). Seeking information, seeking connections, seeking meaning: Genealogists and family historians. *Information Research, 10*(1). Retrieved August 11, 2011 from http://informationr.net/ir/10-1/paper205.html

Zahra, S. (1991). Predictors and financial outcomes of corporate enrepreneurship: An exploratory study. *Journal of Business Venturing, 6*, 259–285. doi:10.1016/0883-9026(91)90019-A

Zahra, S. (1993). Envirnoment, corporate enrepreneurship and financial outcomes: A taxonomic approach. *Journal of Business Venturing, 8*, 319–340. doi:10.1016/0883-9026(93)90003-N

Zahra, S., & Covin, J. (1995). Contextual influences on the corporate enrepreneurship–Performance relationship: A longitudinal analysis. *Journal of Business Venturing, 10*, 43–58. doi:10.1016/0883-9026(94)00004-E

Zampetakis, L., & Moustakis, V. (2007). Entrepreneurial behaviour in the Greek public sector. *International Journal of Entrepreneurial Behaviour & Research, 13*, 19–38. doi:10.1108/13552550710725165

Zhang, Y. (2010). Developing a holistic model for digital library evaluation. *Journal of the American Society for Information Science and Technology, 61*(1), 88–110. doi:10.1002/asi.21220

About the Contributors

Colleen Cool, Ph.D., is a Professor in the Graduate School of Library and Information Studies at Queens College, City University of New York. She joined the faculty in 1997, after completing the Ph.D. in Communication, Information, and Library Studies from Rutgers University. She also holds an M.L.S. from Rutgers, and a Master's degree in Communication from the University of Pennsylvania. At Queens College, Dr. Cool regularly teaches courses in Research Methods, Digital Libraries, and Human-Computer Interaction. Professor Cool maintains an active research agenda, with a focus on studies of human information behavior, in particular help-seeking interactions in the digital library environment. Her research has been federally funded by the Institute for Museum and Library Services. Dr. Cool has published numerous journal articles and presented the results of her research at professional conferences worldwide. Dr. Cool is the co-editor, with Dr. Kwong Bor Ng, of the *International Journal of Digital Library Systems.*

Kwong Bor Ng (Ph D) is an Associate Professor teaching at the Graduate School of Library and Information Studies, Queens College, CUNY. He has also been a consultant for various research projects sponsored by the National Science Foundation and the Defense Advanced Research Projects Agency (DARPA). Dr. Ng's teaching and research areas are in the technical and technological aspects of metadata and information retrieval in the context of digital libraries environment. Dr. Ng has published more than 20 refereed papers in the most prestigious information science research journals, like the *Journal of the American Society for Information Science and Technology* and *Information Processing and Management*. His most recent book publications include: (1) *Using XML*, published by Neal-Schuman in 2007; (2) *Collaborative Technologies and Applications for Interactive Design*, co-edited with S. Rummler, published by Information Science Reference in 2009; and (3) *Digitization in the Real World*, co-edited with J. Kucsma, published by Metropolitan New York Library Council in 2011.

* * *

Norasieh Md Amin obtained her Bachelor Degree in Human Science and Master Degree in Library and Information Science both from International Islamic University Malaysia (IIUM) and served the same university as a Librarian since 2000. Her interest on digital libraries instigated her to pursue her studies. She is currently a PhD candidate at Auckland University of Technology, New Zealand, under the supervision of Dr. Philippa Gerbic and Assoc. Prof. Andy Begg, receiving a fellowship from Universiti Sains Malaysia (USM) to fund her doctoral studies. Her research is on digital library services in blended learning environment: a Malaysian higher education perspective. She has made presentations in

Auckland, New Zealand, and Madrid, Spain, and has produced several conference papers and a journal paper. Her research interests include digital library, blended learning, academic library collaboration, Library 2.0, and blended librarianship. A recipient of AUT Summer Research Assistant Award 2010 and AUT Graduate Assistantship Award 2011, she also served as a reviewer for the Informing Science Institute's conferences in 2009, 2011, and 2012, and was a reviewer for *International Journal of Information, Knowledge, and Management* (IJIKM). Her paper was awarded "Best Paper Award: Humanities Stream" during the 1st Malaysian Research Conference Auckland in 2011.

Dreanna Belden, Assistant Dean for External Relations at UNT Libraries, explores how digital cultural heritage collections can most effectively be used in education, and she collaborates with museums, libraries, and archives to place historic materials online. The American Library Association selected Ms. Belden as a participant in its prestigious Emerging Leaders program in 2007. She recently completed service as a Chair for the Advisory Board for the Texas State Library and Archives Commission's "Train to Share" IMLS funded program. Last year, she became the first librarian elected to the Council of the Texas Association of Museums.

Leonardo Candela is Researcher at the Networked Multimedia Information Systems (NeMIS) Laboratory of the Institute of Information Science and Technologies – Italian National Research Council (CNR-ISTI). He graduated in Computer Science in 2001 at University of Pisa and completed a Ph.D. in Information Engineering in 2006 at the University of Pisa. He joined the NeMIS Laboratory in 2001. Since then, he has been involved in a series of Digital Library-oriented projects including CYCLADES, Open Archives Forum, DELOS, DILIGENT, DRIVER, D4Science, D4Science-II, and DL.org. He was a member of the DELOS Reference Model Technical Committee and of the OAI-ORE Liaison Group. He is currently involved in the iMarine, EUBrazilOpenBio, and ENVRI projects. As part of his research on Digital Libraries, he contributed to the definition of "The Digital Library Manifesto" (2006) and "The Digital Library Reference Model" (2011). His research interests include Digital Library (Management) Systems and Architectures, Digital Libraries Models, Interoperability, Virtual Research Environments, and Data Infrastructures.

Donatella Castelli is a Senior Researcher working at the "Istituto di Scienza e Tecnologie della Informazione" of the Italian National Research Council (CNR-ISTI). She has been the principal investigator of several European and National funded projects on digital libraries and data e-Infrastructure acquiring considerable experience in these domains. In particular, she has acted as scientific director for the series of projects that have developed the D4Science data infrastructure (www.d4science.org) and technical director of those that have realised the OpenAIRE infrastructure (http://www.openaire.eu/). Her scientific interests are centered around digital libraries, data infrastructures, and data interoperability areas.

Maria Gäde holds a Magister (Master equivalent) in Library Information Science and Linguistics from Humboldt-University. She is a researcher and PhD student at the Berlin School of Library and Information Science, Humboldt-Universität zu Berlin. Maria Gäde is currently involved in the PROMISE project, the FP7 European Network of Excellence on the experimental evaluation of multilingual and multimodal information access systems and Europeana v2.0. Her research focuses on digital library evaluation, in particular on user behavior and requirements for multilingual access in digital libraries.

She organized the CHIC 2011 – Cultural Heritage in CLEF workshop dealing with the improvement of systematic and large-scale evaluation of cultural heritage digital libraries and information access systems.

Philippa Gerbic works in the School of Education at the Auckland University of Technology, New Zealand, and has had 25 years experience in the field of adult education. Currently, she teaches and supervises topics within this field and has a special interest in e-learning and learning in a digital age. Her research interests are in the areas of blended learning, especially involving technologies that support interaction and their associated curriculum designs. Other areas of research interest are sustainable innovation in curriculum, and the development of an e-portfolio pedagogy within a blended environment.

Lauren Deborah Harrison (Ph.D) joined Roche in 1979 and has served as an information provider on Pharmaceutical teams (Marketed Products; Global Pharmacovigilance; Discovery and Early Development Oncology, Virology, Inflammation, Metabolic Disease Teams) evaluating and contributing to the design and development of several innovative information tools/processes, providing competitor information, patents, news, biomedical, and marketing information analysis. She holds a BS from Howard University, Washington, DC. She earned both her MLS and Ph.D. in Information Systems and Communication from Rutgers, School of Communication and Information. She has served as Guest Lecturer at the Palmer School of Library and Information School, C. W. Post Campus Long Island University, Brookville, NY, 2010-2011.

William Hicks is the Technology Coordinator for the User Interfaces Unit at the UNT Libraries.

Soohyung Joo is a PhD Candidate in the School of Information Studies at the University of Wisconsin – Milwaukee. He received his B.A. and M.A. from Yonsei University, Seoul, Korea. He has research interests in digital libraries, usability tests, interactive information retrieval, and data mining of user behavioral data. Particular interests are the investigation of system support for users' application of search tactics while using digital library systems. He has published several articles in such journals as the *Journal of the American Society for Information Science and Technology*, *Information Processing and Management,* and *Electronic Library*. He is currently (2012) working on his dissertation research that develops a new evaluation framework focusing on system support for search tactics during the search process in digital library environments.

Iris Lee is the Project Archivist for the CLIR Hidden Collections project at the American Museum of Natural History. For archival collections in the AMNH Library, Iris coordinates cataloging, supervises finding aid work, and batch converts spreadsheet data into MARC records and collection-level EAD-encoded finding aids. Prior to working at AMNH, Iris was the Digital Project Coordinator at the Whitney Museum Library, digitized artists books at the Center for Book Arts, and helped to process records for Coney Island USA, the not-for-profit arts organization responsible for events such as the Mermaid Parade. Iris graduated from the City University of New York, Queens College, earning her M.L.S. with a Certificate in Archives, Records Management, and Preservation. She received her B.A. in Studio Art and Classical Studies from the University of California – Riverside.

Ping Li, Ph.D., is an Assistant Professor in the Graduate School of Library and Information Studies at Queens College, The City University of New York. Her research interests include reference and information services, information literacy and information literacy instruction, users and uses of information systems, health sciences librarianship, and research methods. Her recent publications include, among others, "Science Information Literacy Tutorials and Pedagogy" published in the June issue (2011) of *Evidence Based Library and Information Practice*, "Supporting Evidence-Based Medicine: A Survey of U.S. Medical Librarians" co-authored with Lin Wu (MLIS, AHIP) and published in the 4th issue of *Medical Reference Services Quarterly* in 2011, "What Do They Want? A Content Analysis of Medical Library Association Reference Job Announcements, 2000-2005" co-authored with Lin Wu (MLIS, AHIP) and published in the October issue (2008) of *Journal of Medical Library Association: JMLA*.

Kathleen C. Lonbom is Associate Professor and Art and Theatre Librarian at Milner Library, Illinois State University. She earned a B.F.A. degree in Studio Art from Carnegie Mellon University, M.F.A degree in Sculpture from Illinois State University, and M.L.I.S. degree from the University of Illinois at Urbana-Champaign, completing a practicum in Reader Services at the Art Institute of Chicago's Ryerson and Burnham Libraries. Ms. Lonbom served as the principal investigator and project manager for the LSTA grant-funded digitization project, *Imagine Illinois and Beyond: Celebrating Creativity Through the Eyes of Our Children*. Ms. Lonbom's current research interest is focused on inclusive design, specifically exploring alternate modes of access to digital image collections through audio and verbal descriptions.

Paolo Manghi is Researcher at the Networked Multimedia Information Systems Lab of the Istituto di Scienza e Tecnologie dell'Informazione (ISTI), Consiglio Nazionale delle Ricerche, Pisa, Italy. His interests are in the fields of data models for digital libraries, types for compound objects in digital repositories, digital library systems and services, service-oriented infrastructures for digital libraries, database systems, type systems for XML languages, query languages for XML data, and XML P2P database systems. He is today involved as software architect and researcher in the realization of the Digital Library and Data Infrastructures for the European Commission projects OpenAIRE, OpenAIREplus, EFG1914, and HOPE.

Kathleen Murray is a Postdoctoral Research Associate at the University of North Texas Libraries. In addition to holding a Doctorate in Information Science, she holds a Certificate in Genealogical Studies from the University of Strathclyde. Since 2000, she has conducted user studies for state and national digital library and Web archiving projects. She was project manager for the Portal to Texas History^{SM} reengineering project (2007-2009), and leader of the user studies team. Subsequently, she has been project manager and a principal researcher for the *Classification of the End-of-Term Web Archive* project, a three-year research project funded by a National Leadership Grant from the Institute of Museum and Library Services.

Ruzita Ramly holds a degree in Landscape Architecture from Louisiana State University, USA, and a Postgraduate Diploma in Library Science from Universiti Teknologi MARA, Malaysia. After more than 10 years working as a librarian focusing mostly on reference services and user education programmes, she then obtained her Master of Science in Information Management Education from Syracuse University, USA, and later joined the University of Malaya Library, Malaysia, as the coordinator for the Information

Skills Course. She next joined Open University Malaysia (OUM), the first open and distance learning university in Malaysia and became the Chief Librarian in 2008. While in OUM, she started exploring opportunities in providing library services using Web 2.0 and other related services used by digital libraries. She has made several presentations at national levels in library and information science conferences and has been teaching the Learning Skills for Open and Distance Learners course as OUM part time tutor since 2004. Apart from librarianship and knowledge management, her other interests include open and distance learning, flexible learning, online learning, and quality in education. She is currently the Deputy Director at the Institute of Quality, Research, and Innovation, OUM.

Pasquale Pagano is Senior Researcher at the Networked Multimedia Information Systems Laboratory of the "Istituto di Scienza e Tecnologie della Informazione A. Faedo" (ISTI) of the Italian National Research Council (CNR). He received a M.Sc. in Information Systems Technologies from the Department of Computer Science of the University of Pisa (1998), and the Ph.D. degree in Information Engineering from the Department of Information Engineering: Electronics, Information Theory, and Telecommunications from the same university (2006). The aim of his research is the study and experimentation of models, methodologies, and techniques for the design and development of distributed Virtual Research Environments (VREs) that require the handling of heterogeneous resources provided by Grid- and Cloud-based e-Infrastructures. He has a strong background in distributed architectures. He participated in the design of the most relevant distributed systems and e-Infrastructure enabling middleware developed by ISTI -CNR. He is currently the Technical Director of the Data e-Infrastructure Initiative for Fisheries Management and Conservation of Marine Living Resources (iMarine) and member of VENUS-C European project. He is also involved in the GRDI2020 expert working group and serves the EUBrazilOpenBio initiative as consultant. In the past, he has been involved in the D4Science-II, D4Science, Diligent, DRIVER, DRIVER II, BELIEF, BELIEF II, Scholnet, Cyclades, and ARCA European projects.

Claudia A. Perry, Ph.D., Rutgers University, is an Associate Professor in the Graduate School of Library and Information Studies (GSLIS), Queen College, CUNY, where she teaches courses in the Fundamentals of LIS and Digital Imaging. Student work in the latter course has resulted in the creation of the "Waterways of New York" postcard collection. The database, containing nearly 900 cards with detailed metadata, can be viewed at http://qcpages.qc.edu/GSLIS/digitization.html. Research and professional interests center around the evolving nature of emerging technologies, and the challenges and opportunities presented by the use of digitally based technologies in libraries and other cultural institutions and the society at large. Other areas of interest include library and information services to older adults, and hands-on approaches to learning. Dr. Perry is especially honored to have been chosen to receive the 2005 President's Award for Excellence in Teaching at Queens College, a tribute to the excellent students in the GSLIS.

Vivien Petras holds a PhD in Information Management and Systems from UC Berkeley, USA, and has been an Assistant Professor for Information Retrieval at Humboldt-Universität zu Berlin, Germany, since 2009. She worked for 2.5 years as the Deputy Head of the Information Science R&D department at the Social Science Information Centre in Bonn, Germany, now GESIS. Vivien Petras has been involved with the European Union-funded digital library, museum, and archive Europeana since 2007. Other projects research translation facilities and evaluation methodologies in cultural heritage information systems. Her research interests lie in the areas of information organization to ensure interoperability and (multilingual) information retrieval and evaluation.

Mark Phillips, Assistant Dean for Digital Libraries, has been involved with all stages of digital projects at the UNT Libraries for the past ten years. His division is responsible for the management of over 300,000 unique digital items in the UNT Digital Library and the Portal to Texas History[SM]. His experience includes the areas of digital preservation, born digital collection development, digitization, and Web archiving. He acts as the architect for digital library systems at the UNT Libraries. Born in Oklahoma, Mark attended Oklahoma City University, where he earned a Bachelor's degree in Music Performance (double bass) and went on to earn a Masters of Library Science at the University of North Texas. He was recently selected as a 2012 Mover and Shaker by the *Library Journal*.

Adam Sofronijevic, born in 1973 in Belgrade, Serbia, as of June 2012, he is Department Head at University Library of University of Belgrade. He has a MSc in Management, MSc in LIS, BSc in IT, CISCO CCNA, MITx, and Udacity online IT certificates. His Master theses were on Enterprise 2.0 and on the library business model, both at University of Belgrade. As of June 2012, he earned a PhDc from the Faculty of Philology, LIS department, University of Belgrade. He has seven years of experience in research of Serbian and European libraries and implementation of IT solutions in library environment and three years of experience in management of a department in main Serbian university library. He has implementation experience in kick starting Enterprise 2.0 tools in the library environment. As of 2012, he is a member of the Liber working group for digitization and a member of the Liber annual conference program committee.

Juliane Stiller holds a Magister (Master equivalent) in Library and Information Science from Humboldt-University. Juliane is a Researcher and Doctoral student at the Berlin School of Library and Information Science, Humboldt-Universität zu Berlin. She is currently working in the EU-funded projects GALATEAS (Generalized Analysis of Logs for Automatic Translation and Episodic Analysis of Searches), Europeana v2.0, and the FP7 European Network of Excellence – PROMISE. Her Doctoral research focuses on user interaction and collaboration in multilingual digital libraries and interaction models for cultural heritage information systems. Previous to her research position, she was a Search Quality Analyst at Google Ltd, Ireland.

Cynthia Tobar is the founder of the Welfare Rights Initiative Digital Oral History Project, which is documenting the Welfare Rights Initiative (WRI), a grassroots student activist and community leadership training organization located at Hunter College. Cynthia has also collaborated with the Occupy Wall Street Archives Working Group, where she conducted life history interviews with OWS occupiers. Cynthia is currently a Metadata Librarian/Assistant Professor at the Mina Rees Library, CUNY Graduate Center. Prior to her time at the Graduate Center, Cynthia was Senior Metadata Creator for the Museum of the City of New York and a cataloger, archivist, and metadata creator for the Wilson Processing Project, where she processed archival materials from the collections of the New York Public Library for the Performing Arts. She was also a project archivist for the Lighting Archive © Project, which digitized the theatrical lighting documents of: Tharon Musser, *A Chorus Line*, 1974; Richard Nelson, *Sunday in the Park*, 1984, and Jules Fisher, *HAIR*, 1968. Cynthia earned her M.A. in Political Science at the New

School for Social Research, and received an M.L.S., with a certificate in Archival Management, from Pratt Institute.

Mary Tyson is a recent MLS graduate of City University of New York, Queens College. She has been a Digitization Consultant for the Whitney Museum of American Art and an Acquisitions/Collection Development Intern for the American Museum of Natural History. She is also a fine arts painter and graphic designer, receiving her MFA from Columbia University.

Walter Valero, MLS, MS, Queens College. Walter Valero is a lecturer in the Graduate School of Library and Information Studies (GSLIS), Queens College, CUNY, where he teaches various LIS technology courses, including Digital Imaging, and Introduction to Multimedia. He is also the coordinator for the GSLIS Internship course and for the Technology of Information course. He serves as department Webmaster and manages all departmental listservs. Publications, presentations, and professional interests focus on education for digitization, hybrid/blending learning, and using multimedia as a marketing tool for libraries.

Andrew Weiss earned his B.A. from Kenyon College, his M.A. in English Literature from Temple University, and his MLISc from the University of Hawaii at Manoa. During eight years in Japan, he worked as an ESL instructor, photographer, and translation editor. While at the University of Hawaii at Manoa, he specialized in academic librarianship, digitization, and information literacy. He has formerly worked for the Japanese Cultural Center of Hawaii in Honolulu and the Forsyth Library at Fort Hays State University in Hays, Kansas. He currently works for the California State University, Northridge, Oviatt Library, as Digital Services Librarian, focusing primarily on developing CSUN's institutional repository, *ScholarWorks*. His subject and research interests include data visualization, massive digital libraries (including *Google Books* and the like), digitization best practices, and Japanese language collections.

Neena Weng, as the head of the User Interfaces Unit, providing Web development services to the UNT Libraries and their partners beyond the libraries for more than eight years, has led the team in the analysis of user needs, and in the design and implementation of many Web interfaces and websites for the UNT Libraries and UNT community. In particular, those experiences throughout the years in Web project management and usability studies, along with relationship-building with the students, faculty, team members, upper management, and UNT community, have helped Ms. Weng accrue valuable skills in project management, resource management, cross-organization communication coordination, and user-centered Web interface development.

Iris Xie is Professor in the School of Information Studies at the University of Wisconsin – Milwaukee. Her research interests and expertise focus on interactive information retrieval, design, and evaluation of help mechanisms for different types of systems, human-computer interactions, design and evaluation of digital libraries, IR system evaluation, and user need and behavior studies. Dr. Xie won the dissertation award from the Association for Library and Information Science Education (ALISE) in 1999. She is the principal investigator on many research grants awarded by different agencies, which include Institute for Museum and Library Services National Leadership Grant titled "Designing Interactive Help Mechanisms for Novice Users of Digital Libraries" and ALISE/OCLC research grant titled "Ease of Use versus

User Control: Desired Interface Model and Functionalities for Web-Based Online Database." She has a strong record in publishing refereed articles in *Journal of American Society for Information and Science Technology*, *Information Processing and Management*, and *Journal of Documentation*, and presenting at international and national conferences in the field of library and information science.

Index

E

F

G

H

I

J

L

M

N

O

P

Q

R

S

T

U

V

W

Y

www.ingramcontent.com/pod-product-compliance
Lightning Source LLC
LaVergne TN
LVHW080058220926
848484LV00007BA/1874